A History of the Global Ecor

CW00742425

Why are some parts of the world poor today, while others are rich? At which point in time did they diverge, and what were the reasons? These core questions are addressed in a concise and accessible introduction to global economic development since 1500. Leading economic historians from across the globe provide overviews of major world regions together with global comparison chapters and case studies highlighting key themes, individuals, processes and events. Utilising a set of common developmental indicators, the chapters address crucial issues such as how international trade and migration, institutions and flows of physical and human capital impacted economic growth. Richly illustrated with informative figures, maps, tables and charts, *A History of the Global Economy* summarises the key economic findings, debates and ideas and provides students and the interested public with an up-to-date and engaging introduction to the origins and evolution of today's global economy.

JOERG BATEN is Professor of Economic History at the Department of Economics, University of Tübingen.

A History of the Global Economy

From 1500 to the Present

EDITED BY

JOERG BATEN

University of Tübingen

In co-operation with the
International Economic History Association

CAMBRIDGE
UNIVERSITY PRESS

University Printing House, Cambridge CB2 8BS, United Kingdom

One Liberty Plaza, 20th Floor, New York, NY 10006, USA

477 Williamstown Road, Port Melbourne, VIC 3207, Australia

314–321, 3rd Floor, Plot 3, Splendor Forum, Jasola District Centre, New Delhi – 110025, India

79 Anson Road, #06–04/06, Singapore 079906

Cambridge University Press is part of the University of Cambridge.

It furthers the University's mission by disseminating knowledge in the pursuit of education, learning and research at the highest international levels of excellence.

www.cambridge.org
Information on this title: www.cambridge.org/9781107507180

First published 2016
3rd printing 2019

Printed in the United Kingdom by TJ International Ltd, Padstow, Cornwall

A catalogue record for this publication is available from the British Library

Library of Congress Cataloguing in Publication data
A history of the global economy : from 1500 to the present / edited by Joerg Baten.
    pages   cm
"In co-operation with the International Economic History Association."
Includes index.
ISBN 978-1-107-10470-9 (hardback) – ISBN 978-1-107-50718-0 (paperback)
1. Economic history.   2. Economic development – History.   I. Baten, Joerg, editor.
II. International Economic History Association, sponsoring body.
HC51.H596   2016
330.9′03–dc23   2015026750

ISBN 978-1-107-10470-9 Hardback
ISBN 978-1-107-50718-0 Paperback

Contents

Figures

Maps

Tables

Contributors

Pablo Martín-Aceña

Professor at the University of Alcalá, Madrid.

Franco Amatori

Professor of Economic History at Bocconi University, Milan.

Gareth Austin

Professor at the Graduate Institute of Geneva and professor of Economy History at the University of Cambridge.

Joerg Baten

Professor of Economic History at the Department of Economics, University of Tübingen.

Luis Bértola

Professor at the Universidad de la Republica, Uruguay.

Stephen Broadberry

Professor of Economic History at the University of Oxford.

Sarah Carmichael

Assistant Lecturer at Utrecht University.

Selin Dilli

Postdoctoral Researcher at Utrecht University.

Price Fishback

Thomas R. Brown Professor of Economics at the University of Arizona.

Rima Ghanem

Assistant Lecturer at Tübingen University.

Marjolein 'T Hart

Professor of the History of State Formation in Global Perspective at VU University of Amsterdam and Head of the History Department at Huygens ING, The Hague.

Kris Inwood

Professor at the University of Guelph.

Salomón Kalmanovitz

Professor at the Universidad Jorge Tadeo Lozano Bogotá.

Debin Ma

Associate Professor at the Economic History Department at London School of Economics and Political Science.

Ma Min

Professor at Central China Normal University.

José Antonio Ocampo

Professor in the School of International and Public Affairs and co-President of the Initiative for Policy Dialogue at Columbia University.

Tetsuji Okazaki

Professor at the University of Tokyo.

Kevin Hjortshøj O'Rourke

Chichele Professor of Economic History, All Souls College, Oxford.

Irina Potkina

Professor at the Institute of Russian History, Russian Academy of Sciences, Moscow.

Auke Rijpma

Assistant Lecturer at Utrecht University.

Tirthankar Roy

Professor, Economic History, London School of Economics.

Osamu Saito

Professor Emeritus, Hitotsubashi University.

Catherine Schenk

Professor of International History at the University of Glasgow.

Martin Shanahan

Professor in International Economic and Business History at the University of South Australia.

Knut Sogner

Professor of Economic History at BI Norwegian Business School, Oslo.

Jan Luiten van Zanden

Professor in Global Economic History at Utrecht University.

Jeffrey G. Williamson

Professor at Harvard University and University of Wisconsin.

Introduction: A history of the global economy – the 'why' and the 'how'

Joerg Baten

For many years of our recent past, one's country of birth predicted the income and welfare level of the majority of the population: if you were born in a western European country or a country that was a previous European settlement (such as the US), you would be relatively well off by global standards. If you were born in the developing world, this would often not be the case. Many observers perceived this almost as a natural law. Even if that might still hold on average, the rapid rise of income in China and other threshold economies over the last years cast doubt on the persistence of development differences. This is even truer after the recent crisis in Europe and the US and after the reappearance of territorial war in Europe.

To answer today's questions, it is crucial to understand the economic history of the past: which countries developed positively during the various periods of their history? This book of the history of the global economy will trace the developments of many individual countries and their world regions. The ingredients of success (or failure) will be the main focus. What was a good economic policy? Was there investment in education? Was there an absence of war? Were there growth-promoting institutions?

In this volume, twenty-seven authors of various nationalities and intellectual traditions will present the welfare development of the global economy and its components in a concise and accessible way. The authors will reflect on the considerable increase in knowledge of global economic history and the history of world regions that has occurred over previous years, both in the developed world as well as in countries with traditionally lower research density in Africa, the Middle East, Asia and other world regions. A special focus of this volume will be on developing countries that have received less attention in former world economic histories: was, for example, Africa always a continent of relative poverty, or were there periods of economic growth in some of its regions? Why did Asia fall behind in the early nineteenth and twentieth centuries?

This book will concentrate on the period from 1500 until today but with a slightly stronger focus on the recent past. Ten world region chapters will present an economic history in a balanced way. The aim is to write a non-Eurocentric history; hence, the chapters discuss world regions that have an approximately similar population size currently. Each world region chapter will have circa 500 million inhabitants today.[1]

'Interlinking' chapters will summarize some of the core debates and topics studied recently. These interlinking chapters will also take a global perspective on some of the core indicators and growth determinants. In addition, a number of shorter 'highlight' articles will focus on particular topics in economic history that shed light on especially astonishing developments, such as why Ethiopia was not colonized and the productivity of Second World War industry in Japan.

We decided to consider a set of core indicators in the world regions so that a comparative picture emerges. Among these indicators will be estimates of national income. The political and institutional dimension will be represented by an index of democratic possibilities. In addition, recent research has suggested that indicators of nutrition and health are important. Finally educational – and numerical abilities in particular – will be traced. Indicators for these components of development will be described in the following pages. Their major advantages are as follows: (1) they approximate some of the core dimensions of development such as income, political freedom, health and education; (2) and they are available for a large number of countries also located outside the Western world and for almost the whole nineteenth and twentieth centuries (and often earlier).[2]

In particular, the long-term history of developing countries sometimes required the use of new proxy indicators that are less obvious in their informative values or in the possibility to measure them with a sufficient degree of precision. We will therefore discuss their plausibility in detail in the following.

Gross domestic product (GDP) as an indicator of productive capacity

One indicator that seems not to need much introduction is gross domestic product per capita (GDP/c). This is the total national income of a country, divided by its population, following internationally established rules to measure it. GDP has many advantages: it measures the people's command over produced goods and services. These not only provide direct utility to human beings, but they can also be used indirectly to improve health and education, which again enhances well-being and utility in the future (Bolt *et al.* 2014). Hence, the growth of GDP per capita over the last two centuries in many world regions had important consequences for the standard of living. Looking at various countries, it becomes clear in this volume that lower growth in GDP in many of them caused dissatisfaction in their inhabitants.

In sum, GDP per capita is one of the most important concepts for tracing the development of the global economy. Why, then, should we consider other indicators at all? There are several reasons why GDP should be complemented with other measures of well-being. First, the rules for measuring GDP were designed for recent decades (especially the period after the 1960s). For example, it is more difficult to estimate GDP for the UK in 1800 than in 1960 or for Malawi in 1800.

Second, one big challenge is to construct informative series of prices over long periods, often with large gaps in existing historical sources and documents. A major problem is also the appearance of new products: what would have been the price of an iPhone in 1800? Economists have invested significant thought in these problems and have devised convincing strategies, but any reader of economic history must be aware that a national income estimate in 1800 does not necessarily have the same informative value as a GDP estimate of 2014. Hence, it is helpful to complement it with other measures. Third, while higher income can be used to improve health and education, this was obviously not always achieved in human history. Also, rising inequalities within countries sometimes resulted in lower welfare for the poorer part of the population, while average GDP per capita was increasing. One strategy of economic historians has been to compare other indicators of welfare to countercheck GDP estimates, which we will discuss below.

Height as an indicator of health and the quality of nutrition

Human stature is now a well-established indicator for the so-called 'biological standard of living', positively correlated as it is, along with good health and longevity, with a nutritious diet.[3] In the 1980s, Robert F. Fogel, Richard Steckel and John Komlos pioneered its use in the field of economic history, and a large body of literature in this and other fields has emerged since (Baten and Blum 2014a, Floud *et al.* 1990, Harris 1994, Komlos and Baten 2004, Moradi and Baten 2005, Steckel 2009). Anthropometric studies of individual countries have made a significant contribution to social-welfare economics over the past several decades, particularly in developing countries hitherto neglected because reliable data were lacking, but also in the developed world.

If economists are coming to use height as a valid complement to conventional welfare indicators, this is because it has some specific advantages. A given income level permits the purchase of a given quality as well as quantity of food and medical services, and is thereby correlated with health, which in turn is correlated with height. However, this income–height correlation is not one-to-one, modified as it is by important inputs not traded in the marketplace, but provided as public goods, such as infant-nutrition programmes and public hospitals, which account for slight deviations between purchasing power-based and height-based measures of biological well-being. While height is not without its deficiencies as a measure of the standard of living of a given population, it generates insights into global changes, and is particularly valuable as a countercheck as well as a complement to conventional indicators, permitting more reliable results than might otherwise be the case.

Life expectancy is among the many health indicators with which height is positively correlated. Having analysed height data for the birth cohorts of 1860,

1900 and 1950, Baten and Komlos (1998) concluded that every centimetre above and beyond a given population's average height translates into a life-expectancy increase of 1.2 years. Thus a mere half-centimetre deviation from the average is significant, representing as it does six months of life.

The question of what role genetics, as well as nutrition, may play in determining a given population's average height was often raised in the early years of anthropometric research. It turns out that while genes are a key determinant of an individual's height, when it comes to groups of individuals genetic deviations from the mean cancel each other out. Moreover, there is considerable evidence that it is environmental conditions, not genes, which account for most of today's height gap between rich and poor populations, including those inhabiting a single nation. Habicht *et al.* (1974), for example, found that the height gap between the rich and poor sectors of a less-developed country (LDC), Nigeria, was even wider than that between an LDC's elite and a reference population in the US (see also Fiawoo 1979 on Ghana; Graitcer and Gentry 1981 on Egypt, Haiti, and Togo). What is more, the height-distribution percentiles for children from rich families in this last study are in line with those for a rich country, namely the US. Of course, not all height differentials are due exclusively to environmental conditions: African bushmen and pygmies, for example, spring to mind, although they account for only a small percentage of their respective nations' populations. However, after taking into account protein availability, disease environment, lactose tolerance and food preferences (especially in more affluent countries) the height impact of 'race' seems rather small.

One important issue for all historical indicators, but the recently developed height indicator in particular, are selectivities of the sources. Some of the sources used are samples, and it has to be assessed whether those are a representative mirror of the underlying population, or whether they might be a selected group. How substantial are these issues in the studies used? First, some typically biased samples – such as samples of students – were not included in the national height estimates considered in our study. In general, preference was given to military conscript samples and systematic anthropological measurements. The military conscript samples became available after the concept of general conscription in the French revolutionary and Napoleonic armies spread throughout continental Europe around 1800. Typically, every male of a certain age was measured and medically examined (thereafter, the lot determined who joined the army). The files recorded everyone's height.[4] Hence, height estimates based on this system are more representative than volunteer armies. Measurements recorded by scholarly anthropologists were normally also a very comprehensive source with little underlying social selectivity. However, the earliest anthropological measurements of the late nineteenth century were sometimes more difficult to use because they were often quite localized. Only if a country was documented by a large number of

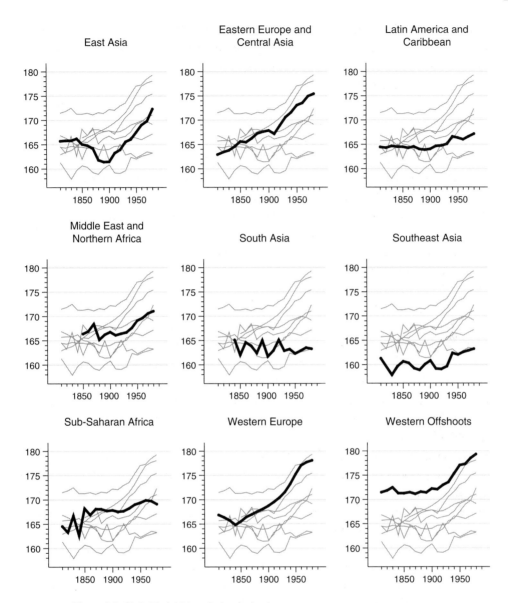

Figure I.1 Global height trends (males)
Source: modified from Baten and Blum (2014b).

regional measurements (representing the various regions) could representativeness for national means be assumed.[5] For some countries and periods, only samples of prisoners, slaves and volunteer soldiers were available. In those cases, selectivities were slightly more difficult to assess. However, for most of the countries, several sources were available, and hence a comparison of height trends and levels recorded in different contexts was possible. Baten and Blum (2014a) also ensured that no substantial regional biases were present in the height series that was ultimately selected for a specific country (especially in large countries where regional height differences can be substantial). One obvious problem in volunteer armies and prison samples is the dependence on the opportunity costs as determined by the labour market. The preferred strategy in this case was to assess height samples that were recorded for only one year (or for a short span of time, such as the US Civil War 1861–65) and that contained different age groups. This allowed to keep the labour market conditions constant at the time of recruitment so that height, when organized by birth cohort, could be analyzed.

Estimates of world-region trends for the entire 1810–1989 period indicate that the Anglo-Saxon settlements had very high anthropometric values for much of the period under study, not converging with lower ones until the late nineteenth century, and then only moderately (Figure I.1). Both western Europe and those countries in eastern Europe and central Asia that had ever experienced socialist rule recorded a strong upward trend after the 1880s. In contrast, levels in Latin America, the Middle East, and north Africa were at relatively high levels in the nineteenth century but during the twentieth century experienced only modest increases. East Asia and Sub-Saharan Africa remained near the global average throughout the entire period, except East Asia during the late nineteenth century. Africa is the only world region in which the average height has steadily declined over the last two decades (Moradi 2009). Finally, both South and Southeast Asia remained at a low level throughout the period under study (Brennan *et al.* 1994; Guntupalli and Baten 2006). In sum, we find that after the 1880s global heights increased on average, but also became more unequal.

We would like to end this overview with an example of research on the economic history of today's developing countries in which anthropometric measures provided new insights. In the economic history of the Middle East, for example, evidence on welfare is particularly difficult to obtain. After reading studies on the deindustrialization of this world region, it was difficult to understand why the governments did not attempt a more protectionist trade policy and why they were not even alarmed. However, looking at anthropometric evidence about relatively high biological welfare levels around the mid-nineteenth century in the Middle East, it became obvious that at first there were no alarm signals from this side (this will be further discussed in Chapter 7 by Ghanem and Baten and in the Interlinking Chapter 5/6 by Williamson).

Basic numeracy as an indicator of education

A considerable number of recent studies have used a proxy of basic numeracy that is based on the so-called 'age-heaping' technique. This is the share of people who were most likely able to report their exact age (with an annual resolution) rather than providing a rounded 'heaped' age. The age-heaping phenomenon applies to historical populations (as well as people in the poorest countries today) when a substantial share of the people were not able to state their exact age and instead gave responses, such as 'I am 30', when they were in fact 29 or 31 (A'Hearn et al. 2009).[6]

Duncan-Jones (1990) employed this technique to study age data from Roman tombstones. Mokyr (1983) suggested utilizing the age-heaping measure as an explicit numeracy indicator in economic history. He employed the degree of age-heaping to assess the labour-quality effect of emigration on the Irish home economy during the first half of the nineteenth century, as emigrants from pre-famine Ireland were less sophisticated than those who stayed behind.[7]

A'Hearn et al. (2009) found that the relationship between illiteracy and numeracy for LDCs after 1950 is very close. They calculated both measures for not less than 270,000 individuals who were organized by 416 regions, ranging from Latin America to Oceania. The correlation coefficient with illiteracy was as high as 0.7. The correlation with the PISA results for numerical skills was even as high as 0.85; hence, the ABCC numeracy index is more strongly correlated with numerical skills. They also employed a large US census sample to perform a very detailed analysis of this relationship. They subdivided by race, gender, high and low educational status and other criteria. In each case, A'Hearn et al. obtained a statistically significant relationship. Remarkable also is the fact that the coefficients are relatively stable between samples, i.e., a unit change in numeracy is associated with similar changes in literacy across the various tests. The results are not only valid for the US: in any country with substantial age-heaping that has been studied so far, the correlation was both statistically and economically significant.

To assess the robustness of those US census results and the similar conclusions that could be drawn from the LDCs of the late twentieth century, A'Hearn et al. (2009) also assessed numeracy and literacy in sixteen different European countries between the Middle Ages and the early nineteenth century. Again, they found a positive correlation between age-heaping and literacy.

There remains some uncertainty about whether age-heaping in the sources contains information about the numeracy of the responding individual, or rather about the diligence of the reporting personnel who wrote down the statements. The age data of the relevant age groups were normally derived from statements from the person himself or herself. However, it is possible that a second party, especially the husband, may have made or influenced the age statement, or even that the enumerator estimated the age without asking the individual. If the latter occurred, we would not be able to measure the numeracy of the person interviewed. In contrast, if the enumerator asked and obtained no response, a round age estimated by him would still measure basic numeracy correctly. A large body of literature has investigated the issue of other persons reporting. Recently, Friesen *et al.* (2013) compared systematically the evidence of a gender gap in numeracy and in literacy for the late nineteenth century and early twentieth century and found a strong correlation between countries. They argued that there is no reason why the misreporting of literacy and age should have yielded exactly the same gap between genders. A more likely explanation is that the well-known correlation between numeracy and literacy also applies to gender differences.

There are various examples of how age-heaping based on estimates of numeracy have improved our understanding of long-term development. One example is the relative decline of numeracy that took place in Latin America and China during the nineteenth century: Latin America had a steep increase in numeracy in the eighteenth century and China had already reached a high level by this time. But during the mid- to late-nineteenth century, both world regions experienced declining or stagnating numeracy, whereas in western Europe and North America levels remained high or increased. This might have contributed to the failure of China and Latin America of participating in the second Industrial Revolution, which depended strongly on abilities in science and mathematics as those were necessary to develop the new chemical and electrical industries.

In sum, age-heaping-based numeracy estimates education and, in particular, is a proxy for numerical skills. As such, it is an important component of human capital and a precondition for more advanced skills. A perfect human capital measure would be a composite index of basic and advanced text-related skills, of basic and advanced numerical skills, of technological skills, of social and organizational creativity and perhaps of other components. However, given that such perfect composite indexes are impossible to construct in most real world situations, scholars often use proxy indicators for more broad concepts. Numeracy has the additional advantage that it is particularly growth-relevant (see Interlinking Chapter I.2 by Baten).

The polity IV index as an indicator of democracy

Marshall *et al.* (2009) suggested approximating the development of democratic values with the polity IV dataset. In this dataset, countries are characterized by a score between +10 (fully democratic) and –10 (fully autocratic). The score is actually a composite index that is based on six component variables because the authors argue that political participation is not only a suffrage right but also access to executive function and constraining mechanisms. Among the six components, there are three that relate to the access possibilities to executive functions in the government: (1) how is the recruitment of the chief executive regulated? (2) Is the recruitment of executives in general competitive, or is it clear from the beginning who will obtain power? (3) How open is executive recruitment? Next, there is a variable (4) that considers the constraints of the executive: can the government executive act at will, or do other political bodies and institutions constrain their activities? Finally, the last two components indicate whether participation in elections is (5) regulated and (6) competitive. Each of the six components is characterized with a numerical index value, and the final polity IV measure is the average of these individual component values.

In many cases, these six variables tend to be correlated with each other. However, there are also cases, for example, in which 'show-case' elections are held, whereas the access to executive power is de facto in the hands of a political or ethnic group; this reduces the democratic value of elections greatly, of course.

In the economic history literature, the component of 'constraining the executive' has received particular attention; Acemoglu *et al.* (2001) argued that an unconstrained executive is more likely to expropriate business enterprises and to develop a climate that is not growth promoting. Therefore, there are at least two dimensions that make this variable so important in our volume: the growth-retarding function of unconstrained executives but also the more general welfare function of democratic participation. The world region trends are characterized by an early lead of the 'Western offshoots', and substantial variability during the twentieth century (Figure I.2).

In sum, this set of four variables allows us to provide evidence on income, health, education and democracy in a large number of countries over past

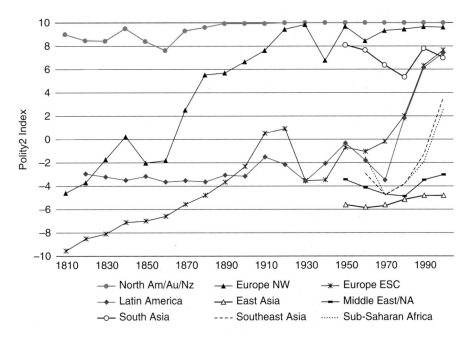

Figure I.2 Regional averages of democracy scores (polity2), 1810–2000s
Source: based on Marshall, Jaggers and Gurr (2011). 'Western offshoots' includes North America, Australia and New Zealand, 'NW' means north-west; 'ESC' means East–South–Central.

centuries. While the indicators are not without potential problems, they allow us to trace a global economic history even for world regions that received less attention before, such as Africa, Asia and Latin America. Of course, these four indicators are not appropriate for all countries and world regions, hence they are not all employed in each chapter. The chapters also differ intentionally in their focus on historical description (of which more is included in Chapter 2, on eastern, south-ern and central Europe) or historical analysis (north-western Europe, for exam-ple), because some world regions such as the latter have been described by many previous authors, hence the descriptive part can be slightly shorter here.

Clearly, there are many measurement issues if these indicators are estimated for individual countries and world regions. In a relatively short book, not all country-specific issues can be discussed. Some general issues have been addressed in this short introduction. Readers who would like to learn more about the data quality and data availability in individual countries can obtain more information using the internet platform www.clio-infra.eu and the recent book by van Zanden *et al.* (2014).

How was the group of twenty-seven authors of this volume formed? An important institution in the discipline of economic history is its global organiza-tion, the International Economic History Association (IEHA). This institution was founded in the early 1960s and regularly organizes world congresses.[8] The authors of this volume meet regularly at these occasions, and the idea to write a balanced history of the global economy was born at one of its meetings (in the Executive Committee); the Secretary General at that time (Joerg Baten) was asked to realize the creation of this volume, acting as editor. Cambridge University Press and its history editor, Michael Watson, agreed to publish the book, for which we are very thankful, and our thanks also go to several readers who reflected on both the initial proposal as well as the whole book manuscript, and to Sevket Pamuk for his comments on the Middle East chapter. Last but not least, we thank all participants at world congresses and all students of economic history for their important input in this volume.

Notes

1. Only China and South Asia are substantially above average as large countries cannot be appropriately split. Chapters on Japan and China were introduced separately. One world region is slightly smaller than the average: north-western Europe. However, as it is likely that much more than half of the whole economic history literature refers to this region, we think that this exception is justified.
2. The historical values for countries whose size changed over time will refer generally to current territory (to make long-run comparisons possible). All world regions and the global average are weighted by their corresponding population size. Additional indica-tors of development – which will be discussed if evidence is available – are life expectancy, real wages, school enrolment, war and civil war occurrence and others.

3. Komlos (1985) suggested the term 'Biological Standard of Living' in 1985. On the following, see Baten and Blum 2014a, Moradi and Baten 2005.
4. Except for the small share of illegal emigrants (clergymen were also exempt).
5. The very earliest anthropological data could sometimes not be used as anthropologists sometimes intended to find certain extremes (such as 'the tallest African tribe', etc.).
6. Around 20 per cent clearly had an age that was a multiple of five; therefore, the numeracy needs to adjust for this. Usually ages 23 to 72 are considered. For further details, see Crayen and Baten (2010). The calculation of the ABCC Index is shown here as a derivation of the Whipple Index:

$$Wh = \left(\frac{(Age25 + Age30 + Age35 + ... + Age70)}{1/5^*(Age23 + Age24 + Age25 + ... + Age72)} \right) \times 100 \qquad (1)$$

$$ABCC = \left(1 - \frac{(Wh - 100)}{400} \right) \times 100 \text{ if } Wh \geq 100 \text{ ; else } ABCC = 100 \qquad (2)$$

7. De Moor and van Zanden (2006) studied the relative numeracy of women during the Middle Ages, and Clark (2007) has recently reviewed the evidence.
8. In spite of this, the present volume is not the 'official' economic history of the IEHA, but a book representing the views of the authors.

References

A'Hearn, B., Baten, J. and Crayen, D. (2009), 'Quantifying Quantitative Literacy: Age Heaping and the History of Human Capital', *Journal of Economic History* 69 (3), 783–808.

Acemoglu, D., Johnson, S. and Robinson, J. (2001), 'The Colonial Origins of Comparative Development: An Empirical Investigation', *American Economic Review* 91, December 2001, 1369–1401.

Baten, J. and Blum, M. (2014a), 'Why are you Tall while Others are Short? Agricultural Production and other Proximate Determinants of Global Heights', *European Review of Economic History* 18, 144–65.

Baten, J. and Blum, M. (2014b), 'Height', in J. L. van Zanden *et al.* (eds.), *How Was Life? Global Well-being Since 1820*, Paris: OECD.

Baten, J. and Komlos, J. (1998), 'Height and the Standard of Living', *Journal of Economic History* 57 (3), 866–70.

Bolt, J., Timmer, M. P. and van Zanden, J. L. (2014), 'GDP per Capita', in J. Baten, M. P. Timmer and J. L. van Zanden (eds.), *How Was Life? A Long-term Perspective on Global Well-being and Development*, Paris: OECD (ch. 3).

Brennan, L., McDonald, J. and Shlomowitz, R. (1994), 'Trends in the Economic Well-being of South Indians under British Rule: the Anthropometric Evidence', *Explorations in Economic History* 31, 225–60.

Clark, G. (2007), *A Farewell to Alms: A Brief Economic History of the World*, Princeton University Press.

Crayen, D. and Baten, J. (2010), 'Global Trends in Numeracy 1820–1949 and its Implications for Long-Run Growth', *Explorations in Economic History* 47 (1), 82–99.

De Moor, T. and van Zanden, J. L. (2006), *Women and the Origins of Capitalism in Western Europe*, Amsterdam: Boom.

Duncan-Jones, R. (1990), *Structure and Scale in the Roman Economy*, Cambridge University Press.

Fiawoo, D. K. (1979), 'Physical Growth and the School Environment: a West African Example', in W. A. Stini (ed.), *Physiological and Morphological Adaptation and Evolution*, The Hague: Mouton (pp. 301–14).

Floud, R., Wachter, K. W. and Gregory, A. S. (1990), *Height, Health, and History: Nutritional Status in the United Kingdom, 1750–1980*, Cambridge University Press.

Friesen, J., Baten, J. and Prayon, V. (2013), 'Women Count. Gender (In-)Equalities in the Human Capital Development in Asia, 1900–1960', *Working Papers in Economics and Finance No. 29, University of Tuebingen*.

Graitcer, P. L. and Gentry, E. M. (1981), 'Measuring Children: One Reference for All', *The Lancet* 2, 297–99.

Guntupalli, A. M. and Baten, J. (2006), 'The Development and Inequality of Heights in North, West and East India, 1915–44', *Explorations in Economic History* 43 (4), 578–608.

Habicht, J. P., Martorell, R., Yarbrough, C., Malina, R. M. and Klein, R. E. (1974), 'Height and Weight Standards for Preschool Children: How Relevant are Ethnic Differences?', *The Lancet* 6, 611–15.

Harris, B. (1994), 'Health, Height, and History: an Overview of Recent Developments in Anthropometric History', *Social History of Medicine* 7, 297–320.

Komlos, J. (1985), 'Stature and Nutrition in the Habsburg Monarchy: the Standard of Living and Economic Development in the Eighteenth Century', *American Historical Review*, 90 (5), 1149–61.

Komlos, J. and Baten, J. (2004), 'Looking Backward and Looking Forward: Anthropometric Research and the Development of Social Science History', *Social Science History* 28 (2), 191–210.

Marshall, M., Jaggers, G. K. and Gurr, T. R. (2011), *POLITY IV Project Political Regime Characteristics and Transitions, 1800–2010 Dataset Users' Manual*. www.systemic peace.org/inscr/p4manualv2010.pdf, last downloaded 1 September 2014.

Mokyr, J. (1983), *Why Ireland Starved: a Quantitative and Analytical History of the Irish Economy*, London: Taylor and Francis.

Moradi, A. (2009), 'Nutritional Status and Economic Development in Sub-Saharan Africa, 1950–1980', *Economics and Human Biology* 8 (1), 16–29.

Moradi, A. and Baten, J. (2005), 'Inequality in Sub-Saharan Africa 1950–80: New Estimates and New Results', *World Development Volume* 33-8, 1233–1265.

Steckel, R. (2009), 'Heights and Human Welfare: Recent Developments and New Directions', *Explorations in Economic History* 46, 1–23.

van Zanden, J. L., Baten, J., d'Hercole, M. M., Rijpma, A., Smith, C., Timmer, M. (eds.), (2014) *How Was Life? Global Well-being since 1820*, OECD, Paris.

1 North-western Europe

Jan Luiten van Zanden

North-western Europe played a crucial role in the world economy: it was the pioneer of the 'modern' market economy and of 'modern economic growth' that resulted from it, and came to control large parts of the world. At the same time, there were quite different roads to modernity, even in this relatively small part of the world; the United Kingdom held the middle in between early developers (in the Low Countries) and latecomers (the Nordic countries and Ireland). The urban, most dynamic core of the region was in Flanders and Brabant in the late Middle Ages, then moved to Holland in the seventeenth century, and crossed the North Sea in the second half of that century, when England started its growth spurt that would result in the Industrial Revolution of the post-1750 period. After 1800 the techniques and institutions of the Industrial Revolution began to spread from the UK to Belgium at first, but within a few decades to almost all parts of north-western Europe. Gradually, the process of economic growth spread to the rest of the region; the nineteenth century saw the 'catching up' of the northern countries, which had not developed rapidly before 1800. In the twentieth century this process of convergence within north-western Europe continued; after 1945 the UK lost its prominent place within the world economy to become the 'sick man' of the region in the 1960s and 1970s, but it rebounded afterwards. The northern countries continued their spectacular advance during the twentieth century, becoming the best examples of welfare states with strong economies based on high levels of human capital formation and innovativeness.

There are many stories to tell about the economic development of this region, but we have to focus on three: (1) why this part of the world experienced rapid economic expansion between 1500 and 1850, resulting in the British Industrial Revolution; (2) how this economic core region developed after 1850, when its model – and in particular its technologies – were increasingly copied elsewhere; and (3) how the more 'marginal' parts of the region (Scandinavia, Ireland) caught up from about the mid-nineteenth century onwards.

Early growth and modernization

It is one of the big questions of economic history why the North Sea region, which was a rather marginal part of the European economy until the high Middle Ages, became the economic powerhouse of Europe (and arguably the world) in the centuries before the Industrial Revolution. Before about 1600 the Mediterranean – and in particular northern Italy – was the most highly developed part of Europe, but already from the thirteenth and fourteenth century onwards, first the Low Countries, then followed by England, developed strongly, first to become an alternative centre of urbanization and growth (1200–1600), and after 1600 to really overshadow the old Mediterranean core. It was the Low Countries and Great Britain that in the long run profited the most from the expansion of the Atlantic economy and the growth of trade with Asia, in spite of the fact that in both regions they were latecomers by about one century, after the pioneering efforts by Portugal and Spain. Why did the Dutch and the English reap where the Iberians sowed?

The most convincing answer is probably that in the North Sea area a set of institutions had emerged that was very conducive to growth. An often used example of this concerns the way in which the commercial empires of Iberia and the North Sea area were organized: in Spain and Portugal it was basically state enterprises in which private entrepreneurship played a limited role; in the north it was the other way around: the state offered encouragement (via monopolies and chartered companies) but the private sector was in charge. This fundamental contrast reflected deep-seated institutional differences. In the late Middle Ages institutions to constrain the power of the king such as Parliaments had emerged almost everywhere in western Europe (the first one was set up in Spain, the Cortez of Leon dated from 1188). At the same time, however, kings built up a stronger power base – a standing army, new sources of taxation and independent bureau-cracy – which allowed them to rule without the 'feudal' parliaments and claim 'absolutist' power. The clash between civil society organized in parliaments (and in cities) and the rising power of the sovereign almost everywhere resulted in victory for the latter – except for two cases: the Dutch Republic after 1572 (born out of an eighty-years war with the absolutism of the Spanish kings), and England after 1640 (or 1688). In both cases Parliament (or the Estates General as they were known in the Netherlands) established a firm grip on power – or even became the supreme authority in the polity. It resulted in an entirely different balance of power between sovereign and civil society – this institutional 'little divergence' helps to explain the economic 'little divergence' that occurred at the same time (van Zanden, Buringh and Bosker 2012).

Another important part of the institutional framework of the North Sea area concerned the way in which family, household and marriage was organized. In the late Middle Ages the region saw the rise of the European marriage pattern (EMP), in which marriage was based on consensus (the boy and girl selected each other voluntarily) and the new couple set up their own household after marriage. This resulted in high ages of marriage (more than 23 years for girls), a relatively large share of singles in the population and the absence of a strong boy preference. This 'delayed' marriage created possibilities for increased human capital formation for both men and women; during their teens and early twenties, many worked as servants or apprentices in the households or crafts shops of others, developing their own networks and building up job experience. As fertility decisions are in most societies heavily influenced by female agency and human capital, this new demographic pattern can be seen as a first step in the switch from 'quantity' to 'quality' of offspring. Its most notable result was a gradual accumulation of human capital through the expansion of formal and informal education (de Moor and van Zanden 2010; Voigtländer and Voth 2012).

The EMP was embedded in a highly developed labour market, with employment opportunities for both men and women. In the North Sea region a large part of the population – both in the cities and in the countryside – was dependent on wage labour, and agricultural activities were increasingly commercialized, also thanks to the high level of urbanization leading to a very dynamic demand for foodstuffs. Capital markets were also highly developed, offering credit to households at interest rates which still would be considered very reasonable (5–6 per cent in Holland in the fifteenth and sixteenth century, dropping even more thereafter) (van Zanden, de Moor and Zuijderduijn 2012). Land markets were equally flexible, resulting, for example, in large changes in the distribution of agricultural holdings towards large units in both England and the Netherlands; in England this process lead to the emergence of large estates and the proletarianization of the farming population (Allen 1992).

Jan de Vries and Ad van der Woude (1997) have analyzed these changes for the northern Netherlands, and concluded that this was the 'first modern economy' that generated a process of 'modern economic growth' leading to the Dutch Golden Age of the seventeenth century. Seen from a broader perspective, the Dutch economic miracle was part of a process of sustained economic growth in the North Sea area that began with the shock of Black Death of 1347 (which lifted gross domestic product [GDP] per capita by about a third), and continued until the early nineteenth century. During these 550 years the average GDP per capita of the region increased by 0.18 per cent per annum; at about 1810 there was a distinct acceleration of growth, to the 'normal' rate for the nineteenth century of about 1 per cent annually (van Zanden and van Leeuwen 2012; Broadberry et al. 2011).

Growth between 1350 and 1800 was partly driven by endogenous changes such as the rise of literacy and other forms of human capital formation, capital accumulation (made possible by the trend towards lower interest rates) and technological change – culminating in the 'wave of gadgets' that resulted in the Industrial Revolution after 1750. But the expansion of commercial empires and the growth of trade also contributed significantly. The highest incomes were earned in international services (trade, shipping, banking), and the cities that managed to become the central hubs in these networks (Antwerp, Amsterdam

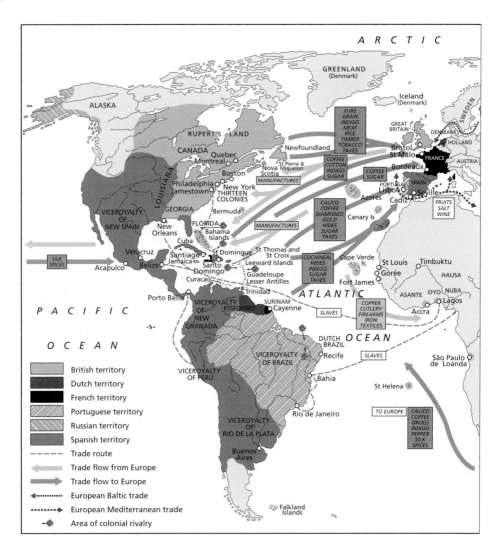

Map 1.1 Trade flows between European Empires and their colonies during the late eighteenth century. Redrawn and modified after *Atlas of World History*, ed. by P. O'Brien, Oxford University Press, 2002.

and London respectively), prospered greatly. Map 1.1 shows the European Empires and their most important trading commodities. It becomes clear that most colonial trade was concentrated in north-western Europe. The Dutch economy was strongly dependent on the Baltic trade for its bread and timber, and the Dutch East India Company set up in 1602 was (initially) extremely successful, highly profitable, a large employer of sailors and soldiers which created an Asian commercial Empire out of proportion with the modest size of the country from which it originated. On an even larger scale Great Britain repeated the experience. It not only put together an Asian Empire (with India gradually becoming the 'jewel in the crown'), but was equally successful in North America and the Caribbean. It

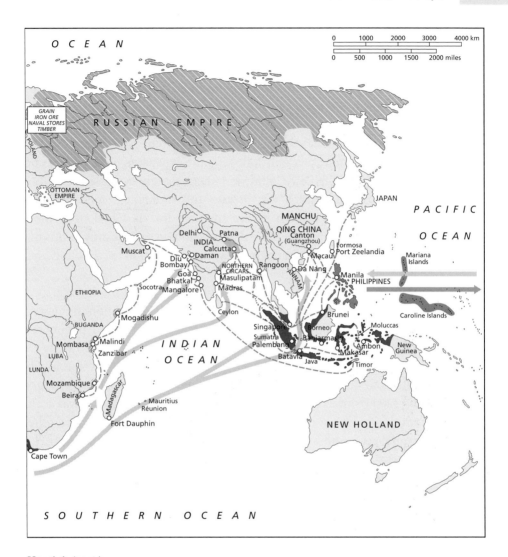

Map 1.1 (cont.)

was the dynamic development of the Atlantic economy that contributed much to the rise of England as the new core of the world economy after 1650 (Acemoglu *et al.* 2005). Political institutions – growing state capabilities to wage war, create a mighty navy, raise taxes – enhanced these commercial developments, an alliance symbolized by Cromwell's Navigation Acts. That the North Sea area in the long run profited the most of the expansion of international trade, and not Portugal and Spain that had pioneered the new trade routes, points to its strong competitive position in this field.

The proceeds of growth were very unequally distributed however. Real wages lagged behind real incomes, and in the most prosperous parts of the region real wages in the eighteenth century were at best at about the same level as they were before the 'price revolution' of the sixteenth century (Allen 2001). Inequality of income and wealth increased rapidly, paralleling the growth of urbanization and average income levels. Both Holland and England became very unequal societies with a huge gap between the rich and the poor, but paradoxically this did not undermine the new political structures that had emerged after 1572 and 1688 respectively. As a counterbalance to growing income gaps, literacy and numeracy were growing rapidly, probably following the expansion of secondary and tertiary activities – first in the Low Countries (where already in the sixteenth century the majority of urban citizens was literate and numerate), followed by England, northern Germany, northern France and Scandinavia. The Reformation with its emphasis on the reading the Bible also contributed significantly to this process – it for example induced governments to pay more attention to schooling (the Swedish case is a well-known example).

The Industrial Revolution – the arguably most important watershed in economic history – was in many respects the logical culmination of the trends set at the end of the Middle Ages. All recent interpretations of the phenomenon start from the situation that already in 1750 Great Britain was a highly developed economy, with a large urban sector, well developed markets and institutions, a skilled labour force earning high wages thanks to their labour productivity. In Allen's (2009) interpretation of the Industrial Revolution it was a process of substitution of labour by capital, made possible by low energy costs (cheap coal), low capital costs and high real wages (in comparison with the rest of the world). In Mokyr's (2002) more 'idealistic' approach the amazing capacity of British engineers to invent new labour saving machines was induced by the spread of Enlightenment ideas of experimentation and rational enquiry. But such favourable conditions were necessary for the industrial transformation – the growth of steam power, the rise of the factory system, the increase of industrial employment, the spectacular expansion of industrial exports – that occurred between about 1750 and 1850, which only after about 1810 led to an acceleration of GDP per capita growth.

The spread of the Industrial Revolution in the nineteenth century

The early nineteenth century acceleration of growth was a remarkable phenomenon, because it not only occurred in Great Britain (as a result of the industrial transformation it was undergoing), but almost everywhere in north-west Europe and, even more surprisingly, in other parts of Europe as well. The reconstructed series of GDP show for most European countries almost no growth between 1500 and 1800; some countries, such as Italy, even show remarkable decline (Bolt and van Zanden 2014). But this suddenly ends at about 1810/1820, and most series show growth during the second quarter of the nineteenth century. Growth is more intensive in the north-west, which forges ahead of the rest of Europe until about 1870, when a process of convergence began.

But the most remarkable fact is the sudden break during the early nineteenth century. For parts of the region it coincided with the diffusion of the new technologies to the continent – to parts of Belgium at first, but soon followed by regional concentrations of modern industry in Germany (Rhineland), northern France and Switzerland. Different regions responded differently: where coal was available, mining and iron industry developed rapidly (such as in Namur and Liège – the rapidly industrializing Walloon parts of Belgium) (Pollard 1981). The existence of widespread proto-industrial activities was the precondition for a rapid growth of factory-based textile industry, often based on water power at first, but gradually coal and steam also took over (see Map 1.2 for proto-industrial textile production all over north-western Europe). But in regions with high levels of agricultural productivity – in the Dutch coastal provinces, for example – incentives to move to labour intensive industry were quite weak, and industrial growth arrived relatively late – that is after 1860.

An alternative interpretation of the break at about 1815 is that it was linked to the ending of the Napoleonic wars. Europe had, finally, after twenty years of almost uninterrupted warfare, found a new more or less stable set of institutions to regulate its international affairs (the Vienna Congress had been quite successful, even in finding a solution for France), which created the right conditions for a long period of peace only ending in August 1914. Moreover, the reforms introduced after the French Revolution in the political and institutional spheres – from the streamlining of the European state system (in particular in Germany) to the introduction of a highly rationalized legal system, the Code Napoleon – also may have had strong positive effects on long-term growth. Conscious policies to reduce transaction costs via the abolishment of all kinds of 'feudal privileges' – such as international treaties to ban the many tolls that restricted free trade on for example the Rhine – also contributed to the freeing of international markets (Acemoglu *et al.* 2011). The same years at about 1820 saw a break in market integration: markets in Western Europe became more integrated, pointing to declining transaction costs. Soon the new technologies of the Industrial Revolution started to kick in as well: steamships and in particular trains that began their expansion in the 1830s, were able to reduce transport costs considerably. The telegraph (an invention of the 1840s) revolutionized information costs and had even more dramatic effects on market integration. The liberalization of international trade in the 1850s and 1860s, following the abolishment of the British Corn Laws, completed the process.

Due to these changes, during the first decades of the nineteenth century a process of 'modern economic growth' began in north-west Europe, based on the

Map 1.2 Regional economic specialization in Europe during the late seventeenth and early eighteenth century
Source: See map 1.1.

new (British) technologies and on a (French) rationalization of institutions. Belgium profited the most from the relatively peaceful century between 1815 and 1913 and developed into a small, open economy focused on industrial exports that competed with Great Britain. It developed strong ties between basic industry and the banking sector and as such was one of the pioneers of the 'organized' capitalism that was a feature of twentieth-century Europe. Denmark was another 'success story', in this case based on agricultural exports and an industrialization process that was largely focused on the growing internal market. Both countries saw their GDP per capita increase threefold (or slightly more) (all GDP estimates from Maddison 2001). Sweden (with a much larger industrial sector thanks to coal, iron and copper mines and related industries) and Norway did almost equally well, only 'distant' Finland lagged behind. The two pioneers of early modern growth, the UK and the Netherlands, started the nineteenth century with real income levels much higher than in the rest of the region, but also saw a more than doubling of GDP per capita. Ireland is obviously a special story: it was the poor cousin of the British during the first half of the nineteenth century, then, in 1845–47, was struck by one of the worst famines in European history due to the sudden collapse of the potato harvest. It led to massive out-migration to the United States, which resulted in a sharp drop in population in the second half of the nineteenth century. Per capita growth, which was not spectacular (the gap with Great Britain remained huge) was as much the result of real growth as of the population decline (O'Grada 1995).

France started at a lower level of GDP per capita in the early nineteenth century, compared to Great Britain and the Netherlands (Figure 1.1). Why was this the case? A number of potential explanations have been discussed and rejected. For example, the lack of nationwide representative institutions has been named a determinant, because it could have reduced the creditworthiness of the government: there was no national parliament as it existed in England (on this and the following, see Hoffman 2003). The forced emigration of Protestants could be another factor causing the lower level of income per capita in France, but Benedict (1996) showed that French Catholics and Protestants before the expulsion tended to have similar thriftiness, although the educational impact has not yet been evaluated. The enclosure movement that took place in England also did not happen in France, but British studies argued that enclosures had only a small effect, if any. Hoffman (2003)

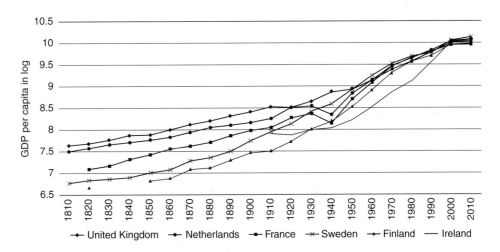

Figure 1.1 Country-specific GDP per capita in north-western Europe (in logs)
Source: www.clio-infra.eu.

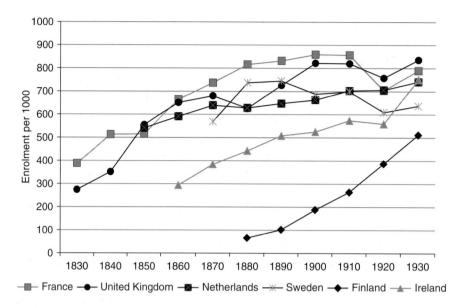

Figure 1.2 School enrolment in north-western Europe
Source: www.clio-infra.eu.

concludes his survey that the lower starting point of France was probably caused by the generally higher transaction costs in France. Fragmented property rights and a legal system that did not favour efficiency increased transaction costs. In addition, the many wars and a military preference in all issues of transaction cost-reducing infrastructure did not help to promote economic growth.[1] However, during the nineteenth century France modernized its institution and also invested heavily in schooling, making it one of the global leaders in school enrolment (Figure 1.2). Towards the end of the century and during the early twentieth century, France also converged in GDP per capita with Great Britain (Figure 1.1).

The 'catching up' of the Scandinavian countries was probably the most remarkable phenomenon in this region during the nineteenth century. These countries had two assets: relative high levels of human capital formation, the result of the Reformation and related government policies, and relatively democratic institutions at the national level, rooted in local democratic traditions. The Swedish Rikstag had developed into a very active Parliament already during the 'Era of Liberty' (1719–72), and this tradition continued into the nineteenth century, laying the basis for the transition towards modern democracy at the end of that century. It was, moreover, relatively well developed 'nation states', culturally homogenous, which mostly were able to keep themselves aside from the conflicts between the great powers. Their economic rise during the nineteenth century was on the one hand based on the – in terms of social and human capital – favourable starting point. The different countries and regions developed their own niches in the expanding international economy: Denmark specialized on agricultural exports, Norway in shipping, Sweden was in a way the 'powerhouse' of the region with a strong industrialization process commencing in the 1860s (Schön 2012), and Finland (and Norway and Sweden) exploited their huge timber resources, first via the exports of the timber itself, towards the end of the century by switching to the end product, paper. But like Ireland, the poor periphery of Scandinavia, Finland, was struck by a major harvest failure, in 1867–68, which wiped out 15 per cent of the population (Hjerppe 1989).

The region as a whole profited from the first wave of globalization of the world economy between 1850 and 1914. Migration flows expanded, not only from Ireland, but also Sweden and Norway, and at a much lower level, from the more prosperous Denmark, Belgium and the Netherlands (O'Rourke and Williamson 1999). International trade grew rapidly: the UK formed the most dynamic market for the agricultural exports from Denmark, the Netherlands and Sweden and for the international shipping services offered by the sizeable Norwegian fleet. But after 1870 Germany became also in this respect the rival of the British. Its rate of growth and the pace of its industrialization was substantially higher than the British, where a mild growth retardation occurred after 1870. In particular British agriculture found it hard to accommodate to the new globalized world, which resulted in much lower agricultural prices due to increased American competition. The sharp reductions in transport costs and the increased migration flows now 'finally' brought relative prices and wages from both sides of the Atlantic much closer together. Moreover, the British state was now totally committed to free trade (whereas other countries, such as Germany and France, increased protection for their agricultural sector). Denmark and the Netherlands also stuck to their free trade policies, as they profited from the cheap imports of cereals (used as feedstuffs for their cattle and pigs) and could increase their exports of butter and meat of which the prices were more stable (Tracy 1989).

Cheap (imported) food and rapid industrial growth resulted in sharp increases in the standard of living in the whole region. Before 1870, workers had hardly profited from the economic growth that occurred, as prices of foodstuffs had increased more rapidly than most other prices. This 'early growth paradox' is clearly evident in the data on heights (the 'biological standard of living') which for this region show a modest decline during the first half of the nineteenth century (see Figure 1.3). Measured in this way, the North Sea area was only marginally more wealthy than the rest of the world, whereas in terms of GDP per capita the gap with the world average was quite big (Figure 1.4). This early growth paradox – the fact that the first decades of industrialization often did not result in a comparable increase in living standards (Komlos 1998) – is probably related to the costs of

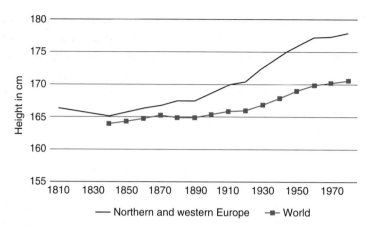

Figure 1.3 Height (male) in north-western Europe
Source: based on Baten and Blum (2014a).

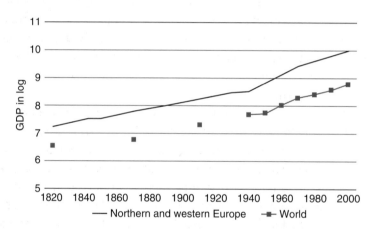

Figure 1.4 GDP per capita in north-western Europe and the world (in log of 1990 dollars)
Source: www.clio-infra.eu.

urbanization (high food prices, high rents). But the 'agricultural invasion' that began after 1870 solved these bottlenecks, and real wages and other indices of the standard of living increased rapidly after that date. To a much lesser extent the next upturn in the agricultural cycle, the increase in the international price level after 1896, had a similar effect, in the sense that real wages also did not increase a lot between 1896 and 1913.

The twentieth century rollercoaster: 1914–45

The various parts of north-west Europe were affected differently by the (largely) exogenous shock of the First World War. Belgium and northern France were devastated by the German forces and by continuous warfare on its territory; the UK was almost as heavily involved – its losses of human lives, physical and monetary capital were huge, and in terms of its international position it never fully recovered from the sacrifice. Scandinavia and the Netherlands, on the other hand, remained neutral and profited from the new circumstances – such as a booming demand for raw materials and foodstuffs and the disappearance of international competition for its exports. Finland, part of the Russian Empire since 1809, used the power vacuum created by the Russian Revolution, to success-fully declare independence. A few years later, in 1919, the Irish followed their example and finally acquired independence in 1921. Social and political upheavals towards the end of the war were an almost universal phenomenon, and reflected the economic problems of these years. On the one hand limited social groups profited from the war, the rising prices and the many (illegal) opportunities for trade and profit. The poor and middle classes suffered: the supply of grains from the US was stopped due to the 'unlimited' naval warfare by the Germans, inter-national markets and transport channels stopped working and scarcity became an urgent phenomenon. The Armistice of November 1918 was the start of an extreme boom on world markets to satisfy these urgent needs, which lasted until the end of 1919. Then, suddenly, the bubble burst, and it was followed by an equally sharp decline of prices on international markets.

In the neutral countries – Sweden, Denmark, Norway, the Netherlands – where the postwar boom was the continuation of strong inflationary tendencies during the war itself, the sudden deflation of 1920–21 led to problems in the financial sector, in banking in particular. Governments and/or central banks had to step in to rescue large banks, and the financial crisis of the early 1920s led to a decade of sluggish growth and high unemployment (Broadberry 1984). The Netherlands was the exception here: it had a modest financial crisis (in 1921–23) but the effect on growth and employment was limited, perhaps because the country profited from the German growth in the same years. Belgium was even less harmed by the downturn of the early 1920s, focused as it was on the rebuilding of its infrastruc-ture and economy; in its monetary policy it followed France (or was forced to follow it), which resulted in a sound undervaluation of its currency after 1926. The UK did not fare much better than the Scandinavian countries: perhaps because of its monetary policy (a return to the gold standard at the old parity), perhaps because of slowly emerging structural problems in its main industrial centres and sectors – coal, iron and cotton – due to sharply increased international competition. Circumstances at international markets had certainly changed fun-damentally during the First World War; the City lost its control over international capital markets to New York, which also made it much more difficult to monitor the gold standard (as the British Central Bank had managed to do before 1914) (Eichengreen 1992).

In the 1930s the tables turned. The countries that had had a poor 1920s, and that were weakened internationally as a result, were the first to be forced off gold in 1931: the UK's position became untenable in September of that year, and the Scandinavian countries (which had kept part of their international reserves in pounds sterling) all followed immediately. In this way they escaped from the second stage of the deflationary shock of 1929–33, and immediately improved their competitive position vis-à-vis the remaining gold block countries. For them, the worst was over by 1932; for Belgium and the Netherlands, which stuck to gold until 1935 and 1936 respectively, the depression continued for another three to four years (Eichengreen 1992).

Towards the end of the 1930s the international rearmaments race lifted the world economy out of its depression. But soon war broke out, and now almost all countries became involved – Sweden being the only 'neutral' exception. War was even more total than between 1914 and 1918, and resulted in huge drops in output and income, in particular towards the end, when scarcity became an extreme problem in regions still occupied by the Germans (the western part of the Netherlands struggled through a 'hunger winter' in 1944–45). Scarcity was and remained for some time a normal feature of life – even in the UK, which profited from the generous supplies from its overseas allies.

Below the surface of these huge swings in economic activity, the region continued to modernize between 1914 and 1945. Labour productivity growth was in general even faster than in the good old days before the First World War, due to the rapid spread of new technologies linked to the second Industrial Revolution. Electricity was perhaps the most important in this respect – the spread of the electric engine, for example, facilitated huge increases in productivity. Other new technologies (internal combustion engine, the radio and the telephone, new 'artificial' fibres such as rayon) continued to spread, in spite of the violent business cycles of the period. Research and development activities were professionalized, and small economies such as Sweden and the Netherlands became relatively important sources of technological change. Only the British economy showed signs of structural problems, particularly in the north which had dominated during the nineteenth century Industrial Revolution. Its turn, during the 1930s, towards closer links with its colonies via a system of 'imperial preference', signalled that this once dominant player in the world economy was now much less confident about the potential and competitiveness of British industry.

Social and political transformations also continued during the interwar period. The revolutionary 1910s saw the final establishment of full participative democracy – including voting rights for women – in almost all countries of the region (Belgium introduced women's suffrage only in 1948); measured by the Polity IV index, the region came close to a full 10 score in 1920 and 1930 (Figure 1.5). The 1910s and 1920s also saw a sharp reduction in income inequality in large parts of

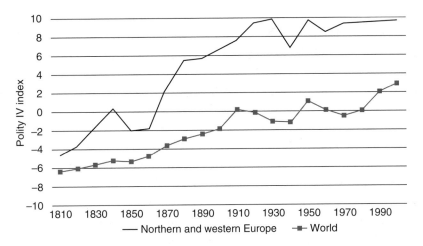

Figure 1.5 Democracy in north-western Europe
Source: calculated from Marshall *et al.* (2011).

the region, and an extension of welfare services supplied by the state. The growth of the trade union movement, and of (related) labourist political parties happened simultaneously. Sweden, ruled from 1917 onwards by governments in which the social-democrats participated, is the classic example, but similar changes – often related to the extension of the franchise in these years – were typical for the whole region. The 1910–40s were therefore no 'lost decades', but years in which the basis was created for rapid growth of the welfare state after 1945.

Peace and welfare: 1945–2010

After the Second World War the region, as the world economy as a whole, entered a new phase of stability, rapid growth and the extension of the welfare state. Until the mid-1970s growth was spectacular in the Scandinavian countries and the Netherlands, and quite fast in Belgium, France, the UK and Ireland. The region as a whole profited from the return of political and economic stability, and the process of European integration that came to symbolize this. But there were large differences in the way in which countries participated in this process.

Growth after 1945 was in many respects the continuation of the economic modernization that had begun after the second Industrial Revolution. One of its most important features was that it was much less tied to the geography of coal – thanks to electricity. The Nordic countries also profited from a different source of energy, water power, as a major source of cheap energy. By contrast, the countries that had pioneered the first Industrial Revolution were handicapped by its legacy – the old industrial districts with coal mining, iron industry and textiles started a long decline due to rising international competition and declining demand. From the 1960s onwards, some of the industries which had dominated earlier growth – shipbuilding, electronics, automobiles – also came under increasing pressure due to the rise as highly efficient producers of first Japan and later Korea and other 'Asian Tigers'. But growth persisted until the mid-1970s, when the oil crisis (a sudden tripling of oil prices by the Organization of the Petroleum Exporting Countries, OPEC), broke the growth cycle.

The 'golden years' between 1945 and 1975 also saw large institutional changes. The US directly after the war initiated (via Marshall Aid) new forms of European cooperation, but these experiments took a more definite shape with the 1957 Treaty of Rome, which established the European Economic Community (EEC). This was an ambitious project to set up a customs union with harmonized external tariffs, with its own agricultural policy. Belgium, France, the Netherlands and Luxembourg were among the six initial members of the EEC, which also included Italy and the economic powerhouse Germany (Milward 1993). The UK preferred to remain outside, more or less expecting an early collapse of the experiment. Ireland and the Scandinavian countries were more closely linked to the UK, and became (with the exception of Finland), members of the alternative European Free Trade Association (EFTA), a free-trade zone set up by the British. The more ambitious EEC model with its supra-national institutions was more effective, however; the EFTA moreover lacked geographic coherence. In the 1960s the UK twice tried to become a member of the EEC, finally succeeding (with Ireland and Denmark) in 1973.

The second dimension of institutional change was national. All countries saw, in varying degrees, the growth of the welfare state. This was partly inspired by the bitter experience of the 1930s and by the new solidarity that emerged during the war; the famous Beveridge report (1942) that created the basis for the British welfare state is a case in point. The implementation of the measures proposed in this report by the new Labour government after 1945 is an example of the 'new settlement' that was realized in most north-western European countries after 1945 (Eichengreen 2007). After long battles between 'capital' and 'labour' a new compromise was reached, in which 'capital' agreed with the extension of social security and other welfare measures that labour had requested for long. In many countries – Sweden, the UK, the Netherlands – the participation of social democracy in government was part of the process. In the Netherlands, a policy of wage moderation was carried out by the government, and trade unions and employers' organizations worked together to implement it. The aim was to create employment for the rapidly growing labour force.

These policies of international cooperation and national reform were successful: rapid growth was until the mid-1970s combined with the rapid expansion of welfare services paid for by progressive taxes, resulting in a dramatic decline of income inequality (again, until the mid-1970s). This 'egalitarian revolution' of the twentieth century had already begun after 1913, but had by and large been the product of the two world wars and the Great Depression, which had had strong levelling consequences (Piketty 2014). What was 'unique' between 1945 and 1975 is that rapid growth went together with an on-going fall in inequality. In previous periods of growth, inequality had often increased, as for example profit income grew more rapidly than wage income. But 1945–75 was different; rapid growth meant that unemployment fell to very low levels, and this labour scarcity drove up nominal and real wages. Labour costs were also increased by the growth of social transfers, often linked to wage income. As a result, from the early 1960s onwards, profits came under pressure, also due to increased international competition from within Europe (thanks to the EEC) and from the global economy (the Asian Tigers). Companies responded by increasing their exports (made possible by EEC trade liberalization), by stepping up investments to save on labour costs and by raising prices (causing an acceleration of inflation). Given the tight labour market, more inflation only led to further wage increases. For a while, declining profits did not 'cool off' the economy, but lead to a wage–price spiral that became characteristic of the late 1960s and 1970s. In the Netherlands these symptoms of economic illness were accompanied by an overvalued exchange rate, made possible by the large reserves of natural gas discovered in the 1960s; it gave rise to the 'Dutch disease', which implied that manufacturing exports (and employment) were crowded out by the easy gains from natural gas exports.

Such was the situation when the oil crisis struck. Its effect was to create a process of 'stagflation' – economic stagnation combined with rapid inflation, a phenomenon not easily explained within the dominant Keynesian paradigm. What had contributed to the hubris of the 1960s and 1970s is that policymakers (and economists) thought that Keynesian demand management had solved the problem of how to stabilize the economy. Supply-side problems were ignored, until the 1970s showed the limitations of the Keynesian ideas. There was in most countries a switch to more liberal and/or monetarist economic policies. In the UK, where politics had an inbuilt tendency to switch from one extreme to another, Margaret Thatcher's rise to power in 1979 was the symbolic end of the postwar period in which the British economy had become the 'sick man' of western Europe. Whereas directly after the war the UK was still the wealthiest country of the region, in 1975 it had been overtaken by all other parts of north-western Europe, with the exception of Ireland and Finland (and the margin with Finland was now reduced to a few per cent). Thatcher's diagnosis included that labour costs were too high and that declining high cost industries such as the coal mines had to be closed down, which implied clashes with the powerful trade unions. More in general, the state had to radically withdraw from attempts to regulate the economy, and the market had to take over. This neo-liberal offensive became in various degrees typical of institutional developments until the early 2000s, when the financial crisis of 2007–08 showed the weaknesses and limitations of this approach. Different countries participated differently in the process: the Thatcherite offensive was probably most dramatic in the UK, although Ireland would be a second candidate of a country most dramatically changed during these years (it also, finally, began to catch up with the rest of Europe in these years, also thanks to the joining of the EU). On the continent changes were more moderate – privatization and liberalization of markets did happen, but there was not the dramatic clash with the trade unions, and the welfare states were only 'streamlined'. During the Mitterand presidency (1981–95) France went through a number of policy experiments, first inspired by left-wing ideas (resulting, for example in nationalization of the big banks), and when this did not work out well, policy switched towards more neo-liberal ideas.

The contrasting developments of the welfare state was reflected in trends in income inequality: in the UK and Ireland inequality increased strongly, whereas it more or less stabilized in the Low Countries and Scandinavia. The EEC developed into the European Union (EU), and more interestingly, from an instrument of government intervention (which is how it originated in the 1950s) into a body that furthered market-oriented reforms, such as the creation of the common market in the early 1990s.

The 1970s–1990s saw a radical transformation of the economic structures of the region. Industrial growth had been until the mid-1960s the engine of economic development, leading to a gradual decline of employment in agriculture and a strong increase in industrial (and tertiary) activities (see for example Schön 2012). In the 1960s–1980s this changed, however; industrial employment first stagnated, then started to fall. Services became the dominant sector in the economy, employing up to 70–80 per cent of the labour force and supplying a more or less equal share of GDP. Education, health care, banking and insurance and government services became the main sources of employment growth, whereas the share of agriculture continued to fall (to less than 5 per cent of the labour force). This transformation towards the postindustrial economy was already well underway when the impact of the information and communications technology (ICT) revolution of the 1990s came to be felt. It further stimulated the transition to a service-oriented economy, and revolutionized the way people did their work and interacted in general. Banking was perhaps the sector that profited most from these changes and from the change in the political climate which favoured free capital flows and markets, and increasingly sophisticated financial services. The 1980s and 1990s saw a remarkable revival of the City of London as the largest financial centre outside the US. It was part of a more general renaissance of the UK, which was also stimulated by North Sea oil, and the renewed flexibility of this typical Anglo-Saxon economy after the Thatcher revolution. Norway, too, profited from the huge oil reserves found in the North Sea, making possible its 'Alleingang' (separate path) outside the

EU. The big boom of the 1990s burst in two steps: the stock market boom driven by ICT companies that only rarely made a real profit, also known as the 'dot com bubble', collapsed in 2001–02; the banking-sector boom driven by sophisticated but highly untransparent financial instruments persisted until 2007 (see Highlight Chapter H1.1 on the debates about banking regulation for which the London City banks were paradigmatic). The financial crisis that began in that year, ended the long (thirty-year) period of growth according to the neo-liberal recipe.

Conclusion

North-western Europe has been among the most successful parts of the world economy, as pioneers of the market economy and Smithian economic growth, being the first region to break through the Malthusian ceiling, and as the leading region to develop the industrial society that came to dominate the world economy after 1800. This long-term success was founded on endogenous institutions and on the acquisition of a central place in the world economy that emerged after 1600. Growth, initially concentrated in the Low Countries and Great Britain, after 1800 also spread to the rest of the region, and France and the Scandinavian countries (and more recently also Ireland) achieved welfare levels which are among the highest in the world.

Note

1. Clearly, the French Revolution and the Napoleonic Wars also reduced incomes per capita, but this could have been a temporary influence on GDP per capita.

Further reading

Allen, R. C. (2009), *The British Industrial Revolution in Global Perspective*, Cambridge University Press; a very accessible interpretation of the British Industrial Revolution.

de Vries, J. and van der Woude, A. (1997), *The First Modern Economy: Success, Failure, and Perseverance of the Dutch Economy, 1500–1815*, Cambridge University Press; still the best book on the pre-1800 development of the region.

Eichengreen, B. (1992), *Golden Fetters: the Gold Standard and the Great Depression, 1919–1939*, Oxford University Press; is still fundamental for the interwar period.

   (2007), *The European Economy since 1945: Coordinated Capitalism and Beyond*, Princeton University Press; for the post-1945 'new settlement'.

Pollard, S. (1981), *Peaceful Conquest: the Industrialization of Europe, 1760–1970*, Oxford University Press; still useful representing the huge literature about industrialization processes in various parts of the region.

van Zanden, J. L. and van Riel, A. (2004), *The Strictures of Inheritance. The Dutch Economy in the Nineteenth Century*, Princeton University Press; covers the atypical experience of the Netherlands.

References

Acemoglu, D., Cantoni, D., Johnson, S. and Robinson, J. (2011), 'The Consequences of Radical Reform: the French Revolution', *American Economic Review* 101 (4) 3286–307.

Acemoglu, D., Johnson, S. and Robinson, J. (2005), 'The Rise of Europe: Atlantic Trade, Institutional Change and Growth', *American Economic Review* 95 (3), 546–47.

Allen, R. C. (1992), *Enclosure and the Yeoman. The Agricultural Development of the South Midlands, 1450–1850*, Oxford: Clarendon Press.

(2001), 'The Great Divergence in European Wages and Prices', *Explorations in Economic History* 38, 411–47.

Baten, J. and Blum, M. (2014a), 'Why are you Tall while Others are Short? Agricultural Production and other Proximate Determinants of Global Heights', *European Review of Economic History* 18, 144–65.

Benedict, P. (1996), '*Un roi, une loi, deux fois*: parameters for the history of Catholic-Reformed co-existence in France, 1555–1685', in O. P. Grell and B. Scribner, *Tolerance and Intolerance in the European Reformation*, Cambridge University Press, pp. 65–93.

Bolt, J. and van Zanden, J. L. (2014), 'The Maddison Project. Collaborative Research on Historical National Accounts', *The Economic History Review* 67 (3), 627–51.

Broadberry, S. N. (1984), 'The North European Depression of the 1920s', *Scandinavian Economic History Review* 32 (3), 159–67.

Broadberry, S., Campbell, B., Klein, A., Overton, M. and van Leeuwen, B. (2011), 'British Economic Growth, 1270–1870: an Output-based Approach', *Studies in Economics 1203*, Department of Economics, University of Kent.

de Moor, T. and van Zanden, J. L. (2010), 'Girl Power: the European Marriage Pattern and Labour Markets in the North Sea Region in the Late Medieval and Early Modern Period', *Economic History Review* 63 (1), 1–33.

Hjerppe, R. (1989), *The Finnish Economy 1860–1985: Growth and Structural Change. Studies on Finland's Economic Growth XIII*. Helsinki: Bank of Finland Publications.

Hoffman, P. T. (2003), 'France: Early Modern Period', in J. Mokyr (ed.), *The Oxford Encyclopedia of Economic History*, Oxford University Press, 363–66.

Komlos, J. (1998), Shrinking in a Growing Economy? The Mystery of Physical Stature during the Industrial Revolution, *The Journal of Economic History* 58 (3).

Maddison, A. (2001), *The World Economy: a Millennial Perspective*, Paris: OECD Publishing.

Marshall, M., Jaggers, G. K. and Gurr, T. R. (2011), *POLITY IV Project Political Regime Characteristics and Transitions, 1800–2010 Dataset Users' Manual*, www.systemic peace.org/inscr/p4manualv2010.pdf, last downloaded 1 September 2014.

Milward, A. (1993), *The European Rescue of the Nation State*, London: Routledge.

Mokyr, J. (2002), *The Gifts of Athena. Historical Origins of the Knowledge Society*, Princeton University Press.

O'Grada, C. (1995), *Ireland: a New Economic History, 1780–1939*, Oxford: Clarendon Press.

O'Rourke, K. H. and Williamson, J. G. (1999), *Globalization and History: the Evolution of a Nineteenth-century Atlantic Economy*, Cambridge, MA: MIT Press.

Piketty, T. (2014), *Capital in the 21st Century*, Cambridge, MA: Harvard University Press.

Schön, L. (2012), *An Economic History of Modern Sweden*, Abingdon: Routledge.

Tracy, M. (1989), *Government and Agricultural Protection in Western Europe, 1880–1988*, New York: Harvester.

van Zanden, J. L., Buringh, E. and Bosker, M. (2012), 'The Rise and Decline of European Parliaments, 1188–1789', *Economic History Review* 65 (3), 835–61.

van Zanden, J. L., de Moor, T. and Zuijderduijn, J. (2012), 'Small is Beautiful: the Efficiency of Credit Markets in late Medieval Holland', *European Review of Economic History* 16 (1), 3–22.

van Zanden, J. L. and van Leeuwen, B. (2012), 'Persistent but not Consistent: the Growth of National Income in Holland, 1347–1807', *Explorations in Economic History* 49 (2), 119–30.

Voigtländer, N. and Voth, H.-J. (2012), 'How the West "Invented" Fertility Restriction', National Bureau of Economic Research (NBER) Working Papers w17314.

The great divergence in the world economy: long-run trends of real income

Stephen Broadberry

I1

The origins of the economic divergence between countries that we observe today can be traced back to the early part of the last millennium, thanks to recent work on historical data. This chapter discusses the roots of the great divergence between European and Asian economies. Divergence is due to the differential impact of shocks that hit economies with different structural features.

As a result of recent work, economic historians have produced historical national accounts reaching back to the early years of the second millennium, derived from data collected at the time. For the major European economies, at least, data are now available on an annual basis back to 1300.

Measuring the great divergence: Maddison revised

This new work presents quite a different picture of the development of European and Asian nations from that surmised by Angus Maddison in his widely used book, *The World Economy: a Millennial Perspective*, where pre-1820 estimates of per capita GDP were based largely on conjecture, and provided only for a small number of benchmark years.

As it turns out, medieval and early modern European and Asian nations were much more literate and numerate than is often thought. They left behind a wealth of data in documents such as government accounts, customs accounts, poll tax returns, parish registers, city records, trading company records, hospital and educational establishment records, manorial accounts, probate inventories, farm accounts and tithe files. With a national accounting framework and careful cross-checking, it is possible to reconstruct population and GDP back to the medieval period. The picture that emerges is one of reversals of fortune within both Europe and Asia, as well as between the two continents.

This means that the great divergence of living standards between Europe and Asia had late medieval origins and was already well under way during the early modern period, contrary to the recent revisionist views of writers such as Kenneth Pomeranz. However, the revisionists are correct to point to regional variation within both continents. Figure I1.1 shows the European little divergence, or reversal of fortunes between the North Sea area and Mediterranean Europe, as Britain and Holland began

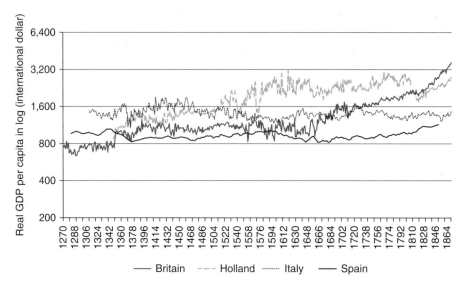

Figure I1.1 Real GDP per capita in European countries, 1270–1870 (1990 international dollars, log scale)
Sources: Álvarez-Nogal and de la Escosura 2013, Bassino *et al.* 2014, Broadberry *et al.* 2011, 2014, 2015a, 2015b, Broadberry and van Leeuwen 2011, Malanima 2011, van Zanden and van Leeuwen 2012.

to catch up with Italy and Spain from 1348 – and then forged ahead from 1500 – led first by the Dutch Golden Age, and later by the British Industrial Revolution.

Putting together the GDP per capita data for these key European economies, with data on a number of important Asian economies in Table I.1, suggests also an Asian little divergence, with Japan overtaking China and India. However, Japan started at a lower level of per capita income than Britain and Holland and grew at a slower rate, so continued to fall behind until after the Meiji Restoration of 1868. Thus the two continents diverged as reversals of fortune occurred within each continent. This picture is not changed dramatically if allowance is made for regional variation within China. Li and van Zanden (2012) estimate GDP per capita in China's richest region, the Yangzi Delta, compared to the Netherlands in the 1820s. This suggests that the Yangzi Delta had a per capita GDP of around $1,000 in 1990 international prices, which is only slightly higher than in Japan, and about the same level as in Spain.

Explaining the great divergence: shocks with asymmetric effects

Economic historians can now, therefore, account for the great divergence, using the word 'accounting' in the sense of measurement – by providing a quantitative picture of when and where the great divergence occurred. However, there is a second sense in which the word 'accounting' can be used – to provide an explanatory narrative.

Much remains to be done on the measurement of the key explanatory factors, but the framework adopted here is to see the divergences as arising from the differential impact of shocks hitting economies with different structural features.

Table I.1 GDP per capita levels in Europe and Asia (1990 international dollars)

	England/GB	Holland/NL	Italy	Spain	Japan	China	India
725					551		
900					476		
980						1,247	
1020						1,518	
1050						1,458	
1086	754					1,204	
1120						1,063	
1150					508		
1280	679			957	552		
1300	755		1,482	957			
1348	777	876	1,376	1,030			
1400	1,090	1,245	1,601	885		960	
1450	1,055	1,432	1,668	889	552	983	
1500	1,114	1,483	1,403	889		1,127	
1570	1,143	1,783	1,337	990		968	
1600	1,123	2,372	1,244	944	605	977	682
1650	1,110	2,171	1,271	820	619		638
1700	1,563	2,403	1,350	880	597	841	622
1750	1,710	2,440	1,403	910	622	685	573
1800	2,080	1,752	1,244	962	703	597	569
1850	2,997	2,397	1,350	1,144	777	594	556

Sources: Álvarez-Nogal and de la Escosura 2013, Bassino *et al.* 2014, Broadberry *et al.* 2011, 2014, 2015a, 2015b, Broadberry and van Leeuwen 2011, Malanima 2011, van Zanden and van Leeuwen 2012.
Notes: The British data refer to the territory of England before 1700 and Great Britain thereafter; the Dutch data refer to the territory of Holland before 1800 and the Netherlands thereafter. Data for all countries except Japan and India are for ten-year averages starting in the year stated (e.g., 1300 = 1300–09).

The economic history literature suggests two important shocks coinciding with the turning points identified above around 1348 and 1500.

- The Black Death – which began in western China before spreading to Europe and reaching England in 1348 – wiped out around one-third of Europe's population within three years, and more than a half over the following century.
- Around 1500, new trade routes were opened up between Europe and Asia around the south of Africa, and between Europe and the Americas.

These shocks had asymmetric effects on different economies because of four important structural factors.

- The type of agriculture.
- The age of first marriage for women.
- The flexibility of labour supply.
- The nature of state institutions.

The effects of the Black Death

The Black Death of the mid-fourteenth century had quite different effects in different parts of Europe. The classic Malthusian response to such a mortality crisis is a rise in incomes for those lucky enough to survive because of an increase in the per capita endowment of land and capital for survivors.

However, as population recovers, it should lead to a corresponding decline in per capita incomes.

- This happened in Italy, but not in Britain or Holland, as a result of the high age of marriage of females (linked to labour market opportunities in pastoral agriculture) and people working more days per year (the industrious revolution).
- The situation was different in Spain, which was a land-abundant frontier economy during the Reconquest, and, hence, did not see a rise in per capita incomes following the Black Death.

Here, population decline destroyed commercial networks and further isolated an already scarce population, reducing specialization and the division of labour, so that Spain did not share in the general west European increase in per capita incomes.

- There are no signs of a positive Black Death effect in Asia, since Japan remained isolated, so that the disease never took root, while the period was marked in China by the Mongol interlude, which destroyed the institutional framework that had underpinned the high per capita incomes of the Northern Song dynasty.

New trade routes

The opening up of new trade routes from Europe to Asia and the Americas accelerated the process of divergence, again through their interaction with structural features of the different economies. It might be expected that Spain and Portugal would have been the gainers from these changes, since they were the pioneers and both had Atlantic, as well as Mediterranean coasts. However, early modern Britain and Holland dominated Spain and Portugal in terms of institutional structures, including both the ability of states to raise taxes to finance the expansion of state capacity (needed for the effective enforcement of property rights), and the control exercised by mercantile interests over the state through parliament (needed to limit arbitrary intervention in business affairs by rulers).

China adopted a restrictive closed-door policy towards long-distance trade after the 'voyages to the western oceans' that had occurred between 1405 and 1433, which had shown China to be technologically ahead in shipbuilding. However, following an initial period of openness to relations with European traders, Tokugawa Japan adopted a policy of seclusion from the 1630s, so any Japanese advantage from the earlier Chinese turn inwards was short-lived.

Although recent work has tended to question the extent to which trade really was closed off by these policies, the contrast with the outward orientation of the European states which sponsored the voyages of discovery from the fifteenth century remains striking. With early modern China and Japan turned inwards, India was the Asian country most open to trade, with its major export business in cotton textiles. However, this did not lead to Indian prosperity because of the low levels of state capacity and its consequences for the enforcement of property rights.

References

Álvarez-Nogal, C. and de la Escosura, P. (2013), 'The Rise and Fall of Spain (1270–1850)', *Economic History Review* 66, 1–37.

Bassino, J. P., Broadberry, S., Fukao, K., Gupta, B. and Takashima, M. (2014), 'Japan and the Great Divergence, 725–1874', London School of Economics.

Broadberry, S., Campbell, B., Klein, A., Overton, M. and van Leeuwen, B. (2011), 'British Economic Growth, 1270–1870: an Output-based Approach", London School of Economics.

(2015a), *British Economic Growth, 1270–1870*, Cambridge University Press.

Broadberry, S., Custodis, J. and Gupta, B. (2015b), 'India and the Great Divergence: an Anglo-Indian Comparison of GDP per capita, 1600–1871', Explorations in Economic History 56, 58–75.

Broadberry, S., Guan, H. and Li, D. (2014), 'China, Europe and the Great Divergence: a Study in Historical National Accounting", London School of Economics.

Broadberry, S. and van Leeuwen, B. (2011), 'The Growth of the English Economy, 1086–1270", London School of Economics.

Li, B. and van Zanden, J. L. (2012), 'Before the Great Divergence? Comparing the Yangzi Delta and the Netherlands at the Beginning of the Nineteenth Century", *Journal of Economic History* 72, 956–89.

Malanima, P. (2011), 'The Long Decline of a Leading Economy: GDP in Central and Northern Italy, 1300–1913', *European Review of Economic History* 15, 169–219.

van Zanden, J. L. and van Leeuwen, B. (2012), 'Persistent but not Consistent: the Growth of National Income in Holland, 1347–1807', *Explorations in Economic History* 49, 119–30.

H1.1 International financial regulation and supervision

Catherine Schenk

The crisis was the result of human action and inaction, not of Mother Nature or computer models gone haywire. (The Financial Crisis Inquiry Report, US Congress, 2011)

The global financial crisis of 2007/08 seemed to reveal a phenomenal lack of prudence by bankers, who bought and sold risky assets that they did not fully understand, and by regulators, who let banks operate in ways that risked the stability of the global financial system. The result was costly state bail-outs of banks in many countries and years of restricted lending as banks restored their damaged balance sheets. Renewed effort at regulatory reform has increased interest in the historical development of banking and banking regulations. Reinhart and Rogoff (2009) catalogued the high frequency of financial crises over the past 800 years and emphasized the dangers of ignoring the historical record. Calomiris and Haber (2014) argued that deals among regulators, politicians and special interests produced ineffective regulations. Banking crises are not randomly distributed; they are the result of regulatory systems that arise from specific historical contexts.

The relationship between regulators and the regulated has attracted considerable academic attention. The importance of banks to economic stability and growth makes a strong case for external prudential supervision; but information asymmetry, complexity, the speed of innovation and the high value of private information to banks often prevent transparent prudential supervision. These difficulties are magnified on the international level. Because national banking systems are fundamental to macroeconomic policy, their supervision is a jealously guarded prerogative of national regulators. However, the highly integrated nature of national banking systems, the vulnerability to cross-border contagion and the need to avoid regulatory competition (to the bottom) provides a strong rationale for some form of multilateral oversight.

In the postwar years, capital controls insulated national systems from contagion as governments sought to protect their national policy sovereignty. National systems of regulation became entrenched as part of the international monetary system designed at Bretton Woods that prioritized policy sovereignty and stable exchange rates over free flows of capital. Central banks focused on the balance of payments while their governments sought to restore national prosperity. By the 1960s, however, this framework was under threat from financial innovation. The offshore Eurodollar market attracted global banking to the City of London in an unregulated market condoned by the Bank of England. The increasingly international networks of banks exposed the inconsistencies between national regulatory systems. In particular, the international operations of the City of London were relatively lightly regulated, in contrast to tighter controls in New York. The result was a flood of American banks into London to take advantage of the offshore market. In the early 1970s, this left the system vulnerable to a series of shocks including newly floating exchange rates and commodity price shocks.

The most ambitious attempt to develop robust international banking regulation was the Basel Committee, launched at the Bank for International Settlements in 1975. The failure and near-failure of several banks in the summer of 1974 exposed the risk of gaps in prudential supervision, inconsistent practice in foreign exchange markets and interdependencies between national banking systems that required a fresh approach. The Basel Committee shared best practice and tried to devise a framework to ensure common regulatory oversight of branches and subsidiaries as well as parent institutions (Goodhart 2010). Over the next thirty-five years the Basel Committee became the main forum for negotiated common standards and regulation. After the sovereign debt crisis of 1982/83 threatened to bring down the international banking system, the Basel Committee spent years negotiating capital adequacy standards with the world's banks.

This did not forestall another series of financial crises in emerging markets in the 1990s. This crisis prompted a fresh round of negotiated standards, but failed to forestall the imprudent practices that led to the 2008 global financial crisis. Despite the efforts at Basel, the entrenched protection of national sovereignty over regulating the banking system has meant that banking regulation remains national while the industry became increasingly global. This mismatch lies at the root of the vulnerability to contagion from one national system to another. The collapse of Lehman Brothers in September 2008 was the outcome of a debate about immediate American interests, but it had disastrous effects as Lehman's global network sucked liquidity out of the international financial system. The history of international banking and financial regulation emphasizes the importance of the institutional context in which regulations are developed, the dangers of regulatory capture because of the specific characteristics of financial institutions and the perils of regulating a global industry through national frameworks.

References

Calomiris, C. W. and Haber, S. H. (2014), *Fragile by Design: the Political Origins of Banking Crises and Scarce Credit*, Princeton University Press.

Goodhart, C. (2010), *The Basel Committee on Banking Supervision: a History of the Early Years*, Cambridge University Press.

Reinhart, C. M. and Rogoff, K. S. (2009), *This Time is Different: Eight Centuries of Financial Folly*, Princeton University Press.

2 Southern, eastern and central Europe

Joerg Baten

European countries and regions have followed many different paths to modernity. How were some countries able to achieve significant development accelerations during some periods? Why did living standards in these countries regress during other periods? This chapter focuses on the countries of eastern, southern and central Europe.

The core events of the Industrial Revolution have attracted much attention; however, because these events occurred in England and Scotland, many countries between Portugal and Russia have received less coverage in economic history books. This lack of research is astonishing because the history of these countries is exciting. In fact, it may seem to the historian that these regions were racing towards higher standards of living. There was considerable change over time in which the region was ahead in this race. For example, southern Europe clearly led in productive capacity and education during the late medieval and early modern periods. Recent studies indicate that the national incomes of Spain and Italy were higher than that of the UK in 1500 and that Italy had higher educational levels. Spain was likely also a world leader in quasi-parliamentary participation during the Middle Ages (van Zanden *et al.* 2012). Hence, skilled workers during this period migrated from north to south, especially to Italy, not the other way as some workers migrate today.

Figure 2.1 presents the human capital development of three European regions (north-west, south and east) between 1450 and 1800. Because educational indicators, such as school enrolment and literacy, are unavailable for all countries during this early period, we use the following basic numeracy indicator: the share of people who were able to report their own age correctly (in years).[1] The eventual human capital leadership of north-western Europe was not a given during the late fifteenth century. Rather, southern Europe exhibited higher levels of numeracy than the rest of Europe. Only after the beginning of the sixteenth century was human capital higher in north-western Europe. In general, Europe experienced a human capital revolution between 1450 and 1800. The increase in numeracy from approximately 50 per cent to nearly 100 per cent represents a difference as large as that existing between rich and poor countries during the early twentieth century.

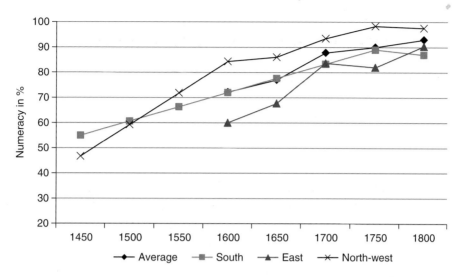

Figure 2.1 The human capital revolution in European regions (numeracy, fifteenth to eighteenth centuries)
Source: based on A'Hearn *et al.* (2009).
Notes: '1450' refers to persons born in 1450–99, etc. We included all countries for which longer series or at least early values were available: 'north-west' includes the UK, Netherlands and protestant Germany; 'south' is Italy (north); 'east' is the average of Russia, Bohemia and Austria. When values between benchmark dates were missing, they were interpolated. Weak estimates were omitted. For the UK and the Netherlands before 1600, the benchmark year of UK 1600 was used and the changes from Germany (Protestant).

The predominance of southern Europe during earlier periods is confirmed by estimates of national income (Figure 2.2). Until the end of the fifteenth century, Italy outperformed both England and Holland and, until the late seventeenth century, it continued to outperform the former. While Spain was richer than north-western Europe during the Middle Ages, this southern European country had been surpassed by 1400.[2] Between 1500 and 1700, north-western Europe experienced significant increases in national income, eventually overtaking Italy.

In the following, we will first discuss the interesting cases of exceptionally high standards of living in Poland during the late sixteenth century, and the equally surprising high human capital and income levels in Italy during the same period. Afterwards, the reasons of their relative decline are studied. To put these cases in perspective, we then consider all regions of southern, eastern and central Europe in a cross-sectional comparison, and we report their development level around 1800. During the late nineteenth century, central Europe overtook the east and south economically, but it became also the epicentre of the political and military catastrophes of the early twentieth century. The history of this large part of Europe during the twentieth century is traced in the last part of this chapter,

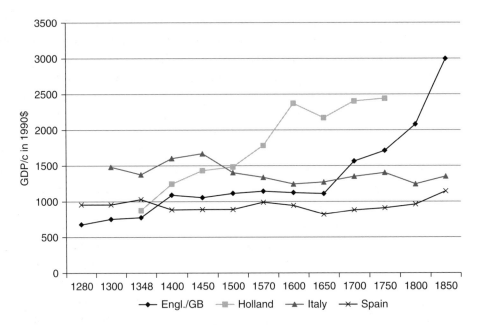

Figure 2.2 Early GDP per capita development
Source: based on Broadberry *et al.* 2014.
Notes: Real GDP in dollars. The British data refer to the territory of England before 1700 and Great Britain thereafter; the Dutch data refer to the territory of Holland before 1800 and the Netherlands thereafter. Data for all countries except Japan and India are for ten-year averages starting in the year stated (e.g., 1300 = 1300–09).

concluding with the transformation of the east from socialism to market economy, and the world economic crisis of the late 2000s that hit southern Europe particularly harshly.

Why did Italy lead during the early modern period?

The economic history of the Italian peninsula illustrates both the high initial level of development in the South as well as its slower growth from the seventeenth to early twentieth centuries compared to north-western and central Europe. The Italian Renaissance was not only astounding in the arts but also in economic development. The economic pioneers were Venice and Genoa. What caused the early development of cities such as Venice and Genoa? Many reasons can be considered, such as the relative military safety of Venetian lagoons and the high population density and urbanization of the Italian peninsula. Acemoglu and Robinson (2012) recently argued that the early development of broader political participation in Venice created an institutional structure in which inspired and talented entrepreneurs had opportunities to succeed. In contrast, in many other European cities, established wealthy merchants excluded newcomers, generating impediments to overall city development. Venice also developed early versions of joint stock capital firms (Acemoglu and Robinson 2012). Typically, two (or more) merchants created a trading enterprise. One merchant was responsible for long-distance transport, while the other provided financing for the enterprise. The famous explorer Marco Polo became an idol of Venetian merchants and other traders in many parts of the world.

Early merchant development paralleled banking activity in Tuscany, first in Siena and Lucca and later in Florence and beyond. Following the early rise of banking and trade, Tuscany developed a highly successful and skill-intensive textile industry. North-central Italian manufacturers began by adding ornaments to Flemish textiles. Soon, they developed new technologies and outperformed the north-west European producers. During the seventeenth and eighteenth centuries, however, the pendulum swung back. Figures 2.1 and 2.2 suggest two main developments. First, southern Europe experienced a gradual but steady decline in relative economic standing; second, the economic dominance of north-western Europe during the eighteenth century – measured by income per capita – was preceded by a significant increase in human capital in this region during the previous two centuries.

What factors were responsible for slower Italian development? A number of factors produced a relative decline in national income and education levels in Italy and the southern European region. Military conflicts, often initiated by foreign powers such as Germany, Spain or France, were traditionally considered driving events of this shift in living standards. In addition, political fractionalization in Italy reduced the ability to defend all city-states and medium-sized principalities. Fiscal capacity was also limited, which otherwise could have facilitated hiring soldiers for defence (Dincecco 2011). A second important factor was the shift of world trade to north-western Europe. While Italian merchant ships had been most active in Mediterranean, Middle Eastern and North African ports, in the seventeenth century, the Dutch and English dominated merchant shipping and the Italians were disconnected from new international trade routes. Alfani (2013) argued that the seventeenth century plague affected Italy much more than other European countries. Therefore, this relatively exogenous event might have contributed to the relative decline of Italy. Finally, the institutional developments that occurred in north-western Europe were more beneficial than those in the southern European countries. Merchants in Amsterdam and London developed new ideas and exploited new economic opportunities and they could be relatively certain that greedy rulers would not expropriate their returns. In contrast, Venice became an aristocratic oligarchy in which rich families excluded new entrepreneurs and hindered further socioeconomic development (Acemoglu and Robinson 2012).

Standards of living in early modern east-central Europe

Interestingly, east-central Europe enjoyed a surprisingly high standard of living during the late sixteenth and early seventeenth centuries. Compared to Italy, this high standard of living was not so much a result of the high incomes of merchants and highly skilled workers but the relatively healthy lives of unskilled urban workers and some farmer groups. Measures such as real wages and human stature are indicators of human welfare. Height is an indicator of health and nutrition, which is particularly well suited to measuring the welfare of lower income groups and farmers.[3] Eastern European males during the sixteenth century were, on average, taller than their southern and northern European counterparts; eastern Europeans were an average of 171.4 cm tall, while the British, southern Germans, and Dutch/west Germans measured 170.4 cm, 169.3 cm and 170.0 cm, respectively (Koepke and Baten 2005, 2008). This height evidence supports the idea of an east-central European golden age of around 1600.

Recent research by Malinowski (2013) notes that if real wages are measured for both urban and rural areas, real wages in Poland were comparable to those in England *c.* 1600 (whereas for earlier and later periods, England's wages were higher). Earlier scholars would not have anticipated this level of income in east-central Europe.[4]

How did east-central Europe maintain relatively high standards of living even for lower income groups? In general, eastern Europe was characterized by low population density during the late medieval period. The local rulers encouraged migration into this area, attracting new settlers by offering relatively favourable conditions. This included also skilled Jewish immigration. During the sixteenth century, this situation began to deteriorate for peasants, but the level of nutrition and health was still relatively high, which can be observed using the indicators discussed above. In addition, during the sixteenth century, Polish kings were constrained by the Polish parliament. Although this parliament consisted mainly of landed nobility and did not necessarily pursue the general welfare, constraints on the executive produced some positive effect during the sixteenth century (for a different view, see Malinowski 2014). For example, the parliament sometimes prevented the king from engaging in costly military adventures. The sixteenth century also produced the Polish Renaissance, which included the construction of remarkably beautiful buildings.

In contrast, during the seventeenth and eighteenth centuries, the government became more extractive. Rent-seeking of the landed nobility characterized national policy. The seventeenth century was also a period of war, epidemic diseases and increasing exploitation of peasants. During the so-called second serfdom, large landowners required increasing labour days from peasants who were often required to postpone their own harvests, which bad weather had often

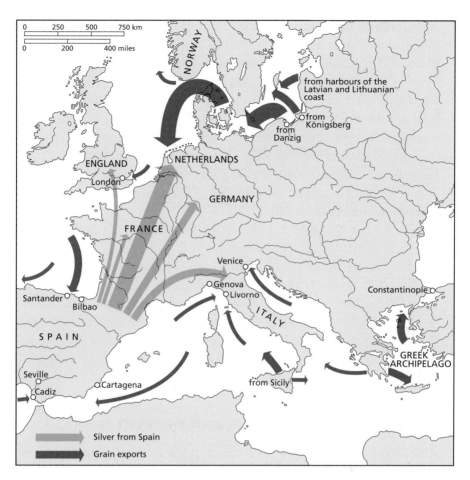

Map 2.1 Trade of grain and silver in Europe during the sixteenth century
Redrawn and modified after *Knaurs historischer Weltatlas*, ed. by G. Barraclough. Knaur 2000.

already partially destroyed. The second serfdom began in the sixteenth century but its negative effects became more visible during the seventeenth century. The most detrimental military events during this period were civil wars of 1605–06 and 1666.

In addition, nutrition and health worsened during the seventeenth century because more grain was demanded and consumed outside of the country. Notably, Polish grain was exported to western Europe (on the trade of grain and silver, see Map 2.1). A portion of the high nutritional status of this country was exported to north-western Europe in exchange for industrial goods of which the nobility consumed a large share.

What was the situation in Russia? During the early-modern period, the principality of Moscow developed into a large territorial state that included much of what is today European Russia. Despite its rapid growth – the principality had one of the highest geographic expansion rates in the world – it was a state facing permanent military challenges: the Polish and Swedish threatened from the west, the Crimean Tatars and Ottomans from the south, and pastoral tribes from the east (Bibikov 2013). Moscow structured its economy according to its military aims; the harvests of both government-owned land (*pomest'e*) and private, inheritable land (*votchina*) were used to support the army. All harvest returns that exceeded the basic subsistence of farmers were consumed by the Russian military. Russia was almost exclusively agricultural; approximately 2 per cent of the population was included in each of the following three groups: townsmen, clergy and military/ administrative. Approximately 5–10 per cent of the population was slaves, mostly in households. The second serfdom gained momentum in Russia after the government prohibited peasant mobility in 1592.

This difficult situation had important implications for Russia's development. Estimates of national income based on real evidence are not yet available, but Mironov´s estimates of human stature suggest that even in the eighteenth century, Russians had relatively low nutritional statuses despite usually beneficial land– labour ratios (Mironov 2012). Additionally, numeracy estimates are low for the seventeenth and eighteenth centuries, although there is some regional variation. Only during the mid-nineteenth century did Russia experience a human capital revolution and substantial modernization of its economy (on the modernization of the legal system, see Highlight Chapter 2.2).

Regional development during the early nineteenth century

After highlighting some of the tectonic shifts in development between the sixteenth and the eighteenth centuries, focusing on Italy, Poland and Russia, we will now examine regional differences around 1800. Substantial variety in economic development existed among regions. Even today, after decades of political attempts to improve standards of living in poorer regions within Europe, these differences persist. For example, if a person is born in Sicily instead of Milan or in Andalusia rather than in Barcelona, their life will typically be quite different. Did development differences among regions characterize earlier periods, such as the nineteenth century? Can we identify some important determinants of early regional differences that are persistent until today?

Unfortunately, some of the usual development indicators are unavailable to describe regional differences during the early nineteenth century, such as regional gross domestic product (GDP), real wages or life expectancy estimates. These indicators have been assessed regionally for some countries, but not for many, and not generally using a common method of measurement. However, one important development indicator is available for many European regions: numeracy. This important component of education has been estimated based on regional census records for many European regions (Map 2.2). Because education is one of

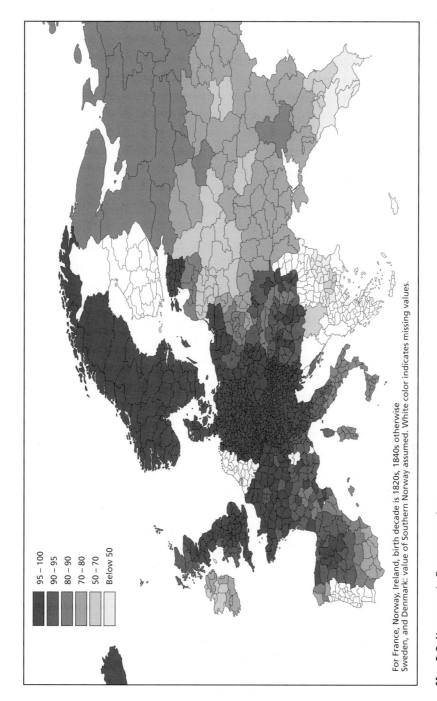

95 – 100
90 – 95
80 – 90
70 – 80
50 – 70
Below 50

For France, Norway, Ireland, birth decade is 1820s, 1840s otherwise
Sweden, and Denmark: value of Southern Norway assumed. White color indicates missing values.

Map 2.2 Numeracy in European regions

Source: Redrawn and modified after Hippe and Baten (2012).

the three components of the Human Development Index (HDI) – income and health are the other two – we will consider this indicator in detail. Education in general and maths skills in particular are important predictors of income during later periods, and this indicator is relevant to the income component of the HDI. The map of European regions indicate that Italy was already divided by the early nineteenth century; numeracy was substantially lower in southern Italy. This finding is also important in the light of arguments that the differences increased after Italian unification in the late nineteenth century (Vecchi 2011).

Before we discuss the other European regional differences, we describe potential influences of numeracy. What caused some regions to be less numerate? One important variable that has been identified in previous research is land inequality. In many regions with high land inequality, powerful elites prevented the public financing of primary education, especially if these elites were primarily involved in agriculture. From the perspective of the landed elite, why should one sacrifice income via taxation for the schooling of poor day labourers who performed mostly manual tasks on one's estate? Even if such a willingness to sacrifice income had existed, labourers who are more educated might threaten land reform or socialist revolution that would eventually reduce elite land and status.

Another factor that can influence the development of numeracy is educational policy and the willingness of the government to invest in education. For example, the Ottoman Empire spent relatively small amounts of public funds on education; in 1860–61, education represented only 0.2 per cent of the total budget. The Russian Empire also lagged in educational development, but some effort was made after the Crimean War was lost. Other possible determinants of human capital, such as proximity to trading ports, personal status (for example serfdom) and religion, can also be important.

The Russian Empire was characterized by marked regional differences (Map 2.2). During this period, it included the Baltic region with its Hanseatic heritage of trade in the urban centres.[5] Numeracy was higher in the Estonian and Latvian parts of the Russian Empire, which might have been influenced by the Protestant religion of the inhabitants (Bible reading was required of all Protestants; see Becker and Woessmann 2009). The western and central portions of the Russian Empire specialized in grain.[6] Interestingly, numeracy was higher in north and north-east Russia than in central Russia and Belarus (Hippe and Baten 2014). The improved legal position and less oppressive serfdom and superior economic situations of frontier farmers in more recent settlements also contributed to numeracy. In addition, in central Russia and Belarus, land inequality was particularly high. This pattern suggests that land inequality is an important variable.

During the early nineteenth century, the Habsburg Empire included modern Hungary, Austria, Czech Republic and Slovakia as well as parts of Poland, Italy, Romania and the former Yugoslavia.[7] The western portion of the Habsburg

Empire was characterized by the highest level of numeracy; however, the Empire was generally characterized by substantial variation. Hippe and Baten (2014) explained these differences by examining the predominance of large estates in some regions.

Among the lowest levels of numeracy are observed in southern Balkan countries, which were long occupied by the Ottoman Empire.[8] This Middle Eastern Empire invested a particularly small share of its budget in education because they viewed education as the responsibility of Islamic schools (for Muslims) or the local initiatives (for other religions). The Ottoman Empire was also characterized by a very low capacity to raise taxes, and the small central budget was spent on the military and government bureaucracies (Karaman and Pamuk 2010). Numeracy, school enrolment and literacy rates were all low in countries under Ottoman rule. In some countries, these low levels of human capital level persisted sometime after Ottoman rule ended.[9] Greece and Cyprus likely faced the same issues of paths taken under Ottoman educational policies (Figure 2.3). In these two countries, numeracy increased rapidly during the twentieth century.[10]

Two countries in the Caucasus interacted intensively with both the Ottoman and Persian Empires: Armenia and Georgia. During the early modern period, these countries were mostly governed by the Persian or Ottoman Imperial forces, although their principalities were sometimes granted semi-autonomous status. During the eighteenth century, Russian territorial expansion included this part of the Caucasus. Given their common Christian religion, local populations sometimes hoped to improve their status under Russian rule. The Russian Empire

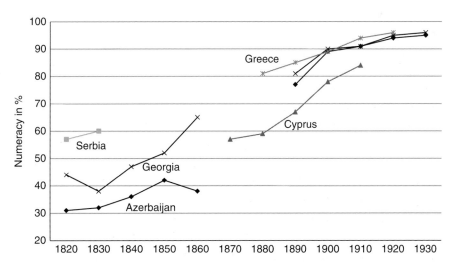

Figure 2.3 Numeracy in selected Balkan and Caucasus countries
Source: based on data from Crayen and Baten (2010).
Note: we include here countries that were previously parts of the Ottoman or Persian Empire.

gradually conquered these two countries during the late eighteenth and nineteenth centuries.[11] Numeracy was relatively low, which might partly be a consequence of Ottoman and Persian educational policies that only gradually improved during the Russian period.

Both Italy and Spain were characterized by strong north–south differences in human capital (Map 2.2). The southern parts of these countries, which specialized in grain production, were characterized by low numeracy and particularly high land inequality.[12] North-western Italy experienced renewed industrial growth centred on the industrial triangle of Genoa, Milan and Turin. The traditional specialization of Spain was the wool produced in the central Meseta region, which declined during the early nineteenth century. In Catalonia, a cotton textile industry developed after the late eighteenth century.[13]

In central Europe, the industrial share was higher in some regions, although agriculture continued to dominate during the early nineteenth century.[14] The industrial centres were located in the Rhineland, the developing Ruhr area and Silesia, with a focus on iron, mining, machinery, tools and textiles (especially during the early period). Among the central European countries, Switzerland was characterized by a long tradition of clock making and, as in much of central Europe, textiles. Numeracy was quite high during the early nineteenth century everywhere in central Europe.

Overall, the European region between Portugal and Russia displayed substantial differences in human capital formation during the early nineteenth century. There was some interaction between agricultural structure and education because regions characterized by large estates developed less human capital. Land inequality explains a substantial part of the differences. However, cultural and institutional influences also had an effect, which the opposite effects of the legacies of the Hanse League and Ottoman Empire demonstrated.

The nineteenth and twentieth centuries: an overview

Before considering development during the nineteenth and twentieth centuries in detail, we first provide an overview and consider core indicators, such as GDP, health and education, for the regions of (1) eastern, (2) southern and (3) central Europe.[15] Figure 2.4 indicates GDP per capita over the last 200 years. At the beginning of the nineteenth century, Italy dominated the other three countries considered as examples (Germany, Austria and Portugal). However, during the late nineteenth century, central European economies grew quickly, and growth outperformed that of southern Europe. This was the period of the second Industrial Revolution, and human capital was a decisive factor in determining who won or lost this race. Other factors that played a role were access to trade routes, institutional quality and fiscal capacity to build infrastructure.

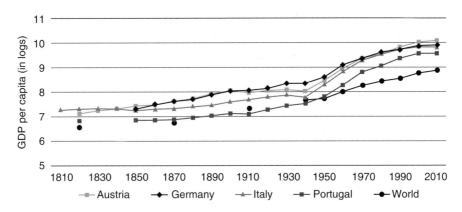

Figure 2.4 GDP per capita during the last 200 years for selected countries
Source: www.clio-infra.eu.

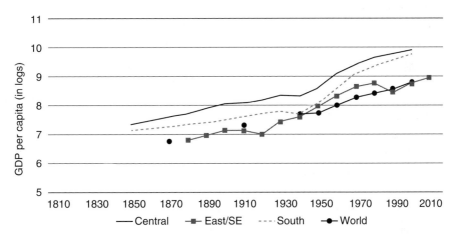

Figure 2.5 GDP per capita in three European regions, 1810–2010
Source: www.clio-infra.eu.

Southern Europe did not participate to the same degree in this second Industrial Revolution and began to trail central and northern Europe. However, southern Europe began to catch up after the Second World War. Even Portugal, which was the poorest country during this period, left the category of average world income behind and converged to that of the richest countries.

Figure 2.5 displays the economic development of the European regions during the last 200 years. During the period 1800–1900, eastern and south-eastern Europe (in which Russia played a dominant role) were characterized by much lower income levels than central Europe (Figure 2.5). The income level of southern Europe was between that of the two other regions during the late nineteenth century. Eastern and south-eastern Europe were on a growth path during the late nineteenth century, but war, civil war and revolution during the early

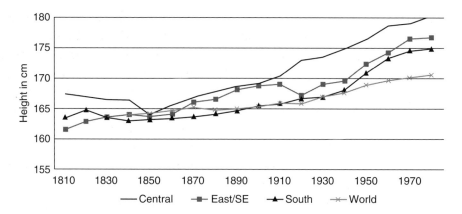

Figure 2.6 Height in three European regions and the World, 1810–1980 (males)
Source: based on Baten and Blum (2014).

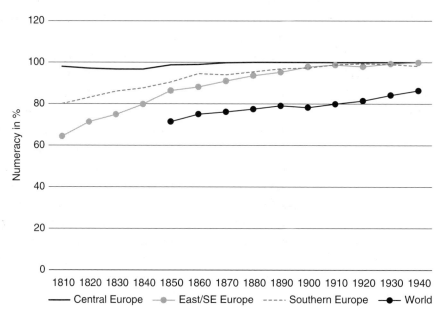

Figure 2.7 Numeracy in three European regions, 1810–1940s
Source: based on Crayen and Baten (2010).

twentieth century derailed their growth (see Highlight Chapter 2.1). In fact, political transformations and wars thwarted eastern Europe during two periods: the 1910–20s and 1990s.

Stature is often used as an indicator of health and nutritional status (see the Introduction to this volume). It is interesting to compare how human stature also reflects economic development in eastern Europe. For example, the crisis in the 1920s is clearly visible in the height records (Figure 2.6).[16] During the early nineteenth century, stature in eastern and south-eastern Europe is quite low; prerevolutionary heights in the late nineteenth century converge to those of central Europe. In contrast, GDP per capita levels indicate a much lower development of production capacity in these regions. However, we must carefully interpret this difference because height is sensitive to the availability of protein in the diet. In eastern Europe, population density was still relatively low during the nineteenth century; therefore, the availability of sufficient protein might have increased heights, while GDP per capita did not follow the same process. Nutritional status tended to be similarly favourable in eastern Europe during the nineteenth century, whereas the productive capacity and consumption of industrial goods were clearly higher in central Europe.

Next, we consider developments in numeracy among the European regions (Figure 2.7). In general, we observe an increase in basic education in all regions, which was at a higher level than the world average. Human capital in eastern and south-eastern Europe increased substantially during the nineteenth century. The improvement in numeracy in eastern Europe between 1810 and 1850 is so dramatic that we can interpret this as the eastern European human capital revolution, which occurred over very few decades. By comparison, the early modern numeracy revolution in western Europe was twice as large and considerably more gradual (from the fifteenth to the eighteenth centuries). This numeracy increase was previously unnoticed because school enrolment evidence for Russia begins in the 1870s (Mironov 2012). These data are consistent with some punctual cohort estimates for literacy in Russia (literacy tripled over the same period but from a relatively low level). In all countries, basic numeracy increased before literacy. Hence, this indicator reflects the first stage of human capital improvement.[17]

All development indicators examined in this summary exhibit improvement: GDP per capita, human stature and numeracy. However, the variation in speed is more interesting. For example, while relatively high numeracy and school enrolment levels were reached quite early, gains in income and stature increased quite slowly during the nineteenth century. Income and stature accelerated especially during the two decades following the Second World War.

Diffusion of industrialization to central and eastern Europe during the nineteenth and early twentieth centuries

In the next section of this chapter, we detail European development during the last 150 years. Which countries experienced faster growth and which experienced slower growth during this period? Which obstacles hindered these countries? The industrial development that had begun in north-western Europe – especially in England and Scotland – during the eighteenth century diffused to central and eastern Europe during the second half of the nineteenth century (Figure 2.8).[18] The heavily industrialized areas of the UK and Belgium were

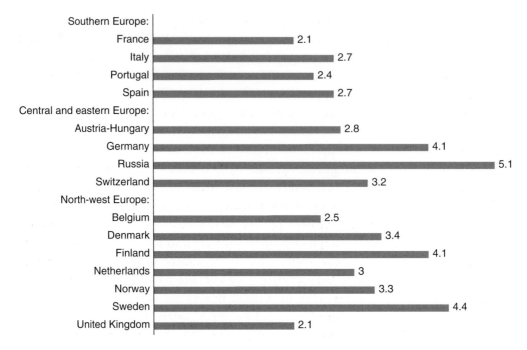

Figure 2.8 Growth of industrial production, 1870–1913 (per cent per annum)
Source: based on Broadberry and O'Rourke (2010), who based it on the following original sources: Belgium: Gadisseur (1973); Denmark: Hansen (1974); Finland: Hjerppe (1996); Netherlands: Smits, Horlings, and van Zanden (2000); Norway: unpublished data kindly made available by Ola Grytten; Sweden: Krantz and Schön (2007); United Kingdom: Feinstein (1972); France: Crouzet (1970); Italy: Fenoaltea (2003); Portugal: Lains (2006); Spain: Prados de la Escosura (2003); Switzerland: unpublished data kindly made available by Thomas David; Austria-Hungary: Schulze (2000); Germany: Hoffmann (1965); Russia: Goldsmith (1961).

characterized by modest industrial growth rates of 2.1 per cent and 2.5 per cent per year, respectively, whereas Germany (4.1 per cent), Russia (5.1 per cent) and Scandinavia (3.3–4.4 per cent) grew considerably faster during this period. In contrast, not all countries with catch-up growth potential achieved high industrial growth rates. Southern Europe advanced quite modestly during the period 1870–1913, and industrial development in these regions had to wait until later in the twentieth century.

Central and eastern European industries were able to grow for many reasons. In the Russian Empire, the government invested heavily in growth relevant infra-structure (such as railroads, banks and imported technologies) and supported industrial development in many ways, including substituting private entrepre-neurship. In central and northern Europe, new industries developed during this period that were highly complementary to the long tradition of substantial human capital investment in these regions, of which chemical and electro-technical industries are the most famous (Landes 1969, see Map 2.3). Although their employment share became only substantial during the twentieth century, these technologies and new 'scientific' style of generating innovations influenced many other fields. However, Broadberry and Burhop (2007) warn against overstating Germany's industrial success relative to Britain and reject a hypothesis of entre-preneurial failure in England for many industries.

Although industry experienced the most remarkable development – and has received the most research attention – the other two sectors should not be neglected, that is, agriculture and services. Agricultural employment declined but total production in this sector increased as new fertilizers were developed by the emerging chemical industry and agricultural machinery gradually improved (from wooden to iron ploughs in poor areas; to threshing machines in richer areas). A number of studies have focused on the dramatic effects of the so-called European grain invasion. As transport costs decreased, a wave of imported wheat from the Russian Empire and North America flooded Europe. The famous response in central Europe was the implementation of agricultural tariffs. In Germany, for example, the imperial government was strongly influenced by east German aristocratic landowners to increase grain tariffs. (However, there is some debate about the quantitative importance of these tariffs. See Broadberry and O'Rourke 2010: p. 68.) The grain invasion also had an important impact on welfare, especially for the poor. Real wages and nutritional levels increased, and stature began to increase during the 1880s, extending over more than a century for the first time in human history (Figure 2.6). Income redistribution, social security programmes, and – during the twentieth century – medical progress supported this trend.

How did the service sector develop during the period 1870–1913? Although the agricultural share of unemployment decreased between 1870 and 1913 from

Map 2.3 Regional economic specialization in Europe during the later nineteenth century
Source: see map 1.1.

just over 50 to just over 40 per cent, and industrialization became a policy goal for most countries, some of the richest countries experienced stronger increases in the service sector than in the industrial sector (Broadberry and O'Rourke 2010). In the UK, service sector employment increased by 9 per cent (while industry grew by only

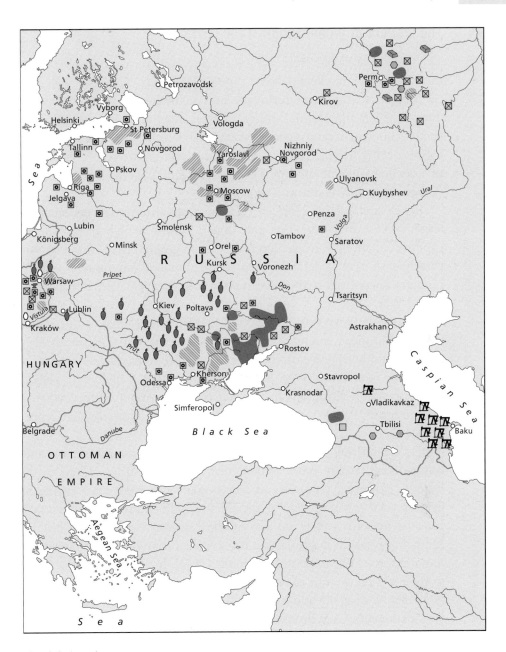

Map 2.3 (cont.)

2 per cent). In Switzerland, service sector employment nearly doubled from 16 to 28 per cent. Cities including London, Zürich and Geneva expanded their central banking and trading positions. Broadberry and O'Rourke (2010) observe a stronger relationship between national income and service sector employment than between income and industrial employment.

The first era of globalization, 1850–1913

The first era of globalization (O'Rourke and Williamson 1999) became visible in three economic markets: labour, capital and goods. The latter two markets are relatively more important during the late twentieth and twenty-first centuries than during the late nineteenth century, whereas integration in labour markets was of primary importance during the first era of globalization, which occurred before the First World War. Migration from the Old World to the New World reached levels of more than one million people per year, considering only transatlantic migration (O'Rourke and Williamson 1999).

Higher land–labour ratios in classical destination countries, such as the US, Canada, Australia, Argentina and Brazil, produced higher real wages in these countries than in Europe. Decreases in migration cost through transatlantic passenger ships considerably increased the number of migrants, especially because immigration policies in these destination countries remained liberal until the First World War.

Germany belonged to the group of first wave of source countries (large-scale western European migration occurred before the mid-nineteenth century). In contrast, southern and eastern European migration occurred in the decades preceding the First World War. Italian emigration was as high as 11 per cent of the total population during the first decade of the twentieth century, whereas typical rates in Spain, Portugal and Austria-Hungary were approximately 5 per cent per decade.[19]

It is astonishing that emigration from relatively poor southern and eastern Europe was initially more limited than migration from richer north-western Europe. However, a number of factors play important roles in the migration process, such as transportation, social and psychological costs. Potential migrants consider not only wages but also hurdles, such as isolation and discrimination. Migration research indicates that the so-called friends-and-family effect plays an important role. The migrant stock in the US was mainly British, Irish and German in the early nineteenth century, and individuals of these nationalities migrated more often during the mid-nineteenth century after the first small communities of their nationalities had been established (and travel costs decreased).

Recently, the selectivity of migrants has been studied more intensively. In contemporary debates over migration, the educational level of immigrants plays an important role, including potential brain-drain effects on the source countries. Did European countries experience brain-drain during the nineteenth century? This phenomenon can be observed for Russia. Partly due to religious persecution during the 1890s, a substantial share of the Jewish inhabitants of the Russian Empire emigrated, which reduced the human capital level of this country (Stolz and Baten 2012). In contrast, German emigrants around the mid-nineteenth century were less skilled than the population that remained. This migration was caused by famine during the so-called hungry 1840s. Local communities were obliged to care for the poor, and it was less expensive for communities to pay for tickets to the New World than for welfare payments. This observation starkly contrasts with the narratives about German migrants in school books, which usually emphasize the political refugees of the unsuccessful revolution of 1848 who were presumably highly educated (but represented few of the total number of migrants).

The war and interwar years

After a relatively consistent increase in welfare in southern, eastern and central Europe, the First World War (1914–18) ended this phase. The loss of human life was unprecedented and the destruction of the war areas immense. Additionally, the war created a climate of distrust and economic disintegration. After the first era of globalization (1850–1913), an era of deglobalization followed (O'Rourke and Williamson 1999). During the war, many of the countries that had been buying European industrial products installed own industrial capacity (e.g., India). Other markets were taken over by US or Japanese exporters, satisfying Latin American and Asian consumer demands. In addition, south-eastern Europe promoted its own industrial development. These processes resulted in a doubling of industrial plants and fierce competition in which governments interfered.[20]

Eastern Europe also experienced a unique development. After the October Revolution in the Russian Empire, the introduction of Soviet-style socialism and later communism with nationalization of the main industries increased heavy industrial production at the expense of consumer-oriented light industries and agriculture. The collectivization of agriculture resulted in harvest failures and the death of a high share of the population, especially in Ukraine during the early 1930s. On the other hand, the Soviet Union engaged in one of the most ambitious expansions of an educational system. Soviet heavy industries were sufficiently developed in the 1940s to defeat the German army that invaded Soviet territory during the Second World War, although imports of weapons and idealism also played a large role.

After this short deviation, we return to central Europe during the interwar period. The deglobalization period after the First World War reached its economic nadir during the Great Depression of the early 1930s. Germany was among the countries most severely affected by the Great Depression because its recovery and rationalization of major industries was financed by unsustainable foreign lending. In addition, war reparation obligations reduced investment propensity and, perhaps most importantly, the government implemented a rigid austerity policy that resulted in deflation (Ritschl 2002). As unemployment rates had

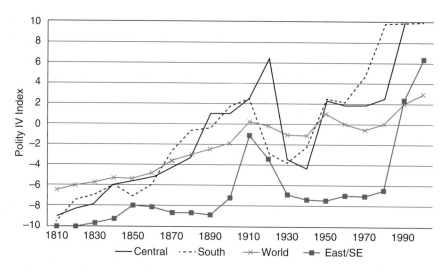

Figure 2.9 Polity IV index for participation in European regions
Source: calculated from Marshall *et al.* (2011).

reached unprecedented heights, the national socialists accumulated government power and began to pursue their inhuman policies against the Jewish minority, political leftists and many other groups. Following their election, the national socialists undertook a series of rapid steps to abolish democracy. Figure 2.9 illustrates the rapid decline of political participation rights in central Europe during the 1930s.[21]

National socialist trade policy in Germany consisted of an autarkic policy regime that aimed to cancel all imports, such as foodstuffs, that could be replaced with domestic substitutes or raw materials for the consumer-oriented industries. Only imports of iron ore and similar items were considered necessary because a main aim of the government was to strengthen the production capacity of military products. Interestingly, both the persecuted and non-persecuted German groups suffered from these autarkic and trade-restraining policies. Mortality rates increased in large cities even before the war. Additionally, the stature growth of children abruptly stagnated despite continuous growth during the half century before and after (except the First World War and immediate post-First World War periods. See Baten and Wagner 2003).

The Great Depression affected all European countries with unpredictable vigour. Reactions to the crisis varied considerably, however. What determined the speed of recovery from the Great Depression among European countries? One important issue was monetary policy. Many countries had adopted the gold standard during the nineteenth century, which guaranteed that all bank notes could be exchanged for gold in the central bank of a specific country. During the First World War, many countries left the gold standard and issued paper money that was not guaranteed. During the postwar period, however, a return to gold was a policy driven by ideology. The gold standard provided important advantages during periods of normal economic development in societies with a modest level of communication technology. For example, investors in one country could be relatively sure that their investments would not be lost in currency devaluations. This effect was one of the building blocks of capital mobility during the first era of globalization during the period 1850–1913.

Eichengreen and Sachs (1985) famously argued that the countries that left the gold standard early (such as the UK in 1931) faced the best prospects for rapid recovery. During the Great Depression, the effect of the gold standard in countries that maintained it for a long period was severe. Italy, Switzerland, France, Belgium and Poland maintained their gold standard policies until the mid-1930s. These countries experienced reductions in their competitiveness because the UK, for example, could offer relatively cheaper products on international markets following the devaluation of the British pound. Similarly, deflationary processes prevented potential investors from stimulating the economy. Investors preferred to maintain their money reserves because the value of money relative to goods increased. Many central and eastern European economies suffered from the agricultural protectionism of industrial countries during the early 1930s, which preferred to stimulate their own agricultural sectors even if it was less efficient to grow foodstuffs domestically than to import these products.

In contrast, the Soviet Union achieved rapid industrial growth, if the statistical evidence can be trusted. For example, pig iron production in 1940 was four times as large as it had been in 1927 (Allen 2003, Buyst and Franaszek 2010). Additionally, countries that generally maintained market economy systems, such as Poland, experimented with nationalized chemical industries, armament and steel production.[22]

The Second World War had severe effects on European economies by redirecting world leadership to the US and, partially, to the Soviet Union. The Nazi army destroyed a considerable portion of European infrastructure and the occupied countries suffered heavily from forced labour, plundering of resources and indirect theft via excessive taxes and 'deliveries' of raw materials. Physical capital in the occupied territories was destroyed by the war, insufficient reinvestment and maintenance, whereas the industrial capacity of Germany increased substantially until the end of the war despite heavy bombing. (However, much of this capacity was useless after the war because it specialized in armament production.)

The golden age of the 1950s and 1960s

The two decades after 1950 are the so-called golden age of European economic growth.[23] In the beginning, some of this growth resulted from the shift from agriculture to industry and services in countries that had not yet fully industria-lized. All European economies became service sector economies with shares of services of approximately 60 per cent, except eastern Europe, which was charac-terized by a slightly smaller share. However, these GDP growth effects of structural change tended to decrease over time. The relatively free markets of southern and central Europe, including bridging some of labour shortages through migration as in Germany's famous 'Gastarbeiter' – the movement of southern Europeans into the country – contributed to the impressive growth of the 1950s and 1960s. The predecessor institutions of the European Union were formed during this period, and they facilitated the economic integration of the initial set of European coun-tries. Additionally, capital shortages did not present major growth obstacles as they had in previous periods because capital was relatively mobile across borders.

In addition to free markets and structural change, marked increases in efficiency resulted from new technologies, especially from North America. These innovations enabled producers to save inputs and provide cheaper products, which experienced increasing demand among larger population segments. Additionally, intermediate goods could be easily imported or bought from domestic producers. Finally, economic policy during this period was Keynesian and aimed to reduce and smooth business cycle effects. During this period of recovery and relatively stable growth, Keynesian policies appeared to have worked well.

How did eastern and south-eastern Europe develop? According to official statistics, which have been used in most previous publications, growth was quite strong in the USSR and particularly strong in Yugoslavia, where the potential for productivity growth and structural change by transitioning from agriculture to industry persisted. In addition, the unique socialist system of Yugoslavia in which factories were owned by workers and decision-making was less centralized than in other socialist countries may have led to stronger growth. According to official statistics, from the 1950s to the early 1980s, Yugoslavia was among the fastest growing countries, approaching the ranges reported in South Korea and other growth miracle countries. However, it is difficult to evaluate the quality of physical capital. This difficulty arises because the type of machinery produced in socialist countries specialized in mass production of sometimes poor quality goods. After the breakdown of the socialist economies in 1989, the evaluation of capital goods changed quickly because these goods were not equally valued in market economies as in socialist economies. Another difficult topic is the evaluation of the quality of services provided in socialist economies. Because prices in general were not always informative, it is difficult to estimate the prices of services provided in these economies. Nevertheless, even if the absolute value of the growth rates was not as high as indicated by the official statistics, both the Soviet Union and Yugoslavia were characterized by surprisingly high growth rates of both income and educa-tion during the 1950s. The American and western European publics experienced a so-called Sputnik shock after the Soviet Union placed the first satellite in space long before the western economies were able to do so. This event might indicate how rapidly human capital had advanced during the first decades of the Soviet Union. However, economic incentives and preferences of the socialist leadership posed severe problems as economic structure changed during the subsequent decades.

Stagflation (1970s–1980s)

After the oil price shock in 1973, the period of European growth ended. The 1970s and 1980s became known for stagflation, i.e., the combination of inflation and stagnation of economic growth. The economic theorists had previously hypothesized that either inflation or stagnation could occur but not that both could occur simultaneously.

The initial turning point, the considerable increase in energy prices following conflict in the Middle East, leads to the following question: was this development driven by resource costs? Could stagflation have been avoided if energy prices had been lower? In fact, during the 1950s and 1960s Europe benefitted from low average costs of energy, foodstuffs and other raw materials. However, other forces were also at work. Crafts and Toniolo (1996) argued that slowing economic growth was simply an adjustment after a period of abnormally high growth rates. The previous growth strategy of adopting North American technology was no longer possible because much of that gap had been closed.

The 1970s were also a period during which European scepticism about unlimited industrial growth increased. The Club of Rome report suggested that the previous strategy of industrial expansion at the expense of ecological deprivation and depletion of resources was unsustainable. In Germany and other countries Green parties for which ecological agendas were central were formed. Even in eastern Germany, the socialist German Democratic Republic (GDR), there was an ecological movement temporarily supported by the government (however, this support was soon terminated). The extreme environmental pollution of the 1950s and 1960s was modestly reduced during the subsequent decades. However, this environmentalism was perceived as a luxury of richer European societies in poorer countries. Southern European countries, such as Portugal, Yugoslavia and Spain, continued to pursue income growth first. In Portugal and Spain, authoritarian regimes were overthrown and democratization began. The Iberian countries were included in the European Community in 1986.

In eastern Europe, the situation differed because the socialist countries possessed their own energy resources and government aims. However, the temptation to sell oil from Azerbaijan and other regions to the West after 1973 strained political-economic relations within the Eastern bloc. During much of this period, the Soviet Union had among the lowest per-capita incomes in the socialist countries. However, Soviets were actually subsidizing its east-central European satellite states through low energy prices. Especially during the 1980s, the inability of the socialist economic system to create appropriate economic incentives became clear. Following political protests in Poland (which were not suppressed to the same degree as earlier protests in the GDR, Hungary and Czechoslovakia) and other signs of dissatisfaction, Mikhail Gorbachev and his followers initiated a drastic change of policy in the Soviet Union in 1986, which transformed not only the political but also the economic systems of the socialist countries.

Finale: the 1990s and 2000s

The transformation from socialist to market economy system was harsh. GDP initially decreased substantially. Life expectancy decreased and crime increased. For example, homicide rates doubled in many former socialist countries and took several years to return to normal levels. Institutional economists moved to Russia and hoped that institutional change would rapidly initiate economic growth; however, other factors also played an important role, such as entrepreneurial traditions and self-images.

The 1990s were characterized by deepening European political-economic integration but also by crisis within the European Union (beginning in 2006). Change in east-central Europe enlarged the EU to twenty-eight member states, including former Soviet republics in the Baltic region. In many European countries, a common currency was introduced that reduced the transaction costs of intra-European trade and increased mobility significantly. The inflationary tendencies of the 1970s and 1980s disappeared. On the other hand, when EU countries, such as Greece, experienced financial crisis, these countries could no longer devalue their currencies to regain competitiveness. In Spain, Portugal, Italy and Greece, the youth unemployment rate was especially high during the 2000s. Even with historically low interest rates, entrepreneurs did not invest sufficiently in new or existing businesses. The global economic crisis that began in 2006 also reinforced some of the north–south differences that began to disappear in Europe. In the 1990s and early 2000s, Germany was often discussed as 'the sick man in Europe'. Germany recovered from the 2006–08 crisis more quickly than the southern European countries did, and many northern and central Europeans professed the belief that southern Europe had always been a difficult area.

Other important developments during the 1990s and 2000s included the economic restructuring that followed the revolution in computer-based information and communication technologies (ICT). Although the trend began in the 1970s and 1980s, during the 1990s almost everybody outside manual workplaces had permanent contact with ICT. Surprisingly, although the change in economic systems was likely as large as the introduction of electricity at the beginning of the twentieth century, the measured productivity effects of ICT in most industries seemed quite limited (Solow 1987). The main effect of ICT was likely making workplaces and services more pleasant for workers by reducing assembly line processes.[24]

Conclusion

One remarkable fact of European economic history since 1500 is the considerable variability in important development and welfare indicators over time. For example, we observe surprisingly high standards of living in southern and eastern Europe c. 1600. The real wages of urban populations benefitted from low cost of grain in Eastern Europe. Nutritional status was also exceptionally high during the sixteenth and early seventeenth centuries by the standards of the early modern period. However, as eastern Europe began to export its grain to north-western Europe, food prices increased. In eastern Europe, the second serfdom resulted in exceedingly unequal distributions of power and income. Consequently, this region trailed in the welfare race.

In Italy, Spain and Portugal, both human capital and national incomes were remarkably high during the fourteenth and fifteenth centuries. During the nineteenth century, central Europe overtook its southern and eastern neighbours in income and began to converge to the levels of north-western Europe. However, this positive economic development was soon overshadowed by the catastrophic World Wars of the early twentieth century. The immediate post-war period produced one of the few eras during which all European regions experienced economic growth at substantial rates. The 1950s and 1960s were truly a golden age for many European countries. In eastern Europe, however, socialism imposed strong constraints on economic development, which ultimately produced transformations to market and mixed economic systems during the late 1980s. This chapter concluded with a discussion of the transformation crisis in eastern Europe, the struggle for reform in central Europe and the global financial crisis of the 2000s.

Notes

1. Hanushek and Woessmann demonstrated that numerical abilities are the most relevant skills to economic development, which also supports the use of this indicator. See the Introduction and Chapter I2, 'The Sputnik shock' for a more detailed discussion.
2. Neighbouring Portugal was a pioneer in the voyages around Africa to Asia, and to the Americas. Portuguese merchants gained considerable wealth through intercontinental trade.
3. See the Introduction for the definition of this indicator.
4. If only urban real wages are considered, Poland always outperformed England due to low cost grain in the surrounding areas. However, agricultural day labourers were relatively poorer than in England.

5. Agriculture in the Baltic region during the nineteenth century was characterized by relatively high numbers of cattle per capita, which might have reduced the malnutrition-related problems of studying that are observed in developing countries today.

6. The part of Poland that was included in the Russian Empire experienced early industrial development in textiles during the early nineteenth century, especially due to the entrepreneurial spirit of its Jewish minority.

7. Land in the western Empire, especially Czech lands and the areas surrounding Vienna (which was also the administrative centre of the Habsburg Empire), industrialized quite early.

8. This can also be observed looking at other indicators. School development was also low in many Balkan countries.

9. In contrast, countries such as Bulgaria invested substantially in education during the early twentieth century and educational indicators increased rapidly during this period. The Balkan region was characterized by a variety of small economies (Serbia, Bulgaria, Romania, Albania, Montenegro, Slovenia and Croatia). In these economies, large export surpluses of wool and other animal products were generated. Bulgaria also developed proto-industrial production of woollen and other household and military goods.

10. Greece specialized in grain, wine, raisins, wool, tobacco and cotton; Greek shipping also dominated eastern Mediterranean commercial routes between the eighteenth and mid-nineteenth centuries.

11. The regional specialization included, to a smaller extent, wine. Agricultural production was characterized by a high share of subsistence farming in the mountainous regions.

12. In northern Italy, specializations varied considerably. For example, the Po Valley developed hard cheese production. In northern Italy, the silk industry had survived since the early modern period and maintained its high quality. Italy generated two-thirds of the world exports of silk during this period.

13. In the Basque country and other parts of northern Spain, the mining and iron industries complemented the agricultural basis.

14. Farmers specialized in dairy farming in north-western Germany and the Alpine regions.

15. We define central Europe not by geographic or historical borders but by the income gap observed during the nineteenth and twentieth centuries. This suggests that only Switzerland, Austria and Germany are included. East-central and south-eastern Europe are included in the eastern region.

16. In contrast, the political crisis of the 1990s cannot be studied using this indicator because the height estimates refer to the period until the 1980s only.

17. Usually, substantial increases in education precede welfare growth. In fact, during the late nineteenth century, eastern and south-eastern Europe were on an upward trajectory, as indicated by their GDP per capita and their height trends.

18. On the following few paragraphs, see Broadberry and O'Rourke (2010).

19. Return migration could reach nearly 30 per cent in the Italian case, whereas the numbers for eastern Europe are smaller. Because most migrants were between the ages of 20 and 30, the size of this age group was dramatically reduced in Italy.

20. New economic activities during this period in the Balkans included the development of the oil industry in Romania.

21. We will discuss the other aspects of this Figure only in passing. During the late nineteenth century, the increase in political participation values was quite slow, while there was a significant shift towards more participation during the first era of globalization (1850–1913) in all three regions. In eastern and south-eastern Europe, levels of political participation remain relatively low. Interestingly, we observe a small increase in eastern and south-eastern Europe c. 1850–60. For example, Serbians obtained some voting rights and Romania temporarily became a partial democracy. Moreover, a short-lived increase can be noted c. 1910–20 (in Poland in 1920, for example). In southern Europe, a dramatic decrease is observed. In Italy, the decrease began during the Mussolini regime, in Spain, the participation index declined during the Franco regime. Fortunately, during the post-Second World War period, democratic values increased (with some support from the US and western European democracies). In central Europe, increases took place slightly later, partially because eastern Germany remained part of the Eastern Bloc until 1989.
22. On this and the following, see Buyst and Franaszek (2010).
23. On this and the following, see Houpt *et al.* (2010).
24. The quality of services also improved – an economic variable that is always difficult to measure.

Further reading

Alfani, G. (2013), 'Plague in Seventeenth-century Europe and the Decline of Italy: an Epidemiological Hypothesis', *European Review of Economic History* 17, 408–30. Thought-provoking article on why Italy declined in relative terms.

A'Hearn, B., Baten, J. and Crayen, D. (2009), 'Quantifying Quantitative Literacy: Age Heaping and the History of Human Capital', *Journal of Economic History* 69–3, 783–808. Measures the human capital of early modern Europe.

Broadberry, S. N. and O'Rourke, K. (eds.) (2010), *Cambridge Economic History of Modern Europe*, Cambridge University Press. The standard for comparative European economic history.

Crafts, N. and Toniolo, G. (1996), *Economic Growth in Europe Since 1945*, Cambridge University Press. Good overview over the recent period.

Dincecco, M. (2011), *Political Transformations and Public Finances*, Cambridge University Press. Explains the interaction between fiscal capacity and executive constraint as growth determinant.

Mironov, B. (2012), *The Standard of Living and Revolutions in Russia, 1700–1917*, Abingdon: Routledge. Impressive and provocative study on Russian welfare development.

Ogilvie, S. C. and Overy, R. (eds.) (2003), *Germany: a New Social and Economic History, Vol. III: Since 1800*, London: Arnold. An English-language overview on German economic history.

van Zanden, J. L., Buringh, E. and Bosker, M. (2012), 'The Rise and Decline of European Parliaments, 1188–1789', *Economic History Review* 65 (3), 835–86. Provocative account of the early history of participation.

References

Acemoglu, D. and Robinson, J. A. (2012), *Why Nations Fail: the Origins of Power, Prosperity and Poverty*, 1st edn., New York: Crown.

Allen, R. C. (2003), 'Progress and Poverty in Early Modern Europe', *Economic History Review* LVI-3, 403–43.

Baten, J. and Blum, M. (2014), 'Why are you Tall while Others are Short? Agricultural Production and other Proximate Determinants of Global Heights', *European Review of Economic History* 18, 144–65.

Baten, J. and Wagner, A. (2003), 'Autarchy, Market Disintegration, and Health: the Mortality and Nutritional Crisis in Nazi Germany 1933–37', *Economics and Human Biology* 1 (1): 1–28.

Becker, S. and Woessmann, L. (2009), 'Was Weber Wrong? A Human Capital Theory of Protestant Economic History', *Quarterly Journal of Economics* 124 (2): 531–96.

Bibikov, M. (2013), 'Russia: Early and Medieval Period', in J. Mokyr (ed.), *The Oxford Encyclopedia of Economic History*, Oxford University Press, 412–14.

Broadberry, S. N. and Burhop, C. (2007), 'Comparative Productivity in British and German Manufacturing Before World War II: Reconciling Direct Benchmark Estimates and Time Series Projections', *Journal of Economic History* 67: 315–49.

Broadberry, S., Campbell, B., Klein, A., Overton, M. and van Leeuwen, B. (2014), *British Economic Growth, 1270–1870*, Cambridge University Press.

Buyst, E. and Franaszek, P. (2010), 'Sectoral Developments, 1914–1945', in S. N. Broadberry and K. H. O'Rourke (eds.), *The Cambridge Economic History of Modern Europe*, Vol. 2, Cambridge University Press, 208–31.

Crayen, D. and Baten, J. (2010), 'Global Trends in Numeracy 1820–1949 and its Implications for Long-run Growth', *Explorations in Economic History* 47 (1): 82–99.

Crouzet, F. (1970), 'Un indice de la production industrielle française au XIXe siècle', *Annales* 25: 92–7.

Eichengreen, B. and Sachs, J. (1985), 'Exchange Rates and Economic Recovery in the 1930s', *The Journal of Economic History* 45 (04), 925–46.

Feinstein, C. H. (1972), *National Income, Expenditure and Output of the United Kingdom, 1855–1965*, Cambridge University Press.

Fenoaltea, S. (2003), 'Notes on the Rate of Industrial Growth in Italy, 1861–1913', *Journal of Economic History* 63: 695–735.

Gadisseur, J. (1973), 'Contribution à l'étude de la production agricole en Belgique de 1846–1913', *Revue Belge d'Histoire Contemporaine* 4: 1–48.

Goldsmith, R. W. (1961), 'The Economic Growth of Tsarist Russia, 1860–1913', *Economic Development and Cultural Change* 9: 441–75.

Hansen, S. A. (1974), *Økonomisk Vaekst I Danmark, Vol. II: 1914–1970*, University of Copenhagen.

Hippe, R. and Baten, J. (2012), 'The Early Regional Development of Human Capital in Europe, 1790–1880', *Scandinavian Economic History Review* 60 (3): 254–89.

(2014), 'Keep them Ignorant. Did Inequality in Land Distribution Delay Regional Human Capital Formation?', Working Paper, University of Tübingen.

Hjerppe, R. (1996), *Finland's Historical National Accounts 1860–1994. Calculation Methods and Statistical Tables*, Jyväskylä: Kivirauma.

Hoffmann, W. G. (1965), *Das Wachstum der deutschen Wirtschaft seit der Mitte des 19. Jahrhunderts*, Berlin: Springer-Verlag.

Houpt, S., Lains, P. and Schön, L. (2010), 'Sectoral Developments, 1945–2000', in S. N. Broadberry and K. H. O'Rourke (eds), *The Cambridge Economic History of Modern Europe*, Vol. 2, Cambridge University Press, 334–402.

Karaman, K. K. and Pamuk, Ş. (2010), 'Ottoman State Finances in European Perspective, 1500–1914', *The Journal of Economic History* 70(03), 593–629.

Koepke, N. and Baten, J. (2005), 'The Biological Standard of Living in Europe During the Last Two Millennia', *European Review of Economic History* 9 (1): 61–95.

(2008), 'Agricultural Specialization and Height in Ancient and Medieval Europe', *Explorations in Economic History* 45: 127–46.

Krantz, O. and Schön, L. (2007), 'Swedish Historical National Accounts, 1800–2000', Lund University Macroeconomic and Demographic Database, www.ehl.lu.se/database/LU-MADD/National%20Accounts/default.htm.

Lains, P. (2006), 'Growth in a Protected Environment: Portugal, 1850–1950', unpublished paper, University of Lisbon.

Landes, D. S. (1969), *The Unbound Prometheus: Technological Change and Industrial Development in Western Europe from 1750 to the Present*, Cambridge, New York: Press Syndicate of the University of Cambridge.

Malinowski, M. (2013), 'East of Eden: Polish Living Standards in a European Perspective, c. 1500–1800', *CGEH Working Paper Series, No. 43*.

(2014), 'Freedom and Decline: Polish State Formation and Rye Market Disintegration, 1500–1772', working paper, University of Utrecht.

Marshall, M., Jaggers, G. K. and Gurr, T. R. (2011), *POLITY IV Project Political Regime Characteristics and Transitions, 1800–2010 Dataset Users' Manual*. www.systemic peace.org/inscr/p4manualv2010.pdf, last downloaded 1 September 2014.

O'Rourke, K. H. and Williamson, J. G. (1999), *Globalization and History: the Evolution of a Nineteenth Century Atlantic Economy*, Cambridge, MA: MIT Press.

Prados de la Escosura, L. (2003), *El progreso económico de España, 1850–2000*, Madrid: Fundaciòn BBVA.

Ritschl, A. (2002), 'Deutschlands Krise und Konjunktur 1924–1934. Binnenkonjunktur, Auslandsverschuldung und Reparationsproblem zwischen Dawes-Plan und Transfersperre', *Jahrbuch für Wirtschaftsgeschichte Beiheft 2/2002*. Berlin: Akademie Verlag.

Schulze, M.-S. (2000), 'Patterns of Growth and Stagnation in the Late Nineteenth Century Habsburg Economy', *European Review of Economic History* 4: 311–40.

Smits, J.-P., Horlings, E. and van Zanden, J. L. (2000), 'Dutch GNP and its Components, 1870–1913', N.W. Posthumus Institute, University of Groningen, www.nationalaccounts.niwi .knaw.nl/start.htm.

Solow, R. (1987), 'We'd Better Watch Out', *New York Times Book Review*, 12 July 1987, p. 36.

Stolz, Y. and Baten, J. (2012). 'Brain Drain in the Age of Mass Migration: Does Relative Inequality Explain Migrant Selectivity?', *Explorations in Economic History* 49: 205–20.

Vecchi, G. (2011), *In ricchezza e in povertà. Il benessere degli italiani dall'Unità a oggi*, Bologna: Il Mulino.

12 The Sputnik shock, the Pisa shock: human capital as a global growth determinant

Joerg Baten

Many pupils in school do not like maths, and those who like it are often despised as 'nerds'. However, maths skills – and education in general – are decisive for the following question: will your country be rich or poor? Some countries follow a path of reinvesting income into education, sustaining more skill-intensive industries. Better education, therefore, does not only increase the current human capital of the labour force, but it also permits the development of additional innovations and adaptation of new technologies that can be imported from foreign countries. Having this relationship in mind, many advanced countries experienced shocks in their histories: the US public suffered from a Sputnik shock during the 1950s, when the Soviet Union demonstrated innovative capabilities in space. The German public experienced a 'Pisa shock' during the early 2000s when testing of problem-solving abilities demonstrated that German school children did not succeed well in maths, reading and natural science tests. East Asian and Scandinavian school children were far ahead in the first tests, suggesting that economic growth would be much more rapid in these world regions. Both the shocked US and Germany initiated expensive educational investment programmes thereafter.

Dramatic shocks like these initiated research projects that also considered long-term developments. The traditional view of economic historians was that human capital could not have played a large role in eighteenth and nineteenth century growth because two of the best-studied countries seemed to be inconsistent with this growth theory. Mitch (1991) noted that Britain experienced stagnating literacy between the mid-eighteenth and mid-nineteenth centuries, whereas France was quite early in its educational development without becoming a driving force of growth in nineteenth-century Europe. Baten and van Zanden (2008) rejected this view by taking a long-term perspective: they found that starting in 1450, there was a substantial influence of advanced human capital on welfare growth, even considering other potential determinants such as institutional development (constraints of the executive), trade and Malthusian forces.

Hanushek and Woessmann (2012) studied the components of human capital and argued that maths and science skills, in particular, are the most important ones. They suggested a new measurement of these components by employing data from the Organization for Economic Co-operation and Development (OECD)

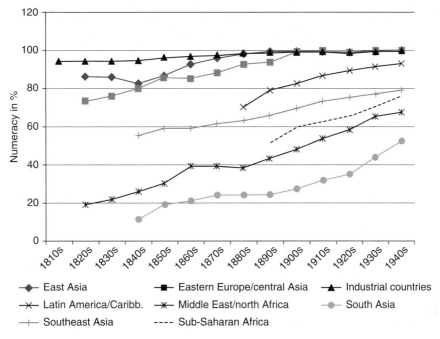

Figure I2.1 Numeracy of the world regions during the nineteenth and twentieth centuries
Source: calculated from Crayen and Baten (2010).
Note: 'industrial countries' represent western Europe, North America, Japan.

and the International Association for the Evaluation of Educational Achievement (IEA), for the period 1964–2003. Hanushek and Woessmann include this new 'measure of cognitive skills', as they call it, as an explanatory variable of economic growth. If this variable is added to a growth model, three-quarters of the variance in growth rates can be explained.[1] In contrast, running a regression with a growth model that utilizes school enrolment rates as an indicator instead, just one-quarter of the variance in growth rates can be explained. If both variables are included as explanatory variables, school enrolment becomes statistically insignificant, whereas the maths and science skills keep their explanatory power. Conditional GDP growth can be explained with conditional ability test scores with an R^2 of 0.98 (although there are only eight world regions).[2]

Additionally, basic maths skills have also been studied for long-run development. In Figure I2.1, we see world regions' trends of basic numeracy (see the Introduction for an explanation of the method). The richest world regions, western European/North American industrial countries, eastern Europe and East Asia, had high numeracy values already, during a period when East Asia was still poor. Relatively low levels of numeracy were found in the Middle East and South Asia (similar rankings can be observed as soon as maths test results can be obtained).

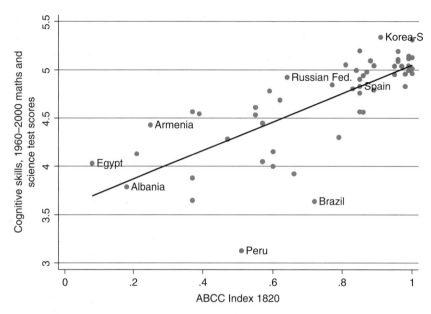

Figure I2.2 Maths and science cognitive skills, 1964–2003, and numeracy, 1820 (ABCC Index)
Source: modified from Baten and Juif (2013). Nigeria added from Cappelli and Baten (2015).

It appears that a high degree of numerical abilities was already developed by some countries before the nineteenth century (Figure I2.2). In addition, basic numeracy in 1820 correlates with maths/science skills during the late twentieth century. However, looking at individual country histories, there was significant mobility; some countries declined in levels of numeracy, others increased (this makes it clear that genetic interpretations are impossible).

However, one of the crucial questions in assessing human capital as a growth determinant is the degree of exogeneity with higher income, which allows for more substantial investment in schooling. Therefore, the direction of causality can potentially run the other way. In addition, another question arises of whether human capital is only a proximate growth determinant, following underlying factors such as institutional design. Some factors related to human capital development have been proposed by the literature stating that human capital is not simply a function of institutional design and not a perfect correlate of income; religious rules can determine education in a relatively exogenous way. Botticini and Eckstein (2007) offered a human capital interpretation of Jewish economic history in which they ascribed Jewish educational rigour to a decisive moment in the first century CE.[3] Although the Jewish religion previously had no specific rules about education, in that century, the religious group of the Pharisees gained dominance over the competing Sadducees, and the main religious rule emerged requiring parents to teach their male children to read the Torah. Botticini and Eckstein argued that this was a relatively exogenous religious decision that was not determined by demand because Jews remained mostly farmers for another seven centuries. Only in the eighth and ninth centuries, when the Middle East became more urbanized, could Jews finally make economic use of their exogenously created human capital. The Jewish elite began to specialize in trade, banking, medicine and similar professions; legal constraints came later.

Similar to this human capital history of the Jewish religion, Becker and Woessmann (2009) offered an alternative explanation to Weber's theory about the Protestant confession. Analysing differences in literacy between nineteenth-century Prussian Protestant and Catholic countries and employing instrumental variable methods, they concluded that human capital was exogenously accumulated by Lutherans. The religiously determined need to read the Bible allowed Protestant regions to prosper economically and caused Catholic regions to fall behind.

A number of other exogenous determinants of human capital have been studied in the literature, which we can only briefly mention here. Such factors include, for example, the following: (1) the curse of natural resources. A number of studies have identified the problems arising from the discovery of natural resources such as oil in a country, because apart from currency effects, inequality and changes in relative prices, the political economy of resource rich countries might also tend towards under-investments in human capital. (2) Similarly, land inequality can be an obstacle to human capital development. Galor et al. (2009) developed a theory in which large landowners normally decided to invest less in the schooling of their day labourers, partly because they tried to avoid additional taxes and partly because they wanted to keep their day labourers on their estates. (3) Some important events in history, like lost wars, were motivators for direct schooling investments, such as the Russian situation after the Crimean war or the French situation after 1871. (4) Malnutrition can be a very important factor as well. Beyond a certain threshold of malnutrition, learning of tedious maths, in particular, is impossible. Baten et al. (2014) recently studied the natural experiment of the Napoleonic blockade in England that resulted in malnutrition. This event delayed numerical development. In other contexts, the factor of malnutrition played a role as well. (5) Additional determinants are demographic behaviour (the decision between quantity of children and more education for fewer children), the relative status of women, contact with immigrants from other countries and a number of other factors.

In sum, education and maths skills, in particular, are a very important determinant of economic growth, and there are many reasons to conclude that the decision for more or less education was exogenous in long-term development.

Notes

1. Only initial GDP level is added in this and the following regression.
2. Hanushek and Woessmann also ensured that endogeneity is not a problem.
3. See also Baten and Juif (2014) on the following.

References

Baten, J., Crayen, D. and Voth, J. (2014), 'Numeracy and the Impact of High Food Prices in Industrializing Britain, 1780–1850', *Review of Economics and Statistics* 96 (3): 418–30.

Baten, J. and Juif, D. (2014), 'A Story of Large Land-owners and Math Skills: Inequality and Human Capital Formation in Long-run Development, 1820–2000', *Journal of Comparative Economics* 42 (2): 375–401.

Baten, J. and van Zanden, J. L. (2008), 'Book Production and the Onset of Modern Economic Growth', *Journal of Economic Growth* 13 (3): 217–35.

Becker, S. and Woessmann, L. (2009), 'Was Weber Wrong? A Human Capital Theory of Protestant Economic History', *Quarterly Journal of Economics* 124 (2): 531–96.

Botticini, M. and Eckstein, Z. (2007), 'From Farmers to Merchants, Conversions and Diaspora: Human Capital and Jewish History', *Journal of the European Economic Association* 5 (5): 885–926.

Cappelli, G. and Baten, J. (2015), 'A Reversal of Fortune in Human Capital: Colonialism and Numeracy in Africa, 1790–1969', Working Paper, University of Tuebingen.

Crayen, D. and Baten, J. (2010), 'Global Trends in Numeracy 1820–1949 and its Implications for Long-run Growth', *Explorations in Economic History* 47 (1): 82–99.

Galor, O., Moav, O. and Vollrath, D. (2009), 'Inequality in Landownership, the Emergence of Human-capital Promoting Institutions, and the Great Divergence', *Review of Economic Studies* 76 (1): 143–79.

Hanushek, E. A. and Woessmann, L. (2012), 'Do Better Schools Lead to More Growth? Cognitive Skills, Economic Outcomes, and Causation', *Journal of Economic Growth* 17 (4): 267–321.

Mitch, D. (1991), *The Rise of Popular Literacy in Victorian England*, Philadelphia: University of Pennsylvania Press.

H2.1 State finances during civil wars

Pablo Martín-Aceña

Economic conditions affect the development and outcomes of wars. The amount of resources available to the warring parties is usually a determinant of the final result. An advantage in resources can be readily transformed into military superiority in order to better meet the needs not only of the war effort, but also of the rearguard, essential for keeping up the morale of the population. Resource superiority usually reflects a higher level of economic development, which in turn allows for greater flexibility in adapting the productive structure to the necessities of the war. This argument has been confirmed for the case of the two world wars where the final outcome has been considered 'primarily a matter of levels of economic development of each side and the scale of resources that they wielded' – and this also applies to the Spanish Civil War, as we will see below.

There are four ways of paying for a war: taxation, public borrowing on the domestic market, borrowing from foreign markets and money creation. All require the intervention of the State. War financing methods have varied greatly, depending on internal and external constraints, institutional factors and on the length and intensity of the conflict. Evidence shows that governments have financed wars by using a mixture of direct contemporaneous taxes, debt and money creation. Adam Smith argued that taxes were the best method of financing because they conveyed the real cost of wars to the general public. A. C. Pigou added debt, although he considered this policy as equivalent to taxation. John Maynard Keynes suggested that money creation would be acceptable until the point of full employment was reached. Moreover, Keynes argued against the use of debt financing and wrote in favour of the use of rationing and price controls.

During the latest two world wars public expenditures increased and governments resorted to all possible means to finance the war effort. Governments used a mix of contemporaneous taxes, debt and money creation. When it was possible taxes were raised. Borrowing was intense and, as a result, government indebtedness multiplied. Deficits were unavoidable and as a result new money was thrown into circulation causing inflation and currency depreciation.

The experience of at least four nineteenth and twentieth century civil wars tells the same story. In the American Civil War, the Union covered its expenses by collecting new taxes, but most of the revenue needed to finance the war came from money creation (the well-known greenbacks) and from the issue of debt. The Confederacy, unable to pay for the war effort through taxation, resorted to selling bonds abroad in either London or Amsterdam and to issuing currency on a huge scale. Inflation both in the north and in the south was the concomitant result of printing money. In the long Mexican Civil War, the two confronted armies tried to raise taxes and to borrow from the public and to sell bonds abroad. However this was not sufficient to meet the expenses and henceforth the printing press was given additional work. Prices skyrocketed and the Mexican peso depreciated sharply. Revolutionary Russia offers a third example, which if anything is even more extreme. The Bolshevik faced insurmountable difficulties to finance the war: the fiscal administration collapsed, the domestic financial market vanished and markets abroad were closed to soviet issues. Paper money became the sole means of financing the deficit caused by the increase in war expenditures. As happened in other instances during civil or international wars, in Russia prices also rose unrelentingly to hyperinflation levels.

For the Spanish Civil War all these same arguments apply. To cover the costs of the war, taxes were an insignificant source of income for either of the two combatant parties in Spain. Neither of the contenders introduced major changes in the tax system. Most of the measures merely raised some tax rates or duties and only in the last month of the conflict was a tax on excess profits introduced. Neither of the two sides resorted to issuing debt, although the Republicans made an attempt in the last year of war, without success. The two contenders made extensive use of confiscation and expropriation of goods and properties of families and firms considered to sympathize with the enemy. The main source of internal financing of both sides was money creation. The Republic resorted to advances and credits from the Bank of Spain: the issue of new money represented 60 per cent of the Republicans' total revenue. On the other side, new money accounted for almost 70 per cent of the acknowledged internal expenses of the civil and military administration of the nationalist state during the war. To pay for foreign supplies, both the Republicans and the Franco administration consumed huge amounts of foreign reserves. The former used up the entire metallic (gold and silver) of the Bank of Spain. The latter received an equivalent amount of funds in the form of so-called aid from the Axis nations (Germany and Italy).

H2.2 Property rights in the Russian Empire
Irina Potkina

Property rights and their regulation are a crucial determinant of economic growth. How did they develop in the Russian Empire, and when were they formulated as binding laws? The laws about the right of property began to take shape in the 1830s. They represented a systematic version of the existing laws. The Russian politician Mikhail Speranskii was the driving force of this legal clarification initiative. In 1832, Article 420 of the Civil Laws delineated the right of ownership precisely, although it lacked sufficient harmony and conciseness. In 1832, the right of ownership was divided into its constituent parts: possession, use and disposal. The separate existence of the generally accepted triad was established in domestic jurisprudence at the turn of the 1860s to the 1870s on account of the Civil Department of the Directing Senate.

In the period of reforms during the 1860s, the legal texts about property rights were further improved, and new content was added to the laws: the socio-economic reforms required the Russian government to clarify its position in the field of property rights and their protection. The judicial practice played a key role in this question, and its results were generalized in corporate resolutions of the Directing Senate. In total it approved 151 definitions concerning the property right on movables and realty for the years 1866–1910. The Civil Department of the Senate focused on the problems of the owner's full authority, protection from invasion by a third person and other co-tenants, the implementation of joint tenancy and the relationship on the basis of dual ownership. All these matters were of paramount importance for doing business. The Senate's activities resulted in the creation of institutions previously unknown to the Russian law.

In the Russian Empire, the property right to land was limited by the strict estate boundaries, while the overwhelming majority of the population, i.e., peasants, could not exercise it unconditionally and without government interference. Such a situation was not compatible with the legal meaning of the law and resulted in the development of a unique system of peasant rights, which lasted until 1917. Moreover, Jews and Poles also suffered under the law and in most cases, the restrictions were of religious and political nature.

Further Russian peculiarities were legal regulations on the purchase and sale of land. The state took on the role of the principal and exclusive initiator of any changes in the conditions of those transactions. Regulations of market relations in the agricultural sector allowed the government to use redistributions of land ownership in the country to fulfil specific objectives of economic policy. Distinctive features of the general land policy of the Russian government were protection of interests of the land-owning nobility in the western parts of the Empire and the local population in the border areas, as well as the proprietary rights of the peasant class.

Rapid development of railways in the nineteenth century forced the state to recognize that it was necessary to alienate immovable property for their construction. The law on expropriation of immovable property and the rules of compulsory purchase of land were adopted on 7 June 1833 and renewed on 19 May 1887. The adopted law had shortcomings, as for example it did not fully consider the interests and benefits of landowners in determining the compensation for the land taken from them by the railway company. In that pivotal question for economic development of the country, the current legislation lagged behind substantially.

By the end of the nineteenth century, the firm as a private legal institution had entered the German legislation only. In Russia, the term 'commercial enterprise' included the entire relationship relevant to a person's business. Trademarks and firm name were important assets of a company. The initial meaning of the firm name was as follows: a commercial enterprise under which a merchant conducts his business, using signs, labels and advertisements, as well as a name, associated by consumers with the trade reputation of the company. It has since been regarded as a commercial institution having monetary value.

Russia adhered to the principles of genuineness and exclusiveness of the firm. Merely the registration of enterprises allowed the implementation of these two principles. According to Russian company law, only highly confirmed partnerships and joint-stock ventures were recorded officially, but not one-man enterprises, which constituted the vast majority of commercial and industrial establishments. Judicial practice allowed the transfer of company rights to others. The company owner enjoyed protective power, both administrative and judicial, although in the absence of universal registration was hardly attainable.

Property rights regulation remained one of the most complex tasks in the Russian legislation and was not accomplished until the end of the Empire in February 1917. Nevertheless, improving the legal support of owner interests was in progress.

3 The United States and Canada

Price Fishback

The United States and Canada have been among the richest nations in the world for the past two and a half centuries, as shown by the gross domestic product (GDP) per capita estimates in Figure 3.1. The US and Canada are endowed with large amounts of fertile soil and natural resources. Before becoming colonies of European nations after 1500 and the countries they are today, the areas were lightly populated relative to many other areas. Seeing opportunities to obtain access to land, large numbers of people have migrated from the rest of the world. The populations in the US and Canada were able to take great advantage of these resources by establishing governments and economies that gave people extensive political and economic freedoms, strong protection of property rights and largely unbiased rule of law. Both countries have managed largely to avoid the destructiveness of warfare on their home territories, although their participation in various wars elsewhere have involved sacrifices that slowed their progress. The nature of the governments led to broad-based educational systems designed to educate the whole population, first at the elementary school level in the mid-1800s then to the high school level in the early 1900s and with broad-based university educational opportunities after the Second World War. The combination of all these factors have allowed their populations to develop a wide range of innovations in goods and services, productive processes and organization of the economy. Economic growth has not been positive in every year, as the economies have gone through a variety of short-lived recessions and one decade-long Depression. Despite these hiccups the economies of Canada and the US have experienced growth patterns that have led them to maintain their statuses as being among the richest nations in the world.[1]

Pre-colonial development

Most scholars believe that the early populations of North America first moved across a land bridge near Alaska into the continent thousands of years ago. People lived in relatively small groupings of hunters and gatherers distributed throughout

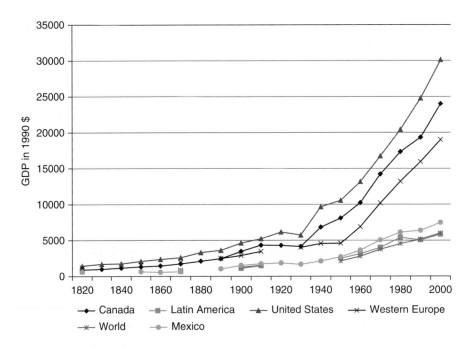

Figure 3.1 Real GDP per capita in North America (in 1990 dollars)
Source: Maddison (2001); www.clio-infra.eu.

North America with lifestyles strongly tied to their local environments. Native Americans in the eastern United States and Canada often trapped game in forests and produced some maize and other crops. North-west Indian tribes near rivers that ran to the sea often had stable food sources. The Plains Indians often travelled over large swaths of territory while hunting and gathering. Many of these tribes seemed to have diets with many calories from meat and other sources and were not typically scarred heavily by disease. One measure of the net gain from nutrition after losses due to work and disease as children is adult height. The Plains Indians in the nineteenth century were among the tallest populations in the world (Steckel and Prince 2001).

European colonialization

European contact began with the Norsemen in the tenth century along the north-east seacoast of Canada. The settlements appear to have been short-lived, possibly due to the similarity of outputs producible in Scandinavia and northern Canada and the problems of navigating trade routes at that time.

Migrations of Europeans from Spain, England, France and the Netherlands most heavily influenced the path of North American development from the sixteenth century onwards. Spaniard Hernando Cortez first arrived in the Aztec nation in Mexico in 1513. After Cortez's discovery of gold and silver there and his success in taking control of the Aztecs, the Spaniards continued to arrive. Ponce de Leon explored Florida, and Coronado searched for mythical seven cities of gold in the American south-west in the 1540s.

Meanwhile, English, French and Dutch explorers discovered that the areas that became Canada and the US were lands with enormous diversity of natural resources. Settlers from these countries began establishing colonies along the Atlantic coastline and further inland along larger rivers. After some fighting, the local Indian tribes made peace with the settlers or more often the tribes moved westward. This pattern of encroachment by people of European ancestry, short-lived fighting, accommodation and eventual moves westward would continue for nearly three centuries. Unfortunately for the Native American tribes, the respect and protection of private property described below did not carry over to the Native American's resource claims.

One key to colonial expansion appears to have been the development of a 'staple' that was demanded in the trade with Europe and its colonies. In the first half of the 1600s Virginia initially expanded with the production of tobacco using indentured servants and then increasing numbers of slaves after 1660 (see Map 3.1 for the most important imports and exports c. 1750). South Carolina produced rice using slave labour. Canada offered fur, timber and fish. New England's tall trees were used to produce ships and Pennsylvania and the middle colonies produced many foodstuffs. Colonial cities specialized in trading services. Over the course of the 1700s the data on price fluctuations in Pennsylvania and many European ports show increases in market integration that was slowed and interrupted whenever wars broke out (Dobado-Gonzales *et al.* 2012).

The structure of the political economy of the colonies and regional differences in the early 1800s were influenced by the nature of staple production, among many factors. Slavery dominated tobacco, rice and later cotton agriculture in the south. Consequently, the income distribution was skewed heavily towards large plantation owners, with a sizeable group of smaller farmers in the middle class, and a large share of slaves at the bottom. The plantation owners between 1780 and 1860 were among the wealthiest people in the world based on the value of the slaves they owned. The owners insured that their own children were educated with tutors and access to universities, and did not push for widespread public education. The planters in many southern areas banned the education of slaves (North 1966).

The gains to slaveholding in the northern and middle colonies diminished over time and their governments eventually banned slavery in the last quarter of the 1700s. Production of wheat and foodstuffs for market and subsistence was characterized by smaller family farms outside the south, which led to a more equal

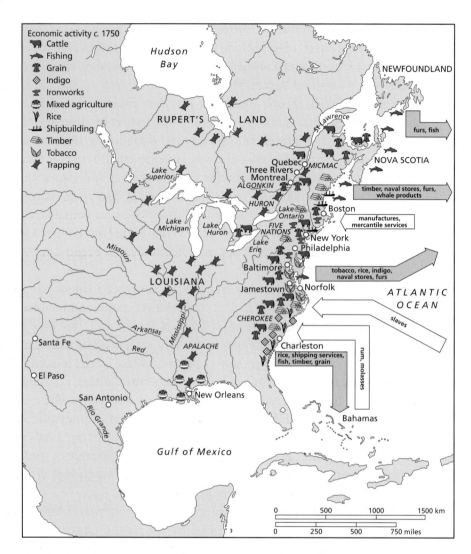

Map 3.1 Trade in North America during the eighteenth century
Source: See map 1.1.

income distribution than in the south. Many northern states offered private elementary schools after 1800 and most northern states offered public education by the 1840s.[2]

Creating an independent nation with a broad range of economic freedoms

After the French and Indian War – an extension of the Seven Years War in Europe – ended in 1763, the English gained hegemony over the area along the eastern seaboard north of Florida and further inland in many areas. The English

Crown and Parliament had long regulated colonial activity and trade relatively loosely. When they tightened enforcement and sought to increase the colonists' share of the tax burden of England's defence of the colonies after the war, the colonists in the area that became the US protested that they had had no say in these changes and established temporary trade embargoes against England. Tensions escalated with each new round of regulation, enforcement and protest. In April 1775 shots were fired in Lexington and Concord in Massachusetts, and a revolution erupted. In 1776 a Continental Congress of representatives from each English colony outside Canada sent a Declaration of Independence to King George III. The statement that each individual had the inalienable right to 'life, liberty, and the pursuit of happiness' has become a central tenet of US government. This was true to some extent of Canadian government, even though Canada remained under British control until it began a slow process of independence with Confederation in 1867. By 1781 the American colonists had managed to outlast the British and gain their independence, despite the apathy or opposition of over half of the colonial population and only a handful of victories on the battlefield.

Dissatisfaction with the problems associated with a loose confederation of states in the six years following the war led Americans to call a Convention in 1787. The American Constitution that came out of the debates, negotiations and compromises of the convention delegates has become arguably the most important political and economic document in world history. When combined with the Bill of Rights, added after the Constitution was ratified by the votes of the states, it established a wide range of individual rights and freedoms not granted by any government before: protection of private property, patents and copyrights, free speech, freedom of the press, freedom of religion, the right to sign contracts without government interference, a representative democracy, the right to trial by a jury of one's peers and a series of other individual rights too numerous to mention here. The document gave the national government the right to collect some taxes, to engage in foreign policy and dominion over interstate trade. Many government features were allocated to the states, but the states could not issue their own currency nor could they interfere with trade between states.

Many of the ideas and the institutions supported in the Constitution had been developing in England and in many countries during the Enlightenment, but they came to full fruition in North America. As many countries have discovered since, the document itself was not enough. It was the commitment of the American people and governments to follow the strictures of the document in their policies and in the decisions made by courts, presidents, governors, mayors, legislators and administrators that truly counted. As President, Revolutionary War General George Washington led the way to peaceful transitions to new leaders by not running for a third term as President, and resisting efforts to get him to run again later.

As the nation's government officials at all levels met the day-to-day challenges of running a democracy, cooler heads devoted to the 'Grand Experiment' most often prevailed in debates and controversies. Under Chief Justice John Marshall, the Supreme Court established the principal of judicial review of the laws created by the legislative and executive branches of government and struck down attempts by governments to interfere with private contracts and to limit trade of goods and services across state lines. Imperfect as the process has been, the general trends have been to expand the political rights of the populace in fits and starts. Property requirements for voting were eventually eliminated. Popular votes for Senators and a variety of other reforms were established in the Progressive Era of the early 1900s. Voting rights were given to women by various states in the late 1800s and early 1900s and by the national government in 1920. Slavery was eliminated in the 1860s and eventually the Jim Crow laws that had disenfranchised blacks after slavery were struck down in the 1960s.[3]

Wars and other crises have led to temporary restrictions of freedom for some groups. Since 1900 the expansion of government regulation and social insurance has created some tensions with respect to individual economic freedoms. Economic freedoms have generally been protected, although the search for security against misfortune that has contributed to expanded government regulation and social insurance has limited the freedom of individuals to make their own economic decisions to some degree.

Measures of democracy, like the Polity 2 scores in Figure 3.2 and measures of economic freedom and the unbiased rule and administration of law like those created by the Heritage Foundation, routinely show that the US and Canada (after 1870) led the way initially in these areas and continue to be among the world leaders in economic and political freedoms, the protection of property rights and the unbiased rule and administration of law. Numerous studies show that the economic freedoms, well defined property rights, and the rule of law are strongly and positively correlated with high levels of income and wealth. A variety of economic historians and economists have developed theoretical models and empirical analyses that suggest that these factors were significant factors that led to the advanced development of the countries with the highest per capita incomes in the world today.[4]

The economy from 1790 to 1914

In the early 1800s North America was largely agricultural with more than 80 per cent of the population in farming. Most of the manufacturing centred on

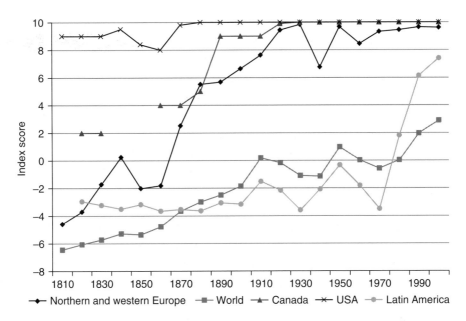

Figure 3.2 Polity 2 scores of democracy in North America
Source: Marshall *et al.* (2011).
Note: the Polity 2 measure (world) is only calculated for non-colonies.

the first stages of transformation of raw materials with lumber and saw mills, textiles and boots and shoes leading the way. Americans borrowed and sometimes stole the methods for textile manufacturing that were being developed in England at the time, and English textiles were considered superior. Prior to 1865 American textile manufacturers fared best when protected from foreign competition through Jefferson's embargo's on trade during the Napoleonic Wars, the War of 1812 and whenever textile tariffs were high. There were a number of American innovators who adapted foreign techniques to an American environment that had much more access to wood and land than the Europeans did. Innovators like Eli Whitney developed manufacturing based on replaceable parts, and Pennsylvanians began to exploit first coal deposits and then oil deposits in the late 1850s for fuel. In Map 3.2, coal and other economic activities in mining and industrial production of the US *c.* 1890 are shown. The rich resource endowments contributed to the rapid economic expansion during the nineteenth century.

The US territory expanded with the purchases of the Louisiana Territory in 1803, Florida in 1819, the Gadsden purchase in the 1850s and Alaska in the 1860s. Americans forcibly took land away from Mexico, as they led the charge in creating a Texas nation in the 1830s and won the south-west and California during the Mexican–American War of 1848. Canada began settling the British Columbia area in the late 1840s. With more and more land available, people migrated westward,

Map 3.2 Regional economic specialization in the US during the late nineteenth century (selected industries and mining)
Source: see map 1.1.

typically along the same latitudes. Ample land availability allowed the number of farmers to keep growing, but activity in manufacturing, services, transportation and other sectors grew at a much faster pace. Thus, by 1860 the share of the farm population in the US had fallen from over 80 per cent to roughly 50 per cent.

Cotton production drove the expansions of agriculture westward in the south and, in fact, accounted for a large share of all American exports (North 1966). Although no more slaves could be imported after 1808, the slave population grew as rapidly as the free population in the south. The emphasis on slavery and the relative lack of railroads and urban areas led many to see the south as a backward economy. However, even after slaves are included in the totals, the per capita incomes in the American south were among the highest in the world behind the American north and some leading countries in Europe. The slave owners were among the wealthiest people in the world. The irony was that in the country that has always been a world leader in establishing and protecting individual freedoms, a large region relied on slave labour through the early 1860s. The conditions under which slaves lived were better than in many slave societies in the Caribbean, but the lack of freedom was a harsh reality (Eltis 2000, Fogel 1994). Limitations on the education of slaves and the low levels of their wealth and property when they were freed by the Civil War, combined with the development of postwar unequal political economic settings, contributed to relatively low incomes for the ex-slaves and their offspring for many decades afterward (Higgs 1977, Margo 1990, Wright 2013).

Population growth, 1800–1940

Much of the economic growth of real GDP in North America prior to the Civil War came from the expansion of the population. In an environment with ample land and heavy reliance upon farming, birth rates were substantially higher than in Europe. Meanwhile, ample supplies of food and less crowding of the population into cities led to lower death rates. Most of the population growth in the colonial period and the first half of the nineteenth century came from these high natural rates of increase; yet the native growth was supplemented by migrants from Europe, who themselves were seeking new lands and often came in increasing numbers during famines in Ireland and Germany in the late 1840s and early 1850s.

From the colonial period through the 1930s, the population growth rate slowed down progressively from a high of about 3–3.5 per cent per year in the colonial era to around 2 per cent per year by 1900. The crude birth rate declined from 55 births per thousand people *c.* 1800, to 30 by 1910, to 19 in 1940 (Atack and Passell 1994: Table 8.2). Birth rates remained higher on farms than in cities, but the birth rate declined in all areas over time with occasional surges when new frontiers opened up. Farm families had more incentives to have children because they could help around the farm at relatively young ages and women were not pulled away from productive activity on the farm while minding the children. Yet, birth rates declined even on farms as more and more mechanical and biological changes allowed farmers to rely less on labour (Haines 2000).

The death rate also declined on a long-term trend from around 25 per 1,000 people in 1800 to 11 by 1940, although there were fluctuations around the decline. The most spectacular short-run spike in death rates occurred during the Spanish influenza epidemic of 1918, when the death rate spiked from about 14 to 18 per thousand in less than a year. The declines in infant mortality were even more dramatic, as the number of infant deaths per thousand live births fell from over 200 prior to 1850, to 120 in 1900, to 43 in 1940. After the Civil War, much of the decline in death rates came from improved diets and standards of living. Improvements in water treatment and sanitary facilities in cities led to dramatic drops in death rates after 1890. Similarly, basic public health education relating to hand washing, sterilization in hospitals and a variety of basic techniques

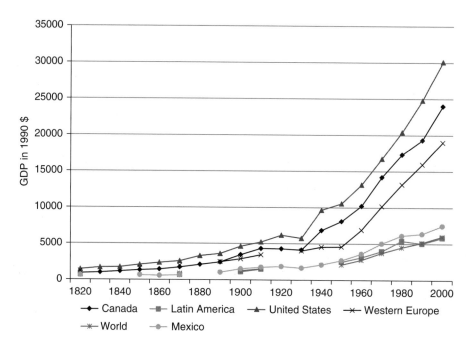

Figure 3.3 Ratio of real GDP per capita of North American countries to real GDP in north-western Europe (1990 dollars)
Source: based on Maddison (2001).

contributed to declines in disease and mortality as the information diffused. On the medical front, most of the gains came from the development of new vaccines and the pasteurization of milk. The decline in death rates associated with medical improvements tended to come after 1920 with vast improvements in medical science.[5]

After the end of the Civil War in 1865, the possibility of high earnings in America and Canada led to large increases in the number of immigrants. As seen in Figure 3.3, real GDP per capita was substantially higher in Canada and the US than in Europe at the time. Even as late as 1910 annual earnings in American manufacturing were 40 to 50 per cent higher than in northern and western Europe, and often double or triple the levels of earnings in southern and eastern Europe (Rosenbloom 2002). The English, Irish, Welsh, Scottish, Germans, French and Scandinavians dominated the immigrant groups prior to 1890. A number brought mining and manufacturing skills that they taught to American workers, and a large share became entrepreneurs. Even though the first immigrants from a family often did not become industrialists, a disproportionate share of their children did. After 1880 immigrants began leaving the farms and unskilled labour work in southern and eastern Europe in droves to come to North America. Roughly one-third returned home to start farms or businesses with the earnings

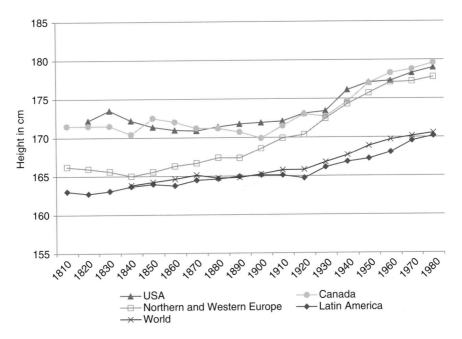

Figure 3.4 Height in centimetres (male) in North America
Source: based on Baten and Blum (2014).

they accumulated. Those who remained were a central reason for the rapid expansion in the industrial sectors of the United States.

Evidence on average adult height in large samples can be used as an alternate measure of relative standards of living because people are taller when they have better nutrition as children and are not stunted by childhood diseases. The average heights in Canada and the US shown in Figure 3.4 were substantially higher than in the rest of the world for most of the nineteenth century, consistent with the better standards of living suggested by earnings differences. In Figure 3.4 heights declined in both countries in the latter half of the nineteenth century, while heights in western Europe grew, so that the height differences in 1890 and 1900 were not as dramatic as the differences in manufacturing earnings and GDP per capita.[6]

The immigration boom was eventually slowed by political and economic restrictions. Chinese and Japanese immigrants were excluded from the US by federal laws in 1882 and 1907, respectively. The First World War slowed immigration to a trickle. In the early 1920s nativist sentiment in the US, partly driven by a desire to restrict the supply of workers and keep wages higher for native workers, led to immigration restrictions that were specifically targeted at slowing the immigration from southern and eastern Europe to a trickle. Within the past thirty years the share of immigrants in the population has risen sharply again based on large legal and illegal flows from Latin America, acceptance of refugees from war-torn countries and expanded immigration from East Asia (Cohn 2002). Some of these flows into the US were slowed by new restrictions aimed to prevent terrorist attacks in the wake of al-Qaeda's use of airplanes to destroy the World Trade Center towers and part of the Pentagon on 11 September 2001.

Long run per capita income growth

Conjectural estimates of growth in income per capita based on census data every ten years suggest that the longer term growth rates slowly rose from roughly 0.5 to 1 per cent per year to around 1.6 per cent per year between 1840 and 1860. However, not all measures of welfare show signs of progress in this period. A number of studies have shown that average height for people born between 1820 and 1860 fell during the ante-bellum period. The difference in the two measures might reflect greater problems with the spread of disease in urban areas and between areas that were trading more regularly than before. Diseases often stunt growth during childhood by putting a greater drain on the nutrition that children receive (Baten, Crayen and Voth 2014).

The growth rate of 1.6 per cent per year from 1840 to 1860 has been the long-run average growth rate ever since, despite severe downturns in the 1890s and the Great Depression and a series of other shorter and less deep recessions. The rate implies a doubling of income per capita roughly every forty years in the US. The US and Canada have been among the few advanced nations where advances in standards of living have continued growing enough during good times to much more than offset depressions and slowdowns. In many nations around the world, advances over periods of time have been wiped out by wars and depressions and stagnant periods (North *et al.* 2009: ch. 1).

National measures of agricultural productivity per acre did not grow very fast between 1800 and 1930, but this national aggregate figure hides an enormous amount of activity. Trial and error with various seeds led to the development of a variety of crops. The mixture of a Mexican strand with existing strands of cotton led cotton bolls to open wide like a flat hand at harvest, which dramatically raised the amount of cotton that could be picked per day. New strains of wheat allowed farmers to produce in Canada and the northern Great Plains and opened the door for a wheat boom. Cross-breeding of cattle and sheep expanded the amount of meat, leather and wool that could be extracted from each animal. Farmers constantly had to develop new methods and seeds to combat crop diseases just to keep producing the same amount. Meanwhile, improvements in steel ploughs, the development of mechanical reapers, and a variety of new implements after 1840 allowed farmers to increase the acreage that they worked and also led to the development of new agricultural implements industries in the midwest (Olmstead and Rhode 2008).

The expansions in the ability of farmers to feed more people, new technological and organizational innovations and the availability of immigrant labour when needed helped fuel one of the most impressive expansions in industrial activity in world history. Industrial expansion had begun well before the Civil War but it increasingly accelerated over time. The boom was fuelled by coal, and mining activity continues to ⟨…⟩ ⟨…⟩ the business cycle even to this day. ⟨…⟩ across the country were cut by the ⟨…⟩. Meanwhile, canals and riverboats ⟨…⟩oad traffic throughout the century. ⟨…⟩ several swings from peak to trough. ⟨…⟩ large share of the financial instru-⟨…⟩ had strong influences on financial ⟨…⟩es in 1873 and in the 1890s. These ⟨…⟩s because many British and some ⟨…⟩rican stocks and bonds.

⟨…⟩ The US was ranked fourth in the ⟨…⟩10 with a capacity that was larger ⟨…⟩ inventions and improvements in ⟨…⟩es, electric lights, automobiles, ⟨…⟩al devices opened the door for ⟨…⟩erican and Canadian consumers. ⟨…⟩omies of scale and better commu-⟨…⟩iness history of the time, see also ⟨…⟩s grew still larger with a merger ⟨…⟩es raised fears of monopoly that ⟨…⟩ of these firms were cutting costs ⟨…⟩ more output in these industries. ⟨…⟩cies of Theodore Roosevelt and ⟨…⟩ culminating in the break-up of ⟨…⟩o Company in 1911.

⟨…⟩ firms, which typically offered ⟨…⟩ in most cases workers were not represented by unions, and shared in the gains because a large number of employers competed to hire workers who were relatively mobile throughout the country. Some of the gains were won through collective action, however, despite the fact that US labour law did not force firms to recognize unions when more than 50 per cent of workers voted to organize until the National Labor Relations Act in 1935. US unions tended to be much more business-oriented than most European unions and the US never developed labour parties in the way that many other countries did.

Between 1865 and 1914 the US and Canada became increasingly interconnected with the world economy. Workers flowed into and out of both countries, as did financial capital to fuel the economic expansions. This increased globalization came to a halt with the First World War and the interconnections with the rest of the world economy retracted sharply over the next thirty years during the Great Depression of the 1930s and the devastation of the Second World War that followed until 1945. The fiscal and monetary consequences of the enormous debts and inflationary policies that followed the First World War by the warring nations, and the large reparations payments demanded by Germany, contributed to enormous problems with international financial markets in the 1920s. The US had more success at returning to the gold standard than most countries after the war. The result was a much more patchwork version of the gold standard that fell apart in the 1930s. These global issues contributed to the Great Depression in North America and the rest of the world in the 1930s.

After the First World War and a short but deep recession in the early 1920s, the US domestic economy grew relatively rapidly with low inflation until 1929. Farming, coal mining and shipbuilding showed signs of distress as they declined after rapid expansions during the First World War. The US went through a rapid housing boom between 1920 and 1926 as the housing construction delayed during the First World War combined with rising demand for housing associated with rising incomes. Declines in construction and housing values began in the late 1920s. Meanwhile, hundreds of small banks with assets strongly tied to local economies failed each year when local industry and/or local crops suffered downturns.

A recession that started in the summer of 1929 was worsened first by a stock market crash in October 1929 that harmed household balance sheets and created more uncertainty that slowed durable goods consumption. The adoption of the Hawley-Smoot Tariff Act in 1930 contributed to a downward spiral in American exports and world trade as other countries responded with their own trade restrictions. Federal Reserve Bank officials faced twin dilemmas in dealing with three major clusters of bank failures while at the same time trying to provide support to international attempts to maintain the gold standard. These central bankers thought that low nominal discount rates on loans to national banks were a sign of loose policy supporting troubled banks, and they focused more on offsetting gold outflows, as when Britain went off of the gold standard in September 1931. They waited through three major banking crises until the spring of 1932 to prop up the liquidity of the banking system through a series of large-scale purchases of government bonds in open market operations. In consequence, a large number of banks failed and credit availability seized up as deflation rates of 8 to 10 per cent drove real interest rates above 10 per cent, a level nearly double the real rates seen since. These policy moves combined with a wide range of negative shocks to the economy that are still not measured well contributed to drops in real output in 1933 to 70 per cent of the 1929 level and unemployment rates that exceeded 20 per cent from 1932 through 1935.[7]

One problem faced by US banks was that they were often relatively small in size due to rules against branch banking in many states and branch banking across state lines. In contrast, Canada's banking system experienced problems but no failures in part because they had large-scale banks with offices spread across the entire country and thus were protected more against shocks to local area economies (Bordo *et al.* 1995).

Despite extraordinary policy attempts by first Herbert Hoover and even more extraordinary policies followed by Franklin Roosevelt and the Democratic Congresses of the New Deal Era, the US remained in Depression throughout the decade (Fishback 2010). As in many countries, real output turned upward again after the US left the gold standard, but the US was growing out of a deep hole. The US economy experienced a major setback in 1937–38 after the Federal Reserve attempted to limit the potential for inflation by doubling bank reserve requirements in three steps and the federal government balanced its budget. Real output per capita did not return to its 1929 level again until 1940 and unemployment rates remained above 14 per cent until 1940. Even though American output then rose rapidly during the Second World War and the induction of 10 per cent of the workforce into the military cut unemployment to 2 per cent, real consumption per capita during the war fell and Americans sacrificed in numerous ways. As a result, from a consumer welfare perspective, the Second World War in America was just an extension of the Great Depression. It was not until consumption and private investment boomed after the war that North America truly left the doldrums of the Great Depression (Higgs 1992 and 1999, Edelstein 2000).

The destructiveness of wars

Many Americans have a misguided notion that wars are good for the economy, perhaps because they have not experienced a full-scale war on American soil since the end of the American Civil War in 1865. The expenditures and losses of life from the four years of Civil War amounted to war costs roughly equivalent to a full year of real GDP. The major benefit of the war was the manumission of slaves. The cost of the war was so large that a matching amount could have been used for a peaceful settlement that would have bought all of the slaves at 1860 peak market prices from their owners, given each slave family '40 acres and a mule' to give them some land and capital for a good start and paid about half of the GDP in 1860 as back wages to the slaves (Goldin and Lewis 1975).

During the world wars of the twentieth century North Americans fared better than the rest of the combatants. Aside from the attack at Pearl Harbor on 7 December 1941, neither world war was fought on North American territory.

Americans and Canadians entered both wars relatively late and helped turn the tide towards victory for their allies. Meanwhile, between 55 and 100 million lives were lost in the rest of the combatant countries, millions more became displaced refugees and huge amounts of physical capital were destroyed. One sign of the horrendous damage is the sharp spikes between 1940 and 1950 in the ratios of real per capita GDP in the North American countries relative to western Europe in Figure 3.3. Five years after the Second World War ended, the western European countries had still not recovered to the 1940 level shown in Figure 3.1, while in North America the growth had been rapid since the war.

Yet, even in North America, the wars meant sacrifice. The effect was much larger in the Second World War, because North American participation lasted two to three times as long. Even before entering each war, the US federal government shifted production from normal civilian goods to war-time goods. During the peak of Second World War activity, nearly 40 per cent of US GDP was devoted to war production. Decisions about large swaths of the economy were largely made for military purposes and nearly all relevant inputs were allocated to the war effort. Many goods were rationed, prices and wages controlled and many durable consumer goods were no longer produced. People have underestimated the costs of making the transition from a peacetime economy to a wartime economy and back. Real measures of consumer spending per capita at best stayed the same and, once the rationing and price controls were taken into account, consumption per person may have declined. Large segments of the workforce were inducted into the military, paid half wages, and roughly half of those were sent into harm's way.

Some people gained from the war. Stock prices rose. The people who remained at home did see increases in wages and savings given their limited consumption opportunities, and some groups, notably minorities and women, saw their opportunities expand. Particularly during the Second World War there was a sense of common sacrifice towards a worthy goal that seemed better than the psychological doldrums during the Great Depression of the 1930s. Companies in the war industries did well. Once the war ended, consumption and investment ramped up rapidly, but this was more a sign of the opportunities missed had the war never been fought than a stimulus driven by the war (Higgs 1992 and 1999, Edelstein 2000).

Postwar era

After the Second World War the US spent large resources in providing a significant share of the defences for the non-Communist world. The share of US GDP devoted to its own defence and the defence of its allies averaged above 10 per cent in the 1950s and then declined to 8 per cent in the 1960s, to 6 per cent in the 1970s and 1980s, and below 4 per cent after 1990. At the end of the war, Germany, Japan and Italy disarmed, the Soviet Union established hegemony over eastern Europe and the US established a strong countervailing military presence in western Europe and on the Pacific Rim. After President Truman dropped nuclear bombs in Japan to end the war in the Pacific, an arms race developed between the USSR and the US and its allies in the North Atlantic Treaty Organization (NATO). Over the next several decades both sides developed enough nuclear warheads to destroy the world several times over. As the lunacy of the Cold War continued, there were attempts to reduce the number of missiles through treaty agreements. Meanwhile, the US and to a lesser extent Canada sought to combat the spread of Communism in a 'police action' in Korea in the early 1950s, and misadventures in Vietnam and Southeast Asia in the 1960s and early 1970s, and in various other trouble spots around the world.

During Ronald Reagan's presidency in the 1980s, the US ramped up defence spending from less than 5 per cent of GDP in the late 1970s to above 6 per cent of GDP, and sought to develop a star wars missile defence system that would maintain its advantage. Much to the surprise of nearly everybody, except maybe insiders in the Kremlin, the Soviet Union's focus on military and defence spending turned out to be unsustainable. Mikhail Gorbachev led the way to Perestroika, and the Soviets released their hold over eastern Europe, most strongly symbolized by the destruction of the Berlin Wall between East and West Berlin, Germany, in 1989.

Even as the Cold War ended, the US retained a policing role. Iraqi leader Saddam Hussein invaded Kuwait in 1990 and the US led a group of allies to stop the invasion and return Kuwait to its independent status. After the end of the Gulf War with no Cold War left to wage, the US tried to figure out what to do with the 'peace dividend' that was said to come from reduced military spending requirements. President Bill Clinton and a Republican Congress after 1994 managed to run a federal government budget surplus for one of the few times in the postwar era. Unfortunately, the fanatic terrorist group al-Qaeda managed to use commercial airliners to destroy the World Trade Center and part of the Pentagon on 11 September 2001. President George W. Bush and Congress responded by declaring a 'war on terror', and sent troops into Afghanistan with additional forces from a variety of allies. Saddam Hussein's boasts that he maintained weapons of mass destruction led Bush and Congress to invade Iraq in 2003. The combination of tax rate cuts, Bush's willingness to expand government spending for compassionate conservatism and the waging of two wars, contributed to a return to federal budget deficits of between 1.5 and 3.5 per cent of GDP between 2001 and 2008.

Productivity advances after the wars

Even as world military affairs absorbed the attention of many US leaders, there were enormous changes in the domestic economy. North America experienced two rapid eras of growth in productivity, from 1950 to the early 1970s, and then from the late

1980s to the mid-2000s. Invention and innovations in the twentieth century were based both on new mechanical developments and in developments that could only occur through enhanced knowledge of basic sciences. New understanding of engineering has led to extraordinary advances – from radios and phonographs to televisions, compact disk players to personal computers, iPods to the internet, iPads and smart phones. Today, with a satellite connection, a monthly data plan costing $30 and a smart phone, people can listen to the world's greatest music (however each may define it), watch the greatest performers (soon in 3D), access a very large share of the world's books, talk to their friends and shoot videos with a device that fits in the palm of a hand. Advances in biology, chemistry, astronomy, numerous other sciences and cross-breeding across disciplines have led to heart transplants, hip replacements, numerous surgeries, cancer treatments and other medical advances that have allowed people to live pain-free and active lives at increasingly advanced ages.

A great deal of the productivity advances have come from the development of human capital. Both countries focused on educating large segments of their societies. Canada and the US led the world in numeracy measures (Figure 3.5), based on the share of people who report their ages without heavily reporting multiples of 5 and 10 until around 1840. By 1900 the average American had a sixth grade education. Forty years later, 50 per cent of Americans of the appropriate age were graduating from high school. North America has offered widespread opportunities for university

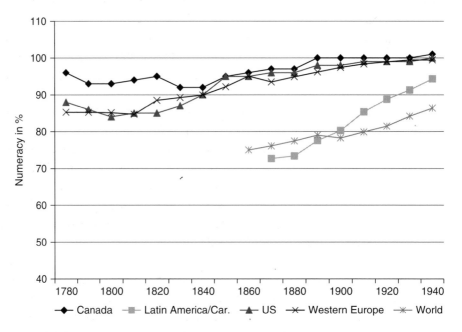

Figure 3.5 Numeracy index in North America
Source: based on Crayen and Baten (2010).
Note: South Asia included in 'world' only from 1840, Africa from 1870.

education with college graduate rates rising from less than 5 per cent for people born in 1900 to roughly 30 per cent for those born in the early 1980s. Both the US and Canada over the past few decades have developed high quality universities, which attract top students from around the world. Both countries have benefitted greatly as significant numbers of foreign students graduate and then stay in the US and Canada, particularly in the sciences and engineering. A disproportionate share of these students have become leading entrepreneurs in companies that have grown among the largest in North America. While North America led the world in widespread high school and university education for much of the twentieth century, the North American lead in high school education has largely been eliminated by the 2000s and many countries around the world are investing to catch up in university and graduate education (Goldin and Katz 2008, Field 2011).

The business cycle

The US economy might best be described as following a path of long-term growth in per capita income with occasional downturns and some serious drops. The US economy has gone through numerous fluctuations and financial crises. The Great Depression of the 1930s was likely the worst drop in terms of percentage output. Earlier downturns were harsh because per capita incomes were at much lower levels. Major downturns occurred in the mid- to late 1830s, the mid-1870s, the early 1890s, 1907–08, the late 1970s and early 1980s, and 2007–09, with shorter and weaker downturns in other periods. Problems in the financial sector were associated with some of these downturns, but the direction of causation was as often from the real sector to the financial sector as it was the other way around.

Canada and the US have maintained strong banking and financial systems. The best illustration of this is when the banks failed. Most of the bank runs in American history were not broad-based runs on all banks but were often narrowly targeted at the bank where a fraud or major drop in asset values occurred. The runs then spilled over to other banks that shared directors or had strong ties to the original bank. In many situations in the nineteenth century, and again in 1907–08, clearinghouses in major cities played a role in maintaining stability by insuring that stronger banks provided liquidity to the weaker banks in the face of bank runs. Even then most of what people have read as 'failures' were actually 'suspensions' of redemptions of bank currency in the nineteenth century or suspensions of withdrawal of deposits in the twentieth century. Most of those banks reopened within weeks or months. In the true failures most people got most of their money but often with a substantial delay. These suspensions were still painful, particularly in the nineteenth century, because delays of a week to a month were scary, and delays of several years in obtaining assets were often ruinous (Wicker 2000).

In the Reemployment Act of 1946 the US federal government took responsibility for ensuring economic growth, low unemployment and low inflation. Such hubris seems odd after the experiences with fiscal and monetary policy in the 1930s, but the economy performed quite well over the next twenty-five years. Real GDP per capita between 1947 and 1969 rose about 2.6 per cent per year with only three years of negative growth, inflation measured by the GDP deflator rose 2.5 per cent per year and the unemployment rate averaged about 4.7 per cent. The second longest expansion in American history occurred in the 1960s. Economists had become confident that they could smooth the business cycle mostly with Keynesian fiscal policy, particularly after the Kennedy tax cut in the early 1960s appeared to stimulate the economy. In hindsight, the tax cut looks more like a supply-side tax rate cut because the deficit actually was smaller during the cut.

Overconfident economic policymakers faced their comeuppance in the 1970s. The long understood negative relationship between inflation and unemployment represented in the Phillips curve no longer held in the 1970s, when the combination of both high unemployment and high inflation, known as *stagflation*, became common. The Nixon administration tried to stop the inflation with wage and price controls, but these at best slightly delayed the rise in inflation. The Organization of Petroleum Exporting Countries (OPEC) nations flexed their muscles by doubling oil prices between 1973 and 1975 and again in the late 1970s. The Federal Reserve responded by using expansionary monetary policy to try to reduce unemployment in the short run. Economic models of adaptive expectations and rational expectations developed in the late 1960s and early 1970s predicted that these attempts would just lead to more inflation with at best temporary effects of reducing unemployment. They were proved right, as inflation rates neared 10 per cent along with unemployment rates above 9 per cent in the late 1970s and early 1980s.

In the early 1980s Federal Reserve Chairman Paul Volcker sharply reduced inflationary expectations with a tightened monetary policy with the consequent cost of a nasty rise in unemployment. Meanwhile, the Reagan administration and Congress cut tax rates for individual households in a move designed to stimulate aggregate supply. Although they continued the push for deregulation of banking, transport and other industries begun in the Carter administration in the late 1970s, the Reagan administration and 1980s Congresses did not control spending as carefully and budget deficits in the Reagan and first Bush administration ranged between 3 and 6 per cent of GDP.

What followed was extraordinary success. Between November 1982 and December 2007 the American economy experienced three of the five longest expansions in its history with minor setbacks at the beginning of 1990 and around 2000–01. Real per capita GDP grew 2.1 per cent per year, and inflation averaged about 2.5 per cent, while unemployment rates fell below 6 per cent from 1995 to 2007. The stock market boomed to record levels as the internet and 'dot com' companies shifted the nature of information and marketing in the late 1990s. After a dot com bust in stocks in the early 2000s, the markets recovered again to new peaks in late 2007. Meanwhile interest rates were extraordinarily low.

Of course, once policymakers and businessmen become convinced that they have the answer to smoothing the business cycle, new troubles appear in a different form. In response to the dot com bust in stocks and the recession that followed, Alan Greenspan and the Federal Reserve drove interest rates down and many people shifted to investing in housing. The Clinton and Bush administrations and Congress pressured Fannie Mae and Freddie Mac to purchase and guarantee riskier mortgage loans in an attempt to increase home ownership among minorities and lower income groups.[8] Meanwhile, investment banks thought they had developed new ways to diversify risk and limit risk on mortgages by combining large numbers of home mortgages into mortgage backed securities (MBSs) that were backed by the value of the homes. These were then combined into collateralized debt obligations (CDOs) to spread the risk further. Finally, the owners of the CDOs and others could buy insurance on these CDOs in the form of credit default swaps (CDSs). With housing prices rising rapidly, particularly in the south-west and Pacific coast and major cities, losses on resales of foreclosed homes were not as large. Thus, the MBSs, CDOs, and CDSs seemed less risky, and ratings agencies gave these securities high ratings because they were backed by real homes that retained much of their value even when borrowers defaulted on the loans.

When housing prices began tumbling in 2006, the investors and investment banks began to discover that their new methods protected them against the risk associated with specific investments but not against wholesale declines in a broad range of the assets. By December 2007 the economy moved into recession, and the stock market began a decline that led values to fall by more than half from its new all-time peak that month. In 2008 the US federal government helped bail out the financial sector by merging failing investment banks into other financial groups, taking over insurance giant AIG, becoming the conservator for Fannie Mae and Freddie Mac, taking ownership stakes in banks and automobile companies and providing Federal Reserve credit for the first time to a broad range of companies. The problems in the US spilled over to banks throughout the world. Canadian banks were level-headed enough to stay mostly out of the fray and Canada's economy performed relatively well.

The US officially came out of recession in early 2009, but the unemployment rate remained at 9 per cent or above to September 2011, and above 8 per cent to May 2012, before finally falling below 6 per cent in 2014. The share of working age population employed fell from around 63 per cent in 2007 to less than 59 per cent in August 2009 and has remained below that level throughout 2014. In one of the few true stated attempts at Keynesian stimulus in American history, the Obama administration and a Democratic Congress pushed through a stimulus package that doubled the deficit from 5 to 10 per cent of GDP, but this did not resolve the unemployment problem. Even though the Federal Reserve has flooded the economy with liquidity with large-scale purchases of government and mortgage-backed securities, interest rates are at record lows and inflation has stayed at a low level. Meanwhile, the S&P 500 stock market index has recovered to reach record highs by 2014. Yet, the problems with housing have not been resolved and many banks still hold a significant number of CDOs that contain troubled mortgages and thus credit has remained tight. Meanwhile, problems with sovereign debt in the euro zone and various disasters in the rest of the world have contributed to a slow recovery in the US.

Growth of government

Likely the biggest change in the North American economy of the twentieth century has been the expansion of the role of government in the economy, particularly the federal government. Circa 1900, large numbers of economic decisions were not much influenced by government regulation. Decisions that were affected were mostly influenced by local or sometimes state regulations. The attitudes of opinion leaders at the time generally avoided reliance on government support. Over the next fifty years these attitudes changed markedly as the federal government expanded its role to large degrees in response to the crises of the two world wars and the Great Depression. In all three periods government activity and regulation expanded to high levels, they retracted after the crises but to higher levels than otherwise would have happened. Since that time expansions of government's role has followed from smaller crises (Higgs 1987, Fishback *et al.* 2007).

The changes have come more through changes in regulation and transfer payments than direct government consumption and expenditures on final goods and services. Despite phases of deregulation of banking and transport in the late 1970s and early 1980s, overall federal regulations have continued to expand in all areas of American life. Pure transfers to the poor have grown from about 1 per cent to 3 per cent of GDP, in part due to rises in health care expenditures associated with Medicaid for the poor. Much of the rise in the 'welfare state' has come in the form of government social insurance, in which a worker or their employer makes payments into a fund that entitles them to benefits when they reach retirement age or become disabled, ill, unemployed or injured on the job. Americans have smaller expenditures on *public* social welfare systems than Canadians and many of the western European countries. The major reason is that about half of American health care spending is private, most often through private insurance with employers. Once this spending is incorporated, Americans spend as much or more on social welfare as any country in the world.

The greatest expansions in the US in public social insurance have come through the social security old-age pension programme enacted in 1935 and the Medicare programme for elderly health care enacted in 1964. Both are operated as pay-as-you-go programmes. Working people and employers pay taxes into a 'trust fund' that is then invested in government bonds, which are basically promises that the federal government will collect enough taxes from future taxpayers to fund pensions and medical care for the current workers when they reach the appropriate age. This would work well if the number of workers always kept pace with the number of retirees.

The demographic changes in the US have led and will continue to lead to increases in the costs of running the programme. The US had a baby boom with a peak in live births in 1957. The rise from 18 to 25 births per thousand people looks small in comparison to the decline in births from 55 per thousand in 1800, but this rise is on the verge of having major consequences. Meanwhile, higher incomes, better medical technologies and better public health practices have led to a very large increase in the share of the population aged 65 and over. Up to 2011 more social security and Medicare taxes have been collected each year than benefits paid out because the tax rates have been raised. For social security, for example, tax rates have risen from 1 per cent each on employer and worker in 1940 to over 6 per cent each in 1988 before the share paid by the worker was 'temporarily' cut to 4.2 per cent in 2011. The extra funds have then been used to fund other projects. As increasing numbers of baby boomers reach social security and Medicare retirement ages over the next two to three decades, the ratio of workers to retirees will continue to fall. This has created a long-run budget problem on top of current budget problems that will lead to either continued increases in tax rates or reductions in benefits. Meanwhile, both federal and state governments have also poorly funded the pension programmes for their workers. Thus, in the future we are likely to see either continued expansion in taxes and transfers based on the social insurance schemes or retractions in their benefits.

The US and Canada are actually in better shape with respect to social insurance than most western European countries and Japan, because the US working age population is growing faster than in those countries, in part due to higher birth rates and also due to more immigration. The western European nations have larger social insurance programmes and a future with even lower worker to employer ratios. The problems with Greece's sovereign debt in 2011 that have created so many problems for the European Community and the countries that use the euro currency, rest in part on exactly these problems with social insurance and may be a harbinger of things to come.

Summary

Since around 1700 the history of Canada and the US has been the history of two of the richest populations in the world. Blessed with a large amount of natural resources relative to the size of the population, both countries developed economic and political institutions that gave them more economic and political freedoms than almost any country. The combination has led to enormous expansions in population and per capita GDP. One important feature to note about the last fifty years is that the US and Canada are still among the richest countries in the world even though growth rates in real GDP per capita are much slower than recent growth rates in China and the rest of the developing world. The reason is that these other countries are starting at a base that is often much lower. Thus, 10 per cent growth in China raises real GDP per capita by $500 to $600 per year currently, while 1.6 per cent growth in the US raises its per capita GDP by over $700 per year. A number of people considered to be poor in the US and Canada have incomes that are above the median in more than half of the world's nations.

Notes

1. For volumes that provide detailed statistical and narrative descriptions of the economic history of the US and Canada, see Carter *et al.* (2006) and Social Science Federation of Canada and Statistics Canada (1983).
2. For discussions of the colonial period in America, see Walton and Shepherd (1979) and McCusker and Menard (1991). For discussions of the role of resource endowments and their impact on institutions see Engerman and Sokoloff (2012) and Acemoglu and Robinson (2012). Go and Lindert (2010) describe the early path of American education.
3. For extended discussion of the role of government in American economic history, see Fishback *et al.* (2007).
4. For examples of studies that show the importance of institutions for economic development, see Barro and Sala-i-Martin (2003), Acemoglu and Robinson (2012), North *et al.* (2009) and a large group of others.
5. See Higgs (1971), Fox (2011), Moehling and Thomasson (2012) and Haines (2000).
6. For discussions on the changing height in the nineteenth century, see Craig *et al.* (2003) and Komlos (1998). Zehetmayer's (2011) findings for US Army soldiers suggest a more positive picture of US heights growing after 1880, which we used.
7. For discussions of monetary and fiscal policy in the Great Depression, see Atack and Passell (1994: ch. 21), Eichengreen (1992), Meltzer (2001), Friedman and Schwartz (1963), Fishback (2010) and Temin (1989).
8. Fannie Mae was created as a government corporation in 1938 to purchase conventional mortgages and to provide more liquidity and stability to the mortgage market. In the late 1960s and early 1970s the US government officially removed its backing and then created Freddie Mac as a competitor in the same role.

Further reading

Atack, J. and Passell, P. (1994), *A New Economic View of American History*, 2nd edn., New York: W. W. Norton and Company. A very good summary of various debates in US economic history that developed out of the Cliometric revolution that began in the 1960s. Cliometrics is the application of economic and statistical methods to the study of history.

Carter, S. B., Gartner, S. S., Haines, M. R., Olmstead, A. L., Sutch, R. and Wright, G. (2006), *Historical Statistics of the United States, Earliest Times to the Present: Millennial Edition*, Cambridge University Press. This is a five-volume cornucopia of statistics and essays about a wide range of socio-economic measures of the American economy that is also available through most university libraries online.

Eichengreen, B. (1992), *Golden Fetters: the Gold Standard and the Depression, 1919–1939*, Oxford University Press. This is a widely cited volume about the role of the gold standard in the world economy in the interwar years.

Engerman, S. and Sokoloff, K. (2012), *Economic Development in the Americas Since 1500: Endowments and Institutions*, Cambridge University Press. This book summarizes the results of their project to understand the relative paths of development followed by the US.

Fishback, P., Higgs, R., Libecap, G., Wallis, J., Engerman, S. *et al.* (2007), *Government and the American Economy: a New History*, University of Chicago Press. A highly readable summary of the literature on the role of government in the American economy from colonial times to 2006.

Fogel, R. (1994), *Without Consent or Contract: the Rise and Fall of American Slavery*, New York: W. W. Norton and Company. This is Nobel Laureate Robert Fogel's summary of the evidence on American slavery generated by twenty years of debate over his book *Time on the Cross*, co-authored by Stanley Engerman. There are four additional volumes of supporting papers.

Goldin, C. and Katz, L. (2008), *The Race Between Education and Technology*, Cambridge, MA: Belknap Press of Harvard University Press. Goldin and Katz examine the long-run role played by education in American development.

Hughes, J. and Cain, L. (2011), *American Economic History*, New York: Addison Wesley. This is the leading textbook in American economic history.

Olmstead, A. and Rhode, P. (2008), *Creating Abundance: Biological Innovation and American Agricultural Development*, Cambridge University Press.

References

Acemoglu, D. and Robinson, J. (2012), *Why Nations Fail: the Origins of Power, Prosperity, and Poverty*, New York: Crown Business.

Barro, R. and Sala-i-Martin, X. I. (2003), *Economic Growth*, 2nd edn., Cambridge, MA: MIT Press.

Baten, J. and Blum, M. (2014), 'Why are you Tall while Others are Short? Agricultural Production and Other Proximate Determinants of Global Heights', *European Review of Economic History* 18, 144–65.

Baten, J., Crayen, D. and Voth, J. (2014), 'Numeracy and the Impact of High Food Prices in Industrializing Britain, 1780–1850', *Review of Economics and Statistics* 96 (3): 418–30.

Bordo, M., Redish, A. and Rockoff, H. (1995), 'A Comparison of the United States and Canadian Banking Systems in the Twentieth Century: Stability Versus Efficiency', in M. Bordo and R. Sylla (eds.), *The Evolution of Anglo-American Financial Markets*, Chicago, IL: Irwin Publishing Company.

Carter, S., Gartner, S. S., Haines, M. R., Olmstead, A. L., Sutch, R. and Wright, G. (2006), *Millennial Edition of the Historical Statistics of the United States*, Cambridge University Press.

Cohn, R. (2002), 'Immigration to the United States', *EH.NET Encyclopedia*, http://eh.net/encyclopedia/article/cohn.immigration.us, downloaded 7 November 2011.

Craig, L., Haines, M. and Weiss, T. (2003), 'The Short and the Dead: Nutrition, Mortality, and the "Antebellum Puzzle" in the United States', *Journal of Economic History* 63 (June), 382–413.

Crayen, D. and Baten, J. (2010), 'Global Trends in Numeracy 1820–1949 and its Implications for Long-run Growth', *Explorations in Economic History* 47 (1), 82–99.

Dobado-Gonzales, R., Garcia-Hiernaux, A. and Guerrero, D. (2012), 'The Integration of Grain Markets in the Eighteenth Century: Early Rise of Globalization in the West', *Journal of Economic History* 72 (3), 671–707.

Edelstein, M. (2000), 'War and the American Economy in the Twentieth Century', in S. L. Engerman and R. E. Gallman (eds.), *The Cambridge Economic History of the United States, Volume III, The Twentieth Century*, Cambridge University Press, 329–406.

Eltis, D. (2000), *The Rise of African Slavery in the Americas*, Cambridge University Press.

Field, A. J. (2011), *A Great Leap Forward: 1930s Depression and US Economic Growth*, Yale University Press.

Fishback, P. (2010), 'Monetary and Fiscal Policy During the Great Depression', *Oxford Review of Economic Policy* 26 (Autumn), 385–413.

Fox, J. (2011), 'Public Health Movements, Local Poor Relief and Child Mortality in American Cities: 1923–1932', unpublished working paper, Rostock, Germany: Max Planck Institute for Demography.

Friedman, M. and Schwartz, A. (1963), *A Monetary History of the United States, 1867–1960*, Princeton University Press.

Go, S. and Lindert, P. (2010), 'The Uneven Rise of Public Schools to 1850', *Journal of Economic History* 70 (March), 1–26.

Goldin, C. and Lewis, F. D. (1975), 'The Economic Cost of the American Civil War: Estimates and Implications', *Journal of Economic History* 35 (June), 299–322.

Haines, M. (2000), 'The Population of the United States, 1790–1920', *The Cambridge Economic History of the United States, Volume II, The Long Nineteenth Century*, in S. L. Engerman and R. E. Gallman (eds.), Cambridge University Press, 143–206.

Higgs, R. (1971), *The Transformation of the American Economy, 1865–1914: an Essay in Interpretation*, New York: Wiley.

(1977), *Competition and Coercion: Blacks in the American Economy, 1865–1914*, Cambridge University Press.

(1987), *Crisis and Leviathan: Critical Episodes in the Growth of American Government*, Oxford University Press.

(1992), 'Wartime Prosperity? A Reassessment of the US Economy in the 1940s', *Journal of Economic History* 52 (March), 41–60.

(1999), 'From Central Planning to Market, the American Transition, 1945–1947', *Journal of Economic History* 59 (September), 600–23.

Komlos, J. (1998), 'Shrinking in a Growing Economy? The Mystery of Physical Stature During the Industrial Revolution', *Journal of Economic History* 58 (September), 779–802.

Maddison, A. (2001), *The World Economy: a Millennial Perspective*, Paris: Development Centre of the Organization for Economic Cooperation and Development (OECD).

Margo, R. (1990), *Race and Schooling in the South, 1880–1950: an Economic History*, University of Chicago Press.

Marshall, M., Jaggers, K. and Gurr, T. R. (2011), *Polity IV Project: Political Regime Characteristics and Transitions*, www.systemicpeace.org/polityproject.html.

McCusker, J. and Menard, R. (1991), *The Economy of British America, 1607–1789, 2nd edn.*, Chapel Hill, NC: University of North Carolina Press.

Meltzer, A. (2001), *A History of the Federal Reserve, Volume 1: 1913–1951*, University of Chicago Press.

Moehling, C. and Thomasson, M. (2012), 'Saving Babies: the Contribution of Sheppard-Towner to the Decline in Infant Mortality in the 1920s', National Bureau of Economic Research Working Paper No. 17996, April.

North, D. (1966), *The Economic Growth of the United States, 1790–1860*, New York: Norton and Company.

North, D., Wallis, J. J. and Weingast, B. (2009), *Violence and Social Orders: a Conceptual Framework for Interpreting Human History*, Cambridge University Press.

Rosenbloom, J. (2002), *Looking for Work, Searching for Workers: American Labor Markets During Industrialization*, Cambridge University Press.

Social Science Federation of Canada and Statistics Canada (1983), *Historical Statistics of Canada*. Updated to more recent years with additional tables at www.statcan.gc.ca/pub/11-516-x/index-eng.htm.

Steckel, R. and Prince, J. (2001), 'Tallest in the World: Plains Indian in the Nineteenth Century', *American Economic Review* 91 (March), 287–94.

Temin, P. (1989), *Lessons from the Great Depression (Lionel Robbins Lectures)*, Cambridge, MA: MIT Press.

Walton, G. M. and Shepherd, J. F. (1979), *The Economic Rise of Early America*, Cambridge University Press.

Wicker, E. (2000), *Banking Panics in the Gilded Age*, Cambridge University Press.

Wright, G. (2013), *Sharing the Prize: the Economics of the Civil Rights Revolution in the American South*, Cambridge, MA: The Belknap Press of Harvard University Press.

Zehetmayer, M. (2011), 'The Continuation of the Antebellum Puzzle: Stature in the US, 1847–1894', *European Review of Economic History* 15, 313–27.

13 The Great Depression of the 1930s and the world economic crisis after 2008

Kevin Hjortshøj O'Rourke

Ever since the Second World War, generations of economic historians have taught their students about the Great Depression of the 1930s and the lessons that we thought we had learned from it (Friedman and Schwartz 1963, Temin 1989, Eichengreen 1992). The experience since 2008 has been both reassuring and unsettling for the profession. Reassuring, because it seems that the lessons of the 1930s still have relevance for today: economic history is a fruitful source of knowledge about the way the economy works. Unsettling, because so many of the mistakes that were made in the 1920s and 1930s were made in the first decade of the twenty-first century, and continue to be made in its second decade.

As always, there are points of both similarity and difference between the two crises. A first point of similarity is that both crises were preceded by a rapid build-up of debt, and associated bubbles in asset markets. When bubbles burst, holes were created in the balance sheets of banks, lending and investment came to a grinding halt and private spending more generally declined sharply as both households and firms attempted to deleverage. The lesson that financial markets require strict regulation was learned during the Great Depression but forgotten from the 1970s onwards. Many commentators have speculated that this can be explained by generational shifts, with the grandchildren or great-grandchildren of those who experienced the Depression first hand forgetting the knowledge that had been gained so painfully by their ancestors.

When the world economic crisis erupted with a vengeance in 2008, commentators were stunned by the rapidity of the collapse in economic activity. Figure I3.1 plots monthly indices of world industrial output from the peaks in 1929 (June) and 2008 (April). It shows that the fall in world industrial output was as rapid in the more recent crisis as in the earlier one, for about a year or so. Figure I3.2 repeats the exercise, this time comparing monthly indices of world trade in the two periods. Strikingly, the collapse in world trade was far more rapid in 2008–09 than in 1929–30.

If the magnitude of the initial shock was the same in both cases, the recovery came much earlier in the more recent crisis, starting after a year or so, rather than only after three or four years. This reflects two lessons that were learned about how to deal with such a macroeconomic crisis, once it erupts.

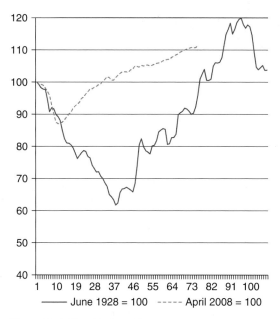

Figure I3.1 World industrial output during two crises (monthly index values, through July 2014)
Source: Eichengreen and O'Rourke (2009), updated.

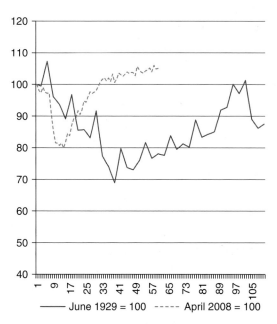

Figure I3.2 World trade during two crises (monthly index values, through July 2014)
Source: Eichengreen and O'Rourke (2009), updated.

The first lesson has to do with the exchange-rate regime, although here the history of how that lesson was absorbed by policymakers is somewhat complicated. The second lesson has to do with appropriate macroeconomic policies when faced with a lack of aggregate demand, and mass unemployment.

In the 1920s, the international economy readopted the gold standard, a system which directly linked money supplies to countries' gold reserves, and which indirectly implied quasi-fixed exchange rates. Fixed exchange rates and internationally mobile capital implied that when the US raised interest rates in 1928, other countries also had to tighten monetary policy, and a deflationary impulse in one country was transmitted across the globe. Worse, countries like France hoarded gold, forcing even tighter monetary conditions elsewhere. Worst of all, once recessions had begun, and turned into depressions, neither monetary nor fiscal policy could be used to increase aggregate demand. Monetary loosening was ruled out directly because of the link with gold reserves. Fiscal loosening was ruled out because of concerns about government deficits leading to trade deficits and gold outflows, and even more so because of a 'gold standard mentality' which advocated orthodox, conservative macro-economic policies in all circumstances, even when they were counterproduc-tive and dangerous (Eichengreen and Temin 2010).

Eventually countries were forced to abandon the gold standard, and recovery swiftly followed. Britain was forced off gold in September 1931, and this was viewed as a catastrophe; but the economy began to recover in 1932. New and very different political leaders abandoned the gold standard in 1933 in Germany and the US, and their economies also started recovering. France stayed on gold in 1936, and only started recovering then.

There are several reasons why going off gold led to recovery during this period. Countries going off gold before the rest benefitted from the increased competi-tiveness that depreciation gave them, and this was 'beggar thy neighbour' in that one country's competitiveness gain was another country's competitiveness loss. More importantly, however, going off gold meant that countries could loosen monetary policy, which in the long run meant bigger markets for other countries to export into. Most importantly, according to several authors (Temin 1989, Romer 1992, Eggertsson 2008) going off gold, and signalling in other ways that the policy regime had definitively shifted away from one based on monetary orthodoxy and pro-cyclical austerity, meant that expectations of deflation were replaced with expectations of inflation, real interest rates declined and investment and expenditure on consumer durables increased. Unfortunately these policy shifts came too late to save democracy in Germany, with tragic consequences for the world.

The two main lessons from the Depression were therefore that flexible exchange rates are preferable to fixed rates, and that countries need to preserve macroeconomic policy flexibility so as to be able to combat recessions and stop these from turning into depressions. The exchange rate lesson took a while to be absorbed: policymakers initially thought that the fluctuating exchange rates that followed the collapse of the gold standard was a problem, focusing on their beggar thy neighbour implications rather than on their systemically beneficial properties. Since the 1970s, however, the world has moved back to floating, as capital movements made it increasingly difficult to maintain the fixed exchange rates of the Bretton Woods era (Obstfeld and Taylor 2004).

The result was that when the crisis hit in 2008, the macroeconomic policy response was far superior to that in 1929. Major country interest rates were immediately cut, in many cases almost to zero. Central banks engaged in large-scale quantitative easing. Automatic stabilizers were allowed to work: fiscal deficits increased, implying that public demand stepped in to fill the gap left by the private sector. There were even some (relatively small, and often ill-targeted) attempts at fiscal stimulus. The effects were impressive, as can be seen in Figures I3.1 and I3.2, with rapid rebounds in production and trade in 2009 and 2010.

There was also a rebound in the Eurozone in 2009 and 2010, in response to these world-wide macroeconomic stimuli. But then Greece was revealed to have lied about its national accounts and the size of its deficits relative to GDP, and the European economies switched wholesale to austerity. Something similar happened in 1937, when monetary and fiscal policy was tightened in the US, and the world went back into recession (as can be seen in Figures I3.1 and I3.2). Between 2010 and the time of writing (2015), the Eurozone has seen a continual policy of austerity, with the result that the crisis that started in 2008 dragged on for more than six years, with no apparent end in sight.

The good news is that economic history can help us to understand why these policies are so destructive. The bad news is that policymakers have not been listening.

References

Eggertsson, G. B. (2008), 'Great Expectations and the End of the Depression', *American Economic Review* 98, 1476–1516.

Eichengreen, B. J. (1992), *Golden Fetters: the Gold Standard and the Great Depression, 1919–1939*, Oxford University Press.

Eichengreen, B. and O'Rourke, K. H. (2009), 'A Tale of Two Depressions', in VoxEU.org.

Eichengreen, B. and Temin, P. (2010), 'Fetters of gold and paper', *Oxford Review of Economic Policy* 26, 370–84.

Friedman, M. and Schwartz, A. J. (1963), *A Monetary History of the United States, 1867–1960*, Princeton University Press.

Obstfeld, M. and Taylor, A. M. (2004), *Global Capital Markets: Integration, Crisis, and Growth*, Cambridge University Press.

Romer, C. D. (1992), 'What Ended the Great Depression?', *The Journal of Economic History* 52, 757–84.

Temin, P. (1989), *Lessons from the Great Depression*, Cambridge, MA: MIT Press.

H3.1 Multi-divisional firms and managerial capitalism

Franco Amatori

At the end of the First World War, the key management characteristic of the large American firm was the unitary-form (abbreviated as U-form) with an organization based on *functions* such as production, marketing and finance. Authority was highly centralized. The difficulty of implementing this type of functional organization was not to be underestimated as firms were *multi-unit* entities.

Important organizational changes continued in the 1920s as the role of professional management took on increasing importance. The appearance of a new form of corporate structure was due to factors within as well as outside of the firm. Income and aggregate demand in the US was quite expansionary in the 1920s. At the same time, in certain sectors growth in research and development (R&D) opened the possibility of developing new products based on the original technologies. Thus was born a process of diversification that could not be managed within the old organizational framework. Top management was especially disoriented.

The pioneers in solving those problems included DuPont and General Motors. The leaders of these corporations understood that the problem was multi-faceted and called for a focus on strategy as well as the ability to allow managers a certain amount of freedom when dealing with their markets. Independent divisions based on product lines or geographic areas were established. The new divisions had all the lines and staff functions that were necessary to operate effectively, but now there was an important difference: top management was no longer occupied in the day-to-day operations. Instead, it concentrated on supervising, coordinating, assessing and allocating resources for the entire entity. To pursue this strategic role, headquarters had to have a sufficient staff to monitor all of the divisions.

This new model became known as the multi-divisional form (M-form), which required a greater diffusion of decision-making powers in the firm. This was generally accepted, but often with initial resistance. The multi-divisional structure adopted by a few pioneers in the United States in the period between the two wars spread through the US business system in the 1940s. Then it was adopted by many large firms in other nations that competed head-on with the United States in the international forum.

But the multi-divisional solution is anything but simple. Henry Ford, probably the greatest entrepreneur of his time, and a man with an aversion to organizational charts and corporate bureaucracy, was unable to make this passage. In 1921, Ford was by far the number one manufacturer of automobiles in the world, covering 55.7 per cent of the US market. General Motors (GM) was a distant second with a 12.3 per cent share. Created in 1908 by an enthusiastic empire builder – William C. Durant – the foundation of GM was the result of a merger of many pioneers of the automotive industry in the United States. Unfortunately, Durant's overly optimistic demand forecasts left GM with increasing financial difficulties in the 1910s. By 1920, GM's major shareholder was the chemical giant DuPont, which decided to appoint Pierre S. DuPont to take over Durant's role and entrust an executive of the company, Alfred Sloan, with its operational management. In a short period in the early

1920s, the two transformed the eclectic mixture of operating units put in place by Durant into a co-ordinated multi-divisional firm. Restructured, GM soon raced ahead of Ford. In the years between 1927 and 1937 Ford had a loss of $15.9 million while GM's net profit in the same years was slightly less than $2 billion. The year 1940 marked the fatal fall: Ford's share of the auto market dropped to 18.9 per cent and GM held almost half of the market with its 47.5 per cent. A well-designed administrative structure was the key component in maintaining a large firm's competitiveness.

The practice of corporate reorganization was of course more complicated and personalized than the theory of the M-form suggests. The owners (primarily the DuPont family) pushed for a strict application of the theoretical model of the multi-divisional firm and, most especially, wanted to exclude the divisional heads from headquarters and concentrate power in an executive committee made up of top management and a few representatives of the stock-holders. Some members of the top management – especially Alfred Sloan – were, however, wary of the idea of completely separating strategic planning from day-to-day operations. In their perspective, the most important thing was to create consensus within the divisions and to stimulate an entrepreneurial spirit within the ranks of middle management. To do so, GM's top executives were expected to involve division managers in strategic planning as well as in decisions regarding the allocation of resources. The preference was based on a profound sense of practicality. Top managers understood that the divisions would undoubtedly oppose any kind of initiative imposed from 'above'. They also understood the high price the company would pay if such a tactic was pursued and they were ready to compromise by offering a say in decision-making in exchange for consensus and support.

Bibliography

Chandler, A. D., Jr. (1962), *Strategy and Structure: Chapters in the History of the American Industrial Enterprise*, Cambridge, MA: MIT Press.

Drucker, P. F. (1946), *Concept of the Corporation*, New York: John Day Company.

Freeland, R. F. (2001), *The Struggle for the Control of the Modern Corporation: Organizational Change at General Motors, 1924–1970*, Cambridge University Press.

H3.2 Business history and innovation
Knut Sogner

Apple's introduction of the iPad gives as good an opportunity as any to define innovation: innovation entails introducing a new product into the economy. The iPad clearly was a new and distinct product that has established tablets as a new product group. Yet everything the iPad did could be done through other means such as computers or mobile phones, only differently. The conceptualization of the product rather than any completely new idea proved to be crucial. Innovations may be radical and creating new paths, but more often innovation comes incrementally. For example, the development of the car consisted of many small improvements in various companies over a long period of time.

Joseph Schumpeter introduced the concept of the entrepreneur as the driving force of innovations. The entrepreneur was not just a businessman behind a company, but a creator of new concepts within the economy. Through entrepreneurial activity the economy could find new paths. A famous concept of Schumpeter is 'creative destruction', or how new products or business concepts outcompete old ones. Another saying is 'add successively as many mail coaches as you please, you will never get a railway thereby' (Schumpeter 1934), thus making clear how radical innovations might be, with all that entailed in terms of creativity. His concept of innovation explains many phenomena for the second Industrial Revolution (*c.* 1880–1930) with the coming of large enterprises, a range of new technologies (electricity, chemical inventions etc.) and products (the light bulb, the car, etc.) and identifiable persons like Thomas Edison, Henry Ford, Werner von Siemens, Lord Lever and other industrialists.

Schumpeter himself in a later article distinguished between 'the creative response' of the entrepreneur and the assumption within economic models of adaptive behaviour.

In one of the most famous business history books of all time, Alfred D. Chandler describes how large American enterprises by building managerial hierarchies and using scale and scope advantages were able to introduce new products at comparatively low prices that appealed to mass markets (Chandler 1977). Chandler's position was that he viewed the large corporations as very important to economic growth and development. They were innovative, with strong competence bases and formidable resources to utilise scale and scope advantages. Schumpeter, too, late in his life, had come to believe in the innovative strengths of big business (Schumpeter 1942). Innovation could be institutionalised within the large corporations. The economic crisis of the 1970s, and ensuing turbulent industrial development in the following decades, was tough for the perception of big business being innovative. The crisis was also a crisis for the widespread belief in economic development as a gradual, controlled process, something big business had been seen as a contributor to.

Students of innovation have gradually seen the potential of Schumpeter's theory of big business being able to institutionalise innovation, but they have turned the theory on its head. Innovation could be encouraged by the surroundings of business, the agglomeration, the industrial town (Lundvall 1992). Concepts like 'systems of innovation' and 'clusters' indicated how businesses' competitive advantages were to be found in interactions between companies and their surroundings, be they universities, government agencies, export organizations etc. Businesses could learn from each other, and adapting to local conditions could give global competitive advantages.

In business history a particular approach that was called 'flexible specialisation' took an almost anti-Chandler approach (Sabel and Zeitlin 1997). Industrial development, according to the argument, was a localized and interactive process that current agglomerations such as Silicon Valley in California proved was still very relevant. The coming of large enterprises to dominate the economy of the twentieth century was, according to this perspective, to a large extent the result of the use of economic power, not necessarily the result of efficiency and innovative performances. The Industrial Revolution in Great Britain could also be understood in this light, as an 'industrial district', as Alfred Marshall had discussed.[1]

'Innovative corporations', 'Industrial districts' and 'creative individuals' – there are many approaches to how business and innovation have developed over time. These approaches need not be mutually exclusive, of course. Companies and their powerful actions do matter. Surroundings, in providing information, competence and opportunities also play significant roles framing the possibilities of action. The different roles that individuals can take do matter. The challenge may be to find the right balance.

Note

1. See for example Lazonick (1991: ch. 5).

References

Chandler, A. D., Jr. (1977), *The Visible Hand. The Managerial Revolution in American Business*, Cambridge, MA: Belknap.

Lazonick, W. (1991), *Business Organization and the Myth of the Market Economy*, Cambridge University Press.

Lundvall, B. (1992), 'Introduction', in B. Lundvall (ed.), *National Systems of Innovation. Towards a Theory of Innovation and Interactive Learning*, London: Pinter Publishers.

Sabel, C. F. and Zeitlin, J. (eds.) (1997), *Worlds of Possibilities: Flexibility and Mass Production in Western Industrialization*, Cambridge University Press.

Schumpeter, J. A. (1934), *The Theory of Economic Development*, Harvard University Press.

(1942), *Capitalism, Socialism and Democracy*, New York: Harper and Bros.

H3.3 Alfred D. Chandler, Jr.: the man behind modern business history
Franco Amatori

In Western culture, the term 'BC' signals one of the most important breaking points in history. Among business historians, however, it has instead come to mean 'before Chandler', when scholars engaged in ideological debates on 'robber barons' or busy producing soulless company histories made up the discipline. In those years, business history was an isolated, peripheral discipline of little interest for economists and the other social sciences.

Alfred D. Chandler, Jr. (1918–2007) started as a historian of the post-Civil War South. During the Second World War, he served in the US Navy, specializing in photographing enemy targets. He experienced first-hand the strength of the huge American war machine and acquired an understanding of the importance of large organizations.

After the war, he started graduate studies at Harvard where he listened to the lessons of Talcott Parsons, defining the sociologist's lessons as the most stimulating intellectual experience of his life. Then he started to follow the activities of the Research Center in Entrepreneurial History founded in 1949 by Joseph Schumpeter and Arthur Cole.

Chandler was a lucky scholar. When it was time to write his PhD dissertation, he found the sources in the attic of the family home. In fact, his great grandfather was Henry Varnum Poor who had left an extensive collection of documents. Poor was an investment advisor who analysed more than one hundred railway companies (the 'blue chips' of his time). From his ancestor, Chandler obtained not only the sources but also the methodology, the comparative one. To these he added a sharp focus in his research.

Chandler had no intention of studying all aspects of the company; he chose to concentrate on one function, administration (decisions at the top level and their materialization). In his first major work (*Strategy and Structure*, MIT Press, 1962), Chandler took the first fifty companies (by assets) of 1908; then, using the same criteria, he analysed the top seventy about four decades later. He found that the most successful ones were those that pursued a strategy of diversification while building up a structure composed of divisions based on products or geographical areas. They were autonomously facing the market relying on all the company's functions, but were also coordinated, evaluated and endowed with resources by *huge headquarters* that were able to utilize adequate staff. Coordination by the headquarters was possible because the strategy of diversification was towards *related* products. In the end, this multi-divisional company based its cohesiveness on technology. *Strategy and Structure* can be considered one of the most innovative economic history books of the twentieth century. But, even more than economic historians, it was students of management who appreciated the work, making it one of the most read textbooks.

The second defining moment in Chandler's career was the 1977 publication of *The Visible Hand* (Harvard University Press). It examines managers of the early twentieth century who took over many of the tasks of the Smithian 'invisible hands' of the market. But the phenomenon only happened in certain sectors, not in all branches of the economy.

The Visible Hand offers a comparison of sectors. The research question is why after the 1880s did large corporations emerge in certain sectors and not others? Why beer and not wine? Why cigarettes and not cigars? Why artificial silk but not silk? For Chandler, the explanation is technology; there were sectors touched by intensive capital, intensive energy, high-speed production processes and the large batch technology of the Second Industrial Revolution, while others remained labour intensive and were not affected in the same way. For Chandler, the former make up the engine of development and are defined as 'core sectors'; they call for large management intensive corporations. The latter are defined as 'peripheral sectors' where small businesses remain perfectly competitive. To those who accused him of technological determinism and of undervaluing the power dimension, Chandler effectively answered that, while this dimension is present in all sectors, only in a few do we find big business between the end of the nineteenth century and the Second World War.

Scale and Scope (Harvard University Press, 1990) was Chandler's third major work. A breathtaking comparison of nations, it picks up where *The Visible Hand* left off. Chandler emphasizes the need for a heroic firm rather than the 'representative firm' of Alfred Marshall. To reach the goal of turning high fixed costs into low costs-per-unit, it was necessary to pursue a difficult and painful three-pronged investment in plants at the minimum efficient scale, in linking production and distribution to make the market more fluid, and in management to govern the entire ensemble. National peculiarities were based on differing dynamicity of the markets, different regulation of competition, and the ability to accept the universalistic rules of big business. Chandler has been criticized for being too focused on the American model. Yet, it is impossible for business historians to ignore his monumental work.

4 Latin America

Luis Bértola and José Antonio Ocampo

It is difficult to talk about the economic history of Latin America as a whole.[1] Latin America is a large world region, a mixture of countries of different sizes, geography, climate, population, socio-economic structures and factor endowments. However, the existence of common features in Latin American history is clear: the Iberian colonial experience, specialization in natural resource-based products and primary export patterns are examples of these common traits that make it possible to distinguish Latin American countries from other regions and to consider them as a unit of analysis.

Latin America is not part of what is regarded as the 'developed world'. None of the countries has attained uniformly high enough living standards. Even more, some of them are still very poor and have large segments of their populations on the sidelines of modern economic and social development processes. Even so, Latin America as a region has made large strides in bringing about very notable economic, social and political changes over the last decades. These transformations have placed the region on a development path that has enabled it to attain middle-income status on a global scale.

Despite these changes in most Latin American countries, there are aspects that remain unchanged. The bulk of the Latin American countries have not been able to leave their natural resource-based production patterns completely behind them. Their pattern of trade specialization has held them back from gaining access to more technologically dynamic segments of the global market or segments in which the growth of demand is more robust. This, coupled with the region's markedly cyclical access to capital markets, has undercut its development efforts.

Conversely, other countries and regions have been able to leverage their natural resource endowments in ways that have enabled them to bring about sweeping economic changes. With differing degrees of success at different stages in their development processes, the United States, Canada, Australia, New Zealand (a group of countries that we will call, using Maddison's terminology, the 'Western offshoots') and the European Nordic countries provide examples of countries that have taken advantage of their natural resource endowments to place themselves upon development paths that have been more successful than those followed by Latin American countries. East Asian countries that have based their development strategies on their abundant labour supply, which shares some traits with some areas of Latin America, have been much more successful in achieving sustained economic growth in recent decades and in improving their population's quality of life.

The Latin American region's limited success in terms of economic development has made it especially difficult for it to sustain broad-coverage welfare policies. This raises the question as to what factors have held Latin America back from making more radical changes in its economy and society and from doing more to improve its population's quality of life. The answers to this question cannot be provided by economic analysis alone. Economic performance is the outcome of a complex constellation of social, cultural and political relationships and of how those factors interact with the geographical setting.

Within the realm of development theory, there is a long-standing debate about the role of institutions and about the ultimate determinants of institutional development. The region's social structures, the distribution of power and wealth, the role and strength of its elites and the complex, often painful process of state-building (which in many cases has resulted in endemically weak nation-states) – in combination with the legacy of colonial times and the economic and political difficulties that the newly independent states had in positioning themselves on the world stage – have all been decisive factors and all have something to do with the successes and failures of Latin America's economies.

In the following we will first clarify Latin America's position relative to Western Europe and North America. We then develop a typology of countries in Latin America that we follow through the painful period of the state-building (1820–70), the export-led growth period (1870–1929) and the remainder of the twentieth century that was characterized by state-led industrialization until about 1980, and then by turning back to the market. In the second large section we will analyze more deeply the obstacles to reaching 'developed world' income levels, focusing on volatility of commodity prices, trade balance issues, education and inequality. Finally, we draw a conclusion about how Latin America could pursue an industrial and technology policy that avoids previous obstacles to growth.

Latin America in the world economy: convergence and divergence in per capita GDP

Historical statistics on gross domestic product (GDP) trends in Latin America are quite limited and do not provide enough evidence to allow us to make categorical statements, especially in regard to the nineteenth and earlier centuries (see Highlight Chapter 4.1 and 4.2 on early developments). While taking care in assessing these data, it can nonetheless be said that, over the past two centuries, per capita GDP in Latin America has fluctuated around the world average while going through three major phases: a decline between Independence and about 1870, although only relative to the world leaders of the industrialization process (the West); an upward trend in 1870–1980, and another decline since the 1980s (see Table 4.1). On the other hand, Latin America has far outpaced Africa in terms of economic growth and continues to do so up to the present day. It also out-distanced Asia until the mid-twentieth century but, since 1980, just the opposite has been true.

Recently, in an effort to understand the uneven economic growth rates of different nations, the concepts of a 'small divergence' and a 'great divergence' vis-à-vis the industrialized world have come into use. The Western economies underwent a major transformation as they transitioned from a pattern of slow economic growth between 1500 and 1820 – during which these economies' expansion was mainly accounted for by the growth of the population and, to a lesser extent, an increase in per capita GDP – to a different pattern, starting in about 1820, in which per capita GDP growth was a far more important factor than population growth. During the first of these periods, the growth pattern of the 'rest of the world' was entirely extensive (i.e., driven by population growth) and was slower than the pace achieved by the West, thereby giving rise to the 'small divergence'.[2] During the second period, the increase in per capita GDP of the 'rest of the world' proved to be, in the long run, no more than a third of that achieved by the West. This was the origin of the 'great divergence'.

Even since the time of Independence, Latin America appears to have followed a growth pattern similar to that of the 'rest of the world', with the upswing in its growth rates being driven by the same factors as the rest: population growth accounts for some 60 per cent of its total economic growth, whereas annual growth rates for per capita GDP have been only three-quarters of the rates achieved by the West. Between 1820 and 2008, the gap between Latin America and the West widened from 0.8 to 2.7 times Latin America's per capita GDP.[3]

According to Maddison's highly speculative assumptions, it would seem that there was a substantial gap between Latin America and the West during the colonial period, although it did not increase to any significant degree during those years. During the early years of colonization, standards of living and, in particular, life expectancy at birth plunged. Then, however, the income levels were recovered, with the result that the gap at the end of the colonial period may not have been much greater than it was at its start.

In sum, while the West's growth pattern entailed fairly slow rates of increase, the gap with Latin America was sizeable but was not widening. When the West's

Table 4.1 Per capita GDP, 1500–2008: regional averages and ratio to the world average

	1500	1820	1870	1913	1929	1940	1950	1973	1980	1990	2008
Per capita GDP ($)											
West	776	1231	2155	4194	5247	5695	6740	13963	15903	19500	26369
Expanded West	702	1102	1877	3671	4590	4991	5642	13067	14950	18750	25285
Rest of the world	538	578	602	859	924	1073	1092	2064	2371	2711	4900
Latin America	416	684	772	1540	2076	1993	2442	4451	5441	5067	7118
Rest (excluding Latin America)	544	575	599	820	865	1003	962	1804	2038	2453	4670
World	566	672	880	1538	1789	1958	2108	4083	4512	5150	7614
Ratios											
Latin America/West	0.54	0.56	0.36	0.37	0.4	0.35	0.36	0.32	0.34	0.26	0.27
Per capita GDP (world mean=1)											
Expanded West	1.24	1.64	2.13	2.39	2.57	2.55	2.68	3.20	3.31	3.64	3.32
Rest of the world	0.95	0.86	0.68	0.56	0.52	0.55	0.52	0.51	0.53	0.53	0.64
Latin America	0.73	1.02	0.88	1.00	1.16	1.02	1.16	1.09	1.21	0.98	0.93

Note: Values are presented in constant 1990 dollars.

'West' includes twelve Western European countries, Australia, Canada, United States and New Zealand.

'Expanded West' includes thirty Western European countries, Australia, Canada, United States, New Zealand and Japan.

growth pattern changed to one marked by larger productivity gains, Latin America began to fall further behind and the gap widened to substantial proportions, even though Latin America's pace of growth also picked up. Consequently, although the original gap and the legacy of the colonial period are subjects that attract a great deal of interest, the fact remains that new growth patterns emerged during the industrial revolution that radically changed the economic landscape and international relations. It would therefore be difficult to argue that the region's more recent history is nothing more than a reflection of its colonial past.

A typology for an analysis of the Latin American countries

It is extremely difficult to find a typology for the Latin American countries that provides equally useful insights into their development process throughout the 200 years that have passed since Independence. One typology may be more informative in one period but may contribute less to the analysis of another. Despite these difficulties, there are a number of specific features in the region that have remained in place over time and that even today have retained a certain explanatory power.

As discussed by Cardoso and Pérez Brignoli (1979), Latin American societies have been shaped by the interaction of three different societies that came together in the Americas: those of the pre-Columbian indigenous population, Europe and Africa. Drawing upon the ideas of these authors, who in turn based their work on many other attempts to construct typologies in this area (Furtado 1976, Sunkel and Paz 1970, Cardoso and Faletto 1971), we will use the following aspects to establish a typology for the Latin American countries.[4]

First, there were different ways in which the transition to the kind of wage-based labour market (typical of modern capitalist economies) was made. Cardoso and Pérez Brignoli (1979) have identified three major types of transitions. The first type was made by the 'Indo-European' regions, where indigenous and mestizo groups constitute a large portion of the population. Located in what were the major centres of pre-Columbian civilization, they became pillars of the colonial structure, in which ranching and farming, indigenous *campesino* communities and mining activities were all combined. Various forms of forced labour were still in use in these areas until well into the twentieth century. Another type of transition was seen in the 'Euro-African' regions where the development of a slave labour-based economy and the complex process involved in the abolition of slavery have been pivotal factors. Finally, the 'Euro-American' societies were located in the temperate zones of the Southern Cone, where European immigration has been the main factor in the growth of the population, or in enclaves within one of the other two types of societies.

Second, the main type of commodity, particularly in export activities, differed between mining, agriculture or forestry. In the case of agricultural products, there is an important difference between temperate and tropical climates, arising by the nature of the production processes and the types of competition or complementarity that production in these climatic zones entails vis-à-vis buyer markets.[5] The capacity of different economies to alter and diversify their export structure in ways that will increase value added is related to the main type of commodity that each country produces.

When these two criteria are combined, a powerful typology can be constructed that captures a large part of the conditions existing in Latin America, especially up to the early decades of the twentieth century (See Table 4.2).

Table 4.2 A simplified typology of Latin American economies

	A	B	C
	Indo-American	Afro-American	Euro-American
(1) Subsistence agriculture and mining			
(1.1) With strong mining export sector			
	Chile		
	Peru		
	Mexico		
	Bolivia		
	Colombia		
	Venezuela		
(1.2) Without strong mining export sector			
	Ecuador		
	Paraguay		
	Guatemala		
	El Salvador		
	Honduras		
	Nicaragua		
(2) Tropical agriculture			
		Brazil	
		Colombia	
		Cuba	
		Dominican Republic	

Table 4.2 (cont.)

	A	B	C
	Indo-American	**Afro-American**	**Euro-American**
		Venezuela	
		Panama	
			Costa Rica
(3) Temperate-zone agriculture			Argentina
			Uruguay
	Chile		

Summary:
(1) A: (except Chile and Venezuela): Bolivia, Colombia, Ecuador, El Salvador, Guatemala, Honduras, Mexico, Nicaragua, Paraguay and Peru.
(2) Brazil, Costa Rica, Cuba, Dominican Republic, Venezuela, and Panama.
(3) A and C: Argentina, Chile and Uruguay.
Source: Simplied version of Bértola and Ocampo (2012).

From the standpoint of the socio-productive structures, the different countries can be grouped in a simplified way into three categories: Group 1 where the hacienda, the indigenous communities and mining activities have predominated in primarily Indo-European societies; Group 2 where tropical plantations have been the predominant economic activity in what are for the most part Afro-American societies; and Group 3 in which Euro-American societies based on temperate-zone agriculture or mining have predominated. The word 'predominant' has been used repeatedly because, in each and every case, there is a mixture of these traits.

The long delay: the decades after Independence, 1820–1870

This typology will also be useful as we describe the historical development during the nineteenth and early twentieth centuries. We can compare the three types of regions with individual country examples. The historical description provides important insights about how the development obstacles were generated.

During the early nineteenth century, most Latin American countries gained independence from the European Emperors. Did the first half century of Independence between *c.* 1820 and 1870 bring about economic growth? There is actually a debate among historians of Latin America on whether at least some countries developed well during this period, or whether the whole era between Independence and the 'first wave of globalization' should be interpreted as a long

Table 4.2a GDP and export growth during the 1820–70 period

	GDP/c growth	Export growth	Domestic market growth	Exports as % of GDP 1830	Exports as % of GDP 1970
Group 1	0	1.4	−0.1	3	5
Colombia	0.1	0.4	0.1	2	3
Mexico	−0.2	1	−0.3	3	6
Group 2	0.4	2	0.3	6	12
Brazil	0.3	1.9	0.1	7	15
Cuba	0.9	2.1	0.9	5	9
Venezuela	0.4	1.7	0.3	10	18
Group 3	1.2	2.5	0.9	13	24
Argentina	0.8	1.9	0.6	12	20
Chile	1.3	3.2	0.8	12	31
Total	0.2	2	0.1	5	13

delay in Latin America's development, caused especially by major conflicts and internal political instability.[6] The aggregate result does not look very good: per capita GDP grew only at an annual rate of 0.2 per cent (Table 4.2a). In contrast, exports per capita grew stronger at around 2 per cent. Using various sources of information on export share of GDP, we arrive at the conclusion, that per capita output for the domestic market was virtually flat. Remember that the starting point for these calculations is 1820, when the wars of independence were coming to a close or were still in full swing. There are evident differences among the per capita GDP growth rates of the three groups of countries, and these differences are similar, but not identical, to those of per capita exports. Bértola and Ocampo (2012) found that Group 3, the Southern Cone countries, realized the greatest increase of exports and it also performed better in terms of per capita GDP, but in the years around 1820, the worst development was not in Group 1 (countries predominated by Indo-European societies) but rather by the tropical economies that relied on slave labour (Group 2).

Around 1870, the per capita GDP of Group 3 was more than double that of Group 1, whereas the difference had amounted to just 16 per cent in 1820 (Table 4.3). Another important difference was that the tropical economies grew more swiftly than those in Group 1, with the result that, by 1870, Group 1 ranked last, although it was not far behind Group 2 (countries predominated by Afro-American societies).

Table 4.3 Per capita GDP in Latin America, 1820–2010 (in 1990 international Geary-Khamis dollars)

	1820	1870	1913	1929	1940	1950	1973	1980	1990	2010
Argentina	998	1468	3962	4557	4342	5204	7966	8367	6433	11820
Bolivia						2045	2604	2695	2197	2987
Brazil	597	694	758	1051	1154	1544	3758	5178	4920	6762
Chile	710	1320	3058	3536	3312	3755	4957	5660	6401	13229
Colombia	607	676	845	1589	1868	2161	3546	4244	4826	6982
Costa Rica				1555	1733	1930	4230	4902	4747	7876
Cuba	695	1065	2327	1688	1244	2108	2313	2724	2957	3997
Ecuador			815	1055	1109	1607	3258	4109	3903	5278
El Salvador				1216	1298	1739	2653	2454	2119	3447
Guatemala				1613	2571	1955	3140	3772	3240	4172
Honduras				1544	1195	1353	1715	1971	1857	2464
Mexico	733	651	1672	1696	1788	2283	4831	6164	6085	7832
Nicaragua				1694	1328	1564	2813	2095	1437	1889
Panama						1854	4068	4824	4466	9198
Paraguay					1569	1419	2015	3218	3281	3819
Peru		840	1024	1892	1895	2289	4001	4248	3008	5844
Dominican Republic						1071	1982	2403	2471	5361
Uruguay		2106	3197	3716	3536	4501	5034	6630	6465	11706
Venezuela	460	570	1010	2813	2879	5310	9788	10213	8313	9434
Average	683	790	1559	1956	1993	2442	4451	5441	5067	7272
Average 'West'	1231	2155	4194	5247	5695	6740	13963	15903	19500	27356
Weighted average by groups										
Group 1	713	692	1373	1963	1780	2220	4163	5072	4890	6674

Table 4.3 (cont.)

	1820	1870	1913	1929	1940	1950	1973	1980	1990	2010
Group 2	588	727	906	1270	1351	1855	4134	5392	5054	6935
Group 3	832	1461	3673	4276	4065	4801	6964	7540	6426	12204
Medium-sized and large countries			1071	1426	1551	2035	4379	5585	5307	7193
Small countries						1663	2779	3204	2941	4398
Ratios										
LA average/'West'	0.55	0.37	0.37	0.37	0.35	0.36	0.32	0.34	0.26	0.27
Group 1/West	0.58	0.32	0.33	0.37	0.31	0.33	0.3	0.32	0.25	0.24
Group 2/West	0.48	0.34	0.22	0.24	0.24	0.28	0.3	0.34	0.26	0.25
Group 3/West	0.68	0.68	0.88	0.81	0.71	0.71	0.5	0.47	0.33	0.45
Medium-sized and large countries/West			0.26	0.27	0.27	0.3	0.31	0.35	0.27	0.26
Small countries/West						0.25	0.2	0.2	0.15	0.16
Coefficient of variation (LA7)	0.24	0.39	0.63	0.52	0.5	0.49	0.5	0.41	0.29	0.37
Coefficient of variation (LA19)						0.53	0.46	0.4	0.38	0.46

Notes:

Group 1 includes Bolivia, Colombia, Ecuador, El Salvador, Guatemala, Honduras, Mexico, Nicaragua, Paraguay and Peru.

Group 2 includes Brazil, Costa Rica, Cuba, Dominican Republic, Venezuela and Panama.

Group 3 includes Argentina, Chile and Uruguay.

The group of medium and large countries consists of Brazil, Colombia, Mexico, Peru and Venezuela.

The group of small countries consists of Bolivia, Costa Rica, Ecuador, El Salvador, Guatemala, Honduras, Nicaragua, Panama, Paraguay and Dominican Republic.

'West' includes twelve Western European countries, Australia, Canada, United States and New Zealand.

LA7 refers to the seven largest Latin American economies.

LA19 refers to all Latin American countries in the sample.

Source: modified from Bértola and Ocampo (2012).

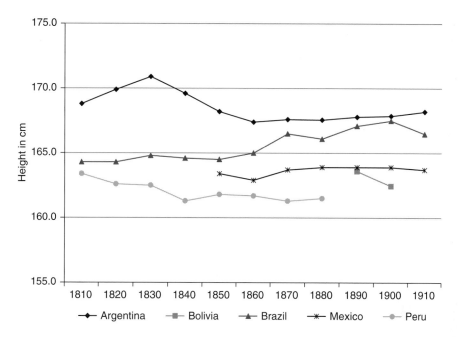

Figure 4.1 Height development in selected Latin American countries during the nineteenth century (male height)
Source: based on Baten and Blum (2014).

Tracing the development of the Latin American countries during this early period, it can be informative to compare GDP estimates with other welfare indicators. The idea that decades following Independence were featured by slow growth and even stagnation is reinforced by anthropometric data (see Figure 4.1). Both in Argentina and Peru, average male stature was lower by the 1870s than at the eve of the colonial period. In Brazil, a stagnating trend is first and slightly reverted after the 1850s.

We will now focus on four country examples (Peru, Mexico, Brazil, Colombia) to explain the difficult situation of the 1820–70 development phase. Peru is a good example of Group 1, and also an example of the central areas of the colonial economy. In 1820, Peru's population was more than two and a half times larger than Argentina's. The Peruvian economy had a large silver mining sector and a vast *campesino*-based sector which was heavily concentrated in subsistence agriculture and produced very little surplus for sale on the market (or, at least, for other than strictly local markets; see also Map 4.1). Peru was one of the countries in which the local elites remained loyal to the Crown. There, the War of Independence was a bloody struggle, and the emerging independent government took political and economic reprisals against the royalists and the local elites who had supported them. The Peruvian economy suffered grievously from the collapse

Map 4.1 Regional economic specialization in Latin America in the nineteenth century
Source: see map 1.1.

of the silver mines. The average output for 1830–70 was 87 per cent of what it had been in 1800 (based on Contreras 2004, Table 4.1). Exports were also flat until the early 1840s, prior to the guano boom, despite the fact that the production diversified into cotton, wool and saltpetre.

The decline of the silver-based economy dampened production activity in the haciendas that provided inputs for that sector, and these haciendas became increasingly self-reliant, a tendency that was heightened by a highly radical form of protectionism. In their turn, the main export activities of the coastal areas

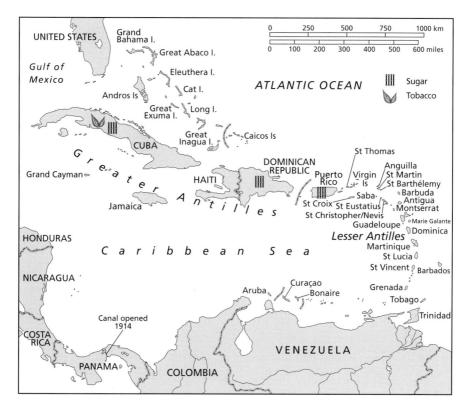

Map 4.1 (cont.)

were hit by the dissolution of the slave-labour system on which they were based (Gootenberg 1989). This downward economic slide was interrupted by the boom in the guano trade (a typical case of the 'commodity lottery'), which had a huge impact on the Peruvian economy. The country's exports jumped by a factor of seven between 1845 and 1860, and guano accounted for over 50 per cent of total exports in the latter year (Contreras and Cueto 2004: 116).

Mexico's (Group 1) short recovery after the War of Independence was soon cut short again by the civil wars and institutional instability of the 1850s, which lasted until the government of Porfirio Díaz reestablished conditions that paved the way for economic growth (Sánchez Santiró 2009b). The conflicts that arose from the mid-1850s had a profound effect because they were widespread and made themselves perceptible in the vast rural areas of the countries, involved clashes between castes, different ethnic groups and haciendas, and entailed a deepening of the political and ideological divisions between radical liberals and conservatives, which was mixed, in turn, with the division between republicans and monarchists (Sánchez Santiró 2009a: 102–03).

The situation in Brazil (Group 2) 1820–72 was also a combination of stagnation and regional diversity. According to Leff (1982, 1997), from the time of Brazil's independence in 1822, its rate of GDP growth failed to outpace its population growth. Thus, while the population did expand at a rapid pace (nearly 2 per cent per annum), the country's efforts to improve its performance in per capita terms were largely frustrating until the start of the twentieth century. This protracted and very difficult period of stagnation was, however, the net result of widely varying trends in different regions of the country. The north-eastern part of Brazil, which was a platform for sugar and cotton exports and which accounted for 57 per cent of the country's exports at the start of this period, saw a steady decline in its external sales (Map 4.2). In 1866–70, these crops represented just 30 per cent of exports, while the share of coffee exports – the leading product in the south-eastern portion of the country – jumped from 26 to 47 per cent (author's estimates; Mitchell 2003).

Leff (1982, 1997) explains the decline experienced in the north-east in terms of Dutch disease. As coffee exports came to play a greater role in the foreign exchange market, the real exchange rate increasingly reflected the importance of that product, which had a negative impact on the less competitive regions, such as the north-east. It was neither possible to restructure the sugar industry very quickly, nor easy to promote large-scale inter-regional migration flows, although a large number of slaves did move from the north-east to the south-east. Throughout this period, the expansion of the coffee industry was not hindered by any increase in labour costs, since up to 1852 (end of the slave trade), wages were depressed by the presence of slave labour and later by subsidized immigration flows, particularly from Italy (Leff 1997: 35). This strengthened the existing pattern in Brazil: an export sector that generated high levels of earnings alongside a large sector that catered to the domestic market and a large subsistence economy, both with very low levels of productivity, with the outcome being low per capita income levels but a high export coefficient relative to the other Latin American economies.

Ocampo (1984, 1990) and Kalmanovitz and López Rivera (2009) indicate that Colombia (Group 2) underwent an economic contraction during the War of Independence that was followed by a period of stagnation, which lasted until around 1850. This was the time of the collapse of gold production along the Pacific coast, which was based on slave labour, but it was also a crisis period for the main colonial port, Cartagena, and the crafts-producing region of Santander. These years were, however, followed by a growth spurt that lasted from the middle of the century until the early 1880s. This expansion was fuelled by the diversification of exports which, despite their volatility, gave a boost to economic activity in different regions of the country. Very short boom-bust

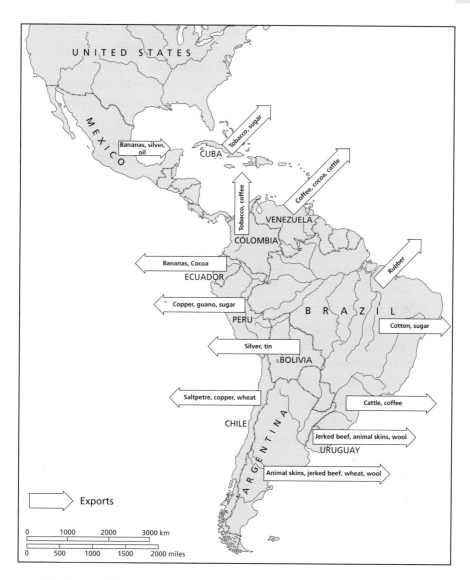

Map 4.2 Exports of Latin America around 1900
Source: see map 2.1.

cycles were experienced in a diverse array of new exports such as tobacco, cotton, indigo, cinchona bark and other forestry products, as well as coffee, which was eventually to become a longer-lasting export crop. In some regions, this growth period began soon after Independence was won. This was particularly the case of Antioquia, where gold production, which had expanded there in the eighteenth century, continued and was turned into a more modern business venture. A long-term improvement in its terms of trade also helped its economic recovery along.

However, in spite of promising regional developments the average growth rates were disappointing. What were the reasons for the difficulties? One of the main reasons was the challenge to build and consolidate the new nation states. This in turn was caused by the weakness of the local elites, which was one of the legacies of the colonial period. In addition, there were severe obstacles against the introduction of liberal reforms that might have improved the growth records. Especially the regions in which the elites considered slavery as economically necessary, such as Brazil's north-east and other regions, the idea of liberal reforms met strong resistance.

In sum, in the early years of Independence Latin America experienced a difficult development. The new freedom certainly allowed rapid institutional change, as the Latin American countries became republics. Some of them experienced rapid population growth, especially those of Group 3, the Southern Cone countries. Argentina could be mentioned as an example of a Group 3 country, but in the beginning there was not a united Argentina. Also the economic development was very different: strong initial decline in the north-west and around Córdoba, and expansion in the Buenos Aires region (Bértola and Ocampo 2012). The experience of welfare and income development during this period was in general quite mixed. It is actually unclear yet whether the 1820–70 period brought at least a modest income growth and whether it was also characterized by slightly improving welfare. Relative to Europe and North America, Latin America clearly fell back: between 1820 and 1870, the per capita GDP gap between Latin America and the West swelled from 0.8 to 1.8 times the level of the former.

Export-led growth during the first globalization boom (1870–1929)

During the final third of the nineteenth century, Latin America embarked on a fairly rapid growth path that allowed it to distance itself from Africa and Asia while more or less keeping up with developed nations. It is important to understand this history of quite successful export-led growth in order to address the basic question of this chapter – namely why Latin America did not change its resource-based economic strategy during the twentieth century. At the same time, Latin America was becoming a region of greater inequalities both between and within countries.

The growth of the population, as in earlier periods, was uneven. The countries that witnessed the sharpest growth were, once again, those in Group 3 (recently settled areas), whereas the Group 1 countries, the traditional centres of the colonial economy and the regions where the economic activity of the haciendas, *campesinos* and mining operations had held sway, experienced slower population growth. Nonetheless, as of 1929 these regions still accounted for 40 per cent of the region's total population. The population in the Group 2 countries expanded more swiftly and outnumbered the population of Group 3 by the end of this period. In fact, while Group 3 had registered the highest growth rate for an entire century, by 1929 it represented just 17.5 per cent of the region's total population.

Argentina and Brazil were the main destinations for European labour. Entrepreneurs and technicians coming from Europe were also important in countries that did not receive massive flows of migrants. Migrants from Asia, and especially from China and India, headed for the plantations of Cuba and Peru, where they worked as indentured labourers. There were also intraregional migration flows, which included the movement of black labourers from the Antilles who went to work on the banana plantations of Central America, the Cuban sugar-cane plantations and the construction of the Panama Canal.

Exports soared between 1870–74 and 1925–29 at an annual rate of 4.2 per cent at constant prices. This forceful expansion of Latin American trade was part of a powerful and more general increase in world trade in which, during certain periods, Latin America was one of the winners. The most striking upswing in exports was experienced in Argentina between the 1870s and the start of the First World War. As time went by, however, all the countries benefitted from the region's increasing integration into the world economy (see Map 4.2 for some of the main export products). Even so, the performance of the different groups of countries was very uneven. Up to 1913, the Group 3 countries continued to outpace the others. If the rates are calculated in per capita terms, however, then Group 1 (whose population grew very slowly during those years) edged past it. The growth of Group 2, dominated by Brazil and Venezuela, was more sluggish, especially in per capita terms.

Until about 1913, the degree of inequality among the Latin American countries increased as part of a tendency that, according to Gelman (2011), had begun at around the time that the countries were winning their independence. Argentina and Uruguay had high income levels from early on and, by 1870, Chile and Cuba had joined the ranks of the high-income countries. Table 4.3 shows that since Independence and until 1913, but especially between 1870 and 1913, the disparities between different Latin American countries were on the rise, as illustrated by the coefficient for the variation in per capita income levels. The increasing divergence that arose between the time of Independence and 1913 is largely a result of the strong growth of the Group 3 countries, which had achieved income levels that were quite close to the average for what is today considered the developed world, while Group 1 and 2 were growing very slowly.

The GDP per capita levels of Latin American countries became more similar after around 1913. This convergence of incomes was a net effect of different factors. On the one hand the growth of the economies of the Southern Cone began to flag, moving them away from the income levels existing in the West, at first at a moderate pace, but then, from the 1950s on (when the developed economies were experiencing a golden age), much more rapidly. The historical trends in Cuba have been even more adverse, moving continuously from its ranking as the economy with the fourth-highest per capita income level in the region in 1913 to one of the lowest-ranking countries now. On the other hand, the convergence of the Latin American economies was due to the strong performance of medium-sized and large countries other than those of the Southern Cone. In sum, the 1870–1929 period was quite successful for Latin America. Some of its economies reached income levels that were quite close to Western European ones. However, this high income was based on commodity exports, which became a big problem in the deglobalization period of the 1930s and 1940s. This in turn motivated Latin America to move away from the global market and try out a state-led industrialization policy in the following period.

How did Latin America develop during the twentieth century relative to the rest of the world?

Overall, between 1870 and 1980, in very different contexts and with some fluctuations, Latin America improved its global ranking, in contrast to the decline registered by the 'rest of the world' up to the mid-twentieth century. What is more, Latin America's share of world output climbed steadily, rising from 2.6 per cent in 1870 to 5.2 per cent in 1929 and to 9.5 per cent in 1980 (see the last row in Table 4.1). Even so, the region was unable to narrow the gap with the West, which remained fairly stable during this period and actually widened somewhat during some years, especially between 1950 and 1973, when the Western economies marked up record-breaking growth rates during what was known as the 'golden age' of capitalism.

Since 1980, Latin America has not only been lagging further behind the developed economies, but has also lost ground vis-à-vis the world average. While many nations, especially in Asia, have joined others on a rapid economic growth path, Latin America has grown at a substantially slower pace. As a result, the region's share of world output slipped from 9.5 per cent in 1980 to 7.8 per cent in 2008.

Analysis: convergence/divergence cycles, financial crises and volatility

After describing some of the main characteristics of Latin American development over the past two centuries, we now turn to a deeper analysis. Two major interrelated factors lie behind the trends of convergence and divergence. The first is the existence of periods of burgeoning growth in some Latin American countries that have reduced the income gap vis-à-vis developed countries but have not been able to sustain the convergence. The other factor is the high levels of volatility of growth rates displayed by all the countries of the region. Experiences at the international level seem to indicate that when economic growth surges, its volatility increases as well. This may be due to the nature of international trade cycles, business cycles, population shifts and international migration, fluctuations in capital flows and even the transition from one style and pattern of technological change to another. But, as shown above, the volatility of the Latin American economies exceeds the norm: the coefficient of variation was 2.63 in 1961–2008, much higher than in the world total (0.42), in the Organization for Economic Cooperation and Development (OECD) countries (0.49) and the low-income countries (0.45).[7]

It is difficult to gauge how much of the sluggishness of the Latin American economies is associated with this factor. A high degree of volatility brings consequences with it in terms of social, corporate, institutional and political stability and the possibility of planning medium- and long-term investments. This situation is compounded by procyclical fiscal and macroeconomic policies, which have tended to exacerbate, rather than dampen, other shocks that adversely affect production activity (Kaminsky *et al.* 2004, Ocampo and Vos 2008).

One significant aspect of Latin America's economic volatility has to do with its position in the international economy. Latin American countries have relied primarily on their natural resources as a means of positioning themselves in the global economy. This strategy seems quite understandable as exporting national resource-intensive commodities brought enormous growth for some countries in the 1870–1929 period, as we saw above. But the supply and demand for these resources have been subject to fluctuation, and the prices that they bring have been extremely volatile. In addition, the fact that these countries' production structures are concentrated in a relatively small number of commodities makes them more vulnerable to changes in demand and price.

The procyclical nature of international capital flows to developing countries also contributes to this excessive volatility. This was pointed out by Triffin (1968) in respect of the first wave of globalization and was also identified during the second (Ocampo 2008). As a result, when international trade has had positive growth effects, economic activity has been boosted further by capital inflows. On the other hand, when the international business cycle enters into a downturn, the effects of the slump in the demand for commodities and in commodity prices are amplified by the sudden stop and even the reversal of capital flows.

The level of volatility has fluctuated and was particularly high during the interwar period of the twentieth century (see Bértola and Ocampo 2012: Table A.3). There has been no downward trend since then. Table 4.4 shows that

Table 4.4 Determinants of volatility, 1870–2008

	Total Volatility (%)	Share of the first product (%)	Average per capita GDP
Argentina	6.90	23	5,129
Brazil	5.40	54	2,170
Chile	7.40	40	4,156
Colombia	2.90	49	2,320
Costa Rica	5.90	53	3,449
Cuba	11.60	77	1,866
El Salvador	6.70	70	1,994
Guatemala	7.90	64	2,613
Honduras	5.40	43	1,604
Mexico	4.80	31	3,500
Nicaragua	9.00	40	1,797
Peru	5.60	29	2,548
Uruguay	7.40	38	4,240
Venezuela	8.40	63	4,408
Correlation coefficient		**0.441**	**0.013**

Note: the correlation coefficient is calculated as the cross-correlation between the variables and total volatility.
Source: calculated from Bértola and Ocampo (2012).

there is no clear-cut correlation between average income levels and the degree of volatility (the correlation coefficient is only 0.013).

Another aspect of volatility is the frequency and severity of financial crises. The upper part of Figure 4.2 depicts the historical variations in the frequency of financial crises. In every case, the peaks follow periods of hefty capital inflows that had their origin, as has been analysed in a vast amount of the literature, in what are essentially international business cycles: the boom in external financing that followed Independence, the boom that preceded the international crisis of 1873, the Great Depression of the 1930s, the Latin American debt crisis of the 1980s and the new series of crises in the developing world that began in East Asia in 1997, with the last two of these crises merging into what can be seen as a single long, drawn-out crisis.[8] These crises enveloped almost all the Latin American countries (and, in some cases, all nineteen of them) in one way or another.[9] Only two of the major international financial booms have not been followed by financial crises in the region: the boom that preceded the First World War, and the

(a) Number of countries on a currency, external debt, or banking crisis

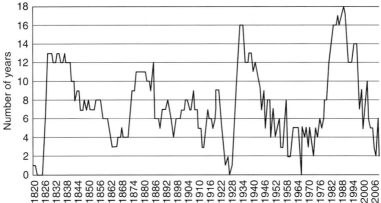

(b) Number of countries/years in crisis by period

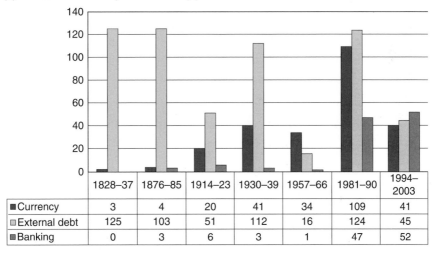

	1828–37	1876–85	1914–23	1930–39	1957–66	1981–90	1994–2003
■ Currency	3	4	20	41	34	109	41
▫ External debt	125	103	51	112	16	124	45
■ Banking	0	3	6	3	1	47	52

Figure 4.2 Economic crises of Latin America, 1820–2008
Source: Database of Reinhart and Rogoff (2009) kindly provided by the authors.
Notes: the definition of crisis according to Reinhart and Rogoff is the following: currency crisis: annual devaluation greater than (or equal) 15 per cent with respect to the US dollar (or the relevant currency); external debt crises: outright default on payment of debt obligations including principal or interest; banking crisis: bank run that leads to the closure, merging, or takeover by the public sector of one or more financial institutions. If there are no runs, the closure, merging, takeover, or large-scale government assistance of an important financial institution (or group of institutions) that marks the start of a string of similar outcomes for other financial institutions.

one that gave way to the severe worldwide recession of 2008–09. In both cases, however, the booms were followed by regional recessions.

The lower part of Figure 4.2 shows how the composition of these crises changed over time. Debt crises have been the most common problem in Latin America since Independence. Steep devaluations associated with balance-of-payments crises have been frequent since the First World War, and this situation was also the main factor behind the crises that occurred between the mid-1950s and mid-1960s, which were not preceded by a boom in external financing. Finally, the most recent type of crisis has been in the banking sector, and these crises have become increasingly frequent since the 1980s. As a result, since the 1930s, most crises have been 'dual' (combined debt and balance-of-payments crises) and, since the 1980s, many of them have been triple crises (the above two plus banking crises). Actually, in recent decades, we should also add in a number of other dimensions, such as high inflation (which, in Latin America, has historically been closely correlated with balance-of-payments crises), balance-of-payments collapses and, in fewer cases, domestic debt crises.[10]

There has also been a notable degree of convergence between external trade cycles and capital flows. Crises are usually triggered by sudden export collapses that occur in the midst of critical international conjunctures (1873, 1890, 1913, 1929, 1973, 1979, 1997, 2008) and that also lead to plummeting commodity prices, which in turn translate into trade deficits. More often than not, these crises coincide with a contraction in the supply of external financing, which is usually abundant when exports are on the rise.

Integration into the world economy: volatility of commodity prices

One hypothesis is that volatility is brought about by external factors – either fluctuations in external markets or fluctuations in the terms of trade of each country.[11] Did the fluctuations occurring in those parts of the world (the 'relevant world') that have an impact on Latin America via its exports and its terms of trade matter?[12] It is important to note that Latin America experiences more volatility than its 'relevant world' does, and the terms of trade appear to be the factor that transmits greater volatility to the region. Table 4.4 indicates that there is a fairly close correlation between volatility and export product concentration (correlation coefficient is 0.44). Table 4.5 provides evidence of the extreme concentration in a very few product categories that has characterized the Latin American economies throughout their history.

The specialization pattern of Latin America has been a subject of debate for many years. In the long tradition of the structuralist school of thought, it has been seen as the main reason for the region's failure to grow more rapidly. If we look at growth trends over the last three decades, it becomes clear that the fastest-growing economies in the developing world have been those that have diversified their production and, in particular, have increased high-technology manufacturing exports (Hausmann et al. 2007; Ocampo et al. 2009).

The first wave of globalization came at a time when world trade was based on an exchange of raw materials and food products for manufactures. At that point,

Table 4.5 Export concentration: share of total exports (%), 1870–1973

Country	Top export product				
	1870–73	1910–13	1926–29	1949–52	1970–73
Argentina	41	21	22	7	26
Brazil	53	52	71	63	29
Chile	52	31	46	5	64
Colombia	8	45	65	74	54
Costa Rica	86	37	61	43	37
Cuba	n.d	71	79	81	75
El Salvador	n.d	76	74	83	45
Guatemala	65	69	79	77	32
Honduras	n.d	12	44	65	50
Mexico	85	22	23	19	8
Nicaragua	n.d	48	54	33	24
Peru	33	18	34	32	18
Uruguay	35	40	33	47	36
Venezuela	42	49	69	92	n.d.
Average	**50**	**42**	**54**	**52**	**38**
1)	Top three export products				
Argentina	74	50	56	19	46
Brazil	82	77	76	78	41
Chile	n.d	34	77	7	67
Colombia	14	47	82	90	69
Costa Rica	n.d	69	92	74	70
Cuba	n.d	92	92	5	90
El Salvador	n.d	n.d	n.d	n.d	62
Guatemala	n.d	n.d	n.d	n.d	51
Honduras	n.d	14	46	73	68
Mexico	91	31	49	38	18
Nicaragua	n.d	56	69	1	53
Peru	57	36	71	56	30
Uruguay	76	69	77	78	63
Venezuela	n.d	n.d	89	94	n.d.
Average	**66**	**52**	**73**	**51**	**56**

Source: calculated from Mitchell (2003).

Latin America was in a good position, given its pattern of specialization. A collapse of the international division of labour followed in the period 1914–45. After the Second World War, intra-industry trade among developed countries dominated. In addition, protectionism was strong against agricultural products and textiles coming from the developing world. In this setting, and given the biases generated by industrialization policies, Latin America's share of world trade sank to a level three percentage points lower than it had been during the boom of the 1920s. When the second wave of globalization began to open up more export opportunities for developing countries in the 1960s, and when Latin American countries began to shift their economic policies towards an emphasis on export growth in the closing decades of the twentieth century, the region was able to regain some of the ground that it had lost, but it was still far removed from the levels that it had reached during the first globalization wave.

Trends in the terms of trade

The trend in the terms of trade for commodities relative to manufactures is an important factor to consider. Starting in the late nineteenth century, but especially during the boom that preceded the First World War, the real prices of agricultural and mineral products trended upward (see Figure 4.3). Then, in the aftermath of the First World War this trend began to reverse, not continuously but in stages (or as the downward phases in long-term cycles). The first strong reduction came in the 1920s and covered all commodities. The second took place in the 1980s and 1990s and was characterized by a sharp drop in the prices of agricultural goods and a more moderate one in mining products. As a result, between the decade leading up to the First World War and 1998–2003, the terms of trade for commodities (other than oil) fell by 60 per cent, with tropical agricultural products being the hardest-hit and mineral products being affected the least. Real oil prices also fell, but that decrease came later than the drop in non-oil commodity prices (the 1930s and 1940s) and, although they also plunged in the 1980s, they maintained a substantial part of the ground gained during the two oil shocks of the 1970s. The commodity price boom that began in 2004, which was driven by demand from China and was stronger in mining and energy products than in agricultural goods, has prompted many people to think that the world may be returning to the patterns observed during the first wave of globalization.

The deeper long-term downturn in tropical goods prices gives us reason to take a serious look at one of the versions of the famous Prebisch-Singer thesis about the terms of trade.[13] This version emphasizes stark structural and institutional differences between the manufacturing sector in industrial countries and the production of tropical goods sectors in more backward regions. In the latter, labour tends to be in ample supply and the history of the labour market institutions has been one of

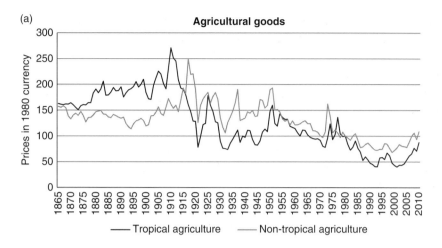

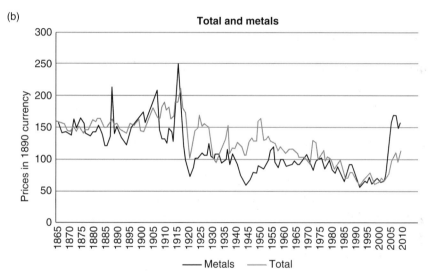

Figure 4.3 Real commodity prices (1980 = 100)
Source: Ocampo and Parra (2010) and updates for 2010.

forced labour and very weak unionization. In the industrial countries, workers have often been better organized than in tropical goods countries.

According to Lewis (1969, 1983), international migration tended to be segmented into two different types of flows: European labourers migrated to new settlement areas of non-tropic climate such as in the Southern Cone countries, and Chinese and Indian workers went to tropical zones. Bértola and Williamson (2006) have underlined the fact that, unlike the temperate zone, new settlement countries elsewhere in the region, tropical Latin American areas have had to compete internationally with countries of low per capita incomes and extremely low wage levels. Especially low-wage tropical countries in Asia and Africa were the competitors of the Brazilian and the Caribbean labourers.

An adjusted version of the Prebisch-Singer thesis suggests that world-wide demand shifts toward higher-quality products caused substantial problems for Latin America. The industrialization process that firstly took place in Europe and North America was based on products that were highly demanded at higher income levels. It was followed by an expansion of the share of services sectors; again the products were compatible with rising income. In contrast, the demand for Latin American products did not always increase at the same pace as income. Until the First World War, rising income levels in Europe and the United States were still favourable for Latin America. Meat and wheat were still highly demanded and Europe's poor labourers consumed Argentinean wheat and beef instead of other, less nutritional products. In other words, the income elasticity of demand for these goods was high in this last period.[14] However, once this 'dietary transition' had been made, the demand curve began to display a low income elasticity, as apparently occurred in the European countries after the 1920s. In periods of income growth consumers did not demand proportionally more Latin American commodities anymore.[15]

The trade balance

What would happen if Latin American consumers and firms at higher income levels demanded more and more foreign products but foreign markets did not proportionally demand more Latin American products (at also higher income levels)? In such a situation, Latin America would run into difficulties of the balance of payments. Structural changes would be needed in such a situation: only if Latin America started to produce other products – namely those with higher income elasticity in foreign markets – the balance of payment problems could be avoided and higher growth rates could be achieved. In this vein, and according to the theory devised by the Economic Commission for Latin America and the Caribbean (ECLAC), the fundamental problem of commodity exporters is that the income elasticity of the demand for imports to Latin America will inevitably be higher than the income elasticity of the demand of their exports abroad.[16] If structural change towards other economic sectors was insufficient, there would be a long-standing tendency to run trade deficits. The economy's growth rate will be determined by its relative propensities to export and import.

Estimates of long-term growth fit in very well with a simple model that explains growth based on the relationship between the income elasticity of demand for exports and imports (Bértola and Porcile 2006). In the aggregate, Latin America's per capita GDP relative to that of the West dropped from 36 per cent in 1870 to

27 per cent in 2008. The relative income elasticity factor (assuming no structural change) may account for the overall drop in Latin America's GDP from 36 per cent to 31 per cent. The remaining four percentage points of the decrease can be accounted for by other factors, such as a decline in the terms of trade, over-indebtedness, or even population growth.[17]

Education and human capital

Latin America as a whole has made significant efforts to bring about improvements in the population's level of education. However, when viewed from a comparative vantage point, those efforts seem to have come too little and too late, and the region has been at a clear disadvantage relative to other regions. This could be another factor explaining why the convergence to Europe and North America was not complete.

Around 2000, Latin America's population had completed an average of 7.1 years of schooling, whereas the populations of the four countries that have dominated the world scene over the last two centuries (France, Germany, the United Kingdom and the United States) had completed an average of 12.5. This means that the region's level of education as of the year 2000 was 59 per cent of the developed countries' level. However, if we look at Latin America's performance during the twentieth century, it becomes clear that it has made a great deal of progress. In fact, at the start of the twentieth century, the region's population had completed, on average, just 1.5 years of schooling (one quarter of the population of the developed countries mentioned above).

Higher educational levels are associated with higher GDP per capita values (Figure 4.4). However, Figure 4.4 shows that Latin America stands out compared to other countries in the sense that, for any given level of per capita income, its level of education is lower than that of other regions. The main explanations that have been advanced for this phenomenon have to do with social structures and power relations. The education system that was set up during colonial times was designed to preserve and legitimize the existing social order. A more modern system of education emerged in Latin America in association with other processes, the most important of which was the creation of independent states. This was accompanied by the appearance of new political parties, the emergence of entrepreneurs, as well as internal and foreign migration. All of this fuelled rapid progress in the creation of education systems, the gradual universalization of primary education and the narrowing of the educational gap between men and women. Nevertheless, as pointed out by Reimers (2006), these processes were all imprinted with a very basic division between those who advocated a democratic, inclusive form of education and those who crafted hierarchical, authoritarian social structures that went hand in hand with a high degree of social exclusion.

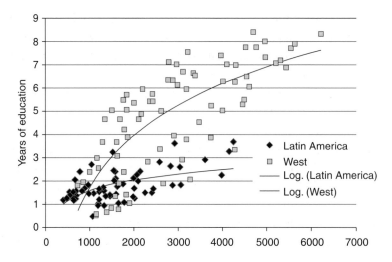

Figure 4.4 Latin America and the West, 1870–1930: per capita GDP (1990 PPP US dollars – x-axis) and average years of education of population aged 15 and above (y-axis)
Source: based on Bértola, Hernández and Siniscalchi (2010).

Frankema (2009), along with other authors, has looked for a relationship between the development of the education system and the concentration of land ownership. Large landholders are not in favour of educating the workforce because they fear that education will build workers' capacities and thus their political power and because they are more inclined to make use of unskilled labour than to use education as a means of boosting productivity.

Lindert (2010) has recently described how the concentration of political power, the concentration of wealth and low levels of education are linked to one another. He also attempts to account for what he calls 'education anomalies' (countries with higher incomes but worse education systems than others) by analysing their tax systems and looking at how fervently opposed high-income sectors are to paying taxes to finance the cost of universal public education.

There is another line of thought that complements this interpretation. Latin America's traditional export pattern shows that the predominant component consists of commodity exports that incorporate relatively low levels of value added but that nonetheless do generate economic rents. This would be the main factor underlying its tendency to have a high level of per capita income relative to its endowment of human capital as measured by levels of education.

Inequality

It is well known that Latin America is the region with the highest levels of income inequality in the world, which is why there has been so much interest in inequality studies in recent years. One of the main questions to be asked is: to what extent does the existence of inequality help to account for the region's relative backwardness? Another question is: to what extent is this characteristic a result of the region's particular style of development?

Most of the inequality research done on and in Latin America in the 1950s, 1960s and 1970s (with, in the second case, the structuralist school of thought leading the way) stressed the importance of the oligarchic aspects of Latin American development, which were manifested in the concentration of political power, wealth and income in elite groups of landowners and financiers who controlled labour relations and trade. The first wave of globalization was associated with the consolidation of the state's political power and a heavy concentration of wealth, along with a stauncher defence of the elites' property rights. The countries that were relying on immigration from Europe were a softer version of the latter rule.

These new elements had their roots in the region's colonial legacy. These new types of relations played out in different spheres, however, owing to the interaction of powerful international forces (the industrial revolution, the independence of the United States, the outcome of the Napoleonic wars) that influenced the liberal reform movement in Latin America.

Neo-institutional theorists have revived this older tradition of research (although they generally ignore the older Latin American structuralist literature), arguing that the institutions set up by the colonial powers immediately following colonization created a long-term equilibrium situation marked by sharp political and economic inequalities, sluggish human capital formation and slow economic growth.

These views have recently come under fire. Coatsworth (2008) contends that the root causes of Latin America's backwardness should be sought in the period between 1770 and 1870, when the Latin American economies missed the opportunity to engage with the industrial revolution and bring about one of their own. In his view, the local elites did not become stronger in the colonial era but only later, towards the end of the nineteenth century, and – contrary to what the neo-institutionalists contend – that reinforcement would not have been possible had it not been for economic growth. Viewed from this standpoint, the concentration of economic power was not an adverse factor but instead one that fostered development.

Unlike the advocates of earlier traditions, the neo-institutionalists looked to local conditions as the sole explanation for the region's development path and inequalities, while turning away almost entirely from an analysis of how those inequalities were reproduced at the international level and how they influenced the existence of inequalities at the national level. Similarly, the emphasis on colonial institutions has diverted attention from research into how institutions have been altered by their interaction with national and international processes of change, with the most significant of those processes undoubtedly being the industrial revolution and the ensuing succession of economic growth impulses, technological change and structural and social transformations (Bértola 2011).

The period of state-led industrialization had differing results in terms of equity in different countries. In those that developed some form of welfare-state, this was a time of declining inequality. This is the case of countries such as Argentina, Chile and Uruguay. In other countries with very large domestic markets and highly segmented labour markets in which a large percentage of the population was made up of the descendants of slaves or of *mestizo campesinos* (i.e., peasants of mixed American-Indian-European ethnicity) or indigenous groups, the industrialization process heightened the concentration of wealth and, even among wage-earners, led to a growing polarization of income levels. Brazil may be regarded as the epitome of this type of experience. In still others, these kinds of phenomena were in evidence until the industrialization process was quite far along, but at some point distribution began to improve, particularly as the surplus of rural labour began to shrink and the effects of the development of the education system began to be felt. Mexico, Venezuela and Colombia are some of the main examples of this type of pattern. In the long run, a significant effect of industrialization and of the urbanization that went along with it, in conjunction with widely varying types of agrarian reforms, was the erosion and ultimate elimination of long-standing forms of servitude that had existed in rural areas, in particular.

There is a broad consensus, as well as detailed information, about how the market reforms of the late twentieth century led to a significant increase in inequality and about the association between this increase and deregulation, the destruction of state capacity and deindustrialization. In the Southern Cone, the military dictatorships that seized power played a major role in the early phases of the reform process, which they accompanied with a systematic repression of the attempts made by the people to organize, with one of the results being a substantial reduction in real wages. More generally, however, the economic crises that took place had a powerful negative distributional impact, while the restructuring of production generated a demand bias for skilled labour that also had an adverse effect on income distribution. In the first decade of the twenty-first century, however, the trend in distribution improved and inequality declined. The reasons for this are still open to question, but it is clear that at least two types of policies have had a broad impact: the improvement of the distribution of educational opportunities had a cumulative effect, and the newly designed system of social assistance succeeded in reaching the poorest sectors of the population.

Present challenges from a historical perspective

At least four major lessons for the future can be drawn from Latin America's history. The first has to do with the region's achievements in the area of macroeconomic management. Its accomplishments in terms of inflation and fiscal sustainability need to be consolidated, but policymakers are also faced with the immense challenge of managing the Latin American economies' long-standing vulnerability to external shocks. The response to the 2008–09 global crisis was in many ways a positive one for Latin America: there was neither an external nor a domestic financial crisis in any country, and inflation did not spiral out of control. Although it proved impossible to avoid a sharp initial recession in the region, this was, fortunately, turned around quite rapidly, with the region (and especially South America) registering a positive growth rate in 2010 and 2011. Furthermore, the boom that preceded the most recent global crisis and the return of capital flows and high commodity prices since mid-2009 have shown that there is still a great deal to be learned about handling economic booms and, in particular, about averting cyclical currency appreciations (which make even less sense in today's export-oriented economies), upswings in public-sector spending during times of abundance and, especially, the steep increases in lending and private-sector spending that typically occur during such periods.

The second lesson relates to economic growth, which has been a frustrating issue for a majority of Latin American countries during the market reform phase of the 1980s. History tells us that high growth rates cannot be attained solely on the back of a sound macroeconomic situation or patterns of specialization based on static comparative advantages. Proactive production policies – which were explicitly excluded from public-sector agendas during the market reform phase – are also needed. And there is an even more glaring need to fast-forward the design of proactive technology policies, which were also seriously neglected during the period of state-led industrialization. This effort should be coupled with a consolidation of the progress made in education and the introduction of measures to address the education system's failings, especially in terms of quality and of the alignment of curricula with the skills and capacities required in order to change the region's production patterns.

The third lesson refers to institution-building and particularly one dimension of that process which has long been a subject of controversy: the relationship between the state and the market. A related facet of the Latin American development process has been the region's tendency toward rentism, which has been manifested both as a dependence on the rents afforded by natural resource endowments and as a reliance on those to be derived from a 'special relationship' with the state. Education and the development of technology (the two policy areas on which we focused in the preceding paragraph) are the best way to overcome this Latin

American institutional trait. International experience tells us that an appropriate mix of the state and the market is vital, but it also shows us that there is no single design that is best for achieving positive synergies between the two.

Contrary to what many have thought in recent decades, the greatest weaknesses in this area may be in the development of the state's capabilities. This question was also of importance in the early years of the Latin American republics. The greatest strides in this regard were made during the phase of state-led industrialization, even though the state that was created at that time often fell victim to its own inefficiencies and its inability to stand up to powerful interest groups. Latin America clearly fell further behind not only the industrialized nations but also the Asian countries (where the development of the state has deep historical roots). History shows us that forward progress is perfectly feasible, however. When strong policy initiatives are taken, they make important inroads. Examples include the creation of social-service delivery mechanisms and the development of the production sector during the period of state-led industrialization, or the actions of the region's finance ministries and the development of social assistance programmes during the market reform phase, or the steps taken to build strong central banks during both periods. Education and technological development should therefore be at the centre of state reform efforts in the future.

The last and most important lesson has to do with the enormous social debt that Latin America has built up over its history. The colonial legacy of extreme economic and social inequality, which has been analysed in classic works of Latin American economic historiography, has been perpetuated and, in some cases, heightened in subsequent periods of the region's history, which have added new dimensions to this phenomenon. In the past few decades, more ground has been lost in this respect, and an entire quarter of a century was lost in terms of poverty reduction before advances again began to be made in 2002–08. What is more, the contrast between these results and the advances made in human development indicate that social policy is not enough, in itself, to make headway in terms of social equity – not as long as the economic system continues to produce and reproduce high level of inequality in income distribution.

Herein lies Latin America's greatest historical debt. The return to an equity agenda, the new discourse around 'social cohesion' and the forward movement in this area observed during the first decade of the twenty-first century are all promising signs. The future will show whether or not these trends herald the first steps towards correcting the most grievous aberration of the Latin American development process. As history has shown us, however, these advances will not be lasting ones unless they are combined with the changes in education, technology and production that are needed in order for the region to be able to integrate itself into the global economy in a more dynamic manner, while at the same time deepening the integration of its own economies and societies.

Conclusion

At the beginning of this chapter Latin America's position was described relative to western European and northern American economies. Afterwards a typology of Latin American countries was developed by the analysis of three distinctive periods, among them the state-building period, the export-led growth period and the later state-led industrialization period until the economies finally turned back to the market. With these insights in mind, a subsequent analysis of volatilities of commodity prices, trade balance issues, education and inequality aimed at explaining the income gap between Latin American countries and higher developed countries in western Europe or North America. In sum, Latin America was on the one hand falling farther behind the Western countries over the past two centuries. This can be explained by Latin America's high concentration on primary commodities as well as the state of the educational system and institutional structure, some of which are still closely related to its colonial past, others to recent political developments. Consequently, further improvements in technological and industrial policies need to be achieved to successfully integrate Latin America's economies and societies into the global markets and to converge to the richest world regions.

Notes

1. This chapter heavily relies on Bértola and Ocampo (2012).
2. We exclude 'the larger West', which as well as what we call 'the West' (the leaders of the industrialization process, made up of the major European powers and the 'Western offshoots') also includes other Western European economies and Japan, which joined the ranks of the leaders later on.
3. In contrast, in life expectancies Latin America fared somewhat better, especially in the twentieth century. The reduction in mortality rates that raised life expectancy stemmed from four main processes: the improvement of public health systems, advances in medical theory and practice, improved personal hygiene and higher income levels and living standards. In Latin America, the mean life expectancy in twelve countries for which information was available jumped from 29 to 71 years during the twentieth century.
4. Additional criteria that we discuss in Bértola and Ocampo (2012) could be: (1) the type of colonial power; (2) the type of market into which each society is most fully integrated (export economies, economies that are subsidiary to export economies, national markets and border or marginal zones); and (3) size, another important variable which influences the possible scales of production and the available opportunities for diversifying production.
5. This covers the entire range, from products in which some of the countries of the region have monopolies or oligopolies (usually for a limited period of time), such as nitrates, coffee or rubber, to those commodities (mainly tropical or subtropical agricultural goods) in which Latin American countries compete with regions with

abundant, relatively inexpensive labour (Asia and Africa), to agricultural products in which the region competes with developed countries that are less rich in natural resources and have higher wage levels (wheat, maize, meat, wool), see Lewis (1969, 1983); Bértola and Williamson (2006).

6. The terminology used here is in line with the recent tendency to refer to the worldwide economic expansion of the late nineteenth century and early twentieth century as the first wave of globalization.

7. Calculated from GDP growth rates (PPP) from World Bank (2014).

8. See, particularly for Latin America, Bacha and Díaz-Alejandro (1982), Marichal (1989), Stallings (1987) and, for the more specific case of the debt crisis of the 1980s and the years leading up to it, Devlin (1989). For the global situation, see also the now classic work of Charles Kindleberger (a recent edition can be found in Kindleberger and Aliber 2005) and the more recent analysis of Reinhart and Rogoff (2009), which is the source of the data used to construct Figure 4.2.

9. From the 1960s on, the figure does not include Cuba and thus covers eighteen, rather than nineteen, countries.

10. These are the different dimensions covered in the analysis of financial crises presented by Reinhart and Rogoff (2009).

11. In other words, how much did the changes of export relative to import prices fluctuate?

12. The 'relevant world' for each Latin American country has been identified on the basis of annual variations in the GDP of each of the destination countries for its exports, weighted according to the share of total exports that it represents from year to year.

13. The original Prebisch-Singer thesis argues that over the long run the price for primary commodities declines in proportion to manufactured goods.

14. The income elasticity of demand is a measure that informs us about how much the consumption of a good increases (in per cent) if income increases by 1 per cent.

15. This trend was heightened by the agricultural protectionist policies introduced at that time, which are still in evidence today in the developed world. The situation with respect to mineral products, including fossil fuels, is different, however. Many mineral products are not renewable and subject to strong supply constraints. These markets are also subject to strong rigidities, particularly after periods when investment has been low, which have an impact on prices for what are sometimes quite lengthy periods of time, since the lead-time for investments can be quite long. This production sector is also more likely to be taken over by monopolies or oligopolies than (tropical or non-tropical) agriculture.

16. This idea has been expressed by Prebisch, Singer, Seers and others and has been taken up by Thirlwall, who sees it as simply being one of the determinants of convergence and divergence in income levels. See also Bértola and Porcile (2006) and Cimoli and Porcile (2011).

17. It is important to remember that the 'relevant world' for Latin America in this exercise is not the same as it is for the West's per capita GDP as shown in Table 4.1.

Further reading

Bértola, L. and Gerchunoff, P. (eds.) (2011), *Instituciones y Desarrollo Económico en Hispanoamérica*, Santiago: CEPAL. This book, only available in Spanish, contains chapters on six different regions of Hispanic America: Río de la Plata; Bolivia, Chile and Perú; the Great Colombia; Central America; Mexico; and Cuba. It is a good companion to Bértola and Ocampo (2012).

Bértola, L. and Ocampo, J. A. (2012), *The Economic Development of Latin America since Independence*, Oxford University Press. A recent, concise and up-to-date comprehensive economic history of Latin America.

Bethell, L. (ed.) (1995), *The Cambridge History of Latin America. Latin America since 1930: Economy, Society and Politics*, 6 vols, Cambridge University Press. This sample is not an economic history collection, but a history collection. Nevertheless, economic history topics are very well covered. The collection covers all the periods and all the regions of Latin America and many different aspects of Latin American history.

Bulmer-Thomas, V. (2012), *The Economic History of Latin America since Independence*, 2nd edn, Cambridge University Press. Originally written in 1994, this book has become a classic of Latin American economic history.

Bulmer-Thomas, V., Coatsworth, J. H. and Cortés Conde, R. (eds.) (2006), *The Cambridge Economic History of Latin America*, 2 vols, Cambridge University Press. This is a sample of articles covering many different aspects of Latin American Economic History, written by a large number of specialists.

Cardoso, C. F. S. and Pérez Brignoli, H. (1979), *Historia Económica de América Latina*, vols. 1 and 2, Barcelona: Crítica. Only available in Spanish, this book is an outstanding comprehensive analysis of Latin American economic history. It represents the state of the art by the late 1970s and its approach is clearly superior to much of the later literature.

Thorp, R. (1998), *Progress, Poverty and Exclusion: an Economic History of Latin America in the 20th Century*, Baltimore: Johns Hopkins University Press; Inter-American Development Bank. This is a volume written for a large audience. It is based on the contributions of a large number of scholars, published in three books with the title *An Economic History of Twentieth-Century Latin America*, Houndmills: Palgrave.

References

Bacha, E. and Díaz-Alejandro, C. F. (1982), 'International Financial Intermediation: a Long and Tropical View', *Essays in International Finance*, 147. Reprinted in Andrés Velasco (ed.) (1988), *Trade, Development and the World Economy: Selected Essays of Carlos Díaz-Alejandro*, Oxford: Basil Blackwell, ch. 8.

Baten, J. and Blum, M. (2014), 'Why are you Tall while Others are Short? Agricultural Production and Other Proximate Determinants of Global Heights', *European Review of Economic History* 18 (2), 144–65.

Bértola, L. (2011), 'Institutions and the Historical Roots of Latin American Divergence', in J. A. Ocampo and J. Ros (eds.), *The Oxford Handbook of Latin American Economics*, Oxford University Press, ch. 2.

Bértola, L., Hernández, M. and Siniscalchi, S. (2010), *Un índice histórico de desarrollo humano de América Latina y algunos países de otras regiones: metodología, fuentes y bases de datos*, Montevideo: Facultad de Ciencias Sociales (Serie Documento de Trabajo).

Bértola, L. and Ocampo, J. A. (2012), *The Economic Development of Latin America since Independence*, Oxford University Press.

Bértola, L. and Porcile, G. (2006), 'Convergence, Trade and Industrial Policy: Argentina, Brazil and Uruguay in the International Economy, 1900–1980', *Revista de Historia Económica-Journal of Iberian and Latin American Economic History*, 1, 37–67.

Bértola, L. and Williamson, J. G. (2006), 'Globalization in Latin America before 1940', in V. Bulmer-Thomas, J. H. Coatsworth and R. Cortés Conde (eds.), *The Cambridge Economic History of Latin America*, vol. 2, Cambridge University Press, 11–56.

Cardoso, C. F. S. and Pérez Brignoli, H. (1979), *Historia Económica de América Latina*, vols. 1 and 2, Barcelona: Crítica.

Cardoso, F. E. and Faletto, E. (1971), *Dependencia y desarrollo en América Latina*, México, D.F.: Siglo XXI.

Cimoli, M. and Porcile, G. (2011), 'Learning, Technological Capabilities and Structural Dynamics', in J. A. Ocampo and J. Ros (eds.), *The Oxford Handbook of Latin American Economics*, Oxford University Press, 546–67.

Contreras, C. (2004), *El Aprendizaje del Capitalismo: Estudios de historia económica y social del Perú Republicano*, Lima: Instituto de Estudios Peruanos.

Contreras, C. and Cueto, M. (2004), *Historia del Perú Contemporáneo*, Lima: Instituto de Estudios Peruanos.

Devlin, R. (1989), *Debt and Crisis in Latin America: the Supply Side of the Story*, Princeton University Press.

Frankema, E. (2009), *Has Latin America Always Been Unequal? A Comparative Study of Asset and Income Inequality in the Long Twentieth Century*, Leiden; Boston: Brill.

Furtado, C. (1976), *Economic Development of Latin America: a Survey from Colonial Times to the Cuban Revolution*, 2nd edn., Cambridge University Press.

Gelman, J. (2011), 'Dimensión económica de la independencia', in *Las Indepedencias latinoamericanas y el persistente sueño de la Gran Patria Nuestra*, México D.F.: Servicio de Relaciones Exteriores de la Cancillería Mexicana.

Gootenberg, P. (1989), *Between Silver and Guano: Commercial Policy and the State in Postindependence Peru*, Princeton University Press.

Hausmann, R., Hwang, J. and Rodrik, D. (2007), 'What You Export Matters', *Journal of Economic Growth* 12 (1).

Kalmanovitz, S. and López Rivera, E. (2009), *Las Cuentas Nacionales de Colombia en el Siglo XIX*. Bogotá, Universidad de Bogotá Jorge Tadeo Lozano.

Kaminsky, G. L., Reinhart, C. M. and Végh, C. A. (2004), 'When it Rains, it Pours: Procyclical Capital Flows and Macroeconomic Policies', *NBER Macroeconomics Annual* 19, 11–53.

Kindleberger, C. P. and Aliber, R. (2005), *Manias, Panics, and Crashes: a History of Financial Crises*, 5th edn., New Jersey: John Wiley and Sons.

Leff, N. H. (1982), *Underdevelopment and Development in Brazil, vol. I: Economic Structure and Change, 1822–1947*, London: George Allen and Unwin.

  (1997), 'Economic Development in Brazil, 1822–1913', in S. Haber (ed.), *How Latin America Fell Behind*, Palo Alto, CA: Stanford University Press, 34–64.

Lewis, W. A. (1969), *Aspects of Tropical Trade, 1883–1965*, Stockholm: Almqvist Wicksell (Serie Wicksell Lectures).

(1983), *Crecimiento y fluctuaciones 1870-1913*, México D.F.: Fondo de Cultura Económica.

Lindert, P. (2010), 'The Unequal Lag in Latin American Schooling since 1900: Follow the Money', *Revista de Historia Económica/Journal of Iberian and Latin American Economic History* 28 (2), 375–405.

Marichal, C. (1989), *A Century of Debt Crisis in Latin America: from Independence to the Great Depression, 1820-1930*, Princeton University Press.

Mitchell, B. R. (2003), *International Historical Statistics: the Americas, 1750-1993*, New York: Stockton Press.

Ocampo, J. A. (1984), *Colombia y la economía mundial, 1830-1910*, Bogotá: Siglo XXI; FEDESARROLLO.

(1990), Comerciantes, artesanos y política económica en Colombia, 1830-1880, *Boletín Cultural y Bibliográfico*, 22, Bogotá: Banco de la República.

(2008), 'A Broad View of Macroeconomic Stability', in N. Serra and J. E. Stiglitz (eds.), *The Washington Consensus Reconsidered*, Oxford University Press, 63–94.

Ocampo, J. A. and Parra, M. A. (2010), 'The Terms of Trade for Commodities since the Mid-Nineteenth Century', *Revista de Historia Económica – Journal of Iberian and Latin American Economic History* 28 (1), 11–37.

Ocampo, J. A., Rada, C. and Taylor, L. (2009), *Growth and Policy in Developing Countries: a Structuralist Approach*, New York: Columbia University Press, ch. 1.

Ocampo, J. A. and Vos, R. (2008), *Uneven Economic Development*, London: Zed Books; United Nations.

Reimers, F. (2006), 'Education and Social Progress', in V. Bulmer-Thomas, J. H. Coatsworth and R. Cortés Conde (eds.), *The Cambridge Economic History of Latin America*, vol. 2, Cambridge University Press, 427–82.

Reinhart, C. and Rogoff, K. (2009), *This Time is Different: Eight Centuries of Financial Folly*, Princeton University Press, 2009.

Sánchez Santiró, E. (2009a), *Las alcabalas mexicanas (1821–1857): los dilemas de la construcción de la hacienda nacional*, México D.F.: Instituto Mora.

(2009b), 'El desempeño de la economía mexicana tras la independencia, 1821–1870: nuevas evidencias e interpretaciones,' in E. Llopis and C. Marichal (eds), *Latinoamérica y España, 1800–1850: Un crecimiento económico nada excepcional*, Madrid and México, D.F.: Marcial Pons, Ediciones de Historia; Instituto Mora, 65–110.

Stallings, B. (1987), *Banker to the Third World. US Portfolio Investment in Latin America, 1900–1986*, California University Press.

Sunkel, O. and Paz, P. (1970), *Subdesarrollo latinoamericano y la teoría del desarrollo*, 9th edn., México D.F.: Siglo XXI.

Triffin, R. (1968), *Our International Monetary System: Yesterday, Today and Tomorrow*, New York: Random House.

ιere a 'curse of natural resources'?

ιten

Latin America and Africa were the world regions which economic observers after the Second World War expected to be growing quickly because they had many natural resources. In contrast, East Asia was expected to remain poor because of its poor resource endowment. These expectations were quite wrong. When societies simply sell their natural resources abroad in exchange for large transfers of money, it is surprisingly difficult to turn this income into continuous economic development. The availability of oil, diamonds, gold and other natural resources often resulted in specific types of political economies, in which small groups obtain great wealth to the disadvantage of the majority of the population and the income and political participation of the majority remains dramatically low. If revenues are large and sudden, it can be a mixed blessing.

The hypothesis of the 'curse of natural resources' suggests that countries that are overly abundant in natural resources are on average rather unsuccessful in terms of growth (Sachs and Warner 1995, Auty 1993), as it was the case in Nigeria during the second half of the twentieth century, or Venezuela during the early twenty-first century. Since being resource-abundant had been regarded as a positive factor of growth, the empirical evidence for the hypothesis came as a surprise in the 1990s. A number of explanations have been developed for this result. Sachs and Warner observed that the production of industrial goods is often unprofitable in resource-abundant countries due to disadvantageous currency exchange rates. Most industrial goods are thus imported. Oil and other resources also resulted in higher inequality and a large part of the population considers their share of income and political participation to be insufficient (van der Ploeg 2011). This in turn can lead to political instability, high public deficit and a dictatorial government system, as well as underinvestment in education (Gylfason and Zoega 2006).

Finally, resource abundance at home or in a neighbouring country can lead to a 'military bias'. Collier (2007) has recently pointed to the influence of oil and other mineral resources in the genesis of civil wars. On the other hand, Brunnschweiler and Bulte (2008) have pointed out that military conflicts can lead to more resource extraction, hence the direction of causality is not obvious. Observations show that resource-abundant countries and their neighbouring states have relatively high military spending and that the military is regarded as the most attractive field for the elites. Conquering resources in military conflicts is perceived as the easiest way to gain wealth and reputation in resource-abundant economies. However, this means that talented and innovative entrepreneurs are missing in other industries and services and that the actual basis of development in a country is eroding, in particular as the subject of further conquests is increasingly unattainable.

Do we observe effects of a 'curse of natural resources' in the long-run development as well? Pamuk and Williamson (2010) argued that a variant of the curse of resources accounts for the slow development of the Middle East (and in other world regions, similar phenomena might have occurred). As late as 1800, the Ottoman Empire that constituted the core region of the Middle East was completely self-sufficient in textile production (Pamuk and Williamson 2010). But in 1910 its textile production had fallen to less than 20 per cent. Why did this strong deindustrialization occur? British textile imports outperformed many local producers. At the same time, the terms of trade of cash crops were improving strongly. Raw cotton prices increased substantially, for example. This change in terms of trade tempted the Middle East to specialize in this area of primary production. Cotton and other commodity exports were the resource that became a 'curse' as the Middle East deindustrialized. This development was later reinforced by oil exports.

Another important case was the Spanish Empire that obtained enormous wealth in Peru, Bolivia and Mexico in the sixteenth century. Spain was wealthier than England in the fifteenth century. Its resource-rich South American colonies provided large cash inflows from silver, but at the same time reduced incentives for industrial development in Spain. Spanish entrepreneurship seems to be reduced by natural resource abundance, as profits could be made by resource extraction involving less risk and effort. Innovation and investment in education were therefore neglected, so that the prerequisites for successful future development were given up. Thus, Spain soon lost its economic strength in comparison to other countries, such as the Netherlands or Britain.

However, the interaction of rich resources and fairly growth-promoting institutions seems to be rather a blessing in some countries and periods. For example Norway and Botswana were resource-abundant and developed well during the later twentieth century because a good institutional framework allowed them to reinvest resource-income to generate stable future income.

At the same time there are a few more examples of historical economies benefiting from resource abundance. For example, according to Allen (2009), coal reserves fuelled the Industrial Revolution in the UK as technical innovations, such as steam engines, were more economical to use than elsewhere. Allen argued that exceptionally high wages in Britain alongside cheap coal played a decisive role in the Industrial Revolution by inciting an early adoption of technological innovations. Between 1560 and 1800, there was a sixty-six-fold increase in coal

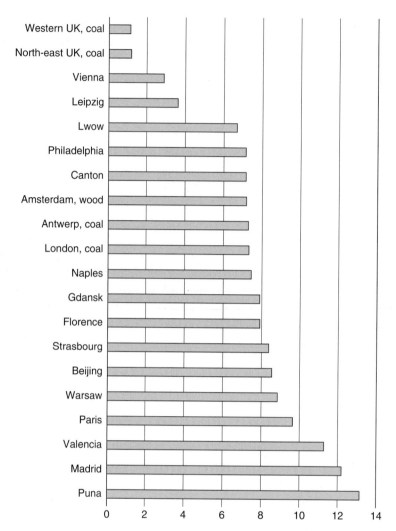

Figure I4.1 Energy prices in different locations, 1750/1800 (gram silver per million British thermal units [BTU])
Source: Allen 2009.

production. In the UK coalfields were available and could be exploited. Belgium, Germany and China only developed similar coal mining techniques much later. The price of coal in London was not exceptionally low compared to other areas of the world, but the coal price in the western areas and in the north-east of Britain was the lowest observed for the pre-1800 period (Figure I4.1).[1]

In sum, it seems that large transfers of natural resource income are quite difficult to digest for countries with imperfect institutions. Only countries with very good institutions or human capital, such as the UK in the early modern period or modern Botswana and Norway, made good use of income from natural resources.

There is much scope for additional historical studies on these issues because the economic historiography of resource-abundant countries is so far constrained to very few examples.

Note

1. Kelly *et al.* (2014) argued that, while the relative cost of energy might in fact be important, there are some doubts about its exogeneity. In some regions of England, such as in Cornwall, coal was really expensive. In this region the high cost of coal influenced technological progress to move into another direction. In Cornwall, the high cost of coal stimulated coal-saving technology such as the one developed by the Cornish engineer Arthur Woolf (Nuvolari and Verspagen 2009). This suggests, in the view of Kelly *et al.*, that there were deeper forces that influenced both high wages and the development of low-cost coal as well as technological progress in England in general. They argued that human capital was a central force that stimulated the British Industrial Revolution and made the adoption of new technologies based on coal possible, instead of falling into a 'curse of natural resources'. Given the high skills of British craftsmen and mechanics and the high health human capital in the UK, this country avoided the trap of natural resources and became the first industrial nation.

References

Allen, R. C. (2009), *The British Industrial Revolution in Global Perspective*, Cambridge University Press.

Auty, R. M. (1993), *Sustaining Development in Mineral Economies: the Resource Curse Thesis*, Routledge, London.

Brunnschweiler, C. and Bulte, E. (2008), 'The Resource Curse Revisited and Revised: a Tale of Paradoxes and Red Herrings', *Journal of Environmental Economics and Management* 55, 248–64.

Collier, P. (2007), *The Bottom Billion: Why the Poorest Countries are Failing and What Can Be Done About It*, Oxford University Press.

Gylfason, T. and Zoega, G. (2006), 'Natural Resources and Economic Growth: the Role of Investment', *The World Economy*, Wiley Blackwell 29 (8), 1091–115, p. 8.

Kelly, M., Mokyr, J. and Ó Gráda, C. (2014), 'Precocious Albion: a New Interpretation of the British Industrial Revolution', *Annual Reviews of Economics* 6, 363–89.

Nuvolari, A. and Verspagen, B. (2009), 'Technical Choice, Innovation, and British Steam Engineering, 1800–50 – Super-1', *Economic History Review* 62 (3), 685–710.

Pamuk, S. and Williamson, J. G. (2010), 'Ottoman De-industrialization, 1800–1913: Assessing the Magnitude, Impact, and Response', *The Economic History Review*, 64 (S1), 159–84.

Sachs, J. D. and Warner, A. (1995), 'Economic Reform and the Process of Global Integration', *Brookings Papers on Economic Activity* 1, 1–118.

Van der Ploeg, F. (2011), 'Natural Resources: Curse or Blessing?', *Journal of Economic Literature* 49 (2), 366–420.

H4.1 Latin America 1500–1800: early contact, epidemics and numeracy development

Joerg Baten

One of the most dramatic moments of world economic history was the encounter at Cajamarca: the Inca Emperor and his large army met a small group of Spanish soldiers and the latter won in the military conflict and conquered the vast Inca Empire. Diamond (1997) has written a widely read book in which he explained the superiority of the Spanish as a result of 'guns, germs and steel': the modern armament, horses and the shock effects of sixteenth-century artillery helped the Spaniards. Even more decisively, though, in the overall conflicts between Europeans and the indigenous people were the germs. The Europeans brought with them a number of diseases such as measles and smallpox from which many American Indians died because they lacked antibodies. In contrast, Europeans had a richer endowment of antibodies due to their frequent contact with cattle, sheep and goats from which many of these diseases originally stemmed. Diamond's conclusions about the long-run effects of this encounter between American Indians, Europeans and their diseases are contested (see Acemoglu and Robinson (2012) among many others). But the importance of the demographic catastrophe caused by imported diseases is obviously a fact. Even lower-bound estimates arrived at a population decline of around 20–50 per cent (McCaa 2000) and high estimates speak of even 90 per cent. This demographic catastrophe had some surprising effects, similar to the fourteenth century pest epidemic in Europe, after which real wages in Europe increased. There was a reaction of wages in Mexico, for example. Arroyo Abad and van Zanden argued that real wages increased substantially after the population catastrophe. While a family could not be nourished even with basic subsistence by one wage earner alone in the sixteenth century, by around 1700 the real wage had tripled. In the Andes, real wages were lower and more stagnant, but even there, wage labour became more important than forced labour (Arroyo Abad, Davies and van Zanden 2012).

Another measure of early modern development is numeracy (Figure H4.1). Initially, numeracy of Indios living in the Inca Empire was substantially lower than Spanish numeracy. After contact, Indios in Lima initially developed substantial numerical human capital quite rapidly. However, the seventeenth century was a crisis period for numeracy development, before the eighteenth century brought positive development again. Argentina, originally a sparsely populated backwater of the Spanish Empire, developed even more rapidly and overtook Peru and Mexico. In fact, eighteenth century Latin America had a remarkably strong development of numerical skills (Manzel *et al.* 2012). Manzel *et al.* (2012) argued that Latin American numeracy development grew as quickly as east-central Europe, but the lack of freedom under the Spanish and other colonial rule led to the independence wars during the early nineteenth century, and many Latin American countries suffered from civil war and political instability. Thus in this period numeracy development decreased.

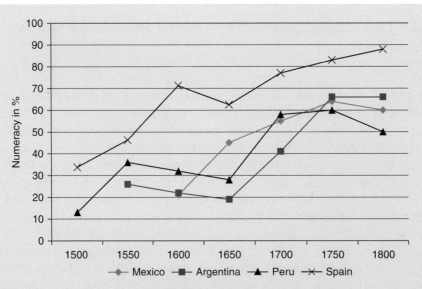

Figure H4.1 Development of numeracy in Latin American countries

In sum, Latin America's history during 1500 to 1800 period was not only characterized by colonial exploitation and inequality (although this was the predominant element), but also long phases of progress and promising development.

References

Acemoglu, D. and Robinson, J. (2012), *Why Nations Fail: the Origins of Power, Prosperity and Poverty*, 1st edn., New York: Crown.

Arroyo Abad, L., Davies, E., van Zanden, J. L. (2012), 'Between Conquest and Independence: Real Wages and Demographic Change in Spanish America, 1530–1820', *Explorations in Economic History* 49, 149–66.

Diamond, J. (1997), *Guns, Germs and Steel: the Fates of Human Societies*, New York: Norton.

Manzel, K., Baten, J. and Stolz, Y. (2012), 'Convergence and Divergence of Numeracy: the Development of Age Heaping in Latin America, 17th to 20th Century', *Economic History Review* 65 (3), 932–60.

McCaa, R. (2000), 'The Peopling of Mexico from Origins to Revolution', in M. Haines and R. Steckel (eds.), *The Population History of North America*, Cambridge University Press.

H4.2 The economic consequences of independence in Latin America
Salomón Kalmanovitz

The actual evil that ruled the Spanish and Portuguese colonies was the political system of absolutism. This monarchical system imposes few constitutional restrictions to the ruler. It is based on corporations that gave raise to strong social hierarchies and economic inequalities. The Catholic church was the ideological backbone of the monarchy by constituting this system with a seemingly divine origin of power.

The most recent Latin American economic history literature on the effects of colonialism can be divided into two broad streams: one that would establish a sort of 'black legend' of the Spanish legacy and another which represents a modern defence for a less negative role of Spain in the development of its colonies.

The former considers Spanish colonial legacy as the source of social and economic inequalities in the economic development of the respective regions. The main representatives of this opinion are Douglass North, Engerman and Sokoloff, and Acemoglu and Robinson. In contrast to this neo-institutional trend, Leandro Prados, Rafael Dobado and others proposed a kind of 'rosy legend' by using neo-classical economic methods to demonstrate that economic growth in the Spanish colonies was quite remarkable during most of the eighteenth century and that independence triggered a sudden stop to this trend. They developed a counter hypothesis stating that without independence the continent would have experienced a long-run trend of positive growth (that was only continued after 1860 when economic growth accelerated). Furthermore, these studies argue that Latin America fares badly when compared with North America, but is better off if compared with other colonies in Africa or Asia. In the Latin American literature critical postures of both orientations can be found: some minimize the role of institutions in economic development by postulating that the latter produces good institutions and not vice versa, like the Argentinean Jorge Gelman. This hypothesis might be plausible since prosperity strengthens economic interests that need in turn political peace. This leads to the tendency to negotiate with all groups in order to enhance democratic reforms. However, once these incentives have vanished, Latin America experienced a frequent resurgence of instability, reflecting the quality of its political institutions. Other scholars question the idea that Latin America achieved a sort of 'consolation prize', when compared with African economic development, like Prados does. They claim that both continents are remarkably different and cannot be easily compared.

These issues can be tackled by posing some fundamental questions: what was in particular the Spanish legacy? What was its role in the framing of a structure of social inequality, modest economic development and authoritarianism? It was obvious that the Spanish incentive structure limited the extent of trade and private businesses, that its social base denied property rights to peasants and gave limited communal property rights to Indian communities. Its legal system defined different rights for Indians, mestizos, slaves and white Creoles. The most frequent social relations consisted of bondages between peasants and labourers and slavery in plantations and some mining districts. Besides these facts, the Iberian Peninsula taxed a large part of the meager economic surplus of its colonies, and impeded the emergence of a commercial bourgeoisie. After independence, the bourgeoisie as such had to compromise with landowners who held in fact the power in the provinces. As a result of this development, nowadays, a big mass of poor landless peasants exists (which has now mostly migrated to the cities).

Having these aspects in mind, a new set of questions arises: until when does the colonial legacy exert its influence? Does the postcolonial course follow a predetermined path set by the colonial institutions, the so-called path of dependency defined by North? It is obvious that the determinants of long-run development are just too different and cannot therefore be reduced only to the past. There are additional demographic and geographic factors, especially immigration, that influence growth. The changes in political and legal organizations, the way in which the new independent nations removed past institutions and the way of building new ones are only few of them. These new republics would follow new trajectories, without being free of certain informal institutions of the past, like religion. They had to go through difficult transitions to arrive at imperfect democratic political systems and to establish economies free of old ties in their labour and land markets. They could modernize their banking sectors, after abolishing the Catholic church monopoly of credit. I take recourse to the old Marxist idea, retaken by Barrington Moore, that the democratic revolution and agrarian reform would facilitate a deeper economic development, for example in Costa Rica or southern Brazil, and deep political reforms that set conditions for a strong economic development early in Chile, Costa Rica and later in Mexico.

5 Japan
Osamu Saito

Many, if not all, Eurasian countries from the late medieval to early modern periods saw their population growing, output expanding and commerce flourishing, despite the notable differences in the ways in which territorial and administrative consolidation proceeded. Japan was no exception: by the seventeenth century the country became densely populated, and the subsequent centuries saw land productivity increasing, and industry and commerce expanding. This chapter begins with an exploration of the population issue: how population growth became sustained. Then, the core sections trace changes in population, urbanization, output growth by sector and per capita gross domestic product (GDP) in the period from 1600 to 1874. Japan's early modern performance will be compared with other Eurasian countries and the ways in which growth was achieved will be discussed. The final section touches on Japan's growth process since the Meiji Restoration of 1868 and the subsequent periods up to 2010.

Population and trade developments before 1600

Located at the eastern end of Eurasia, Japan is an island country, located less than 200 km off the Korean peninsula but 800 km from the coast of China, the civilized pool of both knowledge and parasites in East Asia. This geographical position had a demographic implication. The physical distance 'tended to insulate the archipelago from disease contacts with the world beyond. This was, however, a mixed blessing, for insulation allowed relatively dense populations to develop which were then vulnerable to unusually severe epidemic seizure when some new infection did succeed in leaping across the water barrier and penetrating the Japanese islands' (McNeill 1979: 133). This is what actually happened, says McNeill. The Japanese archipelago remained sparsely populated long after the first contact with mainland China, which 'meant that a number of important and lethal diseases that became chronic in China could not establish themselves lastingly among the Japanese until about the thirteenth century' (McNeill 1979: 133–34). This dating may be debatable. There is a possibility that the critical threshold was passed much later than he assumed. But he was probably right in arguing that: 'As long as the island populations were not sufficient to enable such formidable killers as smallpox and measles to become endemic childhood diseases, epidemics of these (and other similar) infections coming approximately a generation apart must have cut repeatedly and heavily into Japanese population, and held back the economic and cultural development of the islands in drastic fashion' (McNeill 1979: 135). This mechanism may be called the McNeillian trap, which was not unique to Japan. Indeed, similar logic applies to other peripheral areas at both ends of Eurasia, as McNeill demonstrates in relation to the British Isles (McNeill 1979: 135–36). In other words, a real advance in terms of economic development was made only after the demographic threshold had been crossed. For the Japanese archipelago, as I will argue below, it may well have taken place in the sixteenth century.

According to traditional interpretations, the real break with the past pattern is said to have come at the turn of the sixteenth century when a 150-year long period of civil war came to an end: the Tokugawa clan and their allies won a decisive battle with the opponents and cleared the way to form a new shogunate government in 1603 when population stood as low as 12 million, according to Akira Hayami.[1] However, recent estimates suggest that the transformation had started in the mid-sixteenth century, and that the population total in 1600 was *c*. 17 million.[2] The new estimate is consistent with a reconstruction of famine chronology. According to the estimated frequencies of famine, while the eighth and ninth centuries saw a nationwide or cross-regional famine occurring one in less than three years, its probability was still high in the late medieval period: it remained one in three to four years between the fourteenth and the mid-sixteenth century. However, the frequency suddenly declined during that century from that level to an average of once every seven years – in the midst of a long phase of global cooling (Saito 2015a).

Japan's medieval period from the end of the twelfth century onwards may be portrayed as a long decline of Kyoto-based central administration and the corresponding rise of territorially based samurai power. After the collapse of the Kamakura and Muromachi shogunates, two successive samurai regimes, the late-fifteenth century saw the country thrown into a prolonged period of political instability and warfare. Kyoto completely lost control over territorial warlords (daimyo), who started fighting with each other over political and military hegemony. It was in this warring-states period when the drastic decline in famine frequency took place. Although it is difficult to relate any increase in the number of battles to the reduction in famines, this finding seems to suggest that although the frequency of devastating harvest may not have declined noticeably, the probability of the poor harvest resulting in a mass starvation or excess mortality was actually reduced under warlords' rule. What the sixteenth-century warlords brought about is territorial consolidation and administrative integration. An area which came under control of the warlord saw a rudimentary kind of territorial government being formed for the first time in Japanese history, which must have acted as an important factor in preventing any poor harvest from developing into a regional or cross-regional famine, which in turn enabled population to start increasing and, hence, to pass the epidemiological and demographic threshold eventually.

This also implies that state formation began before the establishment of the Tokugawa regime. The policies and schemes which many warring daimyo adopted included not just disaster relief but also extensive projects of land development, especially in lower reaches of the river. It is often argued that the cultivation of farm land extended towards less fertile, marginal areas. However, it was not the case in Japan, nor in many rice-growing Asian countries. There the move was towards fertile alluvial plains of the river delta. In earlier centuries, excess water and, hence, poor sanitation had prevented people from moving into marshy lowland areas. Under the daimyo government, however, investments were made either in the form of civil engineering projects such as land reclamation and the building of dykes and reservoirs, or of introducing new rice varieties which could withstand marshy conditions, or both. It is documented that the very long-run tendency in agricultural progress was associated with a change in the cause of crop failure from drought to cold summer (Saito 2015a); this is because the former, which affects the early growth processes of the rice plant, could be overcome by infrastructural investments whereas the latter could not in earlier centuries. In this respect, the land development projects by sixteenth-century territorial lords might be singled out to have contributed to the general trend. However, their efforts were so erratic and slow that it is not possible to account for the onset of the observed decline in famine frequency with this factor alone. Agrarian progress was a very gradual process.

The sixteenth-century population development coincided with the age of Asia's flourishing maritime trade. Portuguese and, later, Dutch merchants played a decisive role while Chinese, Indian and other Asian traders responded to market opportunities created by an increased volume of intra-Asian trade. In fourteenth-century Japan, licensed trade with China was arranged by the Muromachi shogunate while Japanese trading brigands (*wakō*) had long been active in the China Sea areas. But it was the introduction of a new cupellation technology to Japanese silver mines in the early sixteenth century that touched off a mining and, hence, export boom (see Map 5.1 on Japan's silver export and other trading patterns in East Asia). This enabled Japan's supply of silver onto the world market to rival the mines of Spanish Mexico and Peru. In fact, according to official statistics, average annual silver exports between 1596 and

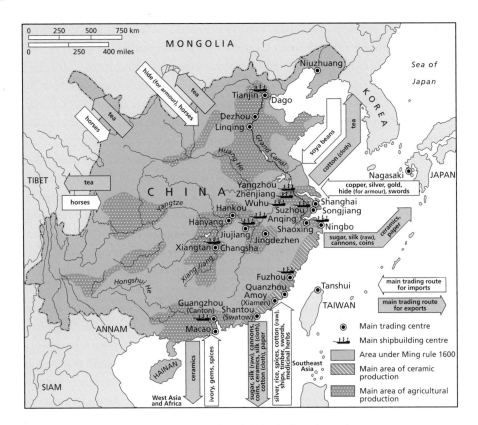

Map 5.1 Trade and production centres in East Asia in the late sixteenth century
Source: see map 1.1.

1623 is said to have amounted to about 10 per cent of the nation's total farm output; with smuggling taken into consideration, the silver share could have been even larger (Hayami 2004: 13, Shimbo and Hasegawa 2004: 167). During this mining boom, the *wakō*'s seafaring trade expanded with an increasing number of Chinese, Korean and Portuguese traders involved, whose activities were sometimes backed by Japanese daimyo. Traders and adventurers crossed the seas: in the early seventeenth century, at least 10,000 Japanese are said to have settled in Cochin-China, Ayutthaya, Manila and other Asian port cities (Lucassen *et al.* 2014: 366). Moreover, some of the daimyo in the Japanese south-west regions sent their own ships to Southeast Asian ports. All this seems to suggest that from the sixteenth century onwards, population growth, state formation and economic development went hand in hand, and this cumulative process produced a large population of settled farmers, on the one hand, and a small but powerful group of merchant adventurers, on the other. By 1600, therefore, having already broken away from the McNeillian trap, Japan set herself on the path to early modern growth.

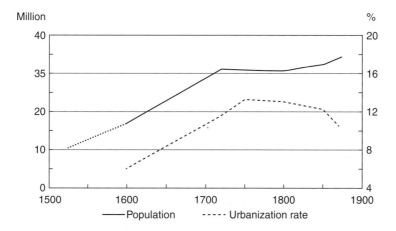

Figure 5.1 Population and the rate of urbanization, 1525–1890
Sources: Saito (2015a), p. 222, for population totals in 1525 and 1600. Other data are from Saito and Takashima (2015a).
Note: the rate of urbanization is calculated for cities with a population of 10,000 or more, and does not cover Okinawa and Hokkaido, the territories which were not under effective control of the Tokugawa shogunate.

Growth performance in the early modern period

Based on the above account, Figure 5.1 shows how population totals changed from 1525 onwards. One notable feature of this new graph is that the rate of increase over the seventeenth century was less rapid than Hayami thought. The estimated annual rate of population increase from 1600 to 1720 stands now at 0.5 per cent, rather than 0.8 per cent.[3] This population growth was accompanied by land development and output growth. Over the same 120-year period, arable land area increased by 40 per cent and farm output by 60 per cent (Miyamoto 2004: 38): clearly, farming became intensified. In per capita terms, however, there occurred no growth. In fact, as the population increased by 80 per cent, farm output per head of national population declined marginally. However, Figure 5.1 indicates that the process was also accompanied by urbanization. Soon after the battle of 1600, the first Tokugawa shogun began constructing new castles and surrounding town facilities by mobilizing manpower and resources from non-Tokugawa daimyo. The project took several decades to complete, which was followed by the other daimyo's own castle town building. This entire building boom created a huge demand for construction workers and, after completion, attracted a number of merchants and craftsmen to settle in the towns and cities (Lucassen *et al.* 2014: 398–403). Thus, the proportion of people living in places with populations of 10,000 or over rose from 6 per cent in 1600 to 12 per cent in 1720, which implies that while rural population grew by 70 per cent, urban population more than tripled. Whether people's overall standard of living declined or not hinges on the estimation of GDP, more specifically on that of output in the secondary and tertiary sectors at both the beginning and the end of the 120-year period.

So far two estimates have been made for per capita GDP in the period before the Meiji Restoration of 1868: Maddison's 2001 estimates and those in a working paper by Jean-Pascal Bassino *et al.* (Maddison 2001: 264, and Bassino *et al.* 2011; the latter is included in the first report of the Maddison Project: Bolt and van Zanden 2014). There are a couple of differences between the two. First, Bassino *et al.* have estimated the level of per capita GDP to be systematically higher than Maddison's for the first half of the Tokugawa period but not for the second, which is at odds with the Tokugawa historiography. It is well known that following the drastic decline in silver mining the export boom ended rather abruptly in the early seventeenth century; while the domestic economy benefited from the shogun's and other daimyo's town building projects, growth lost momentum towards the end of the century as the government's so-called seclusion policy stifled the overseas trade. It is documented that the eighth shogun's government made an effort to 'substitute domestic goods for imports', targeting raw silk, sugar and ginseng (Totman 1993: 311–14). Although it is difficult to substantiate its policy effects, the production of domestic raw silk did expand from the 1920s onwards. More generally, the rural economy appeared to grow from the late eighteenth century onwards – the growth was initially modest and steady but accelerated after the country's reentry into world trade in 1859 – which resulted in the unmistakable decline in the urbanization rate as evident in Figure 5.1 (Smith 1973: 15–49; Saito 1983: 30–54, 2005a, 2005b, 2010: 240–61). Second, Maddison's attempt to include non-primary sector output is based on a reading of non-quantitative works while Bassino *et al.* rely solely on the changing rates of urbanization. Both are thus not quite satisfactory. A new attempt to estimate secondary- and tertiary-sector output has been made by Masanori Takashima and myself. Our method utilizes not only the rate of urbanization but population density as well, both derived from Meiji-period prefectural panel data (based on which regression analysis is conducted for the secondary- and tertiary-sector shares separately; with the estimated parameters, the sectoral shares are back-projected to the Tokugawa period).[4] The point of employing this two-parameter method is that it allows us to measure the impact of proto-industrialization better.[5] As Figure 5.1 makes clear that while both population totals and the rate of urbanization increased until 1721, the two graphs diverged from the late eighteenth century to the 1870s, a period when rural industry and commerce advanced at the expense of the urban sector. Our two-parameter model captures the impact of this trend on both secondary- and tertiary-sector output far better than any one-parameter method.

The new per capita GDP estimates are presented in Table 5.1 and graphically in Figure 5.2 together with Maddison's for comparison (both are in 1990 international

Table 5.1 New estimates of GDP per capita (in 1990 international dollars) and sectoral shares in Japan, 1600–1935

	GDP per capita	Sectoral share (%)		
	(dollars)	Primary	Secondary	Tertiary
1600	556	72	8	20
1721	587	61	9	30
1804	729	61	9	29
1846	788	61	10	30
1874	860	59	11	30
1890	1,012	44	16	39
1913	1,387	33	23	44
1925	1,885	27	26	47
1935	2,120	16	35	49

Sources:
1. GDP per capita for 1600–1874 are from Saito and Takashima (2015b), Fukao *et al.* (2015), 71, and Maddison (2006), 178–79 for 1874–1935. The link is made by projecting Maddison's 1890 estimate in 1990 international dollars back to 1874 with a growth rate calculated from Fukao *et al.*'s 1874 and 1890 estimates. Then, it is linked to Saito and Takashima's 1600–1874 estimates.
2. Sectoral shares are from Saito and Takashima (2015b) for 1600–1874 and Fukao *et al.* (2015), 71, for 1874–1935. The 1913 shares are interpolated from the latter's 1909 and 1925 estimates.

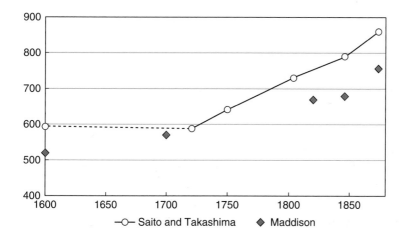

Figure 5.2 GDP per capita, 1600–1874: new estimates compared with Maddison's (both in 1990 international dollars)
Sources: Saito and Takashima (2015b) and Maddison (2001: 264).

dollars). It is interesting to note that the level of both estimates have come very close to each other in the mid-Tokugawa period, i.e., 1700–21. On both sides of this mid-point, however, there emerge differences. From 1721 to the 1870s, the gap between the two widens and ours ends 14 per cent higher than Maddison's level, capturing the effect of proto-industrial progress made during that period. In the 1600–1721 period, the initial gap was non-negligible but narrowed towards the end of the period. This is because our estimates of per capita GDP imply that the trend was stagnant or growing marginally over the 120-year period. To put it differently, while Maddison presented Tokugawa Japan's growth as a steady path, our estimates suggest that there was a turning point from the stagnant to the sustained growth phase.

Does this finding endorse the claim that the early Tokugawa society was under the Malthusian pressure? The observed rate of change in GDP per capita was close to zero. Moreover, given the nature of our estimation methodology, it is likely that the mining and export boom that had started before Tokugawa was not properly reflected in our output estimate for 1600: as hinted earlier, the proportion of silver export to total primary-sector output could have been somewhat higher than the 10 per cent mark. If that amount should be added to our estimate of non-primary products in 1600, then the revised average annual rate of change in GDP per capita between 1600 and 1721 would become negative, –0.01 per cent. Probably, there-fore, we have to accept that it was a period of negative – but still close to zero – growth. It was partially accounted for by moderately high population growth of 0.5 per cent per annum. Additionally, however, the decline was furthered first by the extinction of exportable silver and then by the end of the construction boom. During this process, men of pecuniary fortunes such as long-distance traders and large-scale developer-contractors disappeared from the centre stage; and daimyo too must have squandered away a substantial portion of their wealth on the construction of their castle town. After about 1700, therefore, the market economy became more or less regular and orderly; and the market functioned generally well – even compared with other Eurasian countries.[6] In other words, all this does not necessarily imply that living standards worsened for the peasantry who probably made up more than 80 per cent of the population at the beginning of the seventeenth century. During the first half of the Tokugawa period, as Thomas Smith argued decades ago (Smith 1959), individual farm families became the centre of production organization and decision-making in relation to both exter-nal as well as market conditions. Within this agrarian framework and under a peculiar taxation system of the Tokugawa era, the intensification of agriculture paid: any surplus left was in the hands of the peasants (Smith 1958: 50–70). Moreover, the engagement in non-farm subsidiary employment also paid: it brought in more cash incomes to the household. It was on this basis that proto-industrialization and commercialization proceeded in the second half of the Tokugawa period (Smith 1969: 71–102; Nishikawa 1987: 323–37).

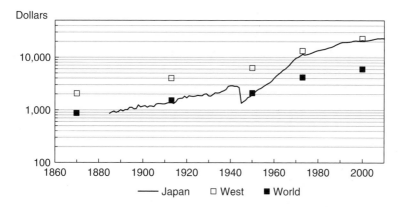

Figure 5.3 Growth of Japan's GDP per capita, 1885–2010: comparison with the West and the world (in 1990 international dollars)
Sources: Maddison (2001: 241, 264), Maddison (2006: 180–85, 234, 236), and Cabinet Office of the Japanese Government (2011, 2012).
Notes: (1) the vertical axis has a logarithmic scale; (2) Maddison's series for Japan ends in 2008, which is extended to 2010 by linking with the *Annual Reports on National Accounts* data. The 'West' is a population-weighted average of western Europe and western offshoots (Australia, New Zealand, Canada and the US).

However, this advance of Tokugawa Japan's labour-intensive mode of agrarian economy should not be taken to imply that the country began to catch up with the West. Our estimates in Table 5.1 indicate that per capita GDP reached the level of 860 dollars by 1874, which turns out to be very close to Maddison's estimate of the world average for 1870 but stands much lower than the level of 2,064 dollars for the wealthy West (see Figure 5.3). Within Asia, it is likely that Japan's per capita GDP surpassed the levels of China and India during the late eighteenth and early nineteenth centuries.

Early modern growth in Eurasian perspective

According to Bolt and van Zanden's survey of recent estimates, Japan's per capita GDP was still very low in 1800 in comparison with other Eurasian countries including India and Ottoman Turkey (Bolt and van Zanden 2014: 637). However, if comparison is to be made on terms of *growth rate* with our new estimates for Tokugawa Japan, then a somewhat different picture emerges. Table 5.2 sets out the average annual rates of GDP per capita for eight countries in both Asia and western Europe in the period before 1700 and also after 1700 (China is added from the Maddison table). In the period before 1700, while England and Holland exhibited comparatively stronger growth, both south European and Asian countries were characterized by either a decline or a

Table 5.2 Average annual growth rates of GDP per capita, 1500–1870: Japan in comparison with other Eurasian countries (per cent per annum)

	England	Holland	Northern Italy	Spain	Ottoman Empire	India	China	Japan
1500–1700	0.15	0.19	−0.02	−0.02	0.03			
1600–1700						−0.08	0.00	0.00*
1700–1800	0.36	0.21	−0.08	0.12	0.05⁑	−0.12	−0.07†	0.24‡

Sources: Table 5.1 for Japan; Maddison (2001: 264) for China; Bolt and van Zanden (2014: 637) for other countries.
Note: * 1600–1720, ⁑ 1700–1820, † 1700–1870, ‡ 1720–1874.

stagnant trend. As noted earlier, Japan was not an exception. The period after 1700 saw the two north-west European countries growing at an even higher pace than in the previous period, but fortune was fickle for the countries in the second group. Italy, India and China were still on the decline, Spain's growth turned positive, and the Ottoman Empire remained steady. What stands out, however, is late Tokugawa Japan's good performance. Not only did it turn positive, but its average growth rate of 0.24 per cent, on a par with Holland's but considerably lower than England's, was well ahead of any other countries' in the second group.

This finding calls for attention, for during much of the 150-year period the country was virtually closed to overseas trade and the growth was distinctly pre-modern, i.e., achieved without machinery and the factory. In this respect, it is interesting to note that Table 5.1 indicates first that the tertiary sector's share was substantially larger than the secondary's throughout the Tokugawa period. Although there remain problems associated with the classification of goods produced, it appears that those engaged in trading, financing and bringing commodities back and forth were numerous probably from the very beginning of the period. Moreover, little structural change occurred despite the steady growth in the period after 1720: the secondary- and tertiary-sector shares did not increase noticeably. Growth of secondary and tertiary output in the final sub-period, 1846–74, was stronger than that of primary goods, reflecting the impact of the reentry into international trade, but as far as the period between 1721 and 1846 is concerned, the sectoral shares hardly changed. This means that sectoral output growth was balanced. Rural industry expanded, especially in textiles, but agriculture, commerce and services also grew more or less simultaneously. What took place was a separation of the cultivation of industrial crops from food crops, the manufacturing of intermediate goods from finished goods and the trading for producers from that for consumers. For example, the rise of silk weaving in any region meant an increase in the demand for raw silk. Under the seclusion regime, there was no option to import raw materials; thus, this went directly to sericulturists and mulberry cultivators in surrounding villages, and resulted in an increase of primary-sector output. At the same time, the marketing of silk fabrics involved more transport and distribution businesses, creating more part-time or by-employment jobs. All these took place in different districts and, sometimes, in remote regions, thus taking the form of regional specialization helped by the well-functioning domestic markets. Since such regional specialization is one form of Adam Smith's division of labour, this type of economic change may be called Smithian growth. Of course, Smithian growth was not unique to Japan. What made Tokugawa Japan's experience rather conspicuous is that it was accompanied by deurbanization. To borrow Thomas Smith's terminology, Japan's Smithian growth was 'rural-centered' as contrasted with 'urban-centered' (Smith 1973: 127–160).

It is suggested, furthermore, that this rural-centred development did not bring any gains to both samurai and the urban wealthy (Smith 1973: 37–41), implying that growth had a *levelling effect* on income distribution. Elsewhere, by having examined wage data, I have shown that in contrast with north-western Europe where real wages tended to decline despite output growth, Tokugawa wage trends did not diverge from per capita GDP growth (Saito 2005a). Moreover, my recent reconstruction of a social table for the Chōshū region in the 1840s has revealed that interclass inequality was surprisingly low (Saito 2015b). Of course we have to take within-class income distribution into account: it was not so egalitarian and in fact much skewed in the case of the samurai case; and now that the growth rate in per capita GDP in the latter half of the Tokugawa period has been reestimated upward, my first statement needs to be revised accordingly. That said, however, it is likely that the income level of the majority of peasants was not particularly lower than that for the median level of urban incomes or even that of lower-rank samurai stipends. In this respect, it is interesting to note that the overall levels of literacy and numeracy in Tokugawa Japan were high by early modern standards, distinctly higher than in many other Eurasian countries. In the area of numeracy, Ma notes in Chapter 6 of this volume that the basic numeracy index – which measures people's ability to report an exact rather than a rounded age – in East Asia was at a level comparable to that for north-west European countries, and moreover, that Japan's index came close to the 100 per cent mark throughout the nineteenth century (Figure 5.2). As for literacy, Ronald Dore estimated that the proportion of boys who would ever had received some kind of schooling was 43 per cent at the end of the Tokugawa period (but 10 per cent for girls). Bold as these estimates may sound, it seems certain that by about 1800 'richer merchants and village headmen were often as learned as the average samurai, and at a lower level the spread of Japanese literacy continued', as a result of which in 1877 a

Frenchman wrote that 'primary education in Japan has reached a level which makes us blush'.[7] This advance in human capital investment in the Tokugawa period must have been an important legacy for the subsequent era of fully fledged industrialization.

Growth acceleration and deceleration, 1868–2010

When Meiji Japan opened up in the wave of nineteenth-century globalization, the attainment of economic growth by industrializing the country became the national goal. Since then Japan has been regarded as a success story of twentieth-century industrialization and, hence, modern economic growth. To check in what sense it was a success, Japan's growth records may be examined in relation to those of the West and the world average (Figure 5.3).

From 1890 to 1935, per capita GDP growth was steady – on average at 1.7 per cent per annum (Table 5.1). The First World War exerted a stimulating rather than depressing effect on the domestic economy, and the impact of the Great Depression was less prolonged in comparison with the Western countries. In the second half of the 1930s, the country enjoyed a brief period of strong growth due to military build-up, but the wartime regime soon faced an economic impasse and then experienced a precipitous decline in people's standard of living (on the wartime economy, see Highlight Chapter 5.1). In 1950 per capita GDP returned to the 1935 level. As is evident from Figure 5.3, however, during the 1890–1950 period Japan's level hardly diverted from the growth path of the world. Japan was an average country in the world until the mid-twentieth century. Even in interwar East Asia Japan's growth performance was not exceptionally superior, either. According to Ma's estimates of average rates of per capita GDP growth between 1914–18 and 1931–36 (Table 6.1 in Chapter 6), Japan's stood at 1.4 per cent while that of the three China Sea areas, i.e., the Lower Yangzi macro-region, Korea and Taiwan, fell in a range of 1.1–1.5 per cent. It was in China proper where economic development faltered. Considering this Chinese situation, Japan's growth performance over the long run was an achievement, to which human capital formation in the late-Tokugawa and institution-building efforts in the Meiji period may well have been conducive. Yet, if the average rate for the pre-1940 period had continued after the Second World War, as Bob Allen noted, 'it would have taken Japan 327 years to catch up to the US. That was not fast enough' (Allen 2011: 126).

The catch-up with the West took place *after* the world war – in a short period between 1950 and 1973, the year of the first oil crisis, during which the average rate of growth stood at 8.1 per cent. As Figure 5.3 shows, it is in this period of strong growth when Japan joined the world's club of rich countries.

Since the political scientist Chalmers Johnson coined the term 'developmental state', an interventionist state whose *raison d'être* is the attainment of economic development (Johnson 1982), Japan's economic success has often been considered a product of the state's planning and guidance. The early Meiji government's industry promotion and the post-Second World War Ministry of International Trade and Industry (MITI)'s industrial policy are said to have been particularly effective and exemplary. However, the early Meiji policy models resulted in a total failure, while many economists emphasize that competitive industries of the 1950s and 1960s grew without any government guidance (Saito 2014: 23–45; Komiya *et al.* 1988). Moreover, almost all those that emerged in the 1950s and 1960s were industries producing consumer durables. In the nineteenth-century West, industries producing intermediate goods for other producers led the tempo of industrialization; in the early twentieth century, therefore, Japan made an effort to promote those industries but yielded only a moderate success. After 1950 the tide changed. The emerging Japanese firms in car making and electronics, targeting an expanding mass consumer market, developed an innovative model of manufacturing methods which tended to be skill-using but *compatible* with the American mode of mass production. Toyota, Sony and Panasonic, to name but a few, were such firms and their growth owed nothing to MITI's industrial policy (Fukao and Saito 2013: 146–48).

Finally, however, high economic growth was short-lived. The average rate of growth declined to 3 per cent per annum in the period from 1973 to 1990 and further to 0.9 per cent in the 1990–2000 period. This phase of deceleration was accompanied by deindustrialization. Before 1973, the proportion of gross value added of the manufacturing sector to GDP stood at 35 per cent or over. Immediately after the 1973 oil crisis it declined by 5 percentage points, which went down again after the so-called bubble years. In 2008, the manufacturing sector's share in output further declined to below 20 per cent, and in 2010 the tertiary sector's share in the workforce reached 70 per cent (Fukao and Saito 2013: 152). This process thus meant a transition to a service economy. However, the post-industrial transition was not occasioned by a rise in productivity in the tertiary sector. According to estimates of industry-specific total factor productivity (TFP), while an increase in manufacturing TFP is still reasonably steady, the tertiary sector's TFP growth has been sluggish since the 1970s. The level of labour productivity in services and construction remains low by international standards (Fukao and Saito 2013: 155–57).

Conclusion

Since 2008, the country's population has begun to shrink. A several century-long population growth cycle has now ended. In the sixteenth century, the country's population started to increase and thus became for the first time in history able to sustain itself. The extent of the market was enlarged, which acted as a stimulus for the division of labour to proceed. Smithian growth thus started in the early eighteenth century when the population is believed to have crossed the 30 million mark. The take-off took place without any external influences, and growth that followed was steady and comparatively stronger by early modern Eurasian standards. While this late-Tokugawa development was sectorally balanced, manufacturing growth was one important component of the process. The transition from the proto-industrial to the subsequent phase of industrialization was more or less continuous, although industries of the classical industrial-revolution type that rose in the Meiji period relied more on borrowed technologies and organizations. The effort of this fully fledged industrialization phase, 1870–1940, had only modest success, however. It was in the post-Second World War period of 1950–73 when Japan became able to catch up with the West, owing largely to the innovative adaptation by Japanese manufacturing firms of American technologies of mass production, which kept – rather than eliminated – skills on the shop floor.

Shortly after this period of very strong manufacturing growth came the sudden onset of deindustrialization. In the domestic economy, the three-century-long process of industrialization seems to have ended. A rapid shift to a service economy began – the trend that became even more apparent in the early twenty-first century. As the population is ageing and fertility remains low, the domestic market is saturated; and as a number of manufacturing companies have opted for relocating their factories to China, Thailand and other Asian countries, employment has drifted towards a less productive service sector. Japan's post-industrial economy now faces challenges totally different from the difficulties the country encountered 150 years ago.

Notes

1. Akira Hayami, the pioneer of Japanese historical demography, has long been arguing that the population in 1600 was substantially lower than 18 million, a guesstimate made a century ago (reprinted in Hayami 2009: 75–98). Hayami's estimate of *c.* 12 million is derived from an extrapolation of regional population trends in one region between the late seventeenth and the eighteenth century but many scholars have accepted Hayami's 1600 estimate until recently. It should be realized, however, that this acceptance of the Hayami estimate implies that given the estimated size of national population being 31 million in 1720, the average annual rate of population

growth was 0.8 per cent during the seventeenth century. This is considered very high by premodern standards, so high that the early Tokugawa economy must have come under mounting population pressure: according to Miyamoto's summary table, farm output per capita is estimated to have decreased as much as 38 per cent from 1600 to 1720. It is odd therefore to suppose, as Hayami does, that such a century saw significant transformations – such as the development of 'land and labour-intensive agriculture' and the emergence of 'a landed proprietor or cultivator seeking to increase productivity or production' – taking place (Hayami 2009: 45). His estimates are summarized with other macroeconomic indicators in Miyamoto (2004: 38).

2. My unpublished estimate is 17 million. My unpublished estimates of population totals are quoted and discussed in Farris (2006). Angus Maddison also argued that the level must have been far larger than the Hayami estimate, saying that the Hayami estimate implied the above-mentioned very high rate of population increase in the seventeenth century, followed by 'more or less complete stagnation' in the eighteenth, a change which he thought is too abrupt to accept. See Maddison (2001: 237).

3. The graph suggests that this seventeenth-century population increase may be traced back to the early sixteenth century. However, as the figure for 1525 is a speculation, the trend for the entire 1525–1720 period remains still uncertain.

4. An earlier version of this chapter was presented as Saito and Takashima (2014). I thank Masanori Takashima for allowing me to make use of our joint research results for this chapter. Note that estimates quoted in the text are revised from the May 2014 version.

5. They are derived from Meiji-period regional panel data. On the basis of this prefectural panel dataset, regression analysis was conducted for the secondary- and tertiary-sector shares separately; then with the parameters estimated, the sectoral shares were back-projected to the Tokugawa period. For details, see Saito and Takashima (2015b). Note that this criticism is accepted by the authors of Bassino *et al.* (2011) and the two-parameter model adopted in its latest revision of early modern GDP per capita estimates (Bassino *et al.* 2015).

6. This is what Jan Luiten van Zanden has found for grain markets in China, India, Indonesia and Japan in comparison with European countries in the North Sea region: see van Zanden (2009). For Tokugawa Japan's factor markets, see Saito (2009: 169–96) and Saito and Settsu (2006).

7. For his estimation of literacy rates, see Dore (1965: 317–22, 31, 291). Herbert Passin went further to break down the national average by social group and gave guesstimates of 50–60 per cent for 'village middle layers' and 30–40 per cent for 'lower peasant levels' (Passin 1965: 57).

Further reading

Allen, G. C. (2013), *A Short Economic History of Modern Japan*, London: Allen and Unwin. Still useful, giving an accessible account of the economic history from the Meiji Restoration to the late 1930s.

Fukao, K. and Saito, O. (2013), 'Japan's Alternating Phases of Growth and Future Outlook', in D. S. Prasada Rao and B. van Ark (eds.), *World Economic Performance: Past, Present and Future*, Cheltenham: Edward Elgar, 136–61. This takes another look at Japan's modern economic growth from a twenty-first century, post-industrial vantage point.

Hayami, A., Saito, O. and Toby, R. P. (eds.) (1999), *Emergence of Economic Society in Japan 1600–1859*, Oxford University Press. Provides scholarly surveys of issues and evidence in the economic history of the early modern period.

Nakamura, T. (1994), *Lectures on Modern Japanese Economic History: 1926–1994*, Tokyo: LTCB International Library Foundation. A chronological overview, placing economic history topics in political, military and international contexts of the day.

Nakamura, T. and Odaka, K. (eds.) (2003), *Economic History of Japan 1914–1955: a Dual Structure*, Oxford University Press. A collection of essays by leading Japanese scholars covers the interwar and postwar reconstruction periods, with special reference to an emerging dual structure of the industrializing economy.

Saito, O. (2014), 'Was Modern Japan a Developmental State?', in K. Otsuka and T. Shiraishi (eds.), *State Building and Development*, Abingdon, England: Routledge, 23–45. Gives a critical reexamination of the role of the state in Japan's economic development, 1859–1938.

Tolliday, S. (ed.) (2001), *The Economic Development of Modern Japan, 1868–1945: From the Meiji Restoration to the Second World War*, 2 vols., Cheltenham: Edward Elgar. A four-volume reprint collection of articles and essays by both Japanese and non-Japanese scholars on various issues covering the entire period of Japan's economic transformation from the Meiji Restoration to the post-Second World War bubble economy. Volume 1 of the first includes some seminal papers on the pre-1868 period.

References

Allen, R. C. (2011), *Global Economic History: a Very Short Introduction*, Oxford University Press.

Bassino, J. P., Broadberry, S., Fukao, K., Gupta, B. and Takashima, M. (2011), 'Japan and the Great Divergence, 730–1870', London School of Economics Working Paper.

Bassino, J.-P., Broadberry, S., Fukao, K., Gupta, B. and Takashima, M. (2015), 'Japan and the Great Divergence, 725–1874', Centre for Economic Policy Research Discussion Paper Series No. 10569, www.cepr.org/active/publications/discussion_papers/dp.php?dpno=10569.

Bolt, J. and van Zanden, J. L. (2014), 'The Maddison Project: Collaborative Research on Historical National Accounts', *Economic History Review* 67, 627–51.

Cabinet Office of the Japanese Government (2011), *Annual Reports on National Accounts 2009*, Tokyo: Ministry of Finance Printing Bureau.

(2012), *Annual Reports on National Accounts 2010*, Tokyo: Ministry of Finance Printing Bureau.

Dore, R. P. (1965), *Education in Tokugawa Japan*, London: Athlone Press.

Farris, W. W. (2006), *Japan's Medieval Population: Famine, Fertility, and Warfare in a Transformative Age*, University of Hawaii Press.

Fukao, K., Bassino, J.-P., Makino, T., Paprzycki, R., Settsu, T., Takashima, M. and Tokui, J. (2015), *Regional Inequality and Industrial Structure in Japan: 1874–2008*, Tokyo: Maruzen.

Hayami, A. (2004), 'Introduction: the Emergence of Economic Society', in A. Hayami, O. Saito and R. P. Toby (eds.), *Emergence of Economic Society in Japan 1600–1859*, Oxford University Press, pp. 1–36.

(2009), *Population, Family and Society in Pre-modern Japan*, Folkestone, UK: Global Oriental.

Johnson, C. (1982), *MITI and the Japanese Miracle: the Growth of Industrial Policy, 1925–1975*, Stanford University Press.

Komiya, R., Okuno, M. and Suzumura, K. (eds.) (1988), *Industrial Policy of Japan*, New York: Academic Press.

Lucassen, L., Saito, O. and Shimada, R. (2014), 'Cross-cultural Migration in Japan in a Comparative Perspective', in Jan Lucassen and Leo Lucassen (eds.), *Globalising Migration History: the Eurasian Experience (16th–21st Centuries)*, Leiden: Brill, 362–409.

Maddison, A. (2001), *The World Economy: a Millennial Perspective*, Paris: OECD.

(2006), *The World Economy: Historical Statistics* (Paris: OECD).

McNeill, William H. (1979), *Plagues and Peoples*, Harmondsworth: Penguin Books.

Miyamoto, M. (2004), 'Quantitative Aspects of Tokugawa Economy', in A. Hayami, O. Saito and R. P. Toby (eds.), *Emergence of Economic Society in Japan 1600–1859*, Oxford University Press, 68–82.

Nishikawa, S. (1987), 'The Economy of Chōshū on the Eve of Industrialization', *Economic Studies Quarterly* 38, 323–37.

Passin, H. (1965), *Society and Education in Japan*, New York: Teachers College Press.

Saito, O. (1983), 'Population and the Peasant Family Economy in Proto-industrial Japan', *Journal of Family History* 8, 30–54.

(2005a), 'Pre-modern Economic Growth Revisited: Japan and the West', Working Paper of the Global Economic History Network 16/05.

(2005b), 'Wages, Inequality, and Pre-industrial Growth in Japan, 1727–1894', in R. C. Allen, T. Bengtsson and M. Dribe (eds.), *Living Standards in the Past: New Perspectives on Well-being in Asia and Europe*, Oxford University Press, 77–97.

(2009), 'Land, Labour and Market Forces in Tokugawa Japan', *Continuity and Change* 24, 169–96.

(2010), 'An Industrious Revolution in an East Asian Market Economy? Tokugawa Japan and Implications for the Great Divergence', *Australian Economic History Review* 50, 240–61.

(2015a), 'Climate, Famine, and Population in Japanese History: a Long-term Perspective', in B. L. Baten and P. C. Brown (eds.), *Environment and Society in the Japanese Islands: from Prehistory to the Present*, Oregon State University Press, 213–29.

(2015b), 'Growth and Inequality in the Great and Little Divergence Debate: a Japanese Perspective', *Economic History Review* 68 (2), 399–419.

Saito, O. and Settsu, T. (2006), 'Money, Credit and Smithian Growth in Tokugawa Japan', Hitotsubashi University Hi-Stat Discussion Paper Series No. 139, http://hdl.handle.net/10086/13705.

Saito, O. and Takashima, M. (2014), 'Estimating the Shares of Secondary- and Tertiary-Sector Output in the Age of Proto-industrialisation: the Case of Japan, 1600–1874', Conference Paper 'Accounting for the Great Divergence', Venice.

(2015a), 'Population, Urbanisation and Farm Output in Early Modern Japan, 1600–1874: a Review of Data and Benchmark Estimates', Hitotsubashi University RCESR Discussion Paper Series No. DP15-3, http://hdl.handle.net/10086/27295.

(2015b), 'Estimating the Shares of Secondary- and Tertiary-sector Output in the Age of Early Modern Growth: the Case of Japan, 1600–1874', Hitotsubashi University RCESR Discussion Paper Series No. DP15-4, http://hdl.handle.net/10086/27294.

Shimbo, H. and Hasegawa, A. (2004), 'The Dynamics of Market Economy and Production', in A. Hayami, O. Saito and R. P. Toby (eds.), *Emergence of Economic Society in Japan 1600–1859*, Oxford University Press, 159–91.

Smith, T. C. (1958), 'The Land Tax in the Tokugawa Period', *Journal of Asian Studies* 18 (1), 3–19.

(1959), *The Agrarian Origins of Modern Japan*, Stanford University Press.

(1969), 'Farm Family By-employments in Preindustrial Japan', *Journal of Economic History* 29 (4), 687–715.

(1973), 'Pre-modern Economic Growth: Japan and the West', *Past and Present* 60 (1), 127–60.

Totman, C. (1993), *Early Modern Japan*, University of California Press.

van Zanden, J. L. (2009), *The Long Road to the Industrial Revolution: the European Economy in a Global Perspective, 1000–1800*, Leiden: Brill.

H5.1 Japanese industry during the Second World War

Tetsuji Okazaki

The period during the Second World War was distinctive in the economic history of modern Japan, in the sense that planning and control by the government substituted for a market mechanism in a substantial part of the economy in this period. Under this regime, the government mobilized huge resource for the war, and the Japanese economy experienced dramatic changes in resource allocation both between industries and within each industry. On the one hand it resulted in a sharp decline in people's living standards, but on the other hand it enabled Japan to increase munitions production rapidly, including aircraft production, which had been at an infant stage before the war.

The extent of the wartime mobilization of resources is clearly observed in the composition of real gross national product (GNP) (Figure H5.1). The outbreak of full-scale war with China in 1937 had a substantial impact on the Japanese economy. Government expenditures, including military expenses, sharply increased, and private capital formation simultaneously increased. This increase of private investment reflected a policy of expanding the productive capacity of munitions and related industries. These two components – government expenditures and private capital formation – continued to absorb an increasing fraction of GNP. In contrast, private consumption and exports continued to decline.

The change in composition of GNP corresponds to the change in the industrial structure. Production of iron, steel, machinery and coal continued to increase until the final stage of the war. It is especially notable that the rate of increase in the production of machinery, including aircraft and ships, accelerated in 1937. Meanwhile, the production of textiles declined sharply from 1938. This reflects the fact that textiles were mainly produced for domestic consumption and export.

From the early stages of the war, the Japanese government substantially intervened in the economy through a system of planning and control, and then it expanded and strengthened the intervention as the war progressed. Given the general price controls imposed in 1938, a number of commodities – including rice, coal, raw cotton, iron ore and steel – were distributed according to the Material Mobilization Plan (*Busshi Doin Keikaku*), which was drawn up by the government, and more specifically by the Cabinet Planning Board (*Kikakuin*) or the Ministry of Munitions (*Gunjusho*) after November 1943. International trade, allocations of funds and the labour market were all government controlled. In order to implement these economic controls, the government often used trade associations, except for the munitions industries that were directly administered by the Army and Navy. From 1941 those associations, which came to be called 'control associations' (*toseikai*), were given legal authority to supervise and instruct the firms under their control (Okazaki and Okuno-Fujiwara 1999).

By this system of planning and control, as we have already seen, resource allocation between industries changed substantially, which in turn had a substantial impact on each industry. Let me focus on the coal and aircraft industries to illustrate how the system worked. Because coal was an important and domestically available energy source, the coal industry was requested to increase its wartime production. Indeed, according to the

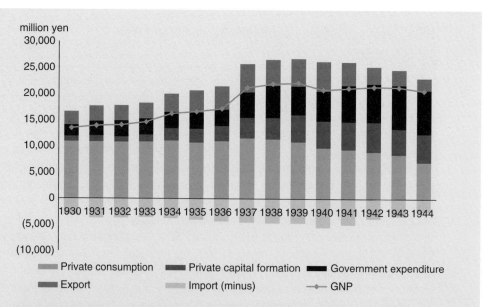

Figure H5.1 Change in the composition of national expenditure in Japan during the Second World War
Source: Economic Planning Agency, *Kokumin Shotoku Hakusho (Whitepaper on National Income)*, 1963 issue, Tokyo: Printing Bureau of Ministry of Finance, 1965, 178–79.

Production Capacity Expansion Plan (*Seisanryoku Kakuju Keikaku*) of January 1939, coal production was expected to increase 1.6 times from 1938 to 1941.

In contrast, the allocation of intermediate goods and capital goods, such as steel and explosives, was not augmented to the same extent, due to shortages of those goods. In this situation, the government and the Coal Control Association (*Sekitan Toseikai*) made great efforts to mobilize the labour force into the coal industry, including workers from Korea. Simultaneously, they concentrated resources on relatively efficient coal mines, whereas inefficient mines were closed and their labour force was moved to relatively efficient mines. This policy of resource reallocation, from inefficient mines to efficient ones, contributed to raising the average productivity of the entire coal industry, thereby mitigating the negative impact of the degenerating economic environment (Okazaki 2014).

The aircraft industry was the industry that expanded most sharply during the war. Indeed, the number of airframes produced increased 5.5 times from 1941 to 1944. As mentioned above, the Army and Navy used their powers to directly administer this industry in order to concentrate resources. The factor critical to aircraft production was the supply of parts, because aircraft require numerous parts. Hence, major aircraft producers including Mitsubishi Heavy Industries Co. and Nakajima Aircraft Co. organized a number of parts suppliers. The rapid expansion of aircraft production was achieved through this extensive outsourcing; however, US strategic bombing eventually destroyed these networks and seriously damaged the industry (Okazaki 2011).

References

Okazaki, T. (2011), 'Supplier Networks and Aircraft Production in Wartime Japan', *Economic History Review* 67 (3): 973–94.

(2014), 'Productivity Change and Mine Dynamics: the Coal Industry in Japan during World War II', *Jahrbuch für Wirtschaftsgeschichte* 55 (2), 31–48.

Okazaki, T. and Okuno-Fujiwara, M. (eds.) (1999), *The Japanese Economic System and its Historical Origins*, Oxford University Press.

6 China

Debin Ma

In the two millennia dynastic history of China, the five centuries of 1500–2000 encompass four political regimes, the Ming (1368–1644), Qing (1644–1911), Republican (1911–49) and Communism since 1949. The five centuries saw regime changes and dramatic ideological shifts and reversals (especially following the collapse of Qing in 1911, the last imperial dynasty) as well as the resilience of historical and political legacy.

This chapter provides a brief account of major economic changes in the last five centuries and offers some major quantitative indicators on long-term welfare. The emphasis of the narrative is on the importance of ideological and institutional changes to China's long-term economic trajectory.

Introduction

The beginning century of our study marked the final century of Ming's imperial dynastic rule. It was a century that also saw the maturing of a highly centralized, unitary political regime governed by an absolutist emperor at the top of the power pyramid, aided by a formal bureaucracy recruited through a highly structured national Civil Service Examination rooted in Confucius classics. But whatever impersonality and neutrality remained of China's imperial regime, they were more than often compromised by the emperor's personal rule, and his personal entourage of eunuchs, consort and other inner court staffs (Ma 2012). Beyond the borders of China, Ming and Qing reigned supreme in East and Southeast Asia throughout the so-called tributary states trade system, where neighbouring small states remained in the status of near protectorate under which limited trade was conducted. China remained more or less isolated politically beyond East Asia until aggressive Western imperialism reached its shore by the mid-nineteenth century.

The claim that China was the world's leading economy in the fifteenth to eighteenth centuries was somewhat misleading based on a conflation of aggregate for the per capita terms. Maddison (2007) was credited with the claim of China being the world's leading economy; based largely on guesstimates, he puts China's annual income at about 500 or 600 international dollars (in 1990 prices), at about 80 per cent (in 1500) and 35 per cent (in 1700) of the world's leading but much smaller economies of the time, Britain and the Netherlands. But Maddison was right in trumpeting the aggregate size of the Chinese economy. Entering into Qing, China saw a doubling of territory and a tripling of population between the fifteenth and eighteenth centuries. No single political entity at the time achieved such size in both geography and population under such stability and durability unified under a single political regime.

Chinese trade with neighbouring Asian states and further beyond remained limited but could be critically important. With the export of silks and tea, China fuelled the fetish of Chinosoirées in western Europe, which formed the basis for import substitution within western Europe. On the other side of the trade equation, inflow of Latin American silver ingots and coins greased the engine of Chinese commerce and supported the monetization of public finance from the sixteenth century. Introduction of new world crops such as maize and potatoes sustained the tripling of population in Qing. But it will be a far cry to claim that any of this gave the Chinese economy the leading position that it may have held in the early centuries of the second millennium as under Song (960–1279). Commercial, financial, political, technological and scientific revolutions that engulfed a fragmented, contentious Europe have largely eclipsed the states of Ming and Qing, only to haunt them by the mid-nineteenth century.

Recent new attempts at constructing new long-term gross domestic product (GDP) series, most notably by Stephen Broadberry, Hanhui Guang and David Li, seem to confirm largely the earlier Maddison estimate (Bolt and van Zanden 2014). We can get a better glimpse of a more comprehensive profile of the evolution of Chinese living standards and human capital in the nineteenth and twentieth centuries based on integrated estimates of real-wage and anthropometric evidences. These confirm a general decline in living standards and human capital after the mid-nineteenth century followed by a recovery only at the turn of the century (Figure 6.1; on the wage evidence, see Allen et al. 2011). Chinese heights fell back relative to Taiwan during the late nineteenth century, for example. Japanese stature was still much lower. The Japanese reached the Chinese height level only during the 1980s although, as argued by Baten et al. (2010), the level of Japanese heights cannot be directly compared to the Chinese as a welfare indicator.[1]

The real wage data also reveal that Chinese living standards were probably closer to the less developed parts of Europe but lower than north-western Europe in the eighteenth and nineteenth centuries. These reviews confirm that the divergence in living standards and per capita incomes between Europe and China already existed before the industrial revolution and only widened from the nineteenth century onwards. However, in contrast to the findings based on real wages and heights, the basic numeracy index – a measure of tendencies to report a rounded rather than an

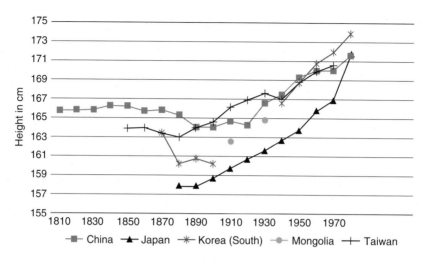

Figure 6.1 Height in East Asian countries (male)
Source: based on Baten and Blum (2014).

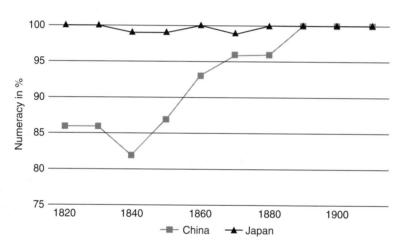

Figure 6.2 Basic numeracy in China and Japan
Source: based on Baten *et al.* (2010).

exact age – reveals a relatively high level of Chinese human capital, closer to that of north-western Europe for the eighteenth and nineteenth centuries, than to countries with a comparable level of living standards, such as India or Turkey (Figure 6.2). In comparison to the high level of Japanese numeracy, Chinese numeracy displayed a slightly lower level during the nineteenth century.[2] In addition, the cohort born during the 1840s, who experienced the Taiping civil war and famine period when they were teenagers and young adults, had lower numerical skills than the generations before and after.

The nineteenth century: an ominous beginning

The beginning of the nineteenth century may have seen the turn of the tide that had once so favoured the fortune of Qing.[3] Population growth sustained by rising agricultural land productivity and the introduction of new crops may have finally stretched the limits of the resource constraint. Beginning with the White Lotus (1796–1804), a series of domestic rebellions, culminating with the vast Taiping uprising (1851–64), both reflected and contributed to the erosion of the Qing regime. Externally, following the collapse of the East India monopoly in 1833, British imperialism driven by private commercial interest intensified on the Chinese trade. The rise of triangular trade, the export of Indian opium to China, reversed China's long-standing trade surplus, draining silver species out of China. This occurred in the background and during the sixteenth and seventeenth centuries fiscal reform under mid-Ming led to the silverization of fiscal revenue and increasing penetration of silver used as a medium of exchange in the next two and three centuries. The increasing scarcity of silver species, as reflected in the rising copper cash–silver ratio, was wreaking havoc on people's livelihoods and governmental tax collection, as well as the morale of the military (Lin 2006). Prompted by an urge to act but armed with little knowledge of the potency of the newly rising Western imperialism, Qing's military confrontation with England in the now famous Opium War of 1842 turned out to be a humiliating defeat and also marked the beginning of the world's largest and most remote empire now in the orbit of Western imperialism. British arms forced the Qing to accept the Treaty of Nanking (1842), which ceded Hong Kong to the British, imposed a regime of virtual free trade, and initiated the 'treaty port' system by opening five Chinese ports to British merchants. This agreement, which set the tone of China's international economic relations during the century prior to the Pacific War, subsequently expanded to include dozens of treaty ports where foreign residents were protected by extraterritoriality at the expense of Chinese sovereignty. The challenge of Western imperialism represented an external threat drastically different from China's traditional nemesis from her northern frontier and hence marked a watershed in Chinese history. The challenge was economic, political, institutional and ideological.

Political accommodation and institutional adjustment to 1895

The new era marked by China's forced opening under Western imperialism started off disastrously for the Qing, who were brought to the brink of collapse by the devastating Taiping Rebellion (1850–62). The Qing under the so-called Tongzhi Restoration (1861–75) also engineered a remarkable economic recovery through the revitalization of traditional institutions: the reinstatement of

Confucian orthodox, the restoration of the National Civil-Service Examination (largely interrupted during the Taiping Rebellion), and the initial exemption of land taxes to lure cultivators back to war-torn agricultural regions.

Neither did the Qing remain entirely passive to Western incursions. As a natural extension to the Tongzhi Restoration, powerful regional bureaucrats such as Li Hongzhang and Zhang Zhidong sponsored the Self-Strengthening Movement (1860–94), a programme that aimed to expand Chinese military strength by developing a small number of Western-style, capital-intensive enterprises financed by the state and directed by prestigious officials who possessed the highest credentials awarded under the Confucian academic system. Although these enterprises, which included arsenals, factories and shipyards, were fraught with inefficiency and corruption, they did manage to record modest achievements. Nonetheless, the overall ideological orientation during this period remained conservative. In contrast to the concurrent Meiji reform in Japan, there was no introduction of any reforms that touched the fundamentals of the traditional regime: no introduction of modern constitution or commercial law; no reform in the currency system; modern banks or modern infrastructures such as railroads were expressly prohibited; and steamships were limited to major river ways such as the Yangzi river.

The direct impact of the treaty port system, where Chinese trade tariff was restricted to a modest 3 or 5 per cent, was the expansion of China's international trade. China's Maritime Customs data show real imports more than doubling in the two and a half decades prior to 1895, and exports increasing by half of this. Trade statistics suggest slower growth of real trade in the range of 2–3 per cent per annum after 1895. Despite its modest scale, trade gradually pulled major domestic commodity markets into close alignment with exchange throughout the Pacific Basin.

The treaty system accelerated the arrival of new technologies, initially to the treaty ports themselves, which in both the nineteenth and twentieth century versions of global entry became staging points for the spread of technologies into the domestic economy. However, it was in this area where we see industrialization lagging far behind the opportunities opened up by the inflow of trade and technology during this era. Attempts by Chinese and European entrepreneurs to take advantage of new opportunities linked to new technologies and new trade arrangements reveal the presence of powerful obstacles to innovation within China's late Qing economy. These barriers were, among others, low investment activity of the government on the one hand, which limited the expansion of key public infrastructure such as modern railroads and inland steam shipping. The second barrier is the resistance of existing vested interests in the form of traditional mercantile and handicraft guilds, who, in connection with local government, defended their traditional monopolistic privilege and obstructed introduction of new technologies and new business arrangements in the processing of agricultural commodities like soybeans and silk larvae. (For details on these obstacles, see section 4.2 in Brandt *et al.* 2014.)

The onset of China's Industrial Revolution 1895–1949

China's defeat in the Sino-Japanese War of 1894–95 by a nation long regarded as a student rather than an equal marked the end of the Self-Strengthening Movement, which events revealed to be feeble and ineffective. This ignominious military failure inflicted a profound mental shock on Chinese elites and the public at large. The immediate economic impact followed the 1896 signing of the Treaty of Shimonoseki, which granted foreigners the right to establish factories in the treaty ports. Eliminating the prohibition against foreign factories in the treaty ports sparked a rapid expansion of foreign direct investment. This new arrangement indirectly legitimized Chinese modern enterprises. Despite some setbacks from the repression of the Hundred Days' reform centred in the southern province of Hunan in 1898, followed by the subsequent debacle surrounding the Boxer Rebellion in 1900, the Qing constitutional movement of 1903–11 was far more comprehensive and ambitious. It aimed at steering China towards a constitutional monarchy by drafting a formal modern Constitution with national, provincial and local level parliaments. Military modernization was high on the reform agenda. Administrative reforms sought to modernize public finance and adopt a national budget. The reform initiative gave birth to new Ministries of Education, Trade and Agriculture and encouraged the founding of local chambers of commerce. There were policy initiatives aimed at currency reform, efforts to establish modern banks and to expand railroads and other public infrastructure (Tables 6.1 and 6.2).

Beginning at the very end of the nineteenth century, activity in mining and manufacturing accelerated sharply from its small initial base. Overall industrial output showed double-digit real annual growth during 1912–36, a phenomenal result for that period, especially in view of China's turbulent political scene and the impact of the Great Depression. Factory production, initially focused on textiles,

Table 6.1 1934–36 East Asian per capita GDP in 1934–36 US dollars and relative to the US

	US	Japan	Taiwan	Korea	China
Per capita GDP based on exchange rate conversion	574.7	77.1	49.2	29.1	20.1
	100%	13.4%	8.6%	5.1%	3.5%
Per capita GDP based on purchasing power parity conversion	574.7	180.8	129.6	70.9	63.6
	100%	31.5%	22.6%	12.3%	11.1%

Source: adapted from Fukao *et al.* (2007), Table 8.

Table 6.2 GDP structure in East Asian countries (%)

		China	Japan	Taiwan	Korea
1914–18	Agriculture	71	29	48	66
	Industry	8	20	29	7
	Services	21	51	23	24
1931–36	Agriculture	65	19	44	53
	Industry	10	28	27	13
	Services	25	53	29	34
Annual per capita net domestic product (NDP) growth rate between 1914–18 and 1931–36		0.53	1.4	1.5	1.1

Source: adapted from Ma (2008), and sources cited therein.

food processing and other consumer products, concentrated in two regions: the lower Yangzi area, where both foreign and Chinese entrepreneurs pursued factory expansion in and around Shanghai, and China's north-east or Manchurian region, where Japanese initiatives predominated (see Map 6.1). By 1935, Chinese factories, including some owned by British or Japanese firms, produced 8 per cent of the world's cotton yarn (more than Germany, France or Italy) and 2.8 per cent of global cotton piece goods production. Despite the importance of foreign investment in Shanghai and especially in Manchuria, Chinese-owned companies produced 73 per cent of China's 1933 factory output growing production of light consumer and industrial goods. This combined with the accumulation of experience in operating and repairing modern machinery, which generated backward linkages that spurred new private initiatives in machinery, chemicals, cement, mining, electricity and metallurgy. Official efforts (including semi-official Japanese activity in Manchuria) also promoted the growth of mining, metallurgy and arms manufacture (Rawski 1989: ch. 2).

China's economic prospects acted as a magnet for trade and investment during the pre-war decades. China's foreign trade rose to a peak of more than 2 per cent of global trade flows in the late 1920s, a level that was not regained until the 1990s (on China's presence on world exhibitions, see Highlight Chapter 6.1). Between 1902 and 1931, inflows of foreign direct investment grew at annual rates of 8.3 per cent, 5 per cent and 4.3 per cent for Shanghai, Manchuria and the rest of China. By 1938, China's stock of inward foreign investment amounted to US$2.6 billion – more than any other underdeveloped region except for the Indian subcontinent and Argentina. Although estimates of pre-war capital flows often blur the distinction between direct and portfolio holdings, it is evident

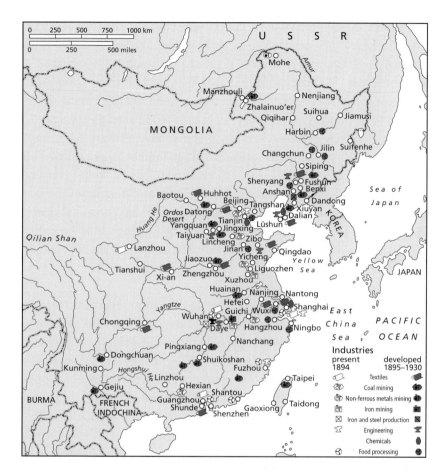

Map 6.1 Regional economic specialization in China 1895–1949
Source: see map 1.1.

that China played a substantial role in global capital flows. The 1938 figure of US$2.6 billion for China's stock of foreign investments amounts to 8.4 per cent of worldwide stocks of outward foreign investment and 17.5 per cent of outward foreign direct investment in that year. By contrast, China's 2001 share of worldwide inward foreign direct investment was only 2.1 per cent. Domestic investment also showed substantial growth. 'Modern-oriented' fixed investment (calculated from consumption of cement, steel and machinery) grew at an average annual rate of 8.1 per cent between 1903 and 1936, outpacing Japanese gross domestic fixed capital formation in mining, manufacturing, construction and facilitating industries, which advanced at an annual rate of 5 per cent. Despite the effects of the Great Depression and political tumult, economy-wide gross fixed investment exceeded 10 per cent of aggregate output during 1931–36 (Brandt *et al.* 2014).

Transport development contributed substantially to economic expansion. China's railway track length grew from 364 kilometers (km) in 1894 to over 21,000 km by 1937, and newly constructed north–south lines slashed economic distances across a landscape dominated by rivers flowing from west to east. Completion of railway and telegraph connections linking Peking (now Beijing) and the central China river port of Wuhan in 1906 reduced the time needed to ship commodities between these cities. In a remarkable triumph of a free banking version of the silver standard, privately held Chinese banks, often cooperating with foreign financial institutions and traditional money shops, transformed the financial face of China by persuading households and businesses to transact with paper banknotes that were convertible into silver on demand. This monetary transformation reduced transaction costs. The expansion of branch networks allowed major domestic banks to attract deposits from all regions and recycle them to the areas of greatest demand, contributing to the emergence of an embryonic national market for funds.

These forces resulted in increased per capita output and structural changes of the sort associated with Simon Kuznets' concept of modern economic growth in two major regions: the Lower Yangzi, where private domestic and foreign investment in and around Shanghai served as the key driver (Ma 2008) and the north-east (Manchuria), where Japanese investment and eventual takeover provided key momentum. All in all, these developments in industry, transport and finance precipitated an episode of modern economic growth at the national level during the early decades of the twentieth century.

Beginning in 1929, China's economy faced a succession of shocks arising from the Great Depression and falling export demand, the severance of Manchuria in 1932 by the Japanese, rapidly rising silver prices triggered by Britain's decision to go off gold and the United States Silver Purchase Act of 1934. Considerable debate persists over how well the Chinese economy weathered the storm and the severity of the combined impact of these events on aggregate economic activity. There is little controversy about what followed. Twelve years of war, with large-scale civil strife following the defeat of Japan's invading armies, battered China's economy and rolled back much of the progress achieved during the preceding decades. Roaring inflation crippled China's financial sector and corruption hobbled the public sector and embittered the populace.

People's Republic of China in 1950–2000

The broad contours of economic change following the establishment in 1949 of the People's Republic of China (PRC) are well understood.[4] The new Communist government quickly implemented an orthodox mix of fiscal and monetary policies to restore fiscal balance and quell hyperinflation, steps that helped facilitate recovery from damage inflicted by twelve years of war and civil strife. Following violent campaigns that expropriated the assets of urban and rural elites, the PRC moved to implement socialist planning. The new regime swept away the remnants of several Qing-era institutional constraints on growth, completing a process that had begun prior to the Second World War. The new government vastly expanded state control over resources, rapidly eliminating the long-standing shortage of fiscal revenue that had prevented earlier governments from financing aggressive development initiatives.

China's plan system, introduced with Soviet advice during the early 1950s, bore strong resemblances to its Soviet counterpart. But starting in 1958, China distanced itself both from Moscow's political leadership and from Soviet economic strategy, as Mao Zedong embarked on a daring campaign to accelerate the pace of development by amalgamating rural households into large-scale collective units, or People's Communes, and by promoting rural industrialization. The communes proved to be a costly failure: poor incentives, false reports of rising crop output, excessive grain procurement and a massive reallocation of labour from agriculture to industry inflicted an immense famine on China's peasantry that cost tens of millions of lives in the so-called Great Leap Famine of 1959–61. Efforts to revive forward momentum in the early 1960s met with some success, but the economy suffered further setbacks in the mid-1960s when a new political campaign known as the Cultural Revolution sparked a new reversal in economic policies and incentive mechanisms.

Mixed economic outcomes characterize China's quarter-century of socialist planning under Mao and his colleagues. The plan era brought notable expansion of industrial and technological capabilities, as well as major improvements in literacy, school attendance, maternal and infant survival rates, public health and life expectancy. Real annual GDP growth of roughly 6 per cent (aggregate) and 4 per cent in per capita terms surpassed gains in India, Pakistan, Indonesia, Egypt, Brazil and other large low-income nations, often by large margins. These successes were accompanied by shortcomings and setbacks, which occurred in part because the PRC government, while eliminating institutional barriers inherited from the past, used its unprecedented administrative capacity to implement a succession of anti-economic policies, including an assault on individual and firm-level incentives, persecution of intellectuals and educators, forced collectivization of farming and a destructive regimen of local self-reliance. In addition, unsuitable technological innovations diffused in both agriculture and industry, and cross-border flows of trade, investment, people and information were severely constricted. A substantial gap emerged between the living standards of urban and rural households. Overall, food supply measured as a percentage of the total population scarcely increased between 1958 and 1978 (Brandt *et al.* 2014).

The death of Mao Zedong (1893–1976) was widely recognized as the end of an era for both the PRC and for China's economy. China's reform initiatives of the late 1970s focused on four areas: rural liberalization, expansion of foreign trade and investment, policies aimed at 'enlivening' state-owned enterprises and fiscal decentralization. Despite obvious limitations, we can see in retrospect that China's initial reforms represent a watershed in Chinese economic history: for the first time, China's economy avoided most of the Qing-era institutional constraints as well as the most restrictive of the fresh obstacles imposed by the PRC. The greatest success occurred in the rural economy, where the explosive response to implementation of the household responsibility system banished the spectre of food shortages and sparked the largest episode of poverty alleviation in human history. Rural economic revival, however, went far beyond an intensification of effort in response to the restoration of individual incentives. The reform unleashed a torrent of entrepreneurship in rural areas and later in the cities. Rapid expansion of international trade and investment eliminated long-standing shortages of foreign exchange, began to tap the wealth and expertise of overseas Chinese and multinational corporations and introduced a long-absent element of economic rationality into investment policies by channelling resources into labour-intensive export production that matched China's resource endowment. Efforts to upgrade state enterprises were far less successful, and losses mounted despite massive direct and indirect subsidies. China's economy throughout much of the 1980s was a halfway house combining elements of old and new. Although the reform process spawned episodes of social unrest – the 1989 Tian'anmen protests in part reflected public anger over inflation and corruption – overall, the first fifteen years of reform produced no substantial group of losers – a rare outcome in episodes of substantial socio-economic change (Naughton 2007, Xu 2011).

Despite fifteen years of GDP growth averaging 8 per cent per annum, China was at a critical crossroads during the early 1990s. Growth had become highly cyclical, with successive periods of liberalization and reform accompanied by high growth but also higher rates of inflation. In the mid-1990s, China's policymakers attacked these difficulties with a remarkable sequence of policy changes. These included a sweeping overhaul of the fiscal system, a reorganization of the financial system, a comprehensive restructuring of the enterprise sector – including the furloughing and eventual dismissal of over 50 million redundant employees, most in the state sector – substantial privatization of both state and collective enterprises, along with further reforms – including virtual elimination of planned allocation of materials – and broad embrace of globalization that reduced tariffs and other trade barriers in advance of its 2001 entry into the World Trade Organization. These reform efforts were far more systematic and aggressive than during the early years of reform. They contributed to China's enormous growth spurt from the 1990s, setting China on course to first surpass the Japanese economy and to possibly become the world's largest economy in due course.

The Chinese economic miracle has stimulated efforts to define a 'Chinese model' of growth or to establish a 'Beijing consensus' of development-enhancing policies. However, China's recent economic success should also be seen by the deep historical roots of China's current institutional structure and the central role of China's unusual legacy of human capital. While historic accumulation of resources and capabilities deserves recognition as an important contributor to China's recent growth, historical legacy may well become a burden to China's economic future as it had impeded China's response to challenges in the past. Despite three decades of near double-digit economic growth and wrenching social transformations, the Chinese political system remains highly centralized, authoritarian, lacking in transparency, rule of law but rife with corruption, with restrictions of public opinion and freedom of information or expression. How the Chinese economy would fare under this political regime in the face of rising expectations and increasing globalization remains to be seen.

differences of Qing vs PRC

1896 - Treaty of shimonoteki; granted foreigner right to establish factories	focused on the revival of rural economy - food
	moving away from Qing's institutional constraints on growth
Constitunal monarchy	
factory production	

similarities Qing & PRC
both attracted FDIS
due to positive economic
prospects on China.
when?

Conclusion

The five hundred years of Chinese economic history are marked by both continuity and radical departures, accompanied by long periods of inertia and stagnation as well as dramatic historical breakthroughs and fundamental transformations. While it is difficult to describe five hundred years in any simplistic categories or terminologies, two features stand out. First, change – or lack therefore – in ideology and political regime are critical to the long periods of economic change and episodes of historical transformation. Second, the rise of mid-nineteenth century Western imperialism proved to be a watershed that shaped and reshaped the Chinese search for a new response and ultimately a new identity in the name of modernization in the centuries to follow. Third, while external influence or shock (such as the Western imperial challenges from the mid-nineteenth century) were critical, given both the immense size of China and the highly authoritarian and centralized nature of the traditional Chinese polity, collective political and institutional responses were often staggered and required significant mobilization of indigenous political capital. A better reading of the Chinese past helps us better understand the enormity of the Chinese transformations in the road ahead, even though China's future may still defy any easy prediction.

Notes

1. The Japanese diet of the nineteenth and early twentieth century is characterized by an absence of animal protein, see Baten *et al.* (2010). The Japanese during this period had lower height levels than most other populations at any level of per capita income.
2. For more details on Japanese living standards, see Chapter 5 on Japan by Osamu Saito in this volume.
3. The narrative from here draws heavily from Brandt *et al.* 2014.
4. For the differential trajectory of post-Second World War Japan, see Chapter 5 in this volume.

Further reading

Brandt, L., Ma, D. and Rawski, T. G. (2014), 'From Divergence to Convergence: Re-evaluating the History Behind China's Economic Boom', *Journal of Economic Literature* 52 (1), 45–123. An extended survey article of Chinese economic history in the last three hundred years with a very comprehensive bibliography.

Brandt, L. and Rawski, T. G. (eds.) (2008), *China's Great Economic Transformation*, Cambridge University Press. A fairly comprehensive collection of important chapters summarizing China's economic transformation during the past three decades.

Ma, D. (2012), 'Political Institution and Long-run Economic Trajectory: Some Lessons from Two Millennia of Chinese Civilization', in M. Aoki, T. Kuran and G. Roland (eds.), *Institutions and Comparative Economic Development*, Basingstoke: Palgrave Macmillan, 78–98. A relatively short but succinct overview of major political episodes in Chinese economic history from the perspective of institutional economics.

Maddison, A. (2007), *Chinese Economic Performance in the Long Run*. 2nd edn., rev. and updated, Paris: Development Centre of the Organisation for Economic Co-operation and Development. A good survey of the Chinese economy offering a quantitative historical profile of economic indicators.

Perkins, D. H. (1969), *Agricultural Development in China, 1368–1968*, Chicago: Aldine. A pioneering book on long-term economic history of China.

(ed.) (1975), *China's Modern Economy in Historical Perspective*, Stanford University Press. A good collection of some important articles on Chinese economic history.

Pomeranz, K. (2000), *The Great Divergence*, Princeton University Press. An important book that set off the so-called Great Divergence debate and offers a comprehensive survey of the Qing economy.

Rawski, T. G. (1989), *Economic Growth in Prewar China*, Berkeley: University of California Press. Remains one of the most comprehensive books on the Chinese economy in the first three decades of the twentieth century.

Rawski, T. G. and Li, L. M. (1992), *Chinese History in Economic Perspective*, Berkeley: University of California Press. A good collection of chapters on Chinese economic history.

References

Allen, R., Bassino, J.-P., Ma, D., Moll-Murata, C. and van Zanden, J. L. (2011), 'Wages, Prices, and Living Standards in China, Japan, and Europe, 1738–1925', *Economic History Review* 64 (S1), 8–38.

Baten, J. and Blum, M. (2014), 'Why are you Tall while Others are Short? Agricultural Production and other Proximate Determinants of Global Heights', *European Review of Economic History* 18, 144–65.

Baten, J., Ma, D., Morgan, S. and Wang, Q. (2010), 'Evolution of Living Standards and Human Capital in China in 18–20th Century', *Explorations in Economic History* 47 (3), 347–59.

Bolt, J., and van Zanden, J. L. (2014), 'The Maddison Project: Collaborative Research on Historical National Accounts', *Economic History Review* 67 (3), 627–51.

Fukao, K., Ma, D. and Yuan, T. (2007), 'Real GDP in pre-War East Asia: a 1934–36 Benchmark Purchasing Power Parity Comparison with the US', *Review of Income and Wealth* 53 (3), 503–37.

Lin, M. (2006), *China Upside Down: Currency, Society, and Ideologies, 1808–1856*. HUAC-Harvard University Press.

(2008), 'Economic Growth in the Lower Yangzi Region of China in 1911–1937: a Quantitative and Historical Perspective', *The Journal of Economic History* 68 (2), 385–92.

Naughton, B. (2007), *The Chinese Economy: Transitions and Growth*, Cambridge, MA: MIT Press.

Xu, C. (2011), 'The Fundamental Institutions of China's Reforms and Development', *The Journal of Economic Literature*, 49 (4).

H6.1 International expositions and East Asia's participation in the modern era
Ma Min

The idea of international expositions was born in the UK during the Victorian Period. In 1851 the UK hosted the unprecedented 'Great Exhibition of the Works of Industry of All Nations', which showcased its overwhelming power to the rest of the world. In the following over 160 years, more than 120 international expositions were hosted by different nations. Among them, the biggest one, participated by all nations, was called World Exposition, and usually held every five years.

After its emergence in Europe, the exhibition exerted great influence on East Asia with the trend of eastward spread of Western culture, while the responses from the East Asian countries varied from each other.

Japan gave the promptest response. In 1862 when the second World Exposition was held in London, the visiting delegation was invited to the opening ceremony, which was the first attendance by the Japanese. When it came to the 1867 Paris World Exposition, the Tokugawa Shogunate sent its representatives to participate and exhibit porcelain, lacquer and copper utensil and local craft works. Japan's first large-scale participation began at the 1873 Vienna World Exposition. During this exposition, the Japanese delegation achieved exceptional success with ninety-two medals. During the Meiji Period, Japan held five domestic industry exhibitions, each larger than the previous one and with more visitors.

In 1965, Japan won the bid for the Osaka World Exposition and became the first country in Asia to organize a World Exposition. The Osaka World Expo achieved unprecedented success and became one of the best World Expositions in history. It surpassed the previous ones both in terms of the number of visitors and the economic revenue, with 64 million visitors and US$150 million. Osaka World Exposition became a milestone in its history of development, technology and culture in contemporary Japan and gave direct boost to the dramatic rise of Japan's economy.

Chinese participation in the World Exposition began in the late Qing Dynasty, officially also with the 1873 Vienna Exhibition in Austria. Although initially less active than the Japanese, the Chinese government, together with businessmen, participated in more than twenty international expositions including the World Expo of 1876 Philadelphia, 1878 and 1900 Paris, 1885 New Orleans and 1903 Osaka. After the 1911 revolution overthrew the Qing Dynasty, participation in the World Expo had been highly valued, aiming at rejuvenating Chinese industry. Particularly, Chinese media reported some sensational news about the 1915 Panama–Pacific International Exposition in San Francisco, which raised unprecedented exposition enthusiasm. The newly founded government of the Republic of China sent an over forty-member delegation to participate in this Exposition. Their main attraction, the China Pavilion, imitated the architecture style of the Hall of Supreme Harmony and embodied distinctive national features. In that World Expo, China achieved great success with fifty-six medallions, sixty-seven Awards of Excellence, and 196 gold medals. However, after the 1933 Chicago World Expo, China took a different path.

Under the circumstance of its reform and opening up, China reappeared in the 1982 Knoxville World Expo. China showed unprecedented vigour and creativity in that Expo, where the China Pavilion mainly displayed arts and crafts. In addition, in order to cater to the theme 'energy', new energy technology was presented by displaying the delicate and convenient solar-powered dinnerware outside the China Pavilion, which drew most of visitors' attention. And the Great Wall bricks and Terracotta Warriors placed under one picture of splendid Great Wall were greatly hailed. During the following years, China had an increasingly important role in making the World Expo splendid. For example, in the 1992 Seville Expo, the China Pavilion integrated ancient culture presentation with modern technology to keep up with the pace of modern international exposition, being awarded 'Five-star Pavilion' for its innovative and rich content as well as unique design. Finally, China won the right to host the 2010 Shanghai Expo, which fulfilled Chinese people's centennial dream of World Expo. And to Chinese people's pride, Shanghai Expo received the most participating countries (242) and the most visitors (over 70 million), which made itself the most brilliant international exposition world-wide.

Other countries in East Asia and Southeast Asia also actively participated in the international expositions either by sending delegations or renting exhibition areas. For instance, in the 1900 Paris World Expo, there were also Korean and Siam (Thailand) Pavilions. The 1993 World Expo was held in Taejŏn, a South Korean Science City, attracting over 14 million visitors.

For more than 160 years, countries in Eastern Asia had switched their roles from observer to participant, from a supporting to a leading role, which enabled them to catch up with other countries. The secret lies in the unique way of Eastern Asia modernization and the common characteristics in Eastern Asia Confucianism Culture Community, which is quite a broad academic issue and beyond the range of this highlight chapter.

Trade and poverty 1820–1913: when the third world fell behind

Jeffrey Williamson

Before Hong Kong, Singapore, South Korea and Taiwan had completed their post-Second World War growth miracle, before China, India and the rest of Asia joined them with double-digit growth rates, and as Africa gained independence from their European colonial masters, there was a *world economic order* in place that had been two hundred years in the making.[1] In 1960, income per capita in Asia and Africa was less than 14 per cent of that of Western Europe. Thus, one characteristic of the 1960 *world economic order* was the wide gap in living standards between the rich industrial core and the poor pre-industrial periphery. The second characteristic of the 1960 *world economic order* was that the poor periphery exported primary products, while the rich core exported manufactures. Indeed, 85 per cent of the poor periphery's exports were either agricultural or mineral products. Commodity exports and poverty were closely correlated.

The 1960 gap between the West and the Rest lingers on even today. What accounts for it? Some economists stress institutions, some geography and some culture, but all agree that we must go back five centuries or more to find the sources of the gap. Let's start by identifying exactly when the great divergence between the West and the Rest emerged. In 1820, when the industrial revolution was just warming up in Europe, GDP per capita in the poor periphery was only half that of the west European leaders. So, whatever explanation one hopes to find for the appearance of the gap must search for it before the industrial revolution. And we see it as early as 1700, when the periphery per capita incomes were only 56 per cent of the core. However, the most notable fact is that the gap rose only very slowly over the centuries before 1820, but rose extremely fast over the century ending at the First World War.

Two things happened between 1820 and 1913. First, the gap between the rich industrial core in the West and the poor commodity exporters in the Rest widened dramatically as we have seen. Second, it was also the first global century, featuring a world trade boom, soaring international financial flows and mass migrations. The correlation between the world trade boom and accelerating divergence during the first global century is suggestive. A world trade boom had never happened before and it would not happen again until after the Second World War. The European economies went open, removing long-standing mercantilist policies and lowering tariffs. Their colonies did the same, and gunboats forced many others to follow suit. Much of the world integrated their currencies by going on the gold standard and other currency unions, lowering exchange risk. Led by new steam engine technologies, the world also underwent a pro-trade transport revolution. As the cost of trade fell dramatically, the ancient barriers of distance began to evaporate. The telegraph stimulated trade still more, lowering uncertainty about prices in distant markets. Most importantly, the industrial revolution in Europe raised GDP growth rates many times faster than what had been common over the previous two millennia, and the demand for everything soared, especially traded goods. To give world trade another nudge, *pax Britannica* brought peace.

The first world trade boom occurred at the same time as the acceleration in the great divergence, and correlations like this invite causal interpretations: did globalization contribute to the great divergence? Before we answer that question, some important issues must be laid to rest. First, Asia and the rest of the periphery did *not* suffer a fall in GDP per capita during the first global century. Furthermore, their GDP per capita growth rates actually rose from 1820 to 1913. However, the rates were much lower in Asia and the Rest than in the core. Second, no economist has ever found any evidence or argument that rejects the belief that all participants gain from trade: by exploiting specialization and comparative advantage, trade raises GDP. But in the long run maybe some countries gain more from trade than others.

Trade can be growth-enhancing. After all, it can be a conduit for knowledge, modern industrial technology, pro-growth institutional reform and political liberalism. It can also enhance agglomeration and scale economies in manufacturing, and foster capital flows and accumulation in capital-deficient countries. Modern economists call this trade-driven endogenous growth.

But were these growth-enhancing forces weaker or even absent in poor countries exporting primary products? Did it cause de-industrialization there? Did commodity price volatility retard their growth? Did trade booms augment the incomes of rent seekers in poor countries, thus suppressing accumulation there? It turns out that that the answer is yes to all of these questions: during the first global century, the growth gains from trade were huge for the West and miniscule for the Rest.

How should we measure trade booms? In exploring the correlation between 'openness' and growth, economists often measure the former by trade ratios, that is, exports plus imports divided by GDP. But trade shares may be high simply because income is high, and trade shares may rise simply because income rises. Thus, a country's openness should be measured by the height of the trade barriers around it, barriers that include tariffs, non-tariff barriers, distance from foreign markets and the cost of transportation to and from foreign markets. All of these fell dramatically between 1820 and 1913, especially in Asia, and it is *changes* in the

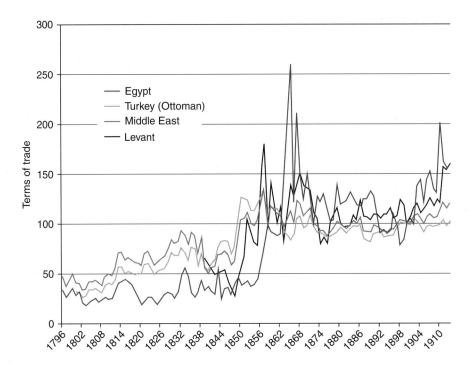

Figure I5/6.1 Middle East: net barter terms of trade, 1796–1913

trading environment that induces *changes* in the domestic economy. How might the trading environment have improved for Asia and the Rest? Two ways: by a decline in those trade barriers, and by an improvement in world market prices for their commodity exports. Both of these induced a rise in their net barter terms of trade (NBTT = the price of exports over the price of imports). So, if we are looking for ways that trade might have fostered or inhibited growth in the Rest, we need to look at the magnitude and duration of improvements in their NBTT.

Figure I5/6.1 shows just how dramatic the rise in the NBTT was in the Rest as their commodity export prices soared and their manufacturing import prices fell. It rose in all poor regions, and it rose very fast. The net result may have been short run gains from trade, but much lower long-run growth gains compared with the West.

The first global century fostered trade and growth, but the latter happened mainly in the West. In short, part of the great rise in the income per capita gap between West and the Rest was due to globalization.

Note

1. This brief summary is taken from my book *Trade and Poverty* (2011), Chinese trans. in paperback (2013 China Renmin University Press: Beijing).

Bibliography

Bhattacharyya, S. and Williamson, J. G. (2011), 'Commodity Price Shocks and the Australian Economy Since Federation', *Australian Economic History Review* 51 (2), 150–77.

Blattman, C., Hwang, J. and Williamson, J. G. (2007), 'The Impact of the Terms of Trade on Economic Development in the Periphery, 1870–1939: Volatility and Secular Change', *Journal of Development Economics* 82 (Jan), 156–79.

Clingingsmith, D. and Williamson, J. G. (2008), 'Deindustrialization in 18th and 19th Century India: Mughal Decline, Climate Shocks and British Industrial Ascent', *Explorations in Economic History* 45 (Jul), 209–34.

Dobado González, R., Gómez Galvarriato, A. and Williamson, J. G. (2008), 'Mexican Exceptionalism: Globalization and De-Industrialization, 1750–1877', *Journal of Economic History* 68 (03), 758–811.

Gómez Galvarriato, A. and Williamson, J. G. (2009), 'Was it Prices, Productivity or Policy? The Timing and Pace of Latin American Industrialization after 1870', *Journal of Latin American Studies* 41 (Dec), 663–94.

Jacks, D. S., O'Rourke, K. H. and Williamson, J. G. (2011), 'Commodity Price Volatility and World Market Integration since 1720', *Review of Economics and Statistics* 93 (3), 800–13.

Milanovic, B., Lindert, P. H. and Williamson, J. G. (2011), 'pre-industry Inequality', *Economic Journal* 121 (551), 255–72.

Pamuk, S. and Williamson, J. G. (2011), 'Ottoman De-industrialization 1800–1913: Assessing the Shock, its Impact and the Response', *Economic History Review* 64 (51), 159–84.

Williamson, J. G. (2006), *Globalization and the Poor Periphery before 1950*, Cambridge, MA: MIT Press.

(2011), *Trade and Poverty: when the Third World Fell Behind*, Cambridge, MA: MIT Press, Chinese trans. in paperback (2013), Beijing: China Renmin University Press.

7 Middle East, north Africa and central Asia

Rima Ghanem and Joerg Baten

In recent years, the Middle Eastern region has been characterized in newspaper reports by its many conflicts between religious and political groups. To understand the present situation, it is important to study the region's development over the last few centuries. The first impression of Middle Eastern history is the great heterogeneity of its development. We cover the geographic region between Morocco and Afghanistan (including the former Soviet Republics in central Asia and the Caucasus that have a substantial Muslim population). These countries have experienced multi-faceted development over the past five centuries. However, prominent economic historians of these world regions, such as Charles Issawi (1982), have distilled some common features that characterized many of the Middle Eastern countries. One common factor was contact with Europe during the nineteenth century, which Issawi described as a 'challenge'. Just before the First World War, European merchants (and sometimes their governments) had taken over many important positions in Middle Eastern economies outside agriculture. In contrast, Issawi interprets the developments during the twentieth century as a 'reaction' in which many Middle Eastern political leaders aimed at reducing the European influence. They also tried to mitigate the role of religious minorities in economic core positions of their countries.

Since Issawi (1982) and Owen (1993) wrote their famous overviews in the 1970s and 1980s, some progress has been made in the quantitative analysis of long-run economic trends of the Middle East. Most famously, Şevket Pamuk has presented his estimates of urban real wages and national income estimates for a number of countries in this region. Coşgel and Ergene (2012) have studied the development of early modern inequality based on tax registers for northern Anatolia and additional sources. Others have focused on complementary issues that are discussed below. Another theme that was studied with considerable effort was the development of the 'biological standard of living'.[1] The development of human stature can serve as an indicator of two key welfare components, nutritional quality and health. This development was reconstructed for a number of Middle Eastern economies. The Middle East actually had a relative advantage over Europe during the middle of the nineteenth century (Stegl and Baten 2009). Since the 1880s, however, there has been a dramatic change in the biological standard of living relative to Europeans. It seems plausible that this shift in relative welfare also influenced a deep feeling of injustice in the Middle Eastern population.

Finally, we draw on new research about trends in education and human capital. Though education in the Middle East was quite developed during the High Middle Ages, various available indicators suggest that Middle Eastern governments and families underinvested in this core determinant of economic growth and competitiveness during the period beginning with the late Middle Ages. Additionally, the differences among countries within this region of the world were substantial, and interesting to study in themselves.

Medieval and early modern period

During the medieval period, the technology of the Middle East was superior to that of Europe and knowledge was flowing from the former to the latter. A good example is medical knowledge. Not only was the ancient knowledge kept in libraries of the Middle East, but physicians also developed it further. This early progress is visible in urbanization rates: Bosker *et al.* (2013) recently estimated the urban share for the geographic area of the Middle East compared to Europe (Figure 7.1). Clearly, urbanization levels were much lower in Europe. They

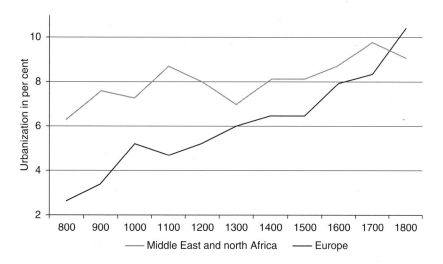

Figure 7.1 Urbanization rates in the Middle East and north Africa, compared with Europe
Source: modified from Bosker *et al.* (2013).
Note: the geographic definition is used, which categorizes the Byzantine Empire as a Middle Eastern economy (though Christian), and Sicily and Muslim Iberia as European (though Muslim in some centuries). Excluded are Russia, the Caucasus, Scandinavia, Iran and Afghanistan. Only cities with population > 10,000 included.

increased at roughly the same pace as in the Middle East until approximately 1100. Even if the Middle East remained more urbanized until 1700, its urbanization apparently reached a plateau after 1100. During the late medieval Mongolian invasion and plague episodes, it even temporarily declined. In contrast, Europe was converging during the period 1500–1800, and finally overtook the Middle East in 1800 (but note that the later Russian Empire and Scandinavia are excluded, which would reduce European urbanization).

As it is typical for world regions that have achieved technological and economic leadership in a certain period, the Middle East saw the formation of large empires, beginning with the Arabic ones of the early medieval period. The Ottoman Empire massively expanded in the fifteenth century toward the Balkans and south-eastern Europe, and in the sixteenth century towards the east and north Africa. In the seventeenth century, it stretched from Bosnia to Iraq and the Arabian Peninsula. In north Africa, only Morocco remained independent (for determinants of imperial expansion, see Highlight Chapter 7.1).

The quantitative evidence on the economic history of the Middle East during the early modern period is quite limited. Many historians have speculated that it was a period of decline. They came to this conclusion by noting that the Islamic Empires of the High Middle Ages were powerful and their scientists very progressive, while travel reports from the eighteenth century largely portrayed an image of backward technology and poverty. However, it is not clear whether the development was really an absolute decline rather than a relative one. It might have been that the level of eighteenth century development was simply somewhat lower than in north-western Europe (that had developed enormously) because the latter was the basis of comparison.

Trade routes between medieval Europe and Asia that had passed the Middle East shifted. This was one of the major events in Middle Eastern economic history (Findlay and O'Rourke 2007: 142). During the Middle Ages, the Middle East earned monopoly profits from the trade of Asian spices and luxury goods with Europe. In the early modern period, these monopoly profits flowed first to the pockets of the Portuguese, then to the Dutch, and finally to the British and French. However, the merchants of the Middle East also found additional sources of trading income such as the trade of Yemenite coffee (Raymond 1973, cited from Owen 1993: 5, see Map 7.1). This change in trade routes could not have had a very large influence on Middle Eastern economies because trading income affects only a small part of the population.

Beside the effects of shifting trade routes, there were medieval and early modern demographic shocks; Borsch (2005) argued that the late medieval plague events and the Mongol invasion hit the Middle Eastern irrigation economies in Iraq and Egypt particularly hard because they needed a critical

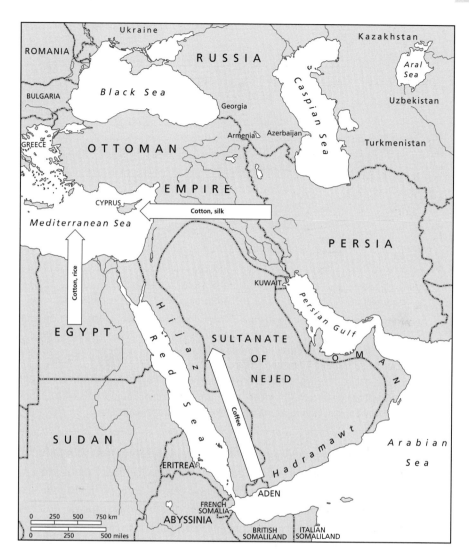

Map 7.1 Trade of the Middle East during the late eighteenth century
Source: Redrawn and modified after İnalcik, Halil, and Quataert, Donald (eds.), An Economic and Social History of the Ottoman Empire, 1600–1914, Vol II, Cambridge University press (1994), 726.
Note: the borders refer to a later period.

mass of population density to keep up the irrigation systems. The Mamluks who were ruling Egypt in a 'predatory' way (Findlay and O'Rourke 2007) were even less willing to invest in the public works that were necessary for irrigation, as the number of peasants and hence the rents for the Mamluks dropped after the great plague. While the plague increased real wages in western Europe, it might have had detrimental effects in the irrigation agricultural parts of the Middle East.

In spite of these interesting hypotheses, information regarding early development in the Middle East is based on quite fragmentary data. Pamuk and Ozmucur

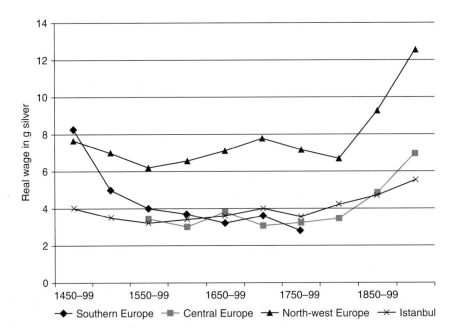

Figure 7.2 Real wages of unskilled urban workers
Source: calculated from Ozmucur and Pamuk (2002).
Notes: for European cities, they used Robert Allen's estimates for unskilled construction workers, wages (in grammes silver) divided by CPI (in grammes silver). Northw. Europe: Amsterdam, Antwerp and London; Central Europe: Leipzig and Warsaw; Southern Europe: Valencia.

developed more solid evidence on real wage developments in Istanbul and other large cities. They found that, in general, the development of urban craftsmen's wages was on a level similar to southern and central Europe during the sixteenth to eighteenth centuries (Figure 7.2). Clearly, the rich European north-west had already left Istanbul behind. However, compared with other European cities, Middle Eastern urban centres maintained a similar welfare level. Ozmucur and Pamuk stressed the fact that their estimates referred to a specific social group, and it might not be so clear how other groups of society were developing. However, we would interpret this evidence as plausible support of the view that living standards were at least equal to most of Europe until the eighteenth century.

Nevertheless, the scant evidence that we have on human capital formation suggests that the Middle East did not participate in the European human capital revolution. Evidence regarding sixteenth-century Maghreb suggests that basic numeracy equalled only 10 per cent in the late fifteenth/early sixteenth century, and reached approximately 50 per cent in the period between the late sixteenth to early eighteenth century (Juif and Baten 2013). For eighteenth-century Turkey and Syria, we have estimates in the range of 10–50 per cent (Baten and Ghanem 2014). In the same period, numeracy in Europe grew from approximately 50 to 90 per cent. Hence, Europe emerged as a dramatically strong competitor.

Limitations to the 'rule of law' at the beginning of the nineteenth century

What characterized the Middle East at the beginning of the nineteenth century? Many contemporary observers noted the complicated institutional structure and sometimes the missing 'rule of law' (reviewed in Kuran 2011). Taxation capability was low and rulers often were exploitative; in many cases their ethnic background differed from those of the ruled (in Iran and Egypt, for example).

However, some regions actually benefited from low levels of the rule of law, such as the Maghreb pirates. In Algeria and Tunisia, an important additional element was the pirate economy of the seventeenth and eighteenth centuries. Originally created by a tradition of holy war against the Christians, privateering was developing into an industry for the Algerian and Tunisian port cities.[2] Ships whose owners were not willing or able to pay a substantial fee were captured, and the surviving personnel sold on slave markets if no ransom was paid. Some Christians who accepted conversion also joined the corsair fleet as renegades. Contrary to the reputation of privateering, corsair activity was a well-organized business. It involved many different actors. As for Tunis' pirates, a pirate crew consisted of at least the ship owner, captain, naval crewmen and armed warriors. The latter were mostly former hostages. Although the hostages were violently taken, many later joined the pirate business and benefited from it. Through the trade of booty, they not only acquired wealth but also rose in social rank. Tunis as an expansionary city of that time welcomed foreigners in its midst and, in return, gained economic profits. Algerian pirates sailed as far as north-western Europe for slave raids.

In the irrigation economies of Egypt and Mesopotamia, clear property rights and the rule of law would have been most important, because irrigation agriculture is particularly dependent on clear institutional settings. But even here, property rights were not always clearly defined. It is very important to understand the structure of property rights to land in the Middle East, and in Egypt and Iraq in particular.[3] In general, land rights were very complicated (Owen 1993: 33). In principle, the state owned most of the land except for some gardens, orchards and the real estate on which the houses and the villages stood. However, many families had already begun using some legal tricks to imitate something like private family ownership at the beginning of the nineteenth century. Generally, the most secure property rights were established in the Mount Lebanon area, and partially so in Anatolia, lower Egypt and parts of Syria. In contrast, in southern Syria, upper Egypt, Mesopotamia and

Palestine, we have communal redistribution of land. Each peasant received a new plot of land after the harvest season. Quasi-private ownership was impossible in this communally organized land tenure system, of course. Only towards the mid-nineteenth century was there a tendency towards imitating private ownership in these regions. While most of the land was owned by the state, local rulers could obtain a large part of the tax revenues. In principle, the rules said that between 10 and 50 per cent of the production should be taxed, plus some additional duties. However, this was only a theoretical tax rate. In practice, a peasant's skill in hiding part of the production was very important, and those who were more skilled at hiding were able to achieve a higher standard of living. Tax evasion was quite common, and tax payers considered this to be legitimate because they received almost no public goods in return. For example, there was little protection except perhaps against other local lords. Therefore, the peasants protected themselves in fortified villages.[4] The roads and other infrastructure were in a relatively poor state at the beginning of the nineteenth century, and the irrigation systems were not centrally surveyed.

Iran, with its long history of early cultures and empires, had suffered particularly hard during the late Middle Ages and the early modern period. Many invasions of nomadic tribes, whose leaders became rulers in this country, affected it negatively. The relationship between these rulers of nomadic origin and the peasants and merchants of Iran was always difficult; therefore, their ability to raise regular taxes was low. Hence, arbitrary confiscations were often used. Relatively unsecure property rights and governmental preference for nomadic tribes resulted in a reduction of irrigated land and an increase of pastures and wasteland before 1800.[5]

Urban craftsmen and transport infrastructure around 1800

In contrast to western European proto-industrial production in the countryside, industrial production in the Middle East was mostly concentrated in the cities (see Map 7.2). Trade in the famous suqs, as well as administration, were the other main functions of the urban centres. With the exception of Istanbul, the cities themselves were all situated next to a substantial area of cultivatable land with reasonable soil quality (see Owen 1993: 45). Textile production was the most important industry, complemented by food-processing, furniture and specialized industries in some places.[6] Even though technological progress in production was slower than in Europe, some industries – such as Turkish armament producers and shipbuilders – could produce goods at similar levels of quality to those produced by Europeans (Owen 1993: 46). Obviously, the military interests of the Ottoman Empire required such exceptions. Most other industries, with fixed price systems and guild systems in which old masters typically commanded

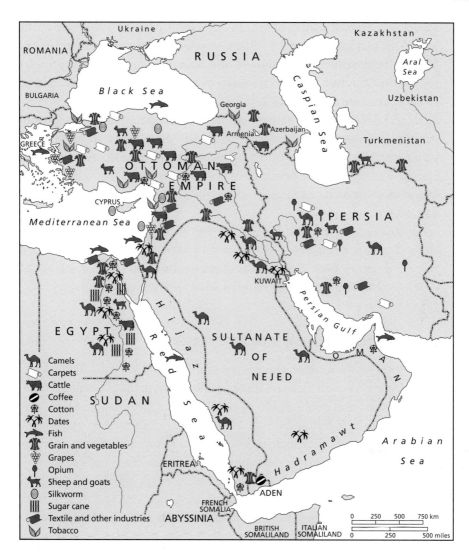

Map 7.2 Regional economic specialization and export products in the Middle East during the nineteenth century
Source: Redrawn and modified after Tübinger Atlas des Vorderen Orients, Vol. A.X.: *Economy during the 19th century*, ed. by SFB 19, Wiesbaden: Reichert, 1980.

younger apprentices, were not conducive to innovation, even if a certain quality of craftsmanship was preserved.

Another very important urban function was to organize caravan trade. Complemented by coastal and river-based trade, the main caravan routes within the Ottoman Empire connected Syria and Mesopotamia (and from there led to Persia and in some periods to China). A caravan artery went east–west in southern and northern Anatolia and from there to central Asia. Trade goods comprised textiles and spices from India and Southeast Asia in exchange for European manufactures, African ivory, skins, ostrich feathers and similar items, as well as a limited variety of Middle Eastern goods (such as Syrian cotton thread and yarn, and Lebanese silk).[7] Black slaves from Africa were traded northward, and white slaves from Russia and the Balkans were traded southward. Trade within the Ottoman Empire consisted of grain, sugar, cotton and other products from Egypt in exchange for textiles, soap, dyestuffs and processed food from Syria and Anatolia. Imports and exports of Mesopotamia were relatively limited, but there was quite some transit trade, and Persia exported opium, carpets and other products. For overland transport, in addition to the regular costs for camels and personnel, safety costs were often large. Bedouin tribes required 'dues' that could be as large as three times the normal transport cost (Owen 1993: 54).

In conclusion, the Middle East at the beginning of the nineteenth century showed complicated property rights and little economic dynamism, although there were exceptions. The systems of production and taxation did not encourage development; nor were land resources completely used.

Reform period: the early nineteenth century

During the early nineteenth century, the situation in the Middle East changed dramatically. We will focus on three development paths of the nineteenth century: mild reforms and problematic openness in the Ottoman imperial core, forced development in Egypt and direct colonization in central Asia and Algeria.

(1) The famous Tanzimat reforms in the Ottoman core (mainly from 1839) fundamentally changed the law, administration, military and economic situation. Although many fields were affected by the reforms, equality of the citizenry was perceived as one of the most important. Previously, the Jewish and the Orthodox and Armenian Christians had a particular status with both advantages (as Muslims saw it) and disadvantages (as the minorities saw it). After the reforms, all citizens of the Ottoman Empire should have been treated equally – in theory at least. As an additional component of the reforms, military service was regulated to a maximum amount of five years.

Tax farming, which had been a problematic economic institution, was successively abolished during the reforms. Previously, a rich tribal leader, merchant or feudal lord could obtain the right to collect taxes after paying a fixed amount to the government. This caused substantial overtaxing, leading to conflict and inequalities of real tax burdens because some tax farmers were more effective – and sometimes violent – in their tax collection efforts (but see Coşgel and Ergene 2012). Finally, an important point was the opening of the Ottoman economy to imports. European governments also influenced the reforms. It soon became clear that in many fields of industrial production, the Middle Eastern craftsmen could not compete with their European counterparts, as trade with Europe was intensified.[8]

(2) Egypt had a special and remarkable development during the nineteenth century, mainly stimulated by political changes initiated by Mohammad Ali Pasha. Since Roman times, Egypt had always been ruled by persons born abroad or with parents from outside of the country, and the Albanian Mohammad Ali Pasha was no exception. During the forty-two years of his reign, Mohammad Ali reformed the Egyptian state and economy in a radical way. One of his main aims was to build a strong army that would be able to protect his new state. Reforms were also applied in the education system, again with the motivation to provide the army with educated leaders but also to train Egyptians in the skills demanded by modern industry, trade and administrative positions. Many factories were built and new industries developed during the Mohammad Ali period. Plants for the construction of ships, the production of chemicals, weapons and other important products were realized. Apart from factories for military purposes, the textile industry also flourished during this period. Imports and exports were severely controlled because much of the government budget stemmed from trade revenues organized by marketing boards. Agriculture was the focus of the reforms. By changing the land property system, building new dams and watering channels, developing the irrigation system, introducing new crops and controlling planted yields, agricultural production increased substantially during the early nineteenth century.

Mohammad Ali also created a law of mandatory military service to expand the army. In the end, it included almost 4 per cent of the population. Egypt had become a military state and participated in many wars during the nineteenth century, such as in Hijaz, Sudan, Greece and Syria. Ali used his oversized army to develop a power position for Egypt. He also intended to provide more raw materials to Egyptian industry. The forced development of military power, agriculture and new industries has similarities to Soviet strategies (but without communism).

Mohammad Ali died in 1848, and his successors adopted different strategies. His son Ismail Pasha encouraged science and agriculture, and decided to ban slavery in Egypt. During the early 1860s, when US cotton producers dropped from the world market due to the American civil war, Egyptian cotton production flourished. During the following period, however, Egypt began to suffer from many disasters including epidemic disease, flood and wars. Ismail Pasha had to rely on foreign debt to solve these problems, and he could not find a solution to pay back the increasing foreign debt. The Egyptian economy weakened, and the English and French colonial powers started to increase interventionist policies, until England transformed Egypt into a protectorate in 1882.

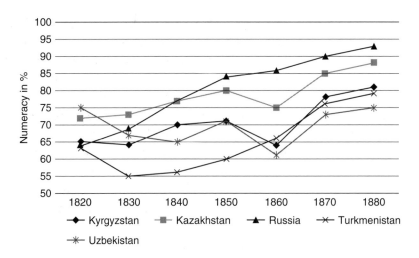

Figure 7.3 Numeracy in central Asia
Source: based on Prayon and Baten (2013).

(3) Direct colonization took place in central Asia, the Caucasus and Algeria: Russia began a territorial expansion, first to the northern steppe of the central Asian region, during the mid-eighteenth century when several Kazakh tribes called Czarist troops for support. While the Kazakhs interpreted this event more as a temporary alliance under Russian supremacy, the Czar now considered the northern steppe to be part of the Russian Empire; however, the imperial administration started to integrate the Kazakh steppe only during the early nineteenth century. Between 1822 and 1848, the three main Kazakh leaders (the Khans) of the minor, middle and major horde were suspended. A number of Russian forts were built to control the conquered territories. Russian settlers were provided with land, reducing the area available for nomadic tribes in the Kazakh steppe. Many of them were forced to adopt sedentary lifestyles. As a result, in the various regions, between 5 and 15 per cent of the population were immigrants. This Russian colonization was accompanied by many conflicts between the 1820s and 1840s, during which the Slavic settlements were often attacked. Russian troops only succeeded in ending this series of rebellions in 1846.

If we consider the numeracy of Kazakhs, it was quite remarkable (Figure 7.3). During the early nineteenth century, Kazakhs were actually more numerate than were Russians. However, Russia experienced a human capital revolution during the nineteenth century, and the colonized Kazakhs could not keep pace. Still, numeracy was higher than that of the more urbanized central Asians in what later became Kyrgyzstan, for example.

What could be the reasons for this remarkable early numeracy level? The settler share can most likely explain part of this, although Russians were a minority in the Kazakh steppe.[9] Another factor could be the relatively good nutritional situation in Kazakhstan. Protein malnutrition that plagued many other populations living in more densely populated settlements was absent in Kazakhstan. Additionally, in later stages of the process of Russian human capital development, Russian settlers of the 1870s and 1880s might have stimulated so-called contact learning (Prayon and Baten 2013). As the Kazakhs observed that Russians were successful with higher investment in human capital, the Kazakhs tended to adopt this strategy as well.

While the northern steppe only had population densities of about one to two persons per square kilometer, the southern part of central Asia was more densely populated; its urbanization rate was as high as 15–20 per cent during the late nineteenth century. This was the region of the old Silk Road, which had connected China with the Middle East and Europe since ancient times. Famous urban centres such as Samarkand had a remarkably developed merchant culture. Politically, the region had experienced many different rulers during the early modern period such as Mongols, Persians and Arabs. Soon after its cities had been conquered and sometimes destroyed, the income of merchant trade and intensive irrigated agriculture allowed reconstructing them once again. The Russian Empire invaded the Khanates of Kokand, Bukhara and Shiva during the 1860s, i.e., much later than it invaded the northern steppe. One motivation was to prevent the British colonial Empire, which had captured Afghanistan, from further expansion northward. In addition, the intensive cotton agriculture was attractive even more during the 1860s when the US civil war led to the cotton famine that also affected the textile factories of Saint Petersburg and Moscow. In contrast to Kazakhstan, military resistance was more limited in the Silk Road region, similar to the northern steppe; however, some regions lost considerably in numeracy relative to Russia (Figure 7.3). The later region of Uzbekistan with its capital Samarkand was the most numerate of the whole region and better educated than Russian or Kazakh regions. However, even before the Russian conquest, numeracy stagnated. During the colonization and accompanying military destruction in the 1860s, numeracy fell dramatically. After modest recovery, the famous centre region of the Silk Road was only 75 per cent numerate in the 1880s, almost 20 per cent lower than was Russia.[10]

In Algeria, numeracy was also quite high initially but stagnated until the 1870s (Baten and Ghanem 2014). In contemporary travel reports of the mid-nineteenth century, the indigenous farmer population is described as unusually industrious and hard-working (*Deutsches Staats-Wörterbuch* 1857). The military conflicts between the French and the indigenous Arabs and Berbers were heavy and long; only after

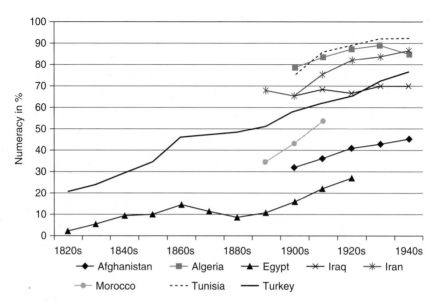

Figure 7.4 Numeracy in selected Middle Eastern countries
Source: based on Prayon and Baten (2013).

the mid-nineteenth century was Algeria really a French colony. Algeria was – apart from twentieth-century Israel – the country most heavily settled by Europeans in the Middle East. During the late nineteenth and early twentieth century, the European share was almost a fifth of the population. The French government aimed at making Algeria an assimilated part of France, and this included substantial educational investments especially after 1900 (Figure 7.4). The indigenous cultural and religious resistance heavily opposed this tendency, but in contrast to the other colonized countries path in central Asia and the Caucasus, Algeria kept its individual skills and a relatively human-capital-intensive agriculture.

In summary, we perceive three types of fundamental change: the Tanzimat reforms that opened many economies to European competition (and deindustrialization); the infant-industry strategy of Mohammad Ali in Egypt; and the direct colonization, which led to a relative decline in human capital in the Silk Road region and stagnation on a high level in Algeria.

Why did the Middle East deindustrialize during the nineteenth century?

Pamuk and Williamson (2010) note that during the eighteenth century, the Ottoman Empire was completely self-sufficient in textile production, which represented a large share of traded industrial goods. There were even small exports of carpets, silk and textiles. The share of the textile market that would be covered by domestic producers in the Ottoman Empire was still close to 100 per cent in

1820; however, between then and 1910, it fell to less than 20 per cent (Pamuk and Williamson 2010).

Pamuk and Williamson (2010) offer a trade-based interpretation of the process during which the Middle East deindustrialized. They argue that not only were imported British textiles during the nineteenth century outperforming many local producers, but another important point was the improving terms of trade of cash crops. Raw cotton prices increased substantially, for example. This change in terms of trade tempted the Middle East to specialize in this area of production. In spite of deindustrialization and the shift to agriculture, real incomes were actually growing during the nineteenth century, albeit much slower than in western Europe (Pamuk 2006). When the terms of trade for these goods declined again during the 1930s, there already was a high degree of path-dependence, which kept Middle Eastern economies in the cash-crop specialization. One could imagine that deindustrialization and concentration on agriculture discourages the development of skills.[11]

Other scholars searched for institutional factors that might have weakened the Middle Eastern economies, leaving them less competitive. Kuran (2011), for example, argued that institutions of Islamic law that were appropriate for early periods tended to become handicaps for growth during the nineteenth century. He criticized the stability of (1) inheritance laws because they did not allow capital accumulation, (2) the lack of legal frameworks for capital firms, and (3) the religious trusts called waqfs, which locked capital resources into relatively inflexible institutions. Kuran was convinced that it was not colonialism or religious attitudes *per se* that was growth retarding, but the excessive stability of these law concepts. Another institutional interpretation was given by Rubin (2011), who also criticized the view that Islam *per se* tended to generate less growth-conducive institutional design. For example, if interest constraints are considered, both the Christian Church and Islam aimed at restricting interest during the Middle Ages. This is an obvious example of an institution that limits capitalist development by constraining credit. In the early phase, Islamic bankers and merchants were actually more successful than Christian ones in circumventing this religious constraint (Rubin 2011). For example, Rubin reports about the Mukhatara institution known in Medina during the eighth century. One person bought a good for a certain price, but the other one bought it back immediately for a higher price to be paid later. However, later on, the development of credit institutions that circumvented religious constraints was more rapid in Christian Europe. Rubin argues that this was caused by the need of rulers to be legitimized by religious leaders. This factor became more important in the Islamic sphere. During the early period of Christianity, the first followers of this religion lived under Roman rule. Christian religious leaders developed doctrines that implied separated religious and governmental power. This was comparable to Jesus' insistence on giving Caesar what belonged to him and God what was his. In contrast, during the early years of the Muslim religion, political power was weak and the first Caliphs gained their legitimization from being relatives of Mohammed. The leaders that later followed them felt legitimized by obeying religious rules very strictly. Although Christian popes and bishops also tried to influence politics – and kings used religion as legitimization – in Christianity, there was always more tension and sometimes competition between religious and political leaders (Rubin 2011: 1316–17).

Another factor that limited industrial competitiveness in the Middle East might have been the interaction between economic segregation and human capital development. Some minorities were considered to be predetermined for occupations in finance and trade in the Middle East; therefore, talented individuals of the majority might have had fewer incentives to develop trade-related skills. This limited human capital development. An important social factor in the economic development of Middle Eastern economies was the minorities of Greeks, Armenians, Jews and Christian Arabs. They were active in the trade sector and played a role in finance, export-oriented agriculture and the modest beginnings of modern industry. European merchants and colonial bureaucrats cooperated with them and partly protected them because these minority members were often more interested in learning foreign languages and developing technical skills.[12] In Turkey, Greeks, Armenians and Jews were most important. In particular, the Galata bankers dominated Turkish financial development during the early twentieth century. Armenians and Greeks were also active in internal trade, industry, crafts and the professions. In Iran, minorities played a smaller role, except for Jews, who were active in both Iranian industry and trade. In Egypt, Copts held a remarkable share of the land, and they worked in the professions as well as government services. In Lebanon, Christians began to dominate foreign trade and the silk industry beginning in the early nineteenth century. This group also took over the traditional Jewish role in Syria in finance and industry. The importance of these minorities was largest in the period at the beginning of the twentieth century. After that, the growing national aspirations of the majorities had the effect of more and more majority members starting to cover positions previously held by the minorities. However, the motivation of talented Arab, Iranian and Turkish majorities to invest in trading skills developed late partly because the minorities had a low social reputation in their eyes and imitating them was not desirable.

Living standards

Pamuk (2006) found that gross domestic product (GDP) development trended upward, but growth was relatively slow in the Middle East. He estimated that

GDP grew from only $611 per capita in 1820 (measured in constant 1990 dollars) to $1,023 in 1913, covering Turkey, Egypt, Arabia and Iran. As a percentage of the US/western Europe national income value, this meant falling back from 49 to 25 per cent. The gulf region developed even more slowly than did the core region of the Ottoman Empire, with Lebanon being the richest country in 1913.

Does this lag in production capacity imply that the overall standard of living was lower relative to Europe? Ozmucur and Pamuk (2002) pointed to the fact that real wages were actually equal or greater in the large Middle Eastern cities. As real wages reflect urban unskilled and skilled craftsmen's welfare, it seems that the richer strata such as merchants and professionals were lagging compared to Europe.

Another approach to analysing welfare is to look at human stature. This reflects health and nutritional quality, which are important components of the standards of living of a population. This is especially informative in data-scarce regions such as the Middle East and north Africa. For the Middle East, some recent estimates have been based on anthropological measurements; a number of famous anthropologists travelled in the Middle East in the eighteenth and nineteenth centuries, systematically measuring many individuals.[13]

The height measurements are organized by birth cohort, and a sufficient number of observations allows assessment of the period from the mid-nineteenth century onward.[14] Stegl and Baten (2009) choose a sample of eight Middle Eastern countries where height data were available for the studied period (Figure 7.5). Turkey, Iraq, Iran, Egypt, Syria, Lebanon, Palestine/Israel, Turkmenistan and Yemen are included. They compare the average heights of these countries with a

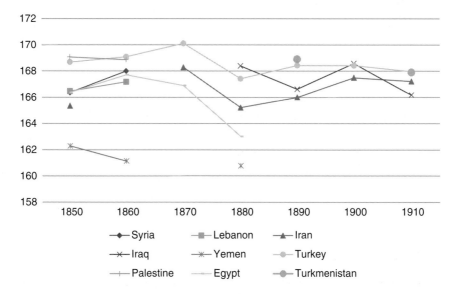

Figure 7.5 Height in Middle Eastern countries (male)
Source: modified from Stegl and Baten (2009). Turkmenistan added from www.clio-infra.eu.

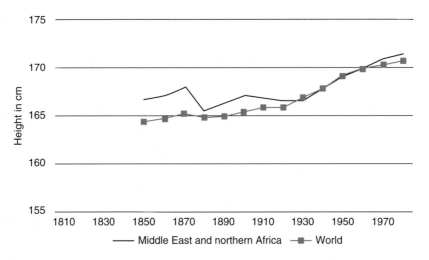

Figure 7.6 Height development in the Middle East and the world (male)
Source: based on Baten and Blum (2012).
Note: see there for interpolation strategies (missing values have been interpolated to avoid artificial 'jumps' caused by data availability).

sample of central and southern European countries. Stegl and Baten showed that people born between 1850 and 1870 in Middle Eastern countries enjoyed on average a favourable nutrition compared to Europe. However, in 1880, the average heights of Middle Eastern people decreased suddenly. European human stature began to exceed it, although with only a small difference for three generations. This difference increased over time, reaching more than 7 centimetres (cm) for the generation born in 1980. Compared with the world height average, the initial lead of the Middle East population vanished during the twentieth century (Figure 7.6).

There were also strong differences between regions within countries; these regional differences shed light on the explanation of the height trend. In Iraq, for example, the average height differed between desert inhabitants and the other inhabitants (both urban and rural). The desert Bedouins were on average 0.85 centimetres taller than were other Iraqis. The reason behind this difference is the low population density in the desert, where people could benefit from the meat and milk of the stock breeding in which the desert tribesmen engaged.

In Turkey during the late nineteenth century, Stegl and Baten (2009) find the shortest population in the western coastal areas, which are now the richest regions in the country, while the tallest people lived in central Anatolia. A likely explanation is again the low population density in central Anatolia. The population specialized on cattle farming. For example, Issawi (1980) analysed tax returns and reported that animal husbandry was most important in the relatively dry inland regions. In this central area, low population density and a part lifestyle allowed protein-rich nutrition.

Egypt is a dry country in general; the agriculture depends mainly on Nile water. Only in the northern coastal region is the rainfall level slightly elevated. The inhabitants of this area had the advantage of obtaining enough rain for their crops, and their height values were greater than were those of other Egyptian areas. The desert inhabitants of Egypt also had a height advantage in comparison with the urban population. For neighbouring Libya, Danubio et al. (2011) found that the heights of nomadic Tuareg born in the 1880s to 1900s were 3 cm greater than the heights of other Libyans; on average, they were even 8 cm taller than were Libyan oasis inhabitants.

In general, between 1850 and 1870, the inhabitants of the Middle East showed a high average stature according to nineteenth century standards (Figure 7.6). This good level first dropped in the 1880s. One potential immediate cause of the 1880s height drop might have been the cattle disease, which originated in Asia in the 1880s and then moved through the Middle East to the eastern part of Africa, which was severely hit in the 1890s.[15] However, there were additional underlying forces affecting the relative decline of Middle Eastern heights. During the nineteenth century, parts of the Middle Eastern population still benefited from the so-called 'proximity advantages' to animal husbandry. Bedouins and other inhabitants of the Middle East who lived close to goats, sheep and cattle could enjoy more protein from milk and meat. Not only rich people could buy this; poor tribesmen also obtained their share, especially of the less-popular parts of the animal. In contrast, Europe with its densely populated urban centres did not have good access to protein sources during the mid-nineteenth century. In the twentieth century, the situation changed. Even perishable foodstuffs such as milk could now be transported, thanks to refrigeration transport technology. European inhabitants of large cities could provide their children with good nutrition, and urban populations became taller than rural ones. Europe also made strong and early progress in public health and medical development. Their GDP level was much higher than in the Middle East during the twentieth century; hence, they could afford good nutrition and health during this later period.

Summing up, the interesting and slightly astonishing fact of this section was that during the mid-nineteenth century, Middle Eastern populations did not necessarily suffer from poor nutrition, relative to Europeans. The fascination of European travellers and writers for the inhabitants of deserts might have originated partly in the special economic situation of nomads during this period. Also life expectancy slightly improved in Turkey from 27 to 31 years between 1820 and 1870 (Baten and Pamuk 2007). The strong relative decline during the twentieth century might have stimulated perception of severe injustice among these tribesmen, who still trained themselves in military activities.

The Middle East in the twentieth century

Issawi (1982) concluded that, for the period just before the First World War, almost all powerful positions in Middle Eastern economies had been taken over by Europeans or minorities such as Armenians, Greeks, other Christian minorities and Jews. He interprets the following century as an attempt to reverse this development. Europeans and entrepreneurial minorities were forced or encouraged to leave, or sometimes killed (such as many Armenians in Turkey). The two world wars that devastated Europe allowed the Middle Eastern reaction to abolish privileges (such as immunities for European merchants) and to nationalize railways, banks, petrol stations and other utilities. The ideology of the interwar and postwar years further promoted government-owned mining and industries. However, even if nationalized industries might have been able to satisfy consumers with relatively simple products during the mid-twentieth century, this way of organizing industries tends to be weak in the quality of goods produced, and in the long run, new investments were missing. For example, countries such as Yemen lost their minority tradesmen (who might have developed into entrepreneurs later on), and the relatively low status of human capital development made it difficult to develop its own Yemenite entrepreneurial groups. Turkey was more successful in developing its own entrepreneurs, given that the status of education had always been higher and the Ataturk reforms placed particular emphasis on education. In addition, Turkey also benefited from the slightly more equal gender distribution of education after the Ataturk reforms.

In Turkey during the time of Mustafa Kemal Ataturk in the first half of the twentieth century, many reforms were initiated in different fields such as politics, economics and culture. Ataturk's reforms can be summarized mainly as abolishing the sultanate and afterwards the caliphate system in the country and converting the republic of Turkey into a secular state. That is, Turkey, although having a Muslim majority, changed from being an Islamic state to a laic country. Ghanem (2014) assessed whether separating the religion from the government had a positive influence on human capital in Turkey. The results confirm that the secular state of Turkey led to a clear increase in numeracy levels in the different Turkish regions. New schools were built and primary schooling became mandatory and free. In addition, Ataturk replaced religious education with a national education system. Turkey did not change to an atheist state; the freedom to worship and follow religions existed. However, the idea was to concentrate on Islam in the mosques and religious places; what mattered at school was science and education (Ghanem 2014).

After the Middle East had deindustrialized during the nineteenth century, the situation started to change during the twentieth century. Political movements in the Middle East not only demanded a political renaissance, but many of its leaders also saw the need for reindustrialization (Issawi 1982). The two world wars also made clear that European imports of industrial goods were not automatically available. The exceptional situation during the wars also allowed experimentation with new production methods within the Middle Eastern countries, even if these were not yet competitive.

Already before the First World War, some industries were growing again in Egypt and Turkey, for example. Soon after the breakdown of the Ottoman Empire, Turkey started to develop more active industrial policies. Indirectly inspired by the Soviet Union, Turkey decided to set up two five-year plans during the 1930s, making clear that the state would play a strong role in this reindustrialization attempt. All Middle Eastern economies lacked entrepreneurs. As suggested by the ideologies of the time, the state was expected to fill the gap. In addition, socialist ideas were important in countries such as Syria, Iraq, Algeria, Afghanistan, Egypt and obviously central Asia, then a part of the Soviet Union.

One different approach to industrial development was taken in Palestine and later Israel. The Sykes–Picot Agreement in 1916 divided a part of the Middle Eastern region – which was previously part of the Ottoman Empire – between England (Palestine, Iraq, Transjordan) and France (Syria, Lebanon). The former Ottoman territory of Palestine became a British mandate in 1920. In 1922, the League of Nations decided that in this territory, a 'national home' for Jews should be established, while still guaranteeing the civil and religious rights of all the inhabitants. Following this political decision (and reinforced by anti-Semitism in Germany and other countries during the interwar period), a strong immigration of Jews from different world regions resulted. Their population share rose from 9 per cent in 1919 to 32 per cent in 1947. Many Jews brought skills and entrepreneurial traditions. Given that the British Mandate aimed at restricting land purchases of previously Arab-owned land by Jewish immigrants, the Jewish population group was initially more urban and had a higher share in industrial occupations than did the Arab majority. This particular development in Palestine, which had terrible political and humanitarian consequences later on, resulted economically in one of the few growth miracles of the region. In addition, the structure of firms was determined much more by private entrepreneurs than by the government as in many other Middle Eastern economies.

Why were twentieth century firms in other countries so often run by the government? Three main reasons come to mind. We already mentioned above that entrepreneurial elites were often foreigners or minorities and that, in the view of Arab, Iranian and Turkish politicians, the influence of both groups was to be reduced during the twentieth century. The other two main reasons were the lack of human capital and skills and the peculiarities of oil production economies.

We first discuss the skills and human capital levels during the twentieth century. Basic numeracy was generally not very high during the nineteenth century and did not converge rapidly to neighbouring European levels (Figure 7.4). Only during the early twentieth century can a strong improvement be noticed. This deficit in the educational component, numeracy, is equally visible in the other components of education, such as literacy. Issawi (1982: 113–14) notes that literacy was only 7 per cent in Egypt in 1907, for example. The governments spent little public funds on education. The 1860/61 Ottoman budget on education was only 0.2 per cent of total expenditure. In Algeria, it was slightly higher at approximately 2 per cent (1890–1914). Even during the early twentieth century, the number of school years was quite low (except in Israel, where it was substantially higher [Barro and Lee 2013]). The most extreme was Yemen, where children received almost no schooling (Figure 7.7). In the Gulf States, the situation was slightly better.

Similar statements could be made about secondary and tertiary schooling. Such a low level of numeracy and school education made it very difficult to develop a class of entrepreneurs because this type of occupation requires substantial abilities to work with numbers. The function of entrepreneurs was, therefore, taken over by the state.

Another reason was the amount of oil revenues. If the Middle Eastern economies reinvested the government share of oil income, they often did this in the form of state-owned companies. In 1908, oil was discovered in the Middle East. This discovery completely changed the landscape of its economies. Oil had always been used in small amounts, for example, in the form of seepage for rubbing of camel sores. In two places in Iraq, crude oil was already extracted in the 1870s with quite primitive methods. However, real development started in the 1900s. The Iranian government decided to give a concession to a British company. Other countries also gave concessions to European and American firms, ultimately resulting in an oligopoly structure of less than ten large oil-mining firms that has persisted until today with varying actors. In Iran, the British monopoly concession was soon debated with great dissatisfaction among the Iranian population. However, Reza Shah again signed in 1933 an unpopular agreement under British pressure. The question about the nationalization of its oil reserves became one of the key issues in the social and political conflicts in Iran during the 1940s and 1950s.

During the pre-Second World War period, most oil extraction took place in Iran and on a much smaller scale in Egypt. Only during the 1940s did Iraq also become a major exporter. To a much smaller extent, Bahrain and other Middle Eastern countries also increased exports. Up to 1940, Middle Eastern and north African oil production was still below 5 per cent of world production. However, it then exploded to 26 per cent in 1960, reaching a maximum of 42 per cent in

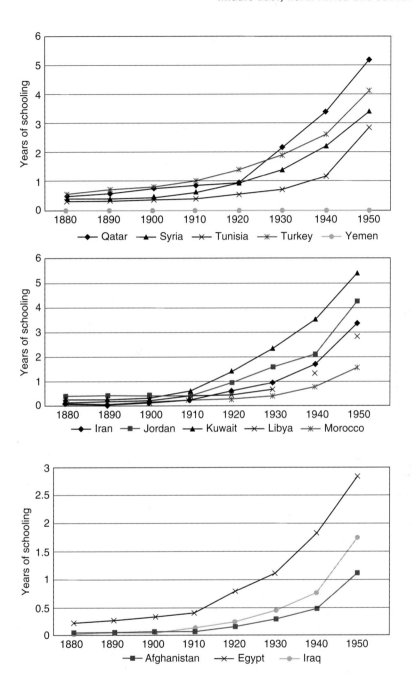

Figure 7.7 Years of schooling in Middle Eastern countries, by birth decade
Source: calculated from the Barro–Lee database (www.barrolee.com) but arranging all data by primary school decade (i.e., the decade in which a cohort was approximately age 10). This assumes no strong survivor-bias distortion and no strong adults schooling (See Baten and Ghanem 2014).

1975. Initially, the Middle Eastern countries did not receive much of this new wealth. However, between 1950 and 1975, direct payments from the petroleum companies to the governments rose from $240 million to $81 billion (and to $163 billion in 1979). The renegotiation of contracts with the petroleum companies and the formation of the Organization of Petroleum Exporting Countries (OPEC) in 1960 resulted in dramatic change. OPEC's cartel policy during the Arab–Israel conflict of 1973 and later in the 1970s generated a flood of revenues for the oil states Iran, Iraq, Kuwait, Saudi Arabia, Qatar, United Arab Emirates, Egypt, Libya, Algeria, Bahrain and Oman (Oman, and also Syria, Israel and Turkey had quite small revenues).

What was the effect of oil production on the economies? Issawi (1982: 207) concludes after carefully weighing many pros and cons that the initial period of the 1950s and 1960s was quite beneficial. In particular, some of the least-developed countries receiving oil revenues served as a stimulus for their economies. In general, only a small part of the population worked in oil production (normally less than 2 per cent), but in the Gulf States, it could be up to one-half. Many persons who left oil companies also created their own firms. Training on the job allowed developing the necessary entrepreneurial skills and the 'spirit'.

However, the 1970s oil price increase and production expansion brought an enormous amount of wealth that resulted in mixed blessings for at least three reasons: (1) Some of the classical 'curse of resources' phenomena occurred. Issawi (1982) speculated that it was difficult for the Middle Eastern people to find agreement on how to distribute the wealth, partly because it was subjectively not 'earned' by the individual population groups in the oil countries.[16] (2) In addition, the view that 'anything could be imported' was shared by many Arabs and Iranians, which was poison for reindustrialization efforts. (3) The high expectations of income generated by the seemingly inexhaustible stream of revenues became unrealistic. Rising inequality between those who benefited and those who perceived themselves as losers created so much dissatisfaction that it could even lead to civil war as in the case of Algeria, or at least extremist political attitudes in other countries.

What could the government do about all this? The only feasible strategy was to try to reinvest much of the oil revenues into firms that would generate income after oil income ended. The owner of those firms was often the state. A major problem was, however, that the state-owned firms tended to be highly inefficient. A government bureaucrat was not necessarily the ideal person to maximize productivity and to reduce costs. When problems of competitiveness appeared, managers demanded import protectionism and monopolies, rather than improving the production side and looking for new markets and new technologies. Only in recent decades have these issues been partly improved and structural reforms initiated. However, perceived injustice in some of the countries was already widespread. In addition, possibilities for democratic participation and improving the situation were limited, which reinforced dissatisfaction. Finally, some of the industrial countries performed interventions to secure oil resources for themselves in recent decades. All these factors resulted in a series of wars and internal conflicts that have had terrible consequences for the Middle East until even today.

To what degree are these developments of the twentieth century reflected in GDP trends and living standards (Figure 7.8)? If we consider the development of GDP per capita in the Middle East between the 1950s and today, we can rely on some informative statistics which are of course not beyond doubt, especially not for the early periods. Some of the governments also had a strong preference for window-dressing of indicator variables. However, in general, we can gain some insight from looking at GDP as an indicator of productive capacity. Given that we have a large number of countries in the Middle East, we reduced the set of the countries we examine in detail to thirteen because, for example, some of the Gulf countries such as the United Arab Emirates, Kuwait and Bahrain developed similarly to Qatar.

If we look first at the six countries which represent the centre and the north (Lebanon, Turkey, Israel, Iran, Afghanistan and Iraq), we see that Israel had a relatively favourable development. Given the relatively good educational status of the Israeli population, this is not astonishing – even though the country did not benefit from oil resources. This is quite different in the cases of Iran and Iraq, both of which had a substantial GDP increase from the 1950s to the 1970s. The oil price explosion and expansion of oil production was clearly a driver here. Especially during the early 1970s, oil prices were at an enormously high level. Later on, Iran had some modest decline during the intensive war of 1980–88 with Iraq. In Iraq, in contrast, we have a substantial decline of GDP per capita in the 1990s following the Kuwait crises and the two Gulf wars with the US. GDP in Iraq has most likely experienced the strongest decline of any of the larger countries of the Middle East. The poorest country in this region is Afghanistan, which always had a very low development level; also, the country's educational values were usually quite low. Interestingly, the second highest level of GDP was initially reached by Lebanon. Despite not having oil reserves, Lebanon, as the banking centre of the Middle East and one of the trading centres, had a high national income in the 1950s.

Moving to the Arabian and Gulf economies, we see again a strong difference in the early period between countries with and without oil. For example, Yemen was very poor, whereas the small oil economies in the Gulf like Qatar started with a quite high GDP per capita. The small population of Qatar combined with very large oil reserves resulted in an enormously high GDP per capita. Saudi

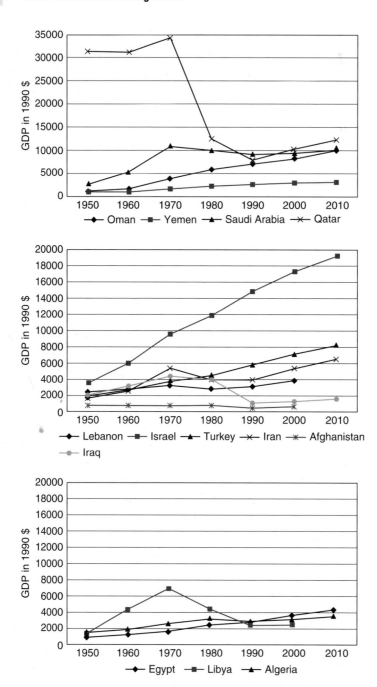

Figure 7.8 GDP per capita in selected countries of the Middle East
Note: the y axes have different scales.

Arabia and Oman benefited from the oil increase. In the 1990s to 2010s period, the three richer countries of this world region had relatively similar GDP values. Finally, we consider three countries of the north African area.[17] We see that Libya shared the strong increase in oil revenues between the 1950s and 1970s. When oil was not a driving force anymore, Libya experienced a decline in GDP per capita up to the 1990s and stagnated since then. There was a gradual increase in Egypt and Algeria. Even during the period of the Algerian civil war (1991–2001), the GDP level did not plummet catastrophically because it was offset by other factors.

Because GDP per capita is strongly dependent on oil revenues and availability, it is important to consider life expectancy as an additional welfare indicator for this period (Figure 7.9). If we compare trends in life expectancy for the same countries, we first observe a steady increase in all the countries, which is mainly driven by worldwide medical progress. Everywhere in the world, we had a strong increase in life expectancy during this period. However, looking a bit more closely, we see some interesting differences in life expectancy. First, slightly different from GDP development, Lebanon develops much better. It starts again at the second highest level directly behind Israel, but in contrast to GDP developments, it stays at a high level, even during the civil wars of the later twentieth century (1975–76, and sporadically thereafter).

The other countries typically developed from values between 35 and 45 years of life expectancy in the 1950s to values of approximately 65 in the 2000s, but some countries deviate from this pattern. The most obvious deviation is Afghanistan, which started at a very low level of approximately 27 years of life expectancy. During its history of civil war and underdevelopment, there was only very modest progress in Afghanistan. Modern technology was not able to diffuse in this country; even in the 2000s, we still only have values of approximately 45 years of life expectancy. In contrast, in Iran, which started even slightly lower than Afghanistan according to these estimates, we see substantial progress in the 1950s to 1970s. Even during the Iran–Iraq war, which many observers compared to the First World War in terms of violence and number of victims, Iran and Iraq did not experience a decrease in life expectancy.[18] In Iran, parallel developments of improving health and nutrition most likely counter-balanced the war effects, although the value of 65 is slightly below what most other Middle Eastern countries achieved during this period. In the Gulf region, Qatar was always slightly ahead of Oman and Saudi Arabia. Unfortunately, we do not have estimates for Yemen during this period. In north Africa, we see a somewhat parallel development in the three countries under study up to the 1970s, after which Egypt had slightly less progress.

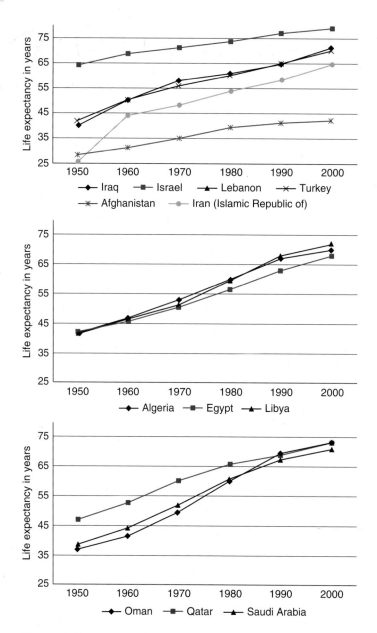

Figure 7.9 Life expectancies in selected countries of the Middle East
Source: www.clio-infra.eu.

Conclusion

The economic history of the Middle East, north Africa and central Asia offers a great amount of variety. Although urban cultures may have lost the world-leading role they had in the high Middle Ages, the urban centres of the region continue to be highly important. Istanbul was the largest city in Europe from around 1600 until 1750. At the other extreme, nomadic economies of the deserts and half deserts display some surprising characteristics. For example, nutritional status was substantially higher in the Middle East than in Europe during the mid-nineteenth century. This can be partly explained by the good access of nomadic people to protein. Only after the cattle plague period of the 1880s and 1890s did health and nutrition development become worse than in Europe. During the nineteenth century, the Middle East became the object of colonialist influences from western European powers after the Ottoman Empire gradually decreased in influence and became the 'sick man of Europe'. In the north-east of the Islamic world, the Russian Empire expanded to include the previous Khanates of Bukhara, Fergana and other Islamic central Asian territories. Cash-crop economies developed, such as cotton in Egypt and what is today Kyrgyzstan.

During the twentieth century, the first substantial oil revenues were earned in Iran and other countries. The economic history of the Middle East, north Africa and central Asia was also a struggle with the 'curse of resources' both during the nineteenth and the twentieth centuries. Pamuk and Williamson (2010) demonstrated that, ironically, favourable development of export prices for Middle Eastern cash crops (such as cotton) lured the region into deindustrialization. Positive price signals had negative long-run consequences.

Another reason why Middle Eastern economies found it difficult to compete with European industrial goods was that human capital and skills to compete with European producers were lacking. The Ottoman Empire had invested almost no public funds in schooling during the mid-nineteenth century; nor did families or religious schools teach abilities useful for industrial development. In addition, low governmental abilities to tax were a factor, as well as institutional developments that interacted with traditional laws and rules of the world region.

The 'curse of resources', of oil in particular, also had the effect that many revenues were reinvested in state-owned firms that became inefficient burdens on the economies. A number of studies have discussed whether oil and other natural resources often result in specific types of political economies in which small groups obtain great wealth while a large part of the population considers their share of income and political participation to be insufficient.

Notes

1. The main indicator is human stature (see below). The term was first used by Komlos; see the Introduction in this volume.
2. See Larguèche (2001).
3. See on the following Owen (1993), Mokyr (2003) and Issawi (1982). Grain was certainly the most important agricultural product. Additional crops included flax, tobacco and opium. The famous Nile inundations helped achieve relatively respectable grain productivity. The other irrigation economy of Mesopotamia (today's Iraq) was also mainly oriented toward grains. However, the rivers were slightly more difficult to handle in Iraq. In particular, they delivered floods in the 'wrong' month, in April and May. This was too late to irrigate the winter crop. However, it could destroy unprotected fields. In addition, the Tigris and Euphrates rivers flooded very quickly in spring, coming from the northern mountains, sometimes causing rivers to move permanently to new channels. In addition to the mentioned grains, large numbers of dates were grown in the south of Mesopotamia around Basra.
4. There were even special towers without doors and windows in Mesopotamia. Some of the peasants also aimed at creating temporary alliances with nomads in order to prevent tax collectors from taxing a large part of their production.
5. During the nineteenth century, the situation of property rights gradually improved, but now population growth was rapid and the imperial interests of Britain and Russia became a challenge for Iran. Although Britain gained considerable influence and Iranian merchants felt that their natural resources were expropriated, Iran never became a formal colony. The Russian Empire was more successful in neighbouring Azerbaijan, which later in the nineteenth century provided substantial oil revenues. Russia also expanded into the steppe of modern Kazakhstan and the 'silk road' area of central Asia.
6. Well-known were muslins from Mosul and damask from Damascus, for example.
7. The wealth of Arabia consisted traditionally mostly of its goats and sheep. Also famous were the horses and camels. Oman developed a significant trading position with up to 2,000 ships moving between India and southern Africa in the early nineteenth century. Some mines for copper and lead existed. Yemen specialized in the production of coffee. This country was politically heavily contested and suffered from several conflicts.
8. Population growth was stimulated by these reforms, as more land was now put to use. Another strong determinant of population growth was the fact that the plague disappeared during the early nineteenth century.
9. Even if migrant selectivity might have been positive, the effect could not be very large.
10. This was a substantial relative decline of human capital during and after colonization. In the later Kyrgyzstan region, development was similar (but from a lower initial value), whereas Turkmenistan had a surprisingly low level during the 1830s and 1840s.

11. We would argue that this is the case if no exogenous motivation for human capital investment exists. However, the cases of Denmark, New Zealand and the early history of the US suggest otherwise; skill-intensive agriculture certainly was an option to develop high income even before later industrialization took place in some of these countries.

12. In addition, the Tanzimat reforms from the 1830s removed many of the constraints under which the minorities ('millets') had been suffering for centuries. They also received support from people of the same religion who lived in Europe and America.

13. The advantage of these samples is that there is no social selectivity in height measurement, although there could be a regional selectivity issue. Stegl and Baten (2009) already accounted for this potential distortion; it seems not to play a large role.

14. All heights are organized by birth cohort, because the strongest influence on final adult stature occurs during the years after birth.

15. In Iran, the decrease happened in 1880 as well. Gilbar (1986) assumes that, in Iran, the boom of crops agriculture such as cotton, opium and grain encouraged people to pay more attention to planting these crops and pushed them away from animal farming.

16. In contrast to industry, for example, where profits went to entrepreneurs and wages to workers.

17. Again we omit Tunisia and Morocco because their development was quite similar to that of Algeria.

18. We assume that there is not misreporting.

Further reading

Coşgel, M. and Ergene, B. A. (2012), 'Inequality of Wealth in the Ottoman Empire: War, Weather, and Long-term Trends in Eighteenth-century Kastamonu', *Journal of Economic History* 72 (2, June), 308–31. Gives a nice snapshot of evidence on inequality.

Issawi, C. (1980), *The Economic History of Turkey*, University of Chicago Press. Rich in details and written accessibly.

  (1982), *An Economic History of the Middle East and North Africa*, New York: Columbia University Press. An accessible and comprehensive economic history of the Middle East.

Kuran, T. (2011), *The Long Divergence: How Islamic Law Held Back the Middle East*, Princeton University Press. A provocative hypothesis about why the Middle East fell back.

Owen, R. (1993), *The Middle East in the World Economy 1800–1914*, London/New York: I. B. Tauris. The trade structure is explained well.

Pamuk, S. (2010), *The Ottoman Empire and European Capitalism, 1820–1913: Trade, Investment and Production*, Cambridge University Press. Pamuk is the pioneer of quantitative economic history of the Middle East.

Pamuk, S. and Williamson, J. G. (2010), 'Ottoman De-industrialization, 1800–1913: Assessing the Magnitude, Impact, and Response', *The Economic History Review* 64 (S1), 159–84. They explain why the rising term of trade lured the Middle East into deindustrialization.

Stegl, M. and Baten, J. (2009), 'Tall and Shrinking Muslims, Short and Growing Europeans: an Anthropometric History of the Middle East, 1840–2007', *Exploration in Economic History* 46, 132–48. The surprising finding of relative high anthropometric welfare around mid-nineteenth century is plausible due to the comparison with similarly high real wages.

References

Barro, R. J. and Lee, J. W. (2013), Data set: www.barrolee.edu, last accessed 15 August 2014.

Baten, J. and Blum, M. (2012), 'Growing Tall but Unequal: New Findings and New Background Evidence on Anthropometric Welfare in 156 Countries, 1810–1989', *Economic History of Developing Regions* 27 (1), 66–85.

Baten, J. and Ghanem, R. (2014), 'Towards a Human Capital History of the Middle East and South Asia 1850–1950', Working Paper, University of Tuebingen.

Baten, J. and Pamuk, S. (2007), 'Inequality in Standards of Living across Europe, 1820–2000: a Preliminary Look', presented at the workshop on Human Capital, Inequality and Living Standards, Measuring Divergence and Convergence in a Globalising Europe, Lund.

Borsch, S. J. (2005), *The Black Death in Egypt and England*, Austin, TX: University of Texas Press.

Bosker, M., Buringh, E. and van Zanden, J. L. (2013), 'From Baghdad to London: Unraveling Urban Development in Europe, the Middle East, and North Africa, 800–1800', *Review of Economics and Statistics* 95 (4), 1418–37.

Danubio, M. E., Domenico Martorella, F., Rufo, E. V. and Sanna, E. (2011), 'Morphometric Distances Among Five Ethnic Groups and Evaluation of the Secular Trend in Historical Libya', *Journal of Anthropological Sciences* 89, 1–12.

Deutsches Staats-Wörterbuch, Bluntschli, J. C. (ed.) (1857), Stuttgart and Leipzig: Giesecke and Devrient.

Findlay, R. and O'Rourke, K. (2007), *Power and Plenty. Trade, War and the World Economy in the Second Millennium*, Princeton University Press.

Ghanem, R. (2014), 'Human Capital Development in the Middle East: Is Secularism a Solution? Evidence from Turkey in the Nineteenth and Twentieth Century', Working Paper, University of Tuebingen.

Gilbar, G. G. (1986), 'The Opening up of Qajar Iran: Some Economic and Social Aspects', *Bulletin of the School of Oriental and African Studies* 49, 76–89.

Juif, D. and Baten, J. (2013), 'A Story of Large Land-owners and Math Skills: Inequality and Human Capital Formation in Long-run Development, 1820–2000', *Journal of Comparative Economics* 42 (2), 375–401.

Larguèche, A. (2001), 'The City and the Sea: Evolving Forms of Mediterranean Cosmopolitanism in Tunis, 1700–1881', in J. Clancy-Smith (ed.), *North Africa,*

Islam and the Mediterranean World: from the Almoravids to the Algerian War, London: Frank Cass, 117–28.

Mokyr, J. (2003) (ed.), *The Oxford Encyclopedia of Economic History*, Oxford University Press.

Owen, R. (1993), *The Middle East in the World Economy 1800–1914*, London/New York: I. B. Tauris.

Ozmucur, S. and Pamuk, S. (2002), 'Real Wages and Standards of Living in the Ottoman Empire, 1489–1914', *The Journal of Economic History* 62 (2), 293–321.

Pamuk, S. (2006), 'Estimating Economic Growth in the Middle East since 1820', *Journal of Economic History* 66, 807–28.

Prayon, V. and Baten, J. (2013), 'Human Capital, Institutions, Settler Mortality, and Economic Growth in Africa, Asia and the Americas', Working Paper, University of Tuebingen.

Rubin, J. (2011), 'Institutions, the Rise of Commerce and the Persistence of Laws: Interest Restrictions in Islam and Christianity', *The Economic Journal* 121 (December), 1310–39.

Women in global economic history

Sarah Carmichael, Selin Dilli and Auke Rijpma

> The existing social relations between the two sexes – the legal subordination of one sex to the other – is wrong itself, and now one of the chief hindrances to human improvement.

> John Stuart Mill, *The Subjection of Women*, 1869

The unequal treatment of women is not only intrinsically problematic, but also detrimental to society. Research shows widespread negative effects of an unequal position for women, including being detrimental to children's educational attainment and economic growth (Carmichael *et al.* 2014). Improving gender equality, therefore, plays an important role in the development process. The comparative study of gender equality, particularly from a historical perspective, is key to understanding current-day gender and development outcomes. For instance, in the Middle East and North Africa (MENA), a woman at the age of 30 is likely to be healthier and more educated than her mother, having benefited from massive investments in the education and health sectors in recent decades. However, she is likely to face greater obstacles in finding a job and playing an active public role in her society than her contemporaries face elsewhere in the world (World Bank 2004: xiv). The MENA region also features unequal inheritance rights of women and has the lowest percentage of female parliamentarians in the world (Carmichael *et al.* 2014). Economic development alone does not seem to sufficiently explain gender inequalities. After accounting for national differences in income, women in the Islamic world are still socially and politically disadvantaged relative to men (Fish 2002; Coffé and Dilli 2014).

A handful of cross-national studies take the historical position of women into account.[1] Alesina *et al.* (2013), for example, show that societies that traditionally practised plough agriculture have less gender equality today. Similarly, Dilli *et al.* (2015) conclude that the institutional arrangement of countries, particularly in terms of historical institutions, is as important as economic development in determining gender equality outcomes. With gender inequalities today the result of historical processes, a historical perspective on the issue is required.

One of the first issues in understanding gender equality is how to capture such a multifaceted concept. Women can be discriminated against in diverse ways, for

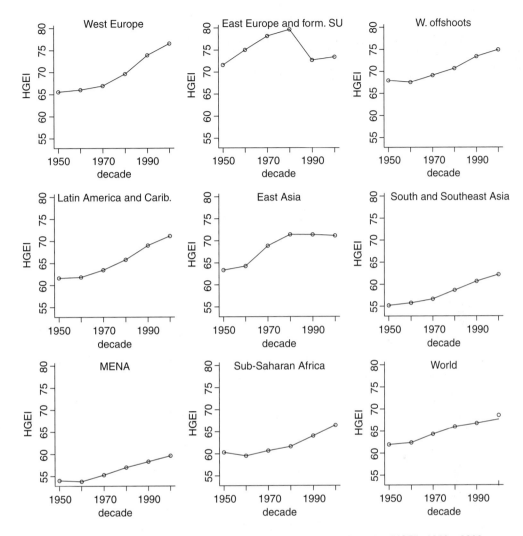

Figure I7.1 Regional averages of the historical gender equality index (HGEI), 1950s–2000s
Source: www.clio-infra.eu.
Note: scaled 100=equality, >100 female advantage.

instance prohibitions on working outside the house, unequal pay, gender-based violence and forced child marriages. Capturing women's position in society thus requires multiple indicators. To create a summary picture of the position of women within a given society, six of these are combined into a composite index by calculating a weighted average of each indicator as a ratio of female to male achievements (Figure I7.1, details in Dilli *et al.* forthcoming). This historical gender equality index shows that progress on a world scale has taken place. However, the gap between high and low performers remains. South and Southeast Asia (SSEA), along with the MENA region are still at the bottom of the pack.

Figure I7.2 The average man and woman in 1900, 1950 and 2000

Turning to the underlying components of the index, the next section illustrates the development of marriage ages of women, sex ratios and the percentage of women in parliament for countries and regions across the world over the course of the twentieth century.

Marriage ages

Marriage ages of women can be used as an indicator of the position of women in society. Hajnal (1965) first suggested a distinct historical difference between marriage ages in western Europe and the rest of the world and linked this to the possibility for women to work in service before marrying. He proposed a division between east and west along a line from St Petersburg to Trieste. Marriage ages to the west of this line were traditionally higher, with women marrying above the age of 24 and closer in age to their spouses, while Eastern Europe displayed lower ages of marriage, and yet further east marriage ages of Asian women indicated the prevalence of child marriages. De Moor and van Zanden (2010) argue, using evidence from early modern Europe, that women's age at marriage influenced economic development, partly because women marrying at higher ages had more opportunities to acquire human capital. Recent scholarship has demonstrated that the line Hajnal proposed is too stark, showing a continuum with a shift towards lower ages from Poland's western to southern border (Szołtysek 2012).

On average, across the world, marriage ages of women have been rising (Figure 17.3). However countries such as China, Mexico, Russia and Egypt have shown a smaller increase in this measure of female empowerment than, say, Japan. India's low ages at marriage are particularly striking (see Gupta 2014). The changes over time in the marriage ages of the UK and the Netherlands both show a similar dip after the Second World War, concomitant with the 'baby boom' and the golden age of the housewife when women retreated into the household.

Sex ratios

Sen (1992) observed that globally there are 100 million women less than the natural ratio at birth (1.05) and survival rates in countries without excess female mortality would suggest. Sen linked this to traditional culture and values, as well as the economic status of women. Work by McNay *et al.* (2005) showed that for nineteenth-century England and Wales excess female mortality varied regionally and depended on demographic conditions and what employment opportunities were open to women.

Here, the so-called 'sex ratio' is calculated as the ratio of girls to boys aged 0–5 to capture discrimination against female infants and sex-selective abortion (Carmichael *et al.* 2014). China and India are among the countries with the most biased sex ratios today – huge countries that impact the global trend. Strikingly, both countries have seen a recent worsening of sex ratios from normal levels in the 1950s (India) and the 1970s (China). This is due to the combination of cultural preferences for boys and, in China, the one-child policy, combined with ultrasound technology enabling sex-selective abortion (Klasen and Wink 2003). This example shows that there is not always linear progress towards gender equality.

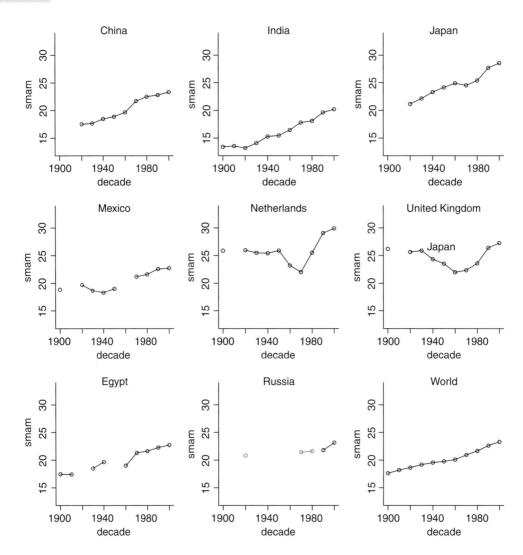

Figure I7.3 Singulate mean age at marriage (smam) in selected countries and world average, 1900s–2000s
Source: www.clio-infra.eu.

Political representation

Although significant progress has been made regarding the political rights of women in the last two centuries, women are still underrepresented in the political decision making processes (Figure I7.4). In 1907, Finland became the first country in world history to elect a woman to parliament. More than a century later, women hold 22.3 per cent of parliamentary seats globally. Countries display very different patterns of growth and decline over time. Sri Lanka has always had

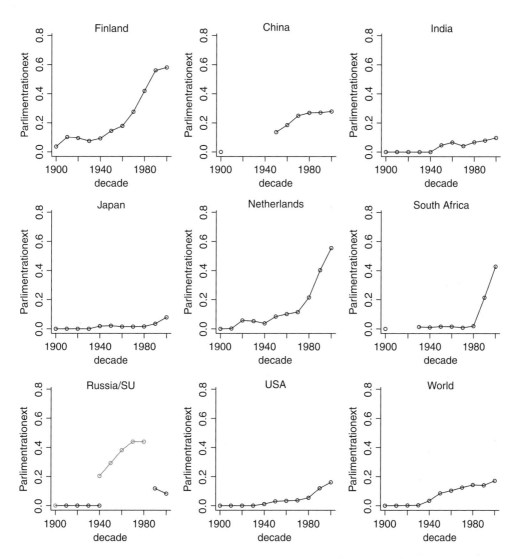

Figure 17.4 Ratio of female to male parliamentarians in selected countries and world average, 1900s–2000s
Source: www.clio-infra.eu.

less than 5 per cent female parliamentarians whereas older democracies, such as Denmark, Sweden and Norway show steady increases in female representation, reaching 30 per cent in the 2000s (Paxton *et al.* 2010). While it took them almost 100 years to reach this threshold, countries like Rwanda and South Africa introduced gender quotas to hasten women's political representation, thereby quickly reaching Scandinavian levels (Dahlerup and Leyenaar 2013). The removal of such quota systems can also have consequences, as is the case in the countries of the former USSR. Once near the top in the world rankings of female representation, the fall of the Berlin Wall brought the removal of the quota system and now most countries of the region rank far behind northern Europe and many developing countries (Saxonberg 2000).

Explanations of the causes of gender equality can be grouped into two strands. The first, modernization theory, attributes gender disparities to countries' levels of development, arguing that as countries become more economically developed, democratic and educated, women can improve their bargaining position (Inglehart and Norris 2003). However this link is not straightforward. Boserup (1970) was among the first to argue that some stages of industrialization worsen gender equality. Goldin (1995) showed women's labour force participation to be U-shaped: declining in the first stage of development, but improving later. Moreover, looking at the low level of parliamentary participation of women in many western European countries, worsening sex ratios in China, or the limited labour force participation of women in the MENA, casts doubt on whether development always translates into gender equality. A second strand of literature therefore focuses on the long-term norms and values as the (deep) causes of the persistent gender inequalities. Family structures, legal traditions, religion and agricultural practices have all been shown to have long-term effects on current gender equality outcomes (Dilli *et al.* 2015, Alesina *et al.* 2013).

It is clear that the position of women has improved since 1900. However, substantial differences remain between regions and countries. Moreover, there has not been much catch-up in gender equality and no country in the world has achieved absolute equality between the sexes. This suggests that improving women's position in society is an area where work remains to be done. Understanding the historical roots of gender inequalities is an important step therein.

Note

1. For a full overview by region, see www.wiwi.uni-tuebingen.de/lehrstuehle/volks wirtschaftslehre/wirtschaftsgeschichte/research.html.

References

Alesina, A., Giuliano, P. and Nunn, N. (2013), 'On the Origins of Gender Roles: Women and the Plough', *Quarterly Journal of Economics* 128: 469–530.
Boserup, E. (1970), *Woman's Role in Economic Development*, London: George Allen and Unwin Ltd.
Carmichael, S., Dilli, S. and Rijpma, A. (2014), 'Gender Inequality', in J. L. van Zanden, J. Baten, M. Mira d'Ercole, A. Rijpma, C. Smith and M. Timmer (eds.), *How was Life: Global Well-being Since 1820*, Paris: OECD.

Coffé, H. and Dilli, S. (2014), 'The Gender Gap in Political Participation in Muslim-Majority Countries', *International Political Science Review*.

Dahlerup, D. and Leyenaar, M. (2013), 'The Move towards Gender Balance in Politics – in Old and New Democracies', paper to the 3rd European Conference on Politics and Gender, Barcelona.

De Moor, T. and van Zanden, J. L. (2010), 'Girl Power: the European Marriage Pattern and Labour Markets in the North Sea Region in the Late Medieval and Early Modern Period', *Economic History Review* 63 (1).

Dilli, S., Rijpma, A. and Carmichael, S. G. (2015), 'Achieving Gender Equality: Development versus Historical Legacies', *CESifo Economic Studies* 61: 301–34.

(forthcoming), 'Gender Equality in a Historical Perspective: Introducing the Historical Gender Equality Index', *GCEH Working Paper Series*.

Fish, S. (2002), 'Islam and Authoritarianism', *World Politics* 55 (1): 4–37.

Goldin, C. (1995), 'The U-Shaped Female Labour Force Function in Economic Development and Economic History', in T. P. Schultz (ed.), *Investment in Women's Human Capital and Economic Development*, University of Chicago Press: 61–90.

Gupta, B. (2014), 'Where Have all the Brides Gone? Son Preference and Marriage in India over the Twentieth Century', *Economic History Review* 67 (1).

Hajnal, J. (1965), 'European Marriage Patterns in Perspective', in D. V. Glass and D. E. C. Eversley (eds.), *Population in History: Essays in Historical Demography*, London: Edward Arnold.

Inglehart, R. and Norris, P. (2003), *Rising Tide: Gender Equality and Cultural Change*, Cambridge University Press.

Klasen, S. and Wink, C. (2003), '"Missing Women": Revisiting the Debate', *Feminist Economics* 9 (2–3): 263–99.

McNay, K., Humphries, J. and Klasen, S. (2005), 'Excess Female Mortality in Nineteenth-century England and Wales: a Regional Analysis', *Social Science History* 29 (4).

Paxton, P., Hughes, M. M. and Painter, M. A. (2010), 'Growth in Women's Political Representation: a Longitudinal Exploration of Democracy, Electoral System and Gender Quotas', *European Journal of Political Research* 49 (1): 25–52.

Saxonberg, S. (2000), 'Women in East European Parliaments', *Journal of Democracy* 11(2): 145–58.

Sen, A. (1992), 'Missing Women', *British Medical Journal* 304 (6827): 587–88.

Szołtysek, M. (2012), 'Spatial Construction of European Family and Household Systems: a Promising Path or a Blind Alley? An Eastern European Perspective', *Continuity and Change* 27 (01): 11–52.

World Bank (2004), MENA Development Report: Women in the Public Sphere, https://openknowledge.worldbank.org/handle/10986/15036, accessed 15 April 2013.

H7.1 Imperial expansion of the Ottoman Empire and its cultural determinants
Rima Ghanem and Joerg Baten

The reasons behind the geographical expansion of the Ottoman Empire have been studied in recent research from a new perspective. Iyigun (2013) analyzed the directions of imperial expansion based on the cultural influences of the Ottoman ruler's family. While male lineage was mostly predetermined, the Sultan mother was typically a former slave, often a convert who was born in Europe. Because the Sultan's mother educated the prince, she provided her son with some cultural preferences that influenced the direction of territorial expansion. For example, fifteenth-century mothers were of Turkish origin, with only one female slave from Albania in between. The ethnic backgrounds of the Sultan's mothers during the sixteenth century were different, as one Polish and two Italian women became concubines and later prince's mothers.[1] During the eighteenth century, the pirates of the western Mediterranean provided French female slaves (as well as Italians and women from the Balkans); some of these later became Sultan's mothers. Iyigun (2013) argues that this composition influenced the direction of territorial expansion, specifically the shift away from Christian target territories between the fifteenth and sixteenth centuries towards the regions of the east, and back again during the seventeenth century.

Note
1. In the seventeenth century, many Serbian women also entered the Harem and became Sultans' mothers, in addition to one Russian and one Greek. However, during this century, there were also Bosnians and one Albanian who might have come from Muslim families.

Reference
Iyigun, M. F. (2013), 'Lessons from the Ottoman Harem on Culture, Religion and Wars', *Economic Development and Cultural Change* 61 (4), 693–730.

8 South Asia

Tirthankar Roy

The region now known as South Asia consists of five large nations – India, Pakistan, Bangladesh, Nepal and Sri Lanka, and several smaller nations. Most debates and controversies in the economic history of South Asia usually relate to the area and population under India, Pakistan and Bangladesh, which together formed a large part of the territory of the British Indian Empire between 1858 and 1947.[1]

This area is geographically very diverse, containing the Himalayan mountains in the north, the huge fertile floodplains of the two great Himalayan river systems, the Indus and the Ganges, the world's largest delta, a long coastline, arid uplands, tropical dry forests and savannah and the Thar desert in the west. It is also socially very mixed, consisting of many language groups, almost all religions of the world and social practices in one region that are vastly different from those in another. Politically, too, the region was never united. The densely populated floodplains and deltas were territories where several large empires formed and disintegrated from before the Christian Era. These empires lived mainly on land taxes. The seaboard and the arid zones, on the other hand, were controlled by smaller and poorer states, usually more dependent on trade. A loose integration of these worlds was achieved during the reign of the great Mughal emperors (1526–1707), but it did not last. The empire fell apart in the early eighteenth century, giving rise to a cluster of semi-independent successor states.

With its geography and history being as varied as just described it is surprising that the economic history of South Asia should exist as a coherent discourse at all. The reason that it does has to do with the trajectory that unfolded after the fall of the Mughal Empire. Two developments imparted a certain unity in the pattern of economic change thereafter. First, the British Empire in South Asia, which rose to power between the mid-eighteenth century and the mid-nineteenth, achieved a degree of political, bureaucratic and military centralization that the region had not seen before. The process of centralization built upon a different system of taxation and, in turn, a different relationship between the state and the elites from before. The current political boundaries of the three nations, as well as persistent problems of achieving a peaceful federal setup in all of them, are both to some extent a result of the way the Empire had forced a union in an otherwise diverse land.

Second, thanks to its prehistory as a trading zone and later the colonial status, colonial India experienced a deep economic integration with the world. Trade, investment and migration rose to higher levels than before. Curiously, the market integration produced paradoxical effects. Colonial India was the only tropical country to have industrialized in the nineteenth century on a truly large scale; employment in factories increased from less than 100,000 in 1860 to two million in 1940. The rise of factory industry owed something to the many-sided links India forged with Britain. On the other hand, South Asia lost a part of its rich craft heritage, and its major livelihood, agriculture, continued to generate small average income, subsistence wages, poor yield and overall gained little from growing export crops for the world market.

The paradox of modernization amid persistent poverty is the origin of many debates in the economic history of South Asia. It will naturally occupy a large part of the present survey too. In order to manage a large scholarship contributed by specialists on many branches of history, I will concentrate on only one segment of it, the one that has handled quantitative data. To this paradox, a new theme has been added in the last ten years. This is the divergence debate of the 2000s. Whereas older discourses on the origin of international economic inequality tended to focus on Europe, the divergence debate foregrounded Asia, Africa and Latin America. Inspired by the new positioning of Asia, and the quantitative nature of the discussion, scholars specializing in India have constructed new estimates of levels of living in the region. The result has been a firmer integration of South Asian history with world history. This second theme will also form a part of the present survey.

The chapter consists of four sections. The next section presents a very brief outline of the major historiographical debates on precolonial and colonial South Asia. The section that follows summarizes the literature assessing the impact of the Empire. The third section focuses on the living standard research in the context of modern debates on inequality. The fourth and the final section deals with post-colonial India, and presents a survey as well as an interpretation of continuity and change between the colonial and the postcolonial times.

A quick tour through the big questions

That the power of the ancient and medieval Empires flowed from control over land is almost an axiom in the literature on precolonial South Asia. The most powerful of these had formed, or tried to control the lands at the intersection of the Indus and Ganges floodplains. This was a strategically important territory being at the crossroads of routes out of South Asia into the territories held by powerful states and military tribes in central Asia, Afghanistan and Iran. It was also near enough to the highly fertile agricultural tracts along the Ganges. The two rivers, especially the

Ganges, provided access to the northern deltas and the Indian Ocean. Large towns formed in these geographical zones. The most famous of these sites were also the capitals of powerful states.

How did property right in land and military privilege combine to maintain such power? Why did such arrangements begin, last a long time and disintegrate? How did politics affect the merchants and artisans? The pioneering work of William Moreland, D. D. Kosambi and, later, interpretive works by the feudalism school led by R. S. Sharma, and the Aligarh historians led by Irfan Habib, address some of these questions with different material.[2] One proposition that finds a great deal of favour now is that these Empires relied on a decentralized system of tax collection and military service. By implication, they were vulnerable to simultaneous outbursts of rebellion by many local agents. Parallel to this set of works interested in the relationship between the land and the state, another set looks at the thriving commercial world of the seaboard. Here Indian and Arab merchants, and from around 1600 Europeans, took part in the Indian Ocean trade in textiles, spices, horses, silks and other commodities (see Map 8.1 showing the centres of South Asian industrial production).[3] The relationship between the maritime world and the land-based world of the interior, however, remains an unsettled issue.

One of the post-Mughal successor states was Bengal where effective political and military power was transferred from the old regime to the British East India Company around 1757–65. Between 1765 and 1818, the Company acquired new territories in western, southern and northern India. These territories passed on to the British Crown in 1858. The link between the land and the sea becomes a major problem in explaining the rise of the Company. The great land-based empires of earlier times – the Mughals and the Sultanates near Delhi, Satavahana or Vijayanagar in the peninsular, the Gupta of central India, the Maurya in the east – had only tenuous control upon the seaboard. The Company was not land-based, it was a merchant firm located on the hitherto politically marginal seaboard. And yet, it formed the most powerful Empire the region had seen. Why did such a dramatic turn happen? Surely, a proximate cause of its success was a standing army maintained from central treasury, and a suppression or marginalization of feudal elements of support. But how much did that revolutionary step owe to the Company's foreign origin, commercial origin or pure chance? What role, if any, did the Company's own internal organization play in its transformation from a multinational trading firm to a territorial state?

Questions like these animate the economic history of 'early modern' India. The core of the discipline, however, is engaged with 'modern' India, or the era of the British Empire, and the long-term legacy that colonialism left upon the modern nations of South Asia. These years saw a number of momentous changes. India's

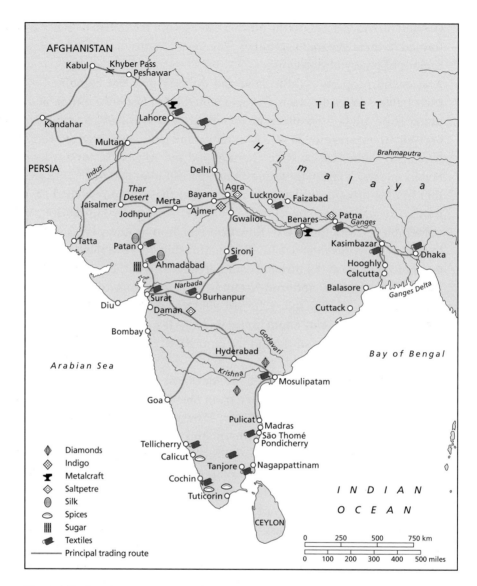

Map 8.1 Trade and manufacturing in South Asia under the Mughals in the sixteenth century
Source: see map 1.1.

status as a trading partner of Britain changed in this time from an exporter of artisanal textiles to an exporter of agricultural commodities and consumer of British textiles, aided by the railways, steamships and the telegraph. The abolition of slavery encouraged New World plantations to organize the import of South Asian labour. The Empire was readier than any previous regime to set up laws governing commercial, financial and labour transactions. From the time of the Mughal collapse, Indian capitalists migrated from the interior world to the port cities established in the seventeenth century by the Company, giving rise to a new cosmopolitan capitalist milieu based on Indo-European partnership and competition, in Bombay, Calcutta and Madras.

As a state, the British Empire in India functioned as if it saw itself as the guardian of a system of connected markets maintained by means of military power, business legislation and monetary management. The flow of goods, money and skills that this order enabled came as an opportunity for Indian capitalists, and generated an industrialization that was quite offbeat in world history. Indian merchants of the port cities, for example, could access British knowhow and services with little difficulty and find it feasible to set up cotton mills in direct competition with Manchester. But having defined its role as a guardian of markets, the Empire withdrew into passivity. Its contribution to infrastructure and welfare was limited. Its only direct contribution was maintaining peace, construction of irrigation canals and running the railways, and even the last two commitments it met fitfully. Most South Asians lived in a village, and if that village was located far away from a canal or a railway line, the land produced just enough value for a bare subsistence. The state did little to transform lives in the remote countryside. To this failure, another one was added late in the interwar period. The political drive to keep India and Britain linked became a blunder in the post-Depression years when the British economy faltered and fewer Indians wanted the dependence to continue. The cynical persistence with the policy led to a fierce backlash among wealthy Indians, who then funded the nationalist movement. Disgruntled peasants in many regions joined in, turning nationalism into a mass movement.

With such a mixed record, was there economic growth during the one hundred years of British rule? Was there increasing inequality in this time? Was the legacy of the Empire to be seen in terms of lasting modernization or lasting retardation?

The debate around these questions became highly politicized and emotionally charged from before independence in 1947. The nationalist movement in the final years of colonial rule had popularized a vision of the past according to which there had been little economic growth and a rise in inequality in the previous century. The early nationalists suggested that India was forced to buy services from Britain that it did not need in exchange for export receipts. This unequal exchange showed up as a net deficit on the services account of the balance of payments, against a net trade surplus with its main partner Britain. The 'drain', it was said, was a politically manipulated payment that compromised India's capacity to make investment. In the 1960s and 1970s, Marxist historians added a second mechanism linking the Empire with Indian underdevelopment. The nineteenth century globalization induced a pattern of specialization wherein India turned into a net exporter of agricultural goods and an importer of manufactures. The process led to deindustrialization, or unemployment among the artisans, on the one hand. And it failed to benefit the peasants on the other hand, because high taxes and excessive risks led to accumulation of rural debts and transfer of landed property from producers to money-lenders. The drain explained stagnation, and the impoverishment or 'immiseration' of the peasants explained inequality.

The main body of statistical research in the field directly or indirectly tests this paradigm of underdevelopment caused by colonial policy. It is only in the last fifteen-odd years that there have been attempts to explore other themes.

The colonial economy

Early statistical work tested the paradigm by means of measurement of production, income and prices; construction of the external accounts; labour force reconstruction to test for deindustrialization and estimates of public saving and investment (Sivasubramonian 2000; Heston 1983; Guha 1992; Banerji 1962; Thorner 1962; Bagchi 1976; Thavaraj 1962). Gross domestic product (GDP) data will be dealt with more fully below. Balance of payments reconstruction produced good estimates of the outflow on the services. And labour force reconstruction showed a fall in the employment of artisans during the census years, 1872–1931.

Overall, however, the evidence for the immiseration model was neither conclusive nor uncontroversial. For example, labour force data revealed an unexplained difference between male and female participation in manufacturing; a decisive fall in participation characterized women more than men. In the nineteenth century, the outflow on the invisibles account contained payment for useful services procured from Britain, which should have contributed to domestic income. If there was deindustrialization in the nineteenth century, the process slowed or even disappeared in the twentieth century. While credit transaction in volume increased in the countryside, the extent of transfer of land ownership was very small. Distress sale of crops, a supposed sign of peasant indebtedness, was questioned in studies that found supply sufficiently responsive to prices, and therefore, profits (Narain 1965).

Recent work has returned to some of these themes, in a more dispassionate way than in the halcyon days of nationalism and global Marxism. Using prices, one of these works pushes back the date of an industrial decline into the eighteenth century, thus attributing its onset to domestic issues rather than trade (Clingingsmith and Williamson 2008). Consumption is the point of interest in new research on the artisan, showing that artisanal production and consumption of craft goods revived after an initial shock (Roy 1999).

Labour force and balance of payments are indirect tests of the hypothesis that the Empire impoverished India. Trends in GDP should supply a more direct test. What does GDP show?

Table 8.1 Average annual growth rates of GDP by sector of origin, 1865–2007

| | GDP at factor cost, constant prices | | | | | |
	Primary sector	Secondary sector	Tertiary sector	Total	Population	GDP per head
1865–1910	1.1	*	*	1.5	0.5	1.0
1910–40	0.0	2.3	2.2	1.1	1.1	0.0

Notes: Indian Union from 1950, British India for periods before. The primary sector consists of agriculture, forestry and fishing; secondary sector of manufacturing, mining, electricity, gas and construction; and the tertiary sector of trade, hotels and transportation, financial and business services and administration and defence. For more details and source, see Roy (2012a).
* These rates are unreliable.

National income of colonial India

National income estimates based on official statistics are available consistently from 1900 onward; and more unevenly between 1860 and 1900. National income estimates for colonial India (1857–1947) establish five propositions about the process of economic change in these years:

(a) GDP, total and per head, increased at modest rates between 1860 and 1914, and at near-zero rates between 1914 and 1947 (Table 8.1).
(b) Agricultural income imparted the strongest effect on GDP (Table 8.1). Agriculture grew by expanding the land frontier between 1860 and 1914. Land became scarce after 1914, and in some of the older agricultural tracts, land was losing natural fertility.
(c) Industry imparted a positive effect on GDP (Table 8.1). This effect was a combination of two distinct processes: a robust growth of modern factories and a slow growth in artisanal industry, which achieved this growth while changing over from traditional household-based production to wage-based production.
(d) Income from the services imparted a positive effect on GDP (Table 8.1). The services too saw a structural change. Traditional non-wage services such as bonded labour in villages declined, and modern wage-based services, such as banking, insurance and foreign trade, expanded.
(e) Labour productivity growth was small throughout, especially so in agriculture (see also Table 8.2). This feature is best summed up in a recent work: 'During the late nineteenth century, labor productivity growth was fastest in industry, as modern industry developed in India, and slowest in services, despite the modernization of the transport network. During the first half of the twentieth century, although there was respectable labor productivity growth in industry

Table 8.2 Average annual growth rates of output per employee (% per year)

	Agriculture	Industry	Services	GDP
1872–73 – 1900–01	0.4	1.1	0.0	0.4
1900–01 – 1946–47	0.0	1.4	1.0	0.5

Source: Broadberry and Gupta (2014).

Table 8.3 Investment ratio and size of government (% of GDP), 1900–2007

	Gross investment			
	Government	Private	Total	Government expenditure
1900–13	2.2	4.7	6.9	
1913–39	2.0	7.3	9.3	5.2

and services, labor productivity growth in the economy as a whole was held back by stagnation in agriculture' (Broadberry and Gupta 2014).

As the cited text shows, the growth process of the colonial period, though unimpressive overall, had strengths that derived from the greater openness of the economy. Industrialization, for example, was financed by private investment (Table 8.3). These investments were partly procured from Britain and partly domestically resourced but used to buy skills and machinery from Britain. In turn, industry was relatively more export-oriented. Without the impetus coming from 'globalization', which would mean in the nineteenth century integration with a Britain-centred world economy, the genesis of Indian industrialization cannot be explained at all.

The real drag on GDP per head was not lack of industrial development, but labour productivity, especially agricultural productivity. With manufacturing and services doing well and agriculture doing badly, did inequality increase?

Inequality

The head of the 1891 census remarked that 'a population spread over such a variety of conditions … cannot be treated statistically as a whole' (Baines 1893). Inequality measures, therefore, are important as descriptions of development, and also as a means to test models of growth or stagnation. Colonial India did see increasing inequality, but not the kind identified by the immiserating model. There is little evidence of land transfer and class-polarization in rural India. On the other hand, rise in inequality almost certainly was an effect of the globalization process, which favoured the resource-rich agricultural tracts and the port cities.

For example, average wage in industry and services increased faster than the average wage in agriculture (compare also the productivity growth rates). Labour markets were not integrated, and agricultural labourers could rarely access the urban labour market. The urban–rural wage gap also points to a sustained trend towards increasing inequality.[4]

Was inequality increasing within agriculture? The extent of actual transfer of land was rather limited, and if the Madras presidency is representative, inequality in land-holding did not change (Kumar 1975). Peasants were famously averse to parting with land. Inequality could still increase in the countryside by another process. Increasing elasticity of labour supply, due to institutional and demographic changes, could depress wages. This effect was present locally in many areas, though wage convergence in the aggregate was a slow process (Collins 1999). A mild rise in inequality does show up when we use the wage–GDP ratio in agriculture, which declined between 1873 and 1939 (Roy 2007).

Fred Atkinson's estimation of national income by occupational classes for 1875 and 1895 is capable of generating a Gini coefficient of personal income inequality, if we are prepared to make the assumption that peasant incomes were distributed equally or almost equally across classes (Atkinson 1902). The only possible defence for such an assumption would be that inequality in agriculture was of low order in colonial South India as well as in the 1950s, by which date consumption surveys became available. Further assuming that agricultural workers were employed for part of the year, we derive Gini coefficients for India in 1895 in the range 0.26–0.32. This is well below the levels Simon Kuznets reported for the 1950s, which ranged between 0.4 and 0.5 (Kuznets 1963). Revision of his analysis of Indian data claimed that Kuznets had over-estimated inequality, and produced ratios that ranged between 0.3 and 0.4 (Ojha and Bhatt 1964). Again, a slight, but only a slight, increase in inequality is plausible.

Atkinson's dataset suggests one further conclusion. Even though urban–rural wages diverged, the distance between the top income and the lowest income narrowed somewhat between 1875 and 1895. Some of the highest individual earners in 1875 were the European officers in the army and the civil service. As the officer corps in the army, the police and the railways 'Indianized', the number of those earning middling incomes expanded. Outside the government, the growth of a middle class was represented by the rising number of merchants, contractors, bankers, money-lenders, doctors, lawyers, managers, clerks and many middle-to-richer peasants who had surplus to sell, could sell it easily, and thus gained from agricultural trade.

If the hypothesis that rising inequality owed to globalization is correct, then we should see increasing regional inequality as well. This is so because India was exporting mainly agricultural commodities and natural-resource-intensive manufactures. Two recent exercises on regional inequality produce slightly contradictory pictures. One of these observes provincial incomes from recon-structed dataset. The other measures inequality in a mixed set of benchmarks (but not income) based on an actual survey of district data (Caruana-Galizia 2013; Roy 2014). The latter finds support for a rise in inequality during 1850–1900, the former does not, for a later time span. Given the different methodology, the two results are not necessarily contradictory, but both are indirect measures at best.

Few historians would conclude from this evidence that the Marxist paradigm of stagnation and inequality has failed. But many would consider that the paradigm has more explanatory power in local contexts than as a global theory of colonialism and development. In any case, current research has moved away from this debate, and has approached the colonial economy by other routes than drain, deindustrialization, or rural credit. Labour productivity and public goods are two of these new themes.

Other themes

The older research on growth and inequality more or less bypassed the issue of productivity trends. An important recent development, led by Susan Wolcott, looks closely at quality and productivity of labour. These works foreground efficiency and work ethic in a discussion on comparative economic growth. An early application of the idea suggests that the Indian cotton mill workers had a cultural norm of low effort. This is reflected, for instance, in high worker-to-machine ratios in textiles. This evidence is viewed differently by others, who see high worker/machine ratios as the profit-maximizing response to the low cost of Indian labour (Wolcott and Clark 1999; Wolcott 1994; Gupta 2008). The low cost of labour is indirectly linked to low agricultural yield.

The older political critique of the colonial state was preoccupied with its role in sustaining unequal exchange. More recent research has explored another dimension, public goods and welfare.[5] That the British Indian state made limited investment in infrastructure and welfare is well known. But the public goods and infrastructure that it did produce was also regionally variable (Map 8.2 shows the highest density of railways near the production centres of wheat in Punjab and along the Ganges). A cluster of recent papers explore the reasons, and emphasize institutions, local autonomy and fiscal resources (Banerjee and Iyer 2005; Iyer 2010; Chaudhary 2010). The major field of public–private investment in British India, the railways, has been the subject of fresh research, and the verdict of this research is rather favourable to the state.[6] A broader notion of efficiency as tradability is explored in two papers on market integration, one on agricultural labour in the colonial period, and the other on

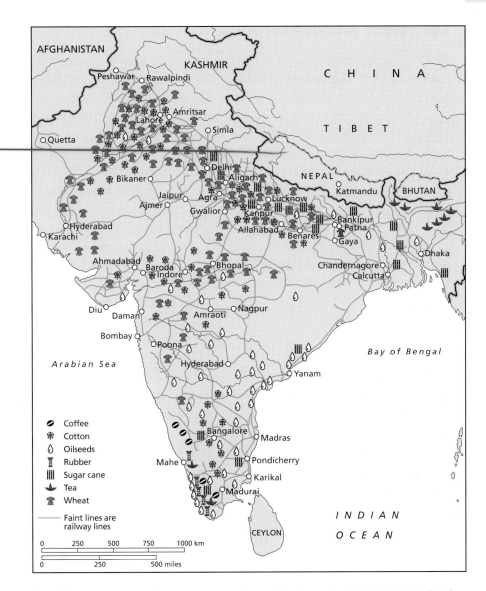

Map 8.2 Regional economic specialization in South Asia during the late nineteenth and early twentieth century
Source: see map 1.1.

grain markets for an earlier period (Collins 1999; Studer 2008). Both papers find the level of market integration relatively small in the aggregate.

Partly, the motivation to seek new research questions in the recent years comes from a desire to integrate India with current discourses on comparative economic development. Institutions, public goods, worker efficiency – all of these themes do this in different ways. But the divergence debate of the last decade achieved a deeper integration.

Living standards in the long run

The divergence debate is significant, among other reasons, because it asks the question of *when* India started falling behind western Europe. Making a useful contribution to that question requires going further back in time than an Empire-focused economic history of South Asia normally does. The major contribution by Kenneth Pomeranz studies early modern China and shows that around 1800 China was like western Europe in many respects (Pomeranz 2000). A similar point was earlier advanced by Prasannan Parthasarathi with Indian data (Parthasarathi 1998). These works, as well as independent advances in the use of anthropometric data, encouraged research on the measurement of living standards in the long run. The material can be divided into four clusters: real wage, height, consumption and morbidity-mortality. Of these clusters, the second (height) is omitted from the current chapter because it is discussed more fully elsewhere in the volume (see the Interlinking Chapter 18 by Baten and Inwood, and the Introduction).

Wage

Using wage data in tests of the welfare implication of colonial rule is not a new practice. The oldest tradition in quantitative history among Indian scholars made use of wage series. But then as now, the wages used were of questionable value because of unresolved sampling bias issues.

The long-term wage-series used most often come from two early twentieth century Indian economists, Brij Narain and Radhakamal Mukherjee (Narain 1929; Mukherjee 1967). Both start from *c.* 1600, and both rely for their earlier wages on English and Dutch East India Company records. For example, based mainly on Dutch reports of wages paid out to unskilled and semi-skilled labourers in the Mughal establishments (Rs. 3–10 per month), and what the Dutch factory paid out to a similar class of workers, one of these authors concluded that 'the most common rate of wages for ordinary unskilled work at the time of Jehangir [1605–27] was about Rs. 3 per month' (Narain 1929: 13). With wheat selling at 84 kg to a rupee, and spring millet at half that price, the wage converts into a quantity of grain that would amount, at 2011 retail prices of wheat or millet, to 4–8 times the poverty line in 2011. The then-and-now comparison enabled Narain, a nationalist, to contend that manual workers in Mughal India were lavishly well-off compared with his own time. Mukherjee reached a similar result using similar data.

These results are questionable. The 'labour market' the Dutch Company accessed in this time could not be a representative one. Being foreigners they had little bargaining power and being the biggest merchant firm, they had deep pockets. It would be unrealistic to expect that these rich and tiny coastal enclaves were in any way representative of any general pattern. The same point would apply to the princely establishments. The market in Delhi or Agra was not integrated with the rural markets, as the Aligarh historians suggest. Migration of peasants and labourers to the Mughal cities, for example, was rare. The city wages would not be comparable with city wages in, say, 1900, when workers did circulate between the village and city more frequently.

Parthasarathi shows that, around 1800, real wages were relatively high in the Kaveri river delta thanks to high productivity of agricultural land (Parthasarathi 1998). With these wages as benchmark, the nineteenth century would have seen a significant regress in conditions of labour. The coastal wages again form a special high-wage sample. How greatly wages could vary between the coast and the interior was illustrated in the evidence of a Madras officer Thomas Cockburn, who collected data on the wages of Madras labourers from around 1800 (British Parliamentary Papers 1812–3: 270). The per head annual expenditure of a labour family was 77 per cent higher than agricultural wages in the interior, confirming his own conjecture that 'in the interior price of labor … must of course be much lower than in Madras'. These differences reflected yield differences between irrigated and dry-land agriculture. The variation was so large when sample surveys were first available that it should be factored in as a fundamental condition of labour markets at all times. Few wage studies acknowledge the point.

In subsequent work using mainly Mukherjee's dataset and reworked prices (silver and millet values were more stable than wheat or rice in the long run), a fall in real wage and welfare is confirmed, but its extent was relatively modest (Allen 2005). Also, some classes of urban wages increased in the long run (Chandra 1983). The general fall is consistent with a global trend in the three centuries outside of England and Holland. But given the quality of the wage data, we should keep an open mind about the extent of the fall over 1600–1900.

The density of agricultural wage data improves greatly around 1800, enabling us to test if the fall happened in the nineteenth century or earlier. Not all of these data have been used yet. Around 1800, the first 'survey' of wages and living conditions that is known to exist was conducted by Thomas Munro, the architect of the ryotwari peasant property system in South India. Munro studied a region of the south the British knew especially well. This was the so-called Ceded Districts, a semi-arid tract of land the Nizam of Hyderabad gifted to the Company to pay for military protection. Soon after possession in 1796, Munro instituted a survey of living conditions. Details of the survey are unavailable, except Munro's own words, that 'a great number of statistical tables were drawn up … containing the price of labor and subsistence'

Table 8.4 Size of the external sector (% of GDP)

	Merchandise trade (export plus import)	Net foreign aid	Net foreign direct investment	Net invisible
1910–14	20.0	0.0	0.0–1.0	−3.0
1956	13.6	0.6	0.0	1.2

Note: Indian Union in 1956, British India for periods before.

Table 8.5 Survey of living conditions in peninsular South India *c.* 1800

	Wage of agriculture labourer (annual, converted from monthly wage)	Consumption per head of the whole population (annual)
Rich		40 s or Rs. 20
Middle		27 s or Rs. 13.5
Poor	48–72 s or Rs. 24–36	18 s or Rs. 9

(British Parliamentary Papers 1812–3: 124). Tables were also drawn showing the average consumption of three classes of inhabitants, the relatively rich, the middling and 'the poorest class of people'. Again, the precise definitions are not available. But from Munro's description, the numbers relate to a notion of subsistence consumption for the poor (including food, shelter and clothing), and average or sufficient consumption for the other two classes. These data are shown in Table 8.5. The wage is available by month, and converted into annual assuming a full year of work available. This was never the case, but annual wage contracts were common in the area in this time. With four members to a labouring family, and one earner, one can see why Munro believed that the wage was 'not more than adequate to the subsistence of a labourer and members of his family'.

Francis Buchanan Hamilton was another Company employee to have carried out something like a systematic wage survey in Bihar in 1809–10 (Majumdar 1934–35). Some of the figures are too low to be believable (possibly referred to adolescents and helpers). The modal number fell in the range Rs. 12–15 per year, after converting grain wages into cash. This is more or less identical with Munro's peninsular wages, adjusted for grain price about double that in Bihar. These numbers are remarkably close to many others that we find elsewhere, for example, Rs. 12–14 in eastern India *c.* 1785, and Rs. 16–22, again in eastern India *c.* 1810 (Roy 2011).

Converting money wages of agricultural workers into annual entitlement of grain in weight, and adding present-day averages, we get Table 8.6, which suggests that the purchasing power of an agricultural labourer wage did not

Table 8.6 Agricultural wage in money and grain, 1784–2011

	Region	Money wage (annual in Rs.)	Kg of wheat per day	Source
1784–88	Bihar and Bengal	12–17	2.2	See text
1809–10	Madras, Bihar	12–15 (Madras) 14–22 (Bihar)	2–2.5	Buchanan Hamilton, Munro (see text)
1875	British India	62	2.6	Atkinson (1902)
1895	British India	72	2.2	Atkinson (1902)
1950	Indian Union	295	2.2	India
2011	Indian Union	29,700	5.7	Gulati, Jain, Satija (2013)

change in any direction from 1784 until the Green Revolution of the 1970s. The one short-lived spike in 1784–1810 can be attributed to the fact that Bengal wages were recovering from the depopulation caused by the 1770 famine. If in the middle decades of the nineteenth century there was a mild increase in real wage, the effect disappeared quickly because of changes in labour supply.

What did this wage mean? The long-term average of about 2 kgs per day per worker is equivalent to barely adequate caloric needs for a family of four, assuming 80 per cent of the wage is spent on food.[7] However, it is a precarious adequacy, a slight fall in employment intensity or slight rise in prices could induce disaster.

Consumption

Conjectures on the long-term trend in consumption would be more difficult to make. The first large-scale family budget surveys did not become available before the interwar years. These surveys, however, produced a startling fact. Nutrition experts who used these surveys set the norm of carbohydrate consumption by an Indian at 437–500 grammes per adult per day (Thomas and Ramakrishnan 1938: 405–6; Bombay 1940: 69–70; Aykroyd 1940). A family of four in 1800 just reached the lower threshold assuming it consumed only grain. Such a diet might generate the required energy in an adult, it was not sufficient to ensure the physical development of children. There is ample evidence that cereals did dominate the Indian diet even when there was money to buy other things. Descriptions of Indian diet we find in European travelogues of the 1600s were consistent with this picture.

In the 1920s, surveys of agricultural labourers in Bihar noted their 'very simple diet consisting practically of rice, pulse and some vegetables. Their children are hopelessly under-nourished inasmuch as they do not get practically any milk at all' (Thakur 1937; Mehta 1938; Sarkar 1948–49; Hossain 1938–39). In South India, excessive rice consumption slowed down protein absorption, and low levels of vegetable and milk consumption led to the prevalence of sub-acute forms of scurvy among working classes and rickets among the working class children, the former a result of Vitamin C deficiency, and the latter of Vitamin D deficiency (Indian Government 1927: 732). In 1936, 94 per cent of the daily calorie intake by an adult male in north India came from grains, 4 per cent from roots and vegetables and 0.7 from animal protein. The corresponding percentages in China were 90, 9 and 1; and in the US, 39, 9 and 39. Dietary habits differed between regions of India. But the high preference for cereal and low protein intake was the norm.

This was changing in the 1930s in one respect, cereal preference diversified. Two surveys of the same village in South India (1917 and 1938) revealed a substitution of high-calorie grain (rice) for coarse grains, increased consumption of milk, clarified butter, sugar, coffee and tea. But the consumption of meat and vegetables rose only slowly. One contemporary study postulated that the preference for cereals was increasing on account of relative price shifts, in turn an effect of the conversion of pastures and commons into grain-producing land. Vegetarianism, according to this author, was reinforced by an ecological imbalance (Mukherjee 1936–37).

Poverty does not explain why Indian food consumption was unhealthy, that is, why it was marginally adequate for working but inadequate for bodily growth. Cultural preference was important too. For example, in the comparison between India, China and US, the reference group came from Punjab and were well-off enough to buy meat, fish or milk. Postcolonial public health picked up the point for discussion. How little nutritional status changed in the next forty years shows the persistence of dietary culture. The green revolution did not solve the nutrition problem. An analysis of 'food balance sheets' concludes that, 'over the entire 1937–95 period, energy supplies increased by only 18 percent, and protein supplies by only 4 percent. It is a poor performance by international standards and by comparison to other nearby Asian countries' (Hopper 1999).

If we look outside of food, there was much sign of dynamism. Cotton cloth consumption per head increased from about 6 yards in 1795 to 15 yards in 1938 (Roy 2012c). The increase in the consumption of clothing was subdued during 1795–1880, but very rapid during 1880–1940. Iron manufactures, not counting railway material, were among the fastest growing items of import. The trade statistics do not permit an estimate of volume. In value, iron articles increased from £0.1 million in 1840 to £5 million in 1914. Some of these articles were used in construction, but some of it went into consumer durables like cooking utensils and cutlery. Consumption of services and many other household articles also increased and became more diverse in quality (Kumar 1987).

Like consumption and wages (and possibly heights), mortality and child mortality changed slowly between the early nineteenth century and the early twentieth.

Mortality and morbidity

Towards the end of the eighteenth century, it was a custom among the European residents of Calcutta to gather together on 15 November every year. The occasion was to congratulate each other for staying alive one more year. The custom was not practised by 1835. But the conditions remained bad. 'There is no city in the world which contains within itself more numerous or deleterious agents prejudicial to health', a Bengali doctor was quoted in an 1850 paper published in the *Journal of the Statistical Society of London* (Finch 1850). He 'does not see in the town of Calcutta any children that are in perfect health'. The source of these statements is a survey done around 1836, certainly the first of its kind, of disease and death rates in India (Finch 1850). The data presented suggest that Calcutta had an average death rate of 51 per 1,000, and an infant mortality rate of 240. In the first census decade 1871–81, the corresponding numbers were 41 and 260 respectively. Of course, the reference areas are completely dissimilar. But there may have been a rise in infant mortality due to the effects of the 1876 famine and the inclusion of northern and central India in the latter figures. On the other hand, the fall in the death rate could reflect some improvement in adult survival rates, at least in the port cities such as Calcutta. In any case, the levels were high, and any change marginal until 1921. The 1836 survey also brought out one remarkably persistent feature of the population, variability of health status between communities. The death rate among the English population was 35; among the Armenians and other Europeans 40–60, among the Indo-Portuguese 125, among Hindus 65 and Muslims 28. To some extent, these differences arose due to the presence of more households among the Portuguese and the Hindus. These figures suggest that the Europeans were not any more vulnerable to the Indian environment than the Indians themselves. In fact, they coped better than some locals.

These conditions did not respond to manmade intervention until the expansion of public health around 1921, suggesting that their source was partly environmental and cultural. In 1901, India belonged in a class of countries, along with Chile and Egypt, with exceptionally high infant mortality rates (Chandrasekhar 1959). Net food availability would have improved between

1836 and 1921, but famines increased the risk of death from epidemics, industrialization and migration to the cities increased the risk of contagion, and neonatal deaths due to avoidable causes such as asphyxia and malnutrition continued to be high. The factory labour settlements and labour colonies in the plantations had above average infant mortality, among other reasons because of congestion.[8]

The overall pattern of the colonial era experience was therefore that of poor, uncertain and almost unchanging lives for many, and highly dynamic commercial and industrial cities on the margins. Did it change after 1947? Did postcolonial India bridge the gap between these two images?

Postcolonial India: revolution or involution?

Despite the much greater density of statistical data in the period after independence (1947), economic historians have rarely tried to connect the postcolonial pattern of change with colonial or precolonial patterns. Most time series, such as GDP, prices or cost of living, have a break around 1947 and the comparability between datasets before that date and those after is not perfect. One obstacle to long-range history is the radical departure of state policy after 1947. But, this section will show, deeper continuity can still be found.

In 1947, the South Asian mainland was partitioned into two countries, India and Pakistan, and in 1971, a further division took place with the birth of Bangladesh. Despite these far from peaceful changes in the map, the transition to a national economy in each case, especially in India, occurred with relatively little friction, owing to substantial continuity in institutions and an indigenization of the bureaucracy effected in the final years of the Empire. The measures included the legislative reforms of 1919 and 1935.

After independence, the Indian Union chose to carry out import-substitution and state-directed industrialization. The strategy, which was a departure from the market system of the Empire era, received immediate support from the nationalist critics of 'drain' and free trade discussed before, the export pessimists ruling the world in the 1950s, and socialist lobbies within the Congress that advocated central planning. It was reinforced further in the 1960s by global Marxism and its offshoots, dependency and world systems school, who rediscovered the Indian nationalist texts. The underlying historiography suggested that free trade had harmed India, that British colonialism extracted surplus value from India and transferred it to Britain, and that in order to carry out this activity colonialism needed collaborators, thus increasing inequality in India. The lesson learnt was that India needed to insulate its economy from trade and investment and build a strong state and closely regulated markets.

There was a large increase in government expenditure and investment. Protection was raised to very high levels and reinforced with non-tariff barriers. Commodity export was discouraged. The fear of a recurrence of famines and shortages led to state control over grain trade. Independent India, thus, set out to replace the Empire's legacy of a small state, free market and open economy with a large state, public control of markets and assets and an insular economy. Faced with a series of macroeconomic crises, the development regime from the 1990s reduced the dominance of the state and reduced barriers to trade and foreign investment. The subsequent period, however, is still too recent to fit into the present chapter, so that the search for deep continuity will stop more or less at the time import-substituting industrialization was partially dismantled, the end of the 1980s.

The differences between the two periods (1857–1947 and 1947–85) are obviously very large. The essential data are shown in Table 8.7, in the same format as in Tables 8.1–8.4, to enable easy comparison. The comparison shows an enlargement of the state, and significant increases in GDP growth rates across the board. But there was limited success in overcoming the productivity barrier. The subsection on GDP growth earlier in the chapter sums up the colonial experience in five propositions. Let me now add five more, exactly parallel, propositions to capture the experience of postcolonial India.

(a) GDP, total and per head, growth rates in 1950–2000 were well above those in the previous ninety years (Tables 8.1 and 8.7).

(b) All three sectors of the economy – agriculture, manufacturing and services – registered acceleration (Tables 8.1 and 8.7). In agriculture, the acceleration owed to the green revolution which took shape in the 1970s. The main difference with the colonial period was that extensive growth utilizing surplus land in 1860–1950 was replaced by productivity-led growth thanks to high-yielding variety seeds, chemical fertilizers and more intensive application of water. The state subsidized all three inputs, seeds, fertilizers and water.

(c) In industry, too, the proximate sources of growth changed. The colonial period had seen an expansion of the relatively labour-intensive sectors financed by private capital. During 1950–85, manufacturing was more capital-intensive, financed significantly by the state and foreign aid, and took place partly in state-owned firms.

(d) Within the services, there was a retreat of foreign trade-related services as the economy became partially closed, whereas a large expansion occurred in the government.

(e) On productivity, a similarity emerges between the colonial and the postcolonial eras (Tables 8.2 and 8.7). The finding confirms the conclusion of a recent

Table 8.7 Consolidated data on economic growth and structural change in India, 1950–2007

Average annual growth rates of GDP by sector of origin, 1950–2007

| | GDP at factor cost, constant prices | | | | | |
	Primary sector	Secondary sector	Tertiary sector	Total	Population	GDP per head
1950–64	3.0	6.8	3.8	4.1	1.9	2.1
1965–85	2.5	4.3	4.4	3.6	2.3	1.4
1986–2007	3.4	6.8	7.1	6.3	1.7	4.6

Average Annual Growth Rates of Output per Employee (% per year)

	Agriculture	Industry	Services	GDP
1950–51 – 1970–71	0.9	3.4	2.8	1.9
1970–71 – 1999–2000	0.9	2.7	2.3	2.5

Investment ratio and size of government (% of GDP), 1950–2007

| | Gross investment | | | Government expenditure |
	Government	Private	Total	
1950–64	5.3	6.1	11.4	12.9
1965–85	7.5	4.6	12.1	16.4
1986–2007	7.5	16.5	24.0	11.7

Size of the external sector (% of GDP)

	Merchandise trade (export plus import)	Net foreign aid	Net foreign direct investment	Net invisibles
1956	13.6	0.6	0.0	1.2
1970	7.0	1.0	0.0	−0.3
1980	14.4	1.3	0.0	2.9
2006	33.4	0.0	1.6	5.6

study on long-range growth in India: 'During the second half of the twentieth century, respectable labour productivity growth in industry and services has again been offset by slow productivity growth in agriculture' (Broadberry and Gupta 2014).

A balanced comparison between the colonial and the postcolonial periods cannot just look at GDP and conclude that the postcolonial statist regime did a great job, but should also look at the productivity problem, and at sources of GDP growth. GDP growth after 1950, though higher than before, was achieved at great cost. The greatest strength of the colonial period growth was that it was funded entirely by private capital, the state merely overseeing the capitalistic system that created opportunities for private accumulation. The postcolonial industrialization and the green revolution, by complete contrast, were largely funded by the taxpayers' money and foreign aid. Economic growth in 1950–85 needed a larger state, and involved a redistribution of taxes from public goods to private goods (mainly subsidies to farmers and state enterprises; note the gap between government expenditure and government investment). The policy involved restraining private investment, a retreat from world trade and foreign capital markets (Tables 8.4 and 8.7), crowding out and a neglect of healthcare and education. The period after 1985 can be seen as a course correction at many levels. It has, however, created its own problems. For example, while private investment and foreign trade revived, subsidy to peasants increased, and a partial withdrawal of the state from infrastructure saw agriculture sink back to slow growth.

To sum up, any comparative assessment of the two periods of history using national income data should confirm that the long-term constraint on Indian development lies in agricultural productivity.

Conclusion

The economic history of South Asia started more or less as a discourse serving political ends, and one preoccupied with the British Empire in the region. Empirical work has shed some of the political drive and diversified research away from politics towards resources, institutions, efficiency, choice and welfare. For historians groomed in a nationalistic tradition in India, or influenced by the neo-Marxist immiseration paradigm, the Empire was the most fundamental force of change, and 1947 represented the end of a dark age and the break of a new dawn. With attention shifting towards a wider range of themes, quantitative economic history suggests that neither was the colonial era a dark age, nor was the postcolonial India a new dawn. In the former era, even as rural wage, GDP and food consumption were stagnant, urban wage rose, there was diversification in consumption, demographic transition and industrialization financed by commercial profits. In the second era, despite much faster GDP growth, there was stagnation in productivity, efficiency and nutrition, and the growth process, being funded by foreign aid and tax-payers' money, was not sustainable. The 1990s liberal economic reforms confirm that point.

Notes

1. In this chapter, I use 'South Asia' and 'colonial India' interchangeably. According to the context of the discussion, 'India' refers to either colonial India or the Indian Union.
2. On these and other historiographical debates on precolonial India, see discussion in Roy (2012a), and Roy (2013).
3. A representative recent collection of essays is Riello and Roy (2009).
4. Roy (2007), on 1875–1939; Williamson (2000), finds a different result for the interwar period.
5. A representative collection of articles on the new turn in the historiography can be found in Chaudhary *et al.* (2015).
6. Donaldson (2010) revisits the welfare effects, and Bogart and Chaudhary (2012) reassess management after state takeover.
7. This is close to what Broadberry and Gupta (2014) also find.
8. On migration, see also Highlight Chapter 8.1.

Further reading

Banerjee, A. and Iyer, L. (2005), 'History, Institutions, and Economic Performance: the Legacy of Colonial Land Tenure Systems in India', *American Economic Review* 95 (4), 1190–213. Applies institutional economics to infer long-term effects of colonial property right reforms – an example of recent quantitative history scholarship.

Broadberry, S. N. and Gupta, B. (2016), 'Indian Economic Performance and Living Standards: 1600–2000', in L. Chaudhary, B. Gupta, A. Swamy and T. Roy (eds.), *A New Economic History of Colonial India*, London: Routledge. An innovative reconstruction of long-range GDP and standard of living data for the South Asian region.

Chaudhary, L., Gupta, B., Swamy, A., and Roy, T. (eds.) (2015), *A New Economic History of Colonial India*, London: Routledge. Contains a set of commissioned critical surveys of a range of themes, contributed by scholars active in the field, and aimed as a handbook for the student.

Parthasarathi, P. (1998), 'Rethinking Wages and Competitiveness in the Eighteenth Century: Britain and South India', *Past and Present* 158, 79–109. An early statement, using Indian evidence, of what is now known as the divergence debate.

Roy, T. (2012a), *The Economic History of India 1857–1947*, Delhi: Oxford University Press. A widely used student text, the book offers a detailed descriptive survey of the field.

(2012b), 'Consumption of Cotton Cloth in India 1795–1940', *Australian Economic History Review* 52 (1), 61–84. A reconstruction of textile data and a measurement of deindustrialization in nineteenth-century India.

(2013), *An Economic History of Early Modern India*, London: Routledge. An attempt at a synthesis of economic history scholarship relating to the eighteenth century, a debated field.

Wolcott, S. and Clark, G. (1999), 'Why Nations Fail: Managerial Decisions and Performance in Indian Cotton Textiles, 1890–1938', *Journal of Economic History* 59 (2), 397–423. An argument about comparative history based on efficiency of the industrial work-force.

References

Allen, R. C. (2005), 'Real Wages in Europe and Asia: a First Look at the Long-term Patterns', in R. C. Allen, T. Bengtsen and M. Dribe, *Living Standards in the Past: New Perspectives on Well-being in Asia and Europe*, Oxford University Press, 111–30.

Atkinson, F. J. (1902), 'A Statistical Review of Income and Wealth in British India', *Journal of the Royal Statistical Society* 65, 209–83.

Aykroyd, W. R. (1940), *Note on the Result of Diet Surveys in India*, Simla and New Delhi: Indian Research Fund Association.

Bagchi, A. K. (1976), 'Deindustrialization in India in the Nineteenth Century: Some Theoretical Implications', *Journal of Development Studies* 12 (2), 135–64.

Baines, J. A. (1893), 'Distribution and Movement of the Population in India', *Journal of the Royal Statistical Society* 56 (1), 1–43.

Banerji, A. (1962), *India's Balance of Payments*, Bombay: Asia.

Bogart, D. and Chaudhary, L. (2012), 'Railways in Colonial India: an Economic Achievement?', Warwick University Working Paper.

Bombay (1940), *Report of the Textile Labour Inquiry Committee, Vol. II (Final Report)*, Bombay: Government Press.

British Parliamentary Papers (1812–3), Select Committee, and Committee of Whole House of Commons, on Affairs of East India Company Minutes of Evidence (Trade and Shipping, and Renewal of Charter).

Caruana-Galizia, P. (2013), 'Indian Regional Income Inequality: Estimates of Provincial GDP, 1875–1911', *Economic History of Developing Regions* 28 (1), 1–27.

Chandra, S. (1983), 'Standard of Living I: Mughal India', in T. Raychaudhuri and I. Habib (eds.), *The Cambridge Economic History of India Vol. 1: c. 1200–c. 1750*, Cambridge University Press.

Chandrasekhar, S. (1959), *Infant Mortality in India 1901–55*, London: George Allen and Unwin.

Chaudhary, L. (2010), 'Land Revenues, Schools and Literacy: a Historical Examination of Public and Private Funding of Education', *Indian Economic and Social History Review* 47(2), 179–204.

Clingingsmith, D. and Williamson, J. (2008), 'Deindustrialization in 18th and 19th Century India: Mughal Decline, Climate Shocks and British Industrial Ascent', *Exploration in Economic History* 45 (3), 209–34.

Collins, W. (1999), 'Labor Mobility, Market Integration, and Wage Convergence in Late 19th Century India', *Explorations in Economic History* 36 (2), 246–77.

Donaldson, D. (2010), 'Railroads of the Raj: Estimating the Impact of Transportation Infrastructure', NBER Working Paper No. 16487.

Finch, C. (1850), 'Vital Statistics of Calcutta', *Journal of the Statistical Society of London*, 13 (2), 168–82.

Guha, S. (ed.) (1992), *Growth, Stagnation or Decline? Agricultural Productivity in British India*, Delhi: Oxford University Press.

Gupta, B. (2008), 'Work and Efficiency in Cotton Mills: Did the Indian Entrepreneur Fail?', University of Warwick Working Paper.

Heston, A. (1983), 'National Income', in D. Kumar (ed.), *The Cambridge Economic History of India, Vol. 2*, Cambridge University Press, 376–462.

Hopper, G. R. (1999), 'Changing Food Production and Quality of Diet in India, 1947–98', *Population and Development Review* 25 (3), 443–77.

Hossain, S. S. I. (1938–39), 'Report of the Family Budget Enquiry into the Conditions of the Weavers of Bihar Sharif', *Patna College Chanakya Society, Annual Report*, 31–7.

Indian Government (1927), *Royal Commission on Agriculture in India, Vol. III, Evidence taken in the Madras Presidency*, Calcutta: India Government Press.

Iyer, L. (2010), 'Direct versus Indirect Colonial Rule in India: Long-term Consequences', *Review of Economics and Statistics* 92 (4), 693–712.

Kumar, D. (1975), 'Landownership and Inequality in Madras Presidency: 1853–54 to 1946–47', *Indian Economic Social History Review* 12 (3), 229–61.

  (1987), 'The Forgotten Sector: Services in Madras Presidency in the First Half of the Nineteenth Century', *Indian Economic and Social History Review* 24 (4), 367–93.

Kuznets, S. (1963), 'Quantitative Aspects of Economic Growth of Nations: Vol. VIII. Distribution of Income by Size', *Economic Development and Cultural Change*, 11 (2), 1–80.

Majumdar, B. B. (1934–35), 'Agricultural Labour in Bihar in the First Half of the Nineteenth Century', *Indian Journal of Economics* 15 (4), 669–76.

Mehta, S. N. (1938), 'General Economic Condition of Shantipur', *Patna College Chanakya Society, Annual Report*, 89–99.

Mukherjee, R. K. (1936–37), 'The Relation between Human and Bovine Population Pressures in India', *Indian Journal of Economics* 17 (2), 249–63.

(1967), *The Economic History of India: 1600–1800*, London: Longmans Green.

Narain, B. (1929), *Indian Economic Life: Past and Present*, Lahore: Uttar Chand Kapur and Sons.

Narain, D. (1965), *The Impact of Price Movements on Areas under Selected Crops in India 1900–1939*, Cambridge University Press.

Ojha, P. D. and Bhatt, V. V. (1964), 'Pattern of Income Distribution in an Underdeveloped Economy: a Case Study of India', *American Economic Review* 54 (5), 711–20.

Pomeranz, K. (2000), *The Great Divergence: China, Europe, and the Making of the Modern World Economy*, Princeton University Press.

Riello, G. and Roy, T. (eds.) (2009), *How India Clothed the World*, Leiden: Brill.

Roy, T. (1999), *Traditional Industry in the Economy of Colonial India*, Cambridge University Press.

(2007), 'Globalization, Factor Prices, and Poverty in Colonial India', *Australian Economic History Review* 47 (1), 73–94.

(2011), 'Economic Conditions in Early Modern Bengal: a Contribution to the Divergence Debate', *Journal of Economic History*, 70 (10), 179–94.

(2012c), *India in the World Economy from Antiquity to the Present*, Cambridge University Press.

(2014), 'Geography or Politics? Regional Inequality in Colonial India', *European Review of Economic History* 18 (3), 324–48.

Sarkar, S. (1948–49), 'Economic Survey of the Village Khirhar', *Patna College Chanakya Society, Annual Report*, 79–89.

Sivasubramonian, S. (2000), *National Income of India in the Twentieth Century*, Delhi: Oxford University Press.

Studer, R. (2008), 'India and the Great Divergence: Assessing the Efficiency of Grain Markets in Eighteenth- and Nineteenth-Century India', *Journal of Economic History* 68 (4), 393–437.

Thakur, R. B. (1937), 'Land Tenure in Taregna', *Patna College Chanakya Society, Annual Report*, 57–64.

Thavaraj, M. J. K. (1962), 'Capital Formation in the Public Sector in India: a Historical Study, 1898–1938', in V. K. R. V. Rao (ed.) *Papers on National Income and Allied Topics*, Delhi: Allied Publishers.

Thomas, P. J. and Ramakrishnan, R. C. (eds.), (1938), *Some South Indian Villages: a Resurvey*, University of Madras.

Thorner, D. (1962) '"Deindustrialization" in India, 1881–1931', in D. and A. Thorner, *Land and Labour in India*, New York: Asia.

Williamson, J. (2000), 'Globalization, Factor Prices and Living Standards in Asia before 1940', in A. J. H. Latham and H. Kawakatsu (eds.), *Asia Pacific Dynamism 1500–2000*, London: Routledge, 13–45.

Wolcott, S. (1994), 'The Perils of Lifetime Employment Systems: Productivity Advance in the Indian and Japanese Textile Industries, 1920–1938', *Journal of Economic History* 54 (2), 307–24.

Human stature as a health indicator in colonial empires

18

Joerg Baten and Kris Inwood

There has been considerable debate about the impact of European colonial empires on other world regions. Karl Marx in the 1850s argued that colonialism had a modernizing function and prepared the countries for later communist take-overs. Modern Marxist writers (Sender and Smith 1986) tend to support this view, as do some economists at the other end of the ideological spectrum (Ferguson 2003). In contrast, most historians identify disadvantages to colonial status including adverse social and economic effects as well as the lack of political freedom (Huillery 2014). Adult stature reflects childhood health and nutrition and thereby provides fresh new evidence for colonial living standards.[1] Admittedly, stature is not the whole story; it reflects important but particular aspects of living standards among the young.[2]

A number of recent studies present a nuanced view of living standards during colonialism. For example, Frankema and van Waijenburg (2012), Moradi (2009), and Cogneau and Rouanet (2011) find evidence in Africa of public health improvements and relatively high real wages (in comparison to Asia at least) under colonial administration. However, the evidence is limited to the colonial period, whereas it would be important to mobilize evidence for the period before colonialism in order to assess fully its effects. Anthropometric evidence may be helpful in this context.

What are the sources of evidence about human stature before, during and after colonialism? The anthropological sciences developed during the nineteenth century; the study of human stature was one of its priority fields. Some European anthropologists undertook extended journeys to Africa, Asia and the Americas, during which they measured the height of many indigenous people.[3] Evidence of this nature sheds light on the development of Africa during the infamous 'Scramble' by European powers for African colonies during the 1880s and 1890s. In Figure I8.1 we report the average stature recorded in various countries according to their colonizing country.

Before the 1880s, most African countries were either uncolonized or the colonial power held only small trading posts. Only the Portuguese colonies, South Africa and the plantation island economies (Mauritius, Réunion, etc.) had been colonized earlier. Hence the majority of Africans born during the 1860s and 1870s grew up

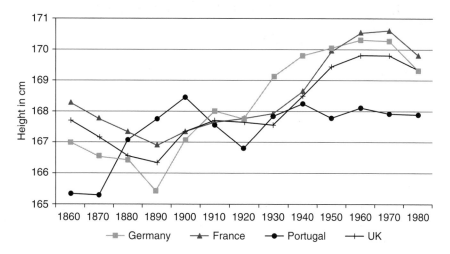

Figure I8.1 African stature by colonizing country of *c*. 1900
Source: based on Baten and Blum (2014) (note for example, 'German' colonies had later other metropoles).

before the advent of direct colonization. We see in Figure I8.1 that their heights were declining during the period of the 'Scramble', reaching a low point during the 1890s. Thereafter, we observe a mild recovery and more or less stagnating height until the 1930s. From the 1940s onwards heights in the colonies of the British and French Empires expanded until the 1960s. In contrast, the Portuguese colonies had been established earlier and show a different profile of stature. Initially heights were low here but in the period from the 1880s they reached a somewhat higher level. The 1920s were a low point. Unlike the British and French colonies, stature in the Portuguese colonies did not improve during the 1930–60s period.

Thus, the first decades of the 'new' colonies of England, France and Germany experienced declining health and nutrition. Towards the end of the colonial period, however, the investments in basic public health and at least basic education bore fruit (Moradi 2009). In addition, African 'rural capitalist' peasants achieved higher income in some colonies (see Chapter 10 in this volume). In contrast, the Portuguese colonies probably suffered from this colonization shock much earlier. Further, the Portuguese did not invest as much in public health and education during the later nineteenth and twentieth centuries and did not see the same growth of stature in this period.

Yet another experience is revealed in Figure 8.2 and Figure 9.3 in Chapter 9 on Southeast Asia by Shanahan in this volume. Stature was large before colonization in Cambodia (colonized 1863) and Myanmar (colonized 1886). Both populations experienced a reduction in stature in the decades following colonization. Thailand, which was never colonized, consistently had the greatest or second-largest stature in the region. Subsequently, after the Second World War, stature rose throughout

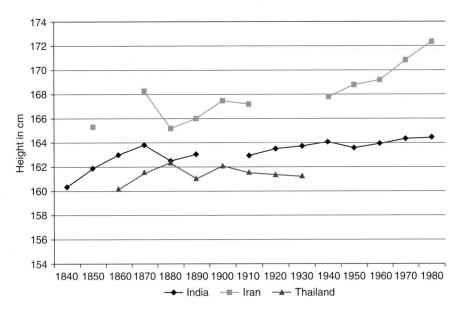

Figure 18.2 Height development in India, Iran and Thailand (male)
Source: based on Baten and Blum (2014).

the region in spite of setbacks originating in military conflict (e.g., the Vietnam War) and severe political regimes (e.g., Cambodia).

A direct comparison of Thailand and Iran with India is interesting because the latter was controlled by Great Britain while Thailand and Iran remained independent (Figure 18.2). Before the 1920s Iranians were taller on average than Indians who were somewhat taller than the Thais, with no tendency for increase or decrease in any of these countries. After the Second World War, however, the two countries that retained political independence were able to realize considerable improvement in stature. India, on the other hand, in spite of gaining independence in 1947, increased stature more slowly. The experience of colonialism may have contributed to a stagnation of Indian stature in the later nineteenth and early twentieth centuries (Brennan *et al.* 1994), just as its legacy may have limited the gain in stature after independence.[4]

An entirely different experience of colonialism is visible in the 'settler colonies', which attracted European immigrants on a large scale in the nineteenth century. Australia, Canada, New Zealand and South Africa inherited similar British institutions in diverse biophysical environments. Their immigrant populations were largely similar although the indigenous peoples of course were distinct. Europeans moving to the settler colonies enjoyed a fundamentally healthy environment with high incomes, cheap food and low population densities. Not surprisingly, the migrants and their descendants were tall, on average. New Zealand and South

African whites were among the tallest in the world, although in both societies the indigenous population fared much worse (Inwood, Oxley and Roberts 2010, 2015; Inwood and Masakure 2013). There was considerable inequality of stature even among the whites (Cranfield and Inwood 2015a, 2015b). Colonial status did not impede the realization of good health, on average, although equally there is no sign of rising stature despite strong economic growth in the nineteenth century, except in particular colonies such as Tasmania (Cranfield and Inwood 2007; Inwood, Maxwell-Stewart, Oxley and Stankovich 2015).

Thus, we see a variety of colonial experience. Colonization hindered the development of stature in Africa although, towards the end of the colonial period, there was some recovery of heights reflecting the impact of medical progress and, in British and French colonies, favourable public policy. In central and southeast Asia countries retaining their independence fared better than their neighbours who were colonized. The settler colonies were able to realize good health and impressive stature, but there was considerable inequality and for the most part stature did not increase as might be expected given the fast rate of income growth. The diversity of experience of stature under colonialism reflects the diversity of the European colonists and the overseas territories into which they expanded in the eighteenth and nineteenth centuries.

Notes

1. The Introduction to this volume discusses the definition and limitations of this indicator.
2. Another limitation is that stature captures direct or short-term effects rather than long-term consequences such as institutional changes or educational investments, which elsewhere in the volume are argued to be important.
3. The Introduction and Baten and Blum (2012, 2014) provide more detail.
4. Roy (Chapter 8 in this volume) mentions the possibility that nutritional culture also play a role.

References

Baten, J. and Blum, M. (2012), 'Growing Tall but Unequal: New Findings and New Background Evidence on Anthropometric Welfare in 156 Countries, 1810–1989', *Economic History of Developing Regions* 27 (sup. 1), S66–85.

(2014), 'Why are you Tall while Others are Short? Agricultural Production and other Proximate Determinants of Global Heights', *European Review of Economic History* 18 (2), 144–65.

Brennan, L., McDonald, J. and Shlomowitz, R. (1994), 'Trends in the Economic Well-being of South Indians under British Rule: the Anthropometric Evidence, *Explorations in Economic History* 31 (2), 225–60.

Cogneau, D. and Rouanet, L. (2011), 'Living Conditions in Côte d'Ivoire and Ghana, 1925–1985: What do Survey Data on Height Stature Tell Us?', *Economic History of Developing Regions* 26 (2), 55–82.

Cranfield, J. and Inwood, K. (2007), 'The Great Transformation: a Long-run Perspective on Physical Well-being in Canada', *Economics and Human Biology* 5(2), 204–28.

(2015a), 'A Tale of Two Armies: the Stature of Australian and Canadian Soldiers in World War One', *Australian Economic History Review* 50 (2), 212–33.

(2015b), 'Genes, Class or Culture? French–English Height Differences in Canada', in P. Baskerville and K. Inwood (eds.), *Lives in Transition: Longitudinal Research from Historical Sources*, McGill-Queens University Press, 231–53.

Ferguson, N. (2003), *Empire: the Rise and Demise of the British World Order and the Lessons for Global Power*, New York: Basic Books.

Frankema, E. and van Waijenburg, M. V. (2012), 'Structural Impediments to African Growth? New Evidence from Real Wages in British Africa, 1880–1965', *The Journal of Economic History* 72 (04), 895–926.

Huillery, E. (2014), 'The Black Man's Burden: the Cost of Colonization of French West Africa', *The Journal of Economic History* 74 (01), 1–38.

Inwood, K. and Masakure, O. (2013), 'Poverty and Physical Well-being among the Coloured Population in South Africa', *Economic History of Developing Regions* 28 (2), 56–82.

Inwood, K., Maxwell-Stewart, H., Oxley, D. and Stankovich, J. (2015), 'Growing Incomes, Growing People in Nineteenth-century Tasmania', *Australian Economic History Review* 55 (2), 187–211.

Inwood, K., Oxley, L. and Roberts, E. (2010), 'Was New Zealand the Land of Milk and Honey? New Evidence on New Zealand Living Standards', *Australian Economic History Review* 50(3), 262–83.

(2015), 'Physical Well-being and Ethnic Inequality in New Zealand Prisons, 1840–1975', *History of the Family* 20 (2), 250–70.

Moradi, A. (2009), 'Towards an Objective Account of Nutrition and Health in Colonial Kenya: a Study of Stature in African Army Recruits and Civilians, 1880–1980', *The Journal of Economic History* 69 (03), 719–54.

Sender, J. and Smith, S. (1986), *The Development of Capitalism in Africa*, London: Methuen.

H8.1 Did brain-drain from India cause underdevelopment? Numeracy of Indian migrants and the Indian population, seventeenth to twentieth century
Joerg Baten

Brain-drain is a crucial economic problem of many countries today. If the most educated and entrepreneurial people leave their country, the remaining population will be less likely to achieve rapid development and growth. For example, in the late twentieth century many Europeans with university education migrated to the US, as skill premia were substantially higher there (see the review in Stolz and Baten 2012). For high-mortality countries in Africa, the recruitment of medical doctors has been severely criticized, up to the point that this recruitment activity was suggested to be treated as a criminal case.

Was brain-drain also a development obstacle for poor countries in the nineteenth century? One candidate for such an effect could be India, as between 200,000 and 600,000 Indians emigrated every year between 1870 and 1930 (Roy 2000: 290). Within the British colonial Empire, Indian agricultural labourers and artisans were recruited to work in plantations and mines in other parts, such as Mauritius, South Africa, the Pacific and the Caribbean. How educated were these migrants? Was there brain-drain from India? In Figure H8.1, we see the basic numeracy of two groups of emigrants and the total Indian population born in the 1830s and 1890s.[1] In addition, some early estimates of Indian numeracy are added to the Figure. The selectivity of migrants during this period was quite mixed. Those who were recruited for Natal (in today's South Africa) were typically slightly more numerate than the Indian average, whereas indentured labourers recruited for the Fiji islands were initially less, later more numerate.[2]

Another interesting fact is the stagnation of Indian numeracy: between the period around 1700 and the mid-nineteenth century, Indian numeracy values remained at around 30–40 per cent, which is relatively low in global comparison. During the 1500–1800 period, Europe experienced a numeracy revolution, growing from around 50 per cent to over 90 per cent numeracy. It should be noted that the early estimates for India rely on very small numbers of observations and have to be considered as being preliminary. Nevertheless, they appear not as unrealistic and the fact that the evidence comes from very difficult institutional contexts, but still yields similar levels, is reconfirming. The earliest estimates are based on inquisition court registers.[3] In the period around 1700 slaves were brought to South Africa, and the census-type registers in Sri Lanka also confirm the picture of stagnating human capital. Finally, the wage evidence presented by Roy in this volume is also compatible with a long-run stagnation of numeracy if we assume that it tends to correlate with wages. This finding has potentially large implications for understanding the issue of competitiveness of the Indian economy with Europe after the transport costs had begun to fall in the nineteenth century.

Returning to our initial question of migrant selectivity, the evidence is also mixed for the early forced migration to South Africa. In addition, an important impact of brain-drain is also less likely, because the majority of Indian labour migrants returned to their home country (Roy 2000). In a similar vein, the number of around 200,000–600,000 per year might seem large, but it has to be taken into account that South Asia had between

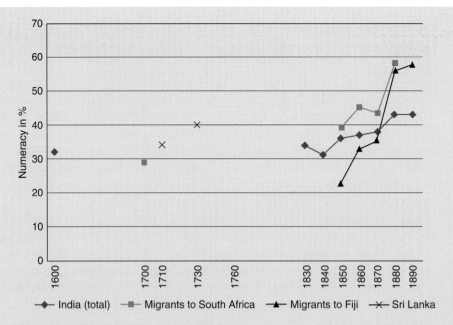

Figure H8.1 Basic numeracy of Indian migrants and the Indian population, seventeenth to nineteenth century
Source: based on Baten and Fourie (2014); www.clio-infra.eu.

250 million (around 1880) and 340 million inhabitants (around 1930, see Roy 2000: 283). In sum, brain-drain was probably not a major issue for India. However, the stagnation of numeracy in the early modern period and during the first period of British colonization might have been a major development obstacle.

Notes

1. See the Introduction to this volume on the method.
2. Regional composition also plays a role: migrants to Natal came more often from coastal districts and cities in the south. In addition, Natal issued a law about language and wealth requirements of immigrants in 1897 (Daniels 1995: 40).
3. Juif and Baten 2013 suggested an adjustment for inquisition source bias.

References

Baten, J. and Fourie, J. (2014), 'Numeracy of Africans, Asians, and Europeans during the Early Modern Period: New Evidence from Cape Colony Court Registers', *Economic History Review* 68 (2), 632–56.

Daniels, R. (1995), 'The Growth of Restrictive Immigrant Restrictions in the Colonies of Settlement', in R. Cohen (ed.), *The Cambridge Survey of World Migration*, Cambridge University Press, 39–44.

Juif, D. and Baten, J. (2013), 'On the Human Capital of "Inca" Indios Before and After the Spanish Conquest. Was there a "Pre-colonial Legacy"?', *Explorations in Economic History* 50 (2), 227–41.

Roy, T. (2000), *The Economic History of India 1857–1947*, Delhi: Oxford University Press.

Stolz, Y. and Baten, J. (2012), 'Brain Drain in the Age of Mass Migration: Does Relative Inequality Explain Migrant Selectivity?', *Explorations in Economic History* 49, 205–20.

9 Southeast Asia and Australia/New Zealand

Martin Shanahan

Some of the countries included in this chapter present the highest living standards in the world (Australia, New Zealand and Singapore), while others stand as the poorest (Papua New Guinea and Timor-Leste). It also includes several middle-ranked countries that even half a century ago were considered to be 'developing' (Malaysia, Thailand, Indonesia), and others that remain in that category (Philippines, Vietnam, Laos, Cambodia). The chapter includes countries that, in the past century, have transformed their societies, over-thrown colonialism, endured wars and invasions and undergone extensive economic change, and others that have developed in comparative peace. The diversity of economic and social conditions in this region, and the problems and opportunities these countries face, serve as a microcosm of the issues facing many countries around the globe.

For most observers, a distinguishing feature of this region has been the rapid economic transformation of a select handful of Asian 'tigers' in the second half of the twentieth century. Remarkable though these changes were, it is worth recalling that all of the nations in this chapter possess deep social and cultural origins; many with foundations in long existent and ancient civilizations that flourished centuries ago. A second factor shaping the economies of this region has been their histories of turbulent, often violent, political, institutional and social change. In some countries this began with the domination of European nations, especially after 1800, and continued in different forms until as late as the beginning of the twenty-first century. The consequences of colonial rule and in some cases war, and struggles for independence, still influence economic attitudes and policies of these countries.

A central theme running through this chapter is the importance of trade and its impact on living standards. Many of the countries of Southeast Asia have a long tradition of trading with others. The marked rise in gross domestic product (GDP) per capita, life expectancy and heights (all of which are indicators of improving material well-being) after the Second World War reflect the importance of trade for a country's living standards. A second theme that emerges is the need for institutional and political stability, and an absence of violence, to advance economic outcomes. Countries with the lowest levels of violence clearly demonstrate higher material outcomes, and those most recently scarred by war lag behind those that have had more time to rebuild. Finally, it is worth reflecting on how economic improvement can be self-reinforcing; populations whose living standards improve devote more resources to education, and enjoy a longer life expectancy. In this respect, the economic histories of Southeast Asian countries provide a significant body of evidence and a range of outcomes.

Geography and latitude

Geographically, it is convenient to cluster the area under discussion into three main regions: mainland Southeast Asia (Cambodia, Laos, Myanmar, Malaysia and Singapore); Australasia (which includes Australia and New Zealand); and those island nations that lie essentially between the two sub-regions (Timor-Leste, Indonesia, Papua New Guinea and the Philippines). Historically and culturally, three of these last four countries are typically viewed as part of Southeast Asia, while the fourth, Papua New Guinea, is more aligned with the Pacific Islands. The land masses, population size and density of inhabitants differ greatly. At one extreme, the city-state of Singapore, home to 5 million people, is around 700 square kilometres in size; while the land mass of Australia, at almost 7.7 million square kilometres, hosts 23 million. The population of Timor-Leste, the newest and smallest country, contains fewer than 1.2 million people; Indonesia, its adjoining neighbour, has a population of more than 250 million.

The geographical region covered here stretches over seventy-five degrees of latitude, from northern Myanmar to the south island of New Zealand, and through eighty-six degrees of longitude. It contains deserts and tropical forest, marsh-lands and stony desert, rolling plains and snow-covered mountains.

Mainland Southeast Asia is heavily shaped by north–south basins surrounding the Irrawaddy, Salween, Chao Phraya, Mekong and Red (Hong) rivers. Mountain ranges such as the Truong Son and other high ground then separate regions such as Thailand and Burma. The physical contrast is thus typically between low flat regions along riverine and alluvial plains, and the uplands; a distinction that also identifies different communities. A single river, the Mekong, influences large parts of Vietnam, Burma, Laos, Thailand and Cambodia. While the Thai-Malay peninsula and the continent of Australia are geologically stable, the island bands of Indonesia, Papua New Guinea and New Zealand are all in areas of volcanic activity.

The countries of Southeast Asia and Australasia occupy around 8 per cent of the world land mass, but receive around 15 per cent of the world's renewable water resources. This water, in the form of rainfall, rivers and surface water, is unequally distributed, as are the approximately 660 million people (just under 10 per cent of world population as measured in 2013). This large variation in population density, land forms, soil fertility, water availability and climate also means that the type of plant-life and agricultural forms also vary. The types of agriculture that are currently supported range from dairy farming in New Zealand, through open low-density cattle and sheep farming and cereal cropping in Australia, to plantations in Indonesia and Malaysia and intensively farmed rice fields in parts of the Philippines, Burma and Vietnam.

The influence and mix of cultures in Southeast Asia is also evident in the mix of religions and governance found across the region. India influenced Burma, Thailand, Cambodia and Laos, and the mixture of Hindu and Buddhist traditions shaped their institutions and supported a semi-Divine monarchy. The Vietnamese, by contrast, were influenced by the Chinese and Confucian values. Islam, dominant in Indonesia, parts of Malaysia and many coastal areas is evidence of the interaction of traders with the Middle East. The Philippines, whose Islamic influences were also influenced by traders, were to be dominated by Christianity only after the arrival of the Spanish in the sixteenth century (on the early history of this world region before 1500, see Highlight Chapter 9.1).

The pre-colonial period 1500–1800

While the period before 1500 saw the rise and fall of empires, the upheavals of wars and peaceful settlements and the continuation of long-distance trade, as well as the usual natural disasters and local change, it was, in comparison to the events of the next 300 years, a period of relative stability.

Before the arrival of the Europeans, the people, empires, and cultures of Southeast Asia comprised a complex mixture of simple and sophisticated societies. The difference in standard of living between the majority of subsistence farmers and elite rulers was great; as was the mix of languages and religions. While peasant farming predominated, there was a small administrative and religious elite in some societies as well as groups of artisans and traders; there was no real middle-class. In short, it was not that dissimilar to the European society of the same period. Only in Australia, and to a lesser extent New Zealand and Papua New Guinea, were the levels of technology, governance, property rights and institutions so different as to be almost unrecognizable for Europeans when they were first encountered.

Maritime Europeans were already familiar with the commercial trading ports such as Cambay (in Gujarat, India), Chittagong (Bengal), Pegu (Lower Burma), Melaka (Malaysian Peninsula), Palembang (Sumatra) and Macao (China). For their locations and the centres of spice production, see Map 9.1. The Europeans' increasing contact with these and other trading regions over the next centuries began slowly, and its effect was most likely confined to the port regions and hinterlands. Even as the Portuguese began to build a chain of fortifications to the Spice Islands in the sixteenth century, in an ultimately failed attempt to monopolize the spice trade, the majority of the indigenous populations would have been comparatively unaffected. The quantity of spices traded via the

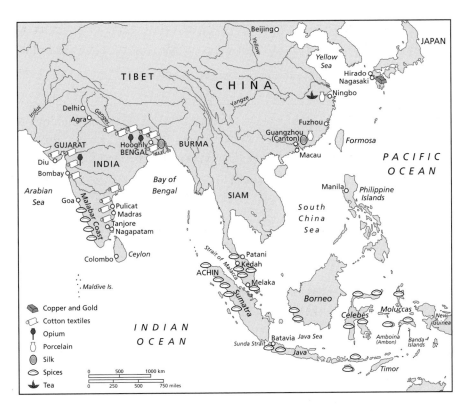

Map 9.1 Trade in Southeast Asia during the seventeenth and early eighteenth century
Source: see map 1.1.

European controlled routes in the sixteenth century grew comparatively slowly and does not appear to have greatly differed from the amounts traded the century before.

While trade quantities increased slowly up to the eighteenth century, or even decreased slightly in the case of some commodities like pepper, the doctrine of mercantilism resulted in a significant expansion of European interests competing to capture control of trade with the 'Far East'. Ultimately, mercantilism saw national interests aligned with trade, so that state power was enhanced through the accumulation of precious metals and trade surpluses. Just as the Portuguese increased their interests in the sixteenth century, the Spanish also began their colonization and religious conversion of much of the Philippines. Despite their early dominance, and in their explorations, the probable European discovery of Papua, by the seventeenth century Portuguese interests were being eclipsed by the Dutch. The Dutch East India Company focused particularly around Malacca and Batavia. The Dutch discoveries of Australia and New Zealand in the seventeenth century were also an indirect consequence of their efforts to find trade routes to the Spice Islands. It was not until the eighteenth century that the British, having

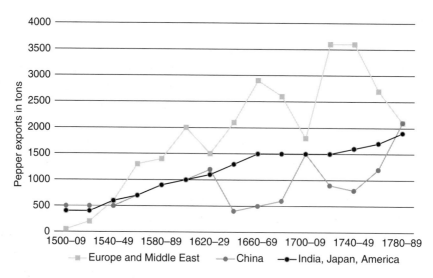

Figure 9.1 Southeast Asian pepper exports, 1500–1790 (tons)
Source: based on Bulbeck *et al.* (1998: table 3.7), cited in Findlay and O'Rourke (2007: 203, 282).

established their interest in India via the British East India Company, turned their attention to colonizing Penang and Singapore. Figure 9.1 presents one dimension of this trade, an estimate of the tons of pepper exported from Southeast Asia from 1500 to 1790.

Despite these expanding trade links with European interests, it is also true that for the majority of the populations in each country, there was comparatively little interaction with Europeans. Some of this was simply because many people lived away from the ports and main points of contact. It was also because, even after European interests had settled in regions for decades or even centuries (as with the Dutch in Java) they had comparatively little interest in local affairs. The three hundred years after 1500 in many ways saw the continuance of traditional social routines and relationships for the majority of people. For most, life was still hard, with subsistence level agriculture, fishing and, in less developed civilizations, hunting and gathering. Typically a country's lowlands were the regions most connected to society; the uplands were less inhabited and far less connected, socially or economically to settlements. Some countries had dominant ethnic groups; Vietnamese in Vietnam; Khmers in Cambodia; the Thais in Thailand. Others, including Burma and the maritime countries, had numerous ethnic populations. In further-flung regions, such as parts of the Philippines, the outer Indonesian islands, Australia, Papua New Guinea and New Zealand, there lived numerous tribes who descended from the earliest inhabitants of those regions.

New imperialism and the colonial period

The transformation of ideas that saw European nations shift from mercantilism to empire building occurred across the eighteenth and nineteenth centuries. In Europe, war and industrial transformation had reshaped attitudes and capabilities. For the rulers in Southeast Asia, this meant increasing pressure on their negotiations, treaties and other forms of compromise with European interests.

For example, the eighteenth century saw Burmese rulers, whose country had not previously been of particular interest to European traders, seek to maintain their traditional influence in the western areas of Assam, Manipur and Arakan. Pressing them, however, was the British East India Company, which was expanding its interests eastwards over the same territory. Over the next sixty years, diplomacy, raids, treaties and compromises continued until, after three successful wars, Britain proclaimed control over most of Burma. In Vietnam, it was the French who invaded in 1850, ostensibly to protect religious missionaries but not unaware of the imperial gains to be had from possession. They also took possession of a weakened Cambodia. While Thailand remained a buffer between British and French interests, and through skilful diplomacy was never colonized, the French also took control of Laos in the late nineteenth century. In Indonesia, the influence of the Dutch East India Company had been transferred to the Dutch government and its influence was to spread across the Indonesian archipelago and New Guinea, with a small neglected Portuguese colony in Timor-Leste. The Spanish had taken possession of the Philippines much earlier, in the sixteenth century, driven by the desire to convert but not unaware of potential economic gain. Their hold was frequently challenged with some islands and their inhabitants resisting conquest and conversion for centuries. Ultimately the Spanish lost possession to the US in 1898. By the end of the nineteenth century the British had taken over effective possession of the Malay Peninsula from the Dutch through their expanding settlements in Singapore, Penang, Malacca and various provinces. They had also taken possession of Australia and New Zealand in the late eighteenth and early nineteenth centuries.

While the effect of this imperialism was to transform the social, political and cultural experiences of these countries, it also transformed their economies. One of the most important shifts was in the production of commodities. The creation of the dairy farms of New Zealand; the sheep farms and wheat fields of Australia; the rubber plantations of Malaysia, Java, Sumatra, Vietnam and Cambodia; the tin mining of Malaya; the rice fields of the Mekong Delta, Menam River (Thailand) and Irrawaddy River delta (Burma), were a response to powerful market demands. In aggregate, millions of acres of land and millions of people were drawn into supplying markets around the world with commodities of all kinds. Production techniques changed. Large-scale production required more intensive use of factor inputs. Much of the capital and finance for this transformation was supplied from outside Southeast Asia and Oceania while labour too was sometimes imported, mostly from other parts of Southeast Asia, to augment local workers. In some cases only land and labour were the locally supplied factors of production.

The period between the Napoleonic wars and the First World War also saw a revolution in transportation technology (from sail to steam; animal drawn carts to railway) and communication. The resulting fall in costs enabled the expansion of trade from regions that from a North Atlantic perspective were at the 'periphery' of global finance and industrialization. In exchange for manufactured goods (used in both production and consumption) the periphery supplied many of the raw commodities and foodstuffs sought by industrialized countries whose affluence and middle-classes were growing rapidly. The opening of the Suez Canal in 1869 served to lower costs further between Europe and Southeast Asia and strengthened the role of trading ports and especially Singapore. Map 9.2 shows some of the main export products of the Southeast Asian countries c. 1920.

In addition to the transformation in production, and the transportation of goods around the world, the nineteenth century also saw an increase in migration. While large numbers of people moved from the old world to the new (including Australia and New Zealand, especially after the discovery of gold) there were also movements of people through Southeast Asia. For example, many Chinese moved rapidly into Singapore shortly after its founding in 1819. The presence of the Chinese and their business skills were encouraged by the French in Vietnam, Cambodia and Laos; the Chinese also supplied much of the labour for the tin mines in Malaya. Other groups, such as Indians, moved in numbers into Burma and Malaysia-Singapore.

One legacy of colonialism was the shaping and defining of many of today's national boundaries. Another was the standardization of record keeping, and internationally recognised (to European eyes) laws, administrative processes and property rights. Colonialism also starkly increased local populations' awareness of the 'outside world', as they had less control over their own affairs. It also changed the aspirations of the local elites as they grew aware of the need for a more 'Western' education to access positions associated with the growing trade economy and political administration. Although the economic consequences of improved trade meant increases in the measured production and consumption of goods, it did not necessarily translate into a more equitable distribution of resources for all members of the country. The political consequences of this differed significantly between regions. Increased market access could advance growth, but it could also increase the transmission of external economic shocks. The nature of these impacts, however, differed between regions.

In Australia (but less so in New Zealand, because of the Treaty of Waitangi) the original inhabitants were ignored, marginalized or killed. The majority of the

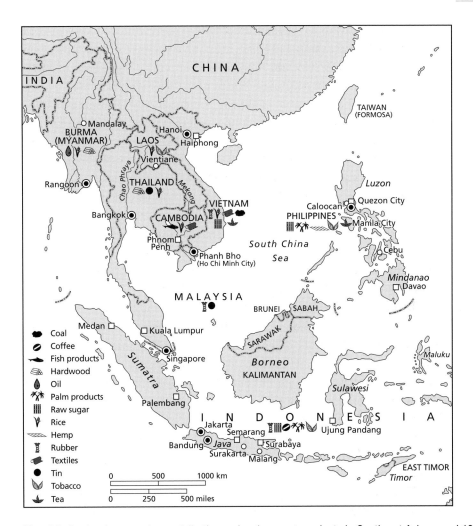

Map 9.2 Regional economic specialization and main export products in Southeast Asia around 1920
Source: see map 1.1.

benefits of global market expansion were captured by the European colonists. In the nineteenth century the result was to raise the measured standard of living of the colonists in both countries to among the highest in the world. Even by the early twentieth century, and after significant immigration, there was, compared to many Southeast Asian countries, a relatively peaceful political transformation from being a series of colonies to becoming the separate nations of Australia (in 1901) and New Zealand (as a 'Dominion' in 1907 and fully in 1947), as the mostly European immigrants gained independence from the British 'motherland'.

In Southeast Asia, by contrast, the path to independent nation status, and a political, social and economic system controlled by native inhabitants was more difficult. The size of local populations and the disenfranchisement of most natives meant any transition to a different political system would require colonial powers to transfer control to non-European local inhabitants. The late nineteenth century and especially the First World War impacted on the perspectives of nationalists in many Southeast Asian countries. The tensions over who benefited from economic growth, colonial attitudes to local people and growing levels of education (if only among elite local members) saw the emergence of increased aspirations for independence. The 1930s depression and subsequent retreat from global trade had significant consequences for those supplying commodity markets – especially those with the least means. Burma and parts of Indonesia were badly affected. As in Europe, economic pressure could produce political change. In Thailand, for example, the deficits caused by the depression saw a military coup to replace the absolute monarch. The Japanese conquests during the Second World War further reinforced the resolve of local people for independence, while demonstrating that European authority was not unsurmountable.

Each country, however, followed a different path to ultimate independence. Thailand negotiated its fate with multiple European interests and, unique to Southeast Asia, managed to avoid major colonial interventions. Burma (now Myanmar) negotiated its independence from Britain in 1948, but was ruled by a military dictatorship from 1962 to 2011. Malaysia negotiated independence from the British in 1957, although not without the violence of the Malayan Emergency that was then followed by the initial union and separation from Singapore (in 1965). The Philippines' transition to independence under the Americans was seen as relatively inevitable, but did not occur until 1946, and even then with a remaining strong American presence. Vietnam only gained independence after extended bloody wars against a series of foreign invaders including the Japanese, French, Americans and their allies, that lasted from 1940 to 1975 and extended into border wars with neighbouring countries for many years. Cambodia gained independence from France in 1953, but was involved in the Vietnam War, and later endured a genocidal regime from 1975–91. Indonesia needed four years of fighting with the Dutch (1945–49) before gaining independence. Laos, too, gained its independence from France between 1945 and 1949 but endured decades of civil war thereafter. Papua New Guinea ceased to be administered by Australia in only 1975, while Timor-Leste was finally released from Portuguese interests in 1975 but endured significant destruction by the Indonesians (who had invaded in 1973) before achieving independence in 2002. Table 9.1 provides one representation of this turbulence, with a nation's form of governance being scored on a scale from minus ten, representing absolute autocracy, to plus ten, representing full democracy. In contrast to many of the other countries of Southeast Asia, it reveals that Australia and New Zealand had long histories of stable and democratic government institutions while several other countries in this region endured institutions well below full democracy. With the exceptions of Laos and Myanmar, institutions

Table 9.1 Polity2 in Southeast Asia (autocracy–democracy on a –10 to 10 scale)

	1900	1950	1955	1960	1965	1970	1975	1980	1985	1990	1995	2000	2005	2010
Australia	10	10	10	10	10	10	10	10	10	10	10	10	10	10
New Zealand	10	10	10	10	10	10	10	10	10	10	10	10	10	10
Papua New Guinea							4	4	4	4	4	4	4	4
Cambodia			–9	–9	–9	–7				1	1	2	2	2
Indonesia												6	8	8
Laos			2	–1			–7	–7	–7	–7	–7	–7	–7	–7
Malaysia				10	10	1	4	4	4	4	3	3	3	6
Myanmar		8	8	8	–7	–7	–6	–8	–8	–7	–7	–7	–8	–6
Philippines		5	5	5	5	2	–9	–9	–6	8	8	8	8	8
Singapore				7	–2	–2	–2	–2	–2	–2	–2	–2	–2	–2
Thailand	–10	–3	–3	–7	–7	2	3	2	2	3	9	9	9	4
Timor-Leste													6	7
Vietnam			–9	–8	–8	–7	–7	–7	–7	–7	–7	–7	–7	–7

Source: Calculated from Marshall, Jaggers, and Gurr (2011), www.clio-infra.eu

Notes: Autocracy–democracy index: –10 (total autocracy), +10 (total democracy). Australia and New Zealand exhibit high levels of democracy from the 1850s, while Thailand was originally an absolute monarchy. Large changes in political governance after 1950 reflect the variety of paths followed post-colonial rule.

and processes in these other nations tended to improve, albeit sometimes slowly, in the second half of the twentieth century. These varying paths to independence, the significant differences in human and capital destruction endured in each country and the different social and economic responses to these challenges, also serve to explain some of the variation in living standards that emerged after the Second World War.

Post Second World War

While the individual countries of Southeast Asia and Oceania found themselves in quite different situations after the Second World War, globally the period was to be marked by a return to more open trade and international cooperation. Despite the fact that wars and civil strife were significant elements of Southeast Asia (in particular the areas of 'Indochina' covering Vietnam, Cambodia and Laos), there was, in other regions, considerable improvement to trade and living standards. This is perhaps less surprising when one considers the long legacy of international trade that existed throughout Southeast Asia from the preceding centuries. It is also worth noting that, with the exception of Australia, New Zealand and the Philippines, earlier European colonial ties did not appear to have much influence on the direction of trade links.

By the 1960s, Singapore was emerging as one of the four 'Asian Tigers' along with Hong Kong, South Korea and Taiwan. Between 1965 and 1995, growth rates for these four economies averaged around 6 per cent per annum, transforming the living standards of their populations. Also in the group of High Performing Asian Economies (HPAE) were Indonesia, Malaysia and Thailand. Of particular interest was their ability to achieve rapid growth, with mostly equitable outcomes, while using quite interventionist government policies. Their unique growth trajectories prompted a range of explanations. Researchers identified several factors including: trade openness (and especially export push policies), financial stability (both macroeconomic and in the banking sector) and international cooperation (particularly in an increasingly globalized world), technology, increased physical and human capital per worker, improved health and education, demographic changes that increased labour supply but also demand for consumer goods, a shift toward manufacturing, cheap energy and interventionist governments. Together these created a 'golden age' of growth. Countries that were able to attract investment to utilize their plentiful, cheap and increasingly educated labour and embrace trade openness were able to grow. A closer focus on the individual HPAEs reveals a more diverse story.

Indonesia's post-1960 economic improvement was quite remarkable when one considers how few indigenous Indonesians in the 1950s had received a formal education under Dutch colonial policies. Political, social and military instability in the early 1960s had resulted in a military coup in 1965. The following forty years, however, saw a military backed government focus relentlessly on uniting and developing the ethnically and culturally diverse archipelago of several thousand islands, using anti-communist, pro-market policies. The sheer size of the population and the diversity of the country meant even small gains would be difficult but, if achieved, that many millions of lives were improved.

Remarkable too was Malaysia's economic development, given its troubled beginnings in the early 1960s and the ethnic partitions that were inherited from centuries of segmented economic development. With an extended period of political stability, however, the government developed a series of policies focused on economic growth. It followed a relatively open economic policy and encouraged the influx of foreign capital. A series of policies and economic targets, such as the New Economic Policy, import-substitution industrialization in heavy industry policy, and the National Development policy, combined with a massive shift to enhance access to education in the mid-1960s, resulted in large advances to Malaysians' standard of living.

In the case of Thailand, the growth path was less straightforward. Significant investment in education in the 1930s, and again in the 1950s, laid the basis for economic growth, as did a liberal approach to trade and investment. Manufacturing, which was given impetus by American requirements for the Korean War and Thailand's ability to supply primary products, also served as the platform for the post-1960s increase in living standards. Nonetheless, the country's proximity to warring states and its own political instability saw multiple devaluations of the currency over several decades. While periods in the late 1980s saw large growth, other decades saw periods of currency speculation, high interest rates and, at different times, a lack of foreign capital.

In the region, the Association of Southeast Asian Nations (ASEAN) was formed in 1967. Initially including only Indonesia, Malaysia, the Philippines, Singapore and Thailand it gradually expanded, as political tensions and differences eased, to include Brunei, Myanmar, Cambodia, Laos and Vietnam. Papua New Guinea currently has observer status and Timor-Leste has applied for membership. Other regional interests, including Australia and New Zealand, are part of the associated ASEAN Regional Forum which now includes twenty-seven countries.

This period of industrialization and growth also saw a massive shift of people from the countryside to the cities. This had occurred early in the case of Singapore, Australia and New Zealand, where half the population lived in cities by 1900. By the 1970s the figure was 80 to 100 per cent (Singapore). By contrast, while millions of people have shifted from the country to the cities since the 1960s, especially in Indonesia, the Philippines, Thailand, Vietnam and Malaysia, only in the 1990s did the percentage living in urban settings reach 50 per cent, and only in the

Philippines and Malaysia. Population size matters in these comparisons. While over 100 million people live in cities in Indonesia, today this still represents less than 50 per cent of their population.

By comparison, the poorest countries of Papua New Guinea and Timor-Leste also have the lowest rates of urbanization. This reflects their lack of the classic pull factor – industrialization – and the movement of people in response to work opportunities. While the move into cities is associated with increased material wealth – industrialization creates more wealth than subsistence farming – it also produces large concentrations of unskilled labour. Cheap labour is critical to basic, large-scale manufacturing but it is also associated with the difficult social issues of poverty, overcrowding, crime and substandard infrastructure. Thus while the shift towards increased urbanization, industrialization and improved aggregate material wealth is a form of catching up with the living standards of more developed economies, it brings with it some of the problems of overly rapid and unconstrained development.

Some aspects of the economic development of these countries are captured in the figures and tables that follow. While none of these figures can reveal all the critical elements impacting on economic growth, they do highlight critical points of similarity and difference in the growth paths and economic outcomes of this widely diverse group of countries.

The long-term transformation of the living standards of these countries can be expressed in a number of ways. The most common measure, GDP per capita, is represented in Figure 9.2. The top panel in Figure 9.2 reveals the high living standards of Australia and New Zealand, throughout the nineteenth and twentieth century. It also shows the rapid improvement to Singapore's material standard of living. One of the four Asian Tiger economies, its spectacular increase in per capita GDP began in the 1960s and has increased to a level that equals (and since 2005 exceeds) that of Australia and New Zealand. Far less spectacular, but also significant, are the improvements in Malaysia and Thailand; their per capita GDPs are now around those of Singapore in the 1970s. The lower panel reveals their growth since the 1960s, as well as the later improvement in Indonesia and the more disappointing increase in the Philippines over the same period. By comparison, the measured standards of living in Laos, Vietnam and Myanmar are only now approaching those of Singapore when it began its take-off over half a century ago. Collectively, however, all of these improvements have meant a transformation in the lives and opportunities of millions of people, and at a rate that was undreamed of a generation ago.

The 1997–98 Asian financial crisis provided a check to both the growth rates of many Southeast Asian countries and their populations' living standards. Caused by a combination of excess borrowing, declining returns and overheating economies, the shock saw growth rates drop dramatically.

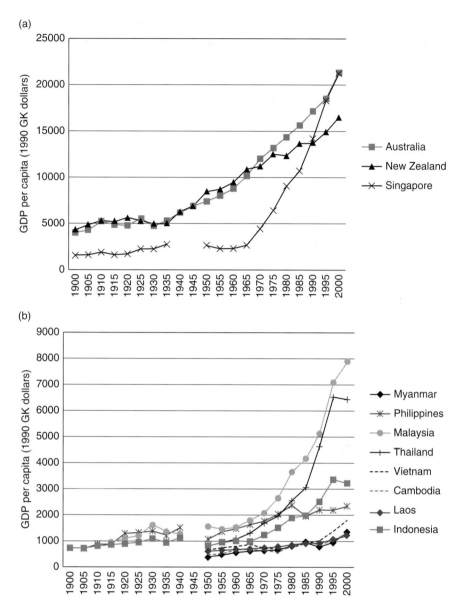

Figure 9.2 GDP per capita in Southeast Asia, 1900–2000
Source: www.clio-infra.eu; Maddison Project: www.ggdc.net/maddison/maddison-project/partici
pants.htm.

National responses to the crisis diverged. Politically, the shock had a significant impact in Indonesia, for example, where many companies were unable to repay their foreign borrowings and several banks collapsed. These events helped precipitate the fall of the government and saw a shift in economic policy, with cuts to projects financed by the government and many import tariffs. Malaysia, on the other hand, responded to the crisis by intervening in its markets, fixing its exchange rate and subsequently expanding government expenditures and refusing aid from the International Monetary Fund (IMF). In contrast, Thailand restricted capital outflows and quickly sought IMF assistance.

While national growth rates subsequently improved, the crisis is now seen as marking a 'turning point' in the region, with the slowing of Japan and the emergence of China, and to a lesser extent India, as new sources of growth. While both China and India had been improving their economic performance for several years before the crisis, the subsequent dominance of China – both globally and as a hub to many of its neighbours' supply chains – has been marked by many as dating from this event. Subsequent to the Asian crisis there was a rapid expansion in bilateral trade agreements, regional capital markets and macroeconomic reforms, as well as significant currency integration. These all enhanced economic growth.

Much of this economic pressure served to integrate the economics of Southeast Asia and Australasia even further. While the mainland Southeast Asian countries have been linked to China both in the process of manufacturing and as importers of China's manufactured goods, Australia and New Zealand have been mostly exporting commodities and agricultural products.

In contrast, the poorest countries in this comparison, Timor-Leste, Papua New Guinea, Myanmar, Cambodia and Laos, remain minimally engaged in trade, often having little to export to others. The reasons behind this vary, although the impact of war and civil unrest are common threads.

Timor-Leste for example, only separated from Indonesia in 2002 and immediately faced the challenge of rebuilding the 70 per cent of homes and schools destroyed by the withdrawing Indonesians. Despite World Bank estimates that countries require fifteen to thirty years to overcome post-conflict trauma, Timor-Leste has been laying the foundations of education, health care, institution building and infrastructure for the past decade, despite significant poverty. Oil reserves off its coast offer the possibility of an important future export commodity. Nonetheless, on all measures, it remains extremely poor.

Self-governing since 1975, Papua New Guinea contains a large number of tradable commodities. Its mountainous geography and tropical climate, fragmented tribal populations and the legacy of previous colonial 'cargo cult' development, have meant that it has not yet developed the level of economic, social or educational infrastructure needed to advance living standards to those of middle-ranked countries.

Myanmar's current levels of poverty and lack of economic progress reflects the impact of decades of violence, military rule, martial law and civil unrest. In stark contrast to the HPAEs, there has been no sustained focus on improving the living standards of the population but instead the nation has been consumed by the struggle between people of different political and economic ideologies. The result has been the neglect of the basic human, social and economic infrastructure required to advance individual living standards.

A similar, though even more violent, set of historical events explains Cambodia's current levels of impoverishment. After modest economic improvement in the early 1960s, Cambodia was drawn into the Vietnam War. While the damage this caused was extensive, the destruction of the Khmer Rouge during the 1970s was the complete antithesis of building factors associated with economic growth. The focus on creating collective agriculture and a nationalized economy was, however, ultimately less destructive than the mass murder of all individuals with any form of education (even including those who simply possessed reading glasses) that occurred throughout the country over several years. After the fall of the Khmer Rouge in 1979, fighting continued at varying intervals and with varying intensity for more than a decade. The result is that, even today, only agriculture, some simple manufacturing, services, tourism and construction serve as the basis of the economy.

The post-Second World War history of Laos, like Cambodia, is inextricably tied to the Indochina Wars and Vietnam. Like Cambodia, the wars resulted in massive destruction of natural and human resources over two decades. Like Vietnam, the economy had also become greatly dependent on external (mainly American) investment which was withdrawn when the Communists came to power in the mid-1970s. For several years a traditional command-based economic system was adopted, although since the late 1980s this has been modified to permit increased international trade and more private sector activity. Nonetheless, agriculture and tourism remain critical to the economy while industrial development plays a relatively minor role in advancing living standards.

The economic consequences of fighting the Indochina wars for over three decades, as well as other border wars, has meant that Vietnam has had far less time than other countries to rebuild. Not only did the human and capital destruction of war need to be addressed, the massive economic distortions caused by a war economy, high levels of aid (in the 1950s and 1960s) and post-war, economic embargoes all created barriers to advancing living standards. As with Laos and Cambodia, a centrally planned economy has dominated, although since 1986 Vietnam has pursued a mixed strategy of socialist planning and market signals. The result has been an increased level of economic growth as the nation has combined private sector growth with planned targets and infrastructure. On several of the indicators described below, Vietnam now outstrips Laos and Cambodia. Vietnam joined the World Trade Organization (WTO) in 2007.

The Philippines, although not suffering the same extremely low average living standards as the above countries, has also struggled with poverty and extreme differences between rich and poor. Before the Second World War government expenditure on education was higher than in several other Southeast Asian countries.

For several decades following the Second World War it followed a relatively open trade policy, but with a policy of import substitution, rather than export growth. Heavy government regulation combined with corruption also discouraged external investment. Subsistence agriculture and lowered levels of investment in education slowed improvements to living standards, while inequality and lack of investment in social infrastructure meant only relatively few areas of export growth. In more recent years, while economic indicators have improved, the distribution of improvements to living standards has remained a significant problem.

In addition to measures of GDP per capita, another way to represent improvements to living standards is by examining the average height of the population. As discussed elsewhere in this book, the average height of the population provides a measure of human well-being that summarizes the total set of factors – economic, social and environmental – that bears down on individuals. The sensitivity of this measure to adversity (and plenty) is remarkable. It is also possible to trace this measure further back in time than many other measures of living standards. As Figure 9.3 reveals, the average height of male (white) Australians and New Zealanders has, for over two centuries, far exceeded the average heights of males in other countries. (Data on male heights are more numerous than female data in the historical record, as they are frequently collected at enlistment, imprisonment or slave sale. Given the external food and disease environment generally impacts equally on men and women they are taken as a reasonable measure of the whole population.) The record also shows some remarkable increases in heights in recent years, as food supplies, medical treatment and the disease environment improved with GDP, particularly in Thailand, Malaysia and, more steadily, in Indonesia. The height record can also reveal the impact of deprivation and adversity. The steep decline in heights in the second half of the nineteenth century in Cambodia and Myanmar, and to a lesser extent in Indonesia in the 1870s, are clearly evident, as are the large declines in Vietnam, Myanmar and Cambodia heights in the second half of the twentieth century. The economic and social ravages of war and civil disruption are ultimately reflected in the very stature of the population. Even the few available observations on male heights in Papua New Guinea confirm that country's ongoing difficulties with low living standards. In contrast, the recent rapid increase in height among male Thais and Malaysians is consistent with a significant improvement in economic and environmental health factors. The more recent improvement in the heights of males in Laos, despite their current low living standards, is also cause for optimism, as it suggests that the basic elements of food and health are being enjoyed by a significant portion of the population.

The ultimate measure of living standard for the individual, life expectancy, also responds to the factors that impact on a person's health and well-being. Like height, it not only reflects the full combination of factors that affect the individual, but also the living conditions of their mothers prior to birth. Before the 1850s,

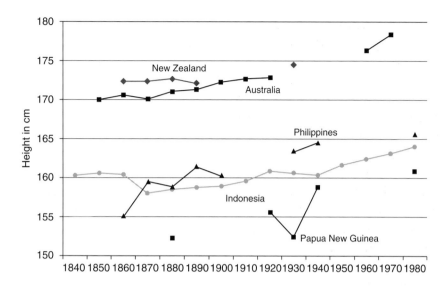

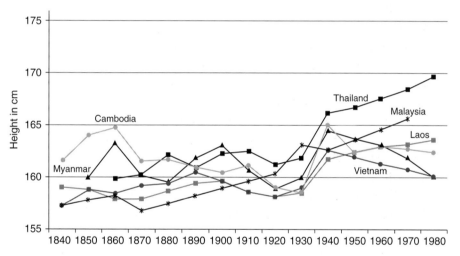

Figure 9.3 Male heights in Southeast Asia, 1800–2000
Source: Baten and Blum (2012).
Note: the y-axes in the upper and lower panel have different minimum and maximum values.

average life expectancy in many European countries was between 30 and 35 years old, a figure that was not achieved in the Philippines even at the beginning of the twentieth century. In Indonesia average life expectancy was below 30 in the 1940s, and in Timor-Leste this was still the average life-expectancy in the 1950s. Figure 9.4 reveals the very rapid improvement in life expectancy that occurred in many countries in the twentieth century. This has been a particular dimension of living standards that has improved in Southeast Asia. In the mid-twentieth century, average life expectancy at birth in Myanmar, Laos, Cambodia and Vietnam

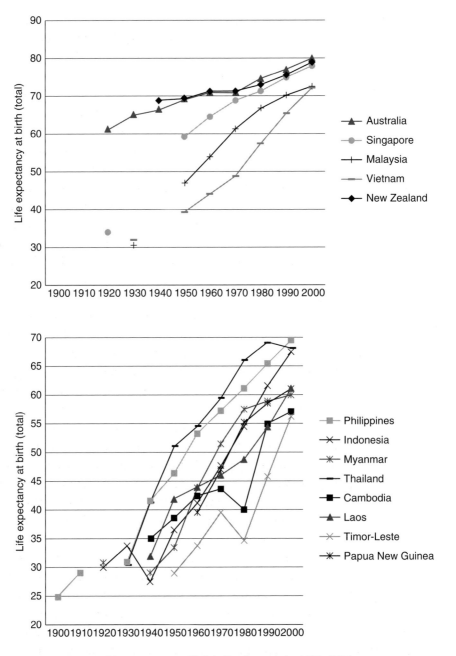

Figure 9.4 Average life expectancy at birth in Southeast Asia, 1900–2000
Source: www.clio-infra.eu. Note: the y-axes in the upper and lower panel have different minimum and maximum values.

were the same as those in more developed nations in the nineteenth century. As recently as the 1960s, average life expectancy at birth in Papua New Guinea and Timor-Leste were equally low, at under 40 years of age, but both countries have exhibited rapid improvements in their populations' life expectancy in recent decades. Nonetheless, there are still clear gaps in life expectancy. More than a decade of life expectancy separates infants born in Australia, New Zealand and Singapore from those born in Thailand, the Philippines or Indonesia. Infants born in Cambodia or Timor-Leste face the prospect of lifetimes that on average will be two decades shorter than their contemporaries in the wealthiest countries.

Just as the closing gap in urbanization and per capita GDP means that more of these countries are encountering the social problems that exist in more developed countries, so increasing longevity means they will, in the future, face the social problems of an increasingly ageing population. In several cases, however, they will not have the time or resources to develop the same levels of health and infrastructure support as the richest countries, suggesting a potentially bleak outcome for many of the aged in the poorest countries.

A critical factor associated with average life expectancy and living standards now and in the future is education. With the transformation of economic development, first from agriculture and commodity production to low-skill industry and manufacturing, and in the second half of the twentieth century to high-skilled manufacturing, the importance of education has increased continuously over the past two centuries. The response of many Southeast Asian nations is represented in Figure 9.5 where the sharp increase in average years of education is clearly evident in most countries, especially after the 1950s. Once again Australia and New Zealand are at the top of the graph. While Singapore and Malaysia have been improving rapidly, the much slower improvement for Cambodia does not bode well for their future. The average number of years of education in Vietnam (despite recent post-war improvements), Laos and Myanmar are still less than half of those achieved by the leading countries.

Commitment and investment in education is one government policy that can be implemented relatively quickly, even though the economic benefit of such investment may take decades to emerge. Even in the more developed countries, it was only after the Second World War that larger proportions of the population began to undertake tertiary education. While the first step in any education investment must be in basic and widespread primary education, for several of the Southeast Asian countries in this study, the creation of larger numbers of highly educated citizens is well within reach.

Many of the economies in this region changed significantly after the 1960s and have changed again in the past decade. Improving their living standards initially via the production and export of labour-intensive, low-cost manufactured goods, many of them achieved high rates of economic growth. More recently, a number of

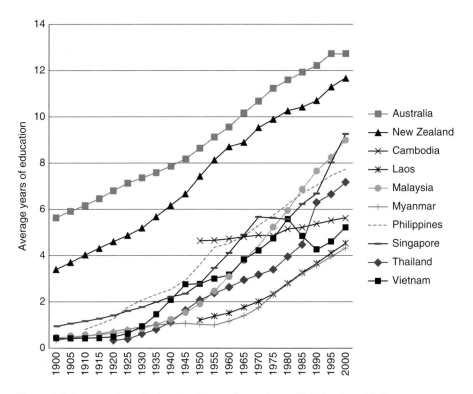

Figure 9.5 Average years of education for people aged over 15 in Southeast Asia
Source: www.clio-infra.eu.

countries have become part of regionally integrated supply chains with a focus on regional co-operation. Through the 1980s and 1990s many of these economies imported capital, had current account deficits and faced pressure to depreciate their currencies. Today, several export capital, have current account surpluses and their currencies are viewed by some as undervalued. Not all, unfortunately, have prospered. Timor-Leste and Papua New Guinea, for example, remain in need of continued external aid to supply their citizens with basic infrastructure.

While Australia, New Zealand and more recently Singapore, have enjoyed high living standards, even these countries have had to adjust their economic settings to maintain those levels. In the case of Australia and New Zealand, for example, the 1970s and 1980s were periods of significant economic adjustment. Tariff barriers, a long time policy of Australia, were significantly lowered, and the exchange rate allowed to float. New Zealand undertook substantial economic reform to lessen regulation. While these policies in many ways followed the trend initiated in other parts of the developed Western world, they also facilitated a more international aspect to these countries' economies and helped sustain their growth rates.

After the retreat from globalization between the First and Second World Wars, the second half of the twentieth century saw trade openness again emerge as a

Table 9.2 Merchandise trade exports per head of population, 1950–2010

	1950	1960	1970	1980	1990	2000	2010
Singapore	1.069		0.749	8.027	19.494	34.297	69.306
Australia	0.220	0.195	0.374	1.505	2.359	3.367	9.517
New Zealand	0.265	0.351	0.427	1.707	2.735	3.473	7.188
Malaysia	0.153		0.192	1.184	2.085		7.030
Thailand	0.017	0.016	0.021	0.145	0.423	1.139	2.827
Vietnam		0.005		0.006	0.037	0.190	0.831
Indonesia		0.009	0.009	0.149	0.143	0.317	0.674
Philippines	0.017	0.023	0.028	0.119	0.134	0.520	0.548
Cambodia	0.008			0.003		0.121	0.360
Papua New Guinea			0.042	0.342	0.313	0.404	
Laos							0.277
Timor-Leste	0.000	0.000	0.000	0.000	0.000		0.015
Myanmar	0.008		0.004				

Source: Exports calculated from WTO (2013), Value of merchandise trade and commercial services and population from Mitchell (2007: table A1, pp. 10–14).
Note: Value of exports per person measured in $US ('000s) per person. Current prices.

critical factor advancing nations' living standards. Countries that were able to participate in trade, that produced goods the world wished to buy, and that developed their human and physical infrastructure to engage with other countries, prospered. Table 9.2 provides one representation of this for the nations of Southeast Asia and Australasia. It measures the value of exported goods, adjusted for population size. The table shows Singapore (as a trading hub with high levels of re-exports), Australia, New Zealand and Malaysia in a group of countries with high levels of exports. Their level of exports, and the fact that their relatively high export levels per capita existed from the 1940s, place them in a different group from the nations of Indonesia, Thailand, the Philippines, Laos or Cambodia. The table also suggests that Thailand has been rapidly improving its export performance, while for Vietnam it took until the cessation of hostilities for it to increase exports. It has been rapidly increasing per capita exports since the 1980s. Unfortunately, the per capita value of exports for Timor-Leste lies well below those of other countries, although the rapid improvement that is seen in many of its Southeast Asian neighbours since the 1970s raises hope for the future. For many of the nations of Southeast Asia, trade would appear to be a critical element for their future well-being; a fact that their forebears many generations earlier would have understood.

Concluding remarks

A generation has passed since the end of the Second World War and while memories of struggles for independence are still fresh in the minds of some citizens, for many born after 1960 their world is unrecognizable from that of their parents. For several countries, the cities, health standards and educational expectations of their citizens are among the highest in the world. The economic well-being of citizens in less developed countries, however, remains decades behind, despite the technology of the internet allowing them to communicate ever more immediately with the rest of the world.

Australia and New Zealand have achieved and maintained some of the highest living standards in the world for over a century. By contrast, the changes that have occurred in Singapore and Malaysia and, to a lesser extent, the Philippines, Indonesia and Thailand over the past half-century have been dramatic and far-reaching; from well below the global average to above many other parts of the globe. The material standard of living enjoyed by the citizens in these countries would have been unimaginable to earlier generations. Lagging behind this surge in economic growth, but for different reasons, are the countries of Thailand, Vietnam, Cambodia and Laos; but even here there has been great improvement, especially, in recent years, in Vietnam. The living conditions and economies of Papua New Guinea, Myanmar and Timor-Leste, however, would still be familiar to an earlier generation, even if the technology would not.

These countries include around 10 per cent of the world's population. Changes to government policy that create even small improvements to their populations' standard of living, therefore, will impact on the lives, health and life expectancy of millions of people. The diversity of growth paths in each country reflects a range of different influences. Trade, war, peace, social and civil unrest, institutions, govern-ance rules, geography, educational opportunities; all have played a role. Fundamental building blocks to improving living standards are common: peace, the opportunity to trade, good governance, property rights, markets, education and good health. Understanding the history of these countries, the paths they have followed and the lessons they have to teach us, will help many countries better address the challenges of the present and future.

Further reading

Asian Development Bank (2014), Country Reports, various issues, www.adb.org/coun tries/main, accessed September 2014.

Baten, J., Stegl, M. and van der Eng, P. (2013), 'The Biological Standard of Living and Body Height in Colonial and Post-colonial Indonesia, 1770–2000', *Journal of Bioeconomics* 15 (2), 103–22. Provides long-run estimates of living standards using human height as a key indicator.

Bellwood, P. (1992), 'From Prehistory to *c.* 1500 CE', in N. Tarling (ed.), *The Cambridge History of Southeast Asia. Vol. 1: From Early Times to* c. *1800*, Cambridge University Press.

Bolt, J. and van Zanden, J. L. (2013), 'The First Update of the Maddison Project; Re-Estimating Growth Before 1820', Maddison Project Working Paper 4.

Booth, A. (1991), 'The Economic Development of Southeast Asia: 1870–1985', *Australian Economic History Review* 31 (1), 20–52. Provides a useful overview of the economic history of Southeast Asia over a critical time of economic change.

Cameron, R. (1997), *A Concise Economic History of the World. From Paleolithic Times to the Present*, 3rd edn., Oxford University Press.

Drabble, J. H. and Booth, A. (2000), *An Economic History of Malaysia c. 1800–1990: the Transition to Modern Economic Growth*, Palgrave Macmillan, Basingstoke.

Fforde, A. (2009), 'History, and the Origins of Vietnam's Post-War Economic Success', *Asian Survey* 49 (3): 484–504.

Hawke, G. R. (1985), *The Making of New Zealand: an Economic History*, Cambridge University Press. With a strong focus on New Zealand post-1890, this provides a comprehensive overview of that country's economic history.

Head, J. W. (2010), 'The Asian Financial Crisis in Retrospect – Observations on Legal and Institutional Lessons Learned after a Dozen Years', *East Asia Law Review* 51 (31), 31–102.

Huang, Y., and Wang, B. (2011), 'From the Asian Miracle to an Asian Century? Economic Transformation in the 2000s and Prospects for the 2010s', Reserve Bank of Australia Conference, www.rba.gov.au/publications/confs/2011/index.html, accessed 20 September 2013.

International Monetary Fund (2014), Economic data, various countries, www.imf.org/external/index.htm, accessed September 2014.

Klein Goldewijk, K., Beusen, A. and Janssen, P. (2010), 'Long Term Dynamic Modeling of Global Population and Built-up Area in a Spatially Explicit Way, HYDE 3.1', *The Holocene* 20 (4), 565–73.

Maddison, A. (2006), 'Asia in the World Economy 1500–2030 AD', *Asian-Pacific Economic Literature*, 20 (2), 1–37. Provides an essentially quantitative overview of Asian economic development.

McLean, I. W. (2012), *Why Australia Prospered: the Shifting Sources of Economic Growth*, Princeton University Press.

Mokyr, J. (ed.) (2003), *The Oxford Encyclopaedia of Economic History*, Oxford University Press.

Montesano, M. J. (2009), 'Revisiting the Rice Deltas and Reconsidering Modern Southeast Asia's Economic History', *Journal of Southeast Asian Studies* 40: 417–29.

Organisation for Economic Cooperation and Development (OECD) (2014), country reports, various, www.oecd.org/countries, accessed September 2014.

Osborne, M. (2013), *South East Asia. An Introductory History*, 11th edn., Sydney: Allen and Unwin. An easily accessible introduction to social and cultural history of Southeast Asia.

Page, J. (1994), 'The East Asian Miracle: Four Lessons for Development Policy', in S. Fischer and J. J. Rotemberg (eds.), *NBER Macroeconomics Annual, Vol. 9*, Cambridge, MA: MIT Press, 219–82.

Prados de la Escosura, L. (2013), 'World Human Development: 1870–2007', Working Papers 0034, European Historical Economics Society.

Shanahan, M. P. (2014), 'Wealth and Welfare', in S. Ville and G. Withers (ed.), *The Cambridge Economic History of Australia*, Cambridge University Press, 489–510.

Slocomb, M. (2010), *An Economic History of Cambodia in the Twentieth Century*, Singapore: NUS Press.

Sugimoto, I. (2011), *Economic Growth of Singapore in the Twentieth Century: Historical GDP Estimates and Empirical Investigations*, Singapore: World Scientific Books.

Tarling, N. (ed.) (1992), *The Cambridge History of Southeast Asia*, 2 Vols., Cambridge University Press. Still one of the most comprehensive historical references for the majority of the countries discussed in this chapter.

United Nations (various issues), *Demographic Yearbook*, http://unstats.un.org/UNSD/Demographic/products/dyb/dyb2.htm, accessed November 2013.

van Zanden, J. L. and Marks, D. (2012), *An Economic History of Indonesia: 1800–2010*, Routledge Studies in the Growth Economies of Asia Series, Abingdon: Routledge.

Ville, S. and Withers, G. (ed.) (2015), *The Cambridge Economic History of Australia*, Cambridge University Press. Recent, up-to-date coverage of Australia's distinct economic history.

Williamson, J. G. (1998), 'Growth, Distribution and Demography: some Lessons from History', *Explorations in Economic History*, 35 (3), 241–71.

(2000), 'Globalization, Factor Prices and Living Standards in Asia before 1940', in A. J. H. Latham and H. Kawakatsu (eds.), *Asia Pacific Dynamism, 1500–2000*, London: Routledge. Focuses on real wages rather than GDP to assess living standards.

(2006), *Globalization and the Poor Periphery before 1950*, Cambridge, MA: MIT Press.

World Bank (1993), *The East Asian Miracle. Economic Growth and Public Policy*, Oxford University Press.

(2014), Various countries, www.worldbank.org/en/country, accessed September 2014.

References

Baten, J. and Blum, M. (2012), 'Growing Taller, but Unequal: Biological Well-being in World Regions and Its Determinants, 1810–1989', *Economic History of Developing Regions* 27, s66–s85.

Bulbeck, D. A., Reid, L., Tan, C. and Wu, Y. (1998), *Southeast Asian Exports since the 14th Century: Cloves, Pepper, Coffee and Sugar*, Leiden: KITLV Press.

Findlay, R. and O'Rourke, K. (2007), *Power and Plenty. Trade, War and the World Economy in the Second Millennium*, Princeton University Press.

Marshall, M. G., Jaggers, K. and Gurr, T.R. (2011), 'Political Regime Characteristics and Transitions, 1800–2010', Dataset Users' Manual, Center for Systemic Peace and Societal-Systems Research Inc, Arlington, www.systemicpeace.org/globalreport.html, accessed 20 July 2015.

Mitchell, B. R. (2007), *International Historical Statistics. Africa, Asia and Oceania 1750–2005*, Basingstoke: Palgrave Macmillan.

World Trade Organization (WTO) (2013), *Statistics. Merchandise Trade and Commercial Services*, www.wto.org/english/res_e/statis_e/trade_data_e.htm, accessed November 2013.

H9.1 Pre-history, ancient and classical periods of Southeast Asia

Martin Shanahan

Little is known about the pre-historical migrations of people through Southeast Asia and Oceania. Archaeological evidence suggests waves of migration, perhaps corresponding to changes in sea levels and climatic conditions. These factors influenced hunter-gatherer communities for over 700,000 years, although archaeological records are only reliable for the past 40,000. The original inhabitants of Australia and Papua New Guinea are believed to have migrated from the Asian mainland perhaps 50,000 years ago, while the Maori in New Zealand, probably originating in Southeast Asia, arrived via Polynesia around 1,000 years ago.

Insights into migration patterns are found through similarities between language groups. Linguistic scholars trace the influence of Tai speakers in Thailand, among the Shans in Burma, in Laos and northern parts of Vietnam and in Cambodia and Malaysia. Austronesian (linked to the Indonesian/Malay language group) is detectable in Timor-Leste, Indonesia, Malaysia, the Philippines and coastal regions of Thailand, Cambodia and Vietnam. The peoples of Papua New Guinea and New Zealand appear to be linguistically distinct.

While there is now considerable diversity in national, ethnic and religious groups across the region, there are also ancient connections. Southeast Asia and its peoples has always been much more than simply off-shoots of Indian or Chinese civilizations, despite these cultures' important long-term influences.

Agriculture emerged in different locations sometime between 11,000 and 6,000 years ago. Climatic conditions meant that more intensive rice farming was favoured in mainland Southeast Asia while in the equatorial regions, tubers, sago palm and some fruits were prominent. Proximity to water and the sea made fish an important source of protein. Notably, the indigenous populations of Australia did not develop intensive agriculture, and their protein sources depended on what they could hunt, fish or gather.

Although it is difficult to reconstruct the history of migration in Southeast Asia, several ancient civilizations are known through their archaeological remains. Mogul invasions and wars, such as the one between the dynasties of Vietnam and China, also shaped today's cultures. These hostilities, for example, ultimately shaped the Vietnamese identity as one quite separate from its northern neighbours. In the west, the interplay was between Indian influences and the emerging Khmer dynasty, and between India and the people of Pagan in northern Burma. While the dynasty in Pagan collapsed in 1289, it was gradually absorbed and replaced by the more northern-based Ayutthaya Empire – an empire modern Thais still regard as a building block of their identity.

The Angkorian (Khmer) Empire in Cambodia, which existed from around 800 AD to 1400 AD, stretched over much of modern Cambodia, southern Vietnam and southern Laos, as well as influencing more distant territories. Today its most famous legacy is the temple complex centred around Angkor Wat. This empire ultimately relied on investment in canals, reservoirs and irrigation that enabled two or three wet-rice crops per year rather than one. Increased climatic and political challenges in the fifteenth century and declining human and physical capital meant the demise of the empire and city that the thirteenth-century Chinese envoy Zhou Daguan had described as the richest in Southeast Asia.

The southern Sumatran trading empire of Srivijaya dominated maritime trade between India and China and especially the western section of the Indonesian archipelago and southern China from the seventh to the thirteenth centuries. Although this empire worked co-operatively with the Chinese, as the Chinese began to use their own fleet, other trading regimes based in Melaka emerged to challenge Srivijaya's dominance. These trading empires were scarcely known to the Portuguese, who arrived more than two centuries later, and who continued rather than founded a tradition of international trade.

Other important and long-standing empires are today also lost from direct view. Majapahit, the last of several trading empires in Java, existed between the eighth and fifteenth century. It influenced trade from the western tip of Sumatra, to the Philippines in the north and New Guinea in the east. Evidence of its inhabitants' wealth and economic control remain in walled terraces and massive monuments.

The importance of trade in spreading populations and linking regions should not be underestimated. Centuries before the empires of Pagan and Angkorian, maritime traders from Southeast Asia were known to the Chinese, Indians, Arabs and Romans. Small quantities of high value goods from cinnamon to gold were traded between Southeast Asia, India, the Middle East and Europe. By the fifteenth century European awareness and demand for these commodities began to match their navigational and shipbuilding ability to reach their source. Motivated by the desire to convert, conquer and consume, the empires of Europe began to send out traders, sailors and soldiers to the Molucca and Banda islands (Spice Islands) and beyond, where they hoped lay opportunities to grasp, wealth to amass and souls to save.

19 Institutional development in world economic history

Joerg Baten

Institutional differences are among the most prominent candidates that might be able to explain the contrast between rich and poor countries and regions. Following a long tradition of institutional economics, Acemoglu and Robinson (2012) recently discussed the role institutional settings played in historical developments. They emphasized that inclusive 'institutions of private property' encourage investment, whereas 'extractive institutions' are poison for economic development. The latter effect occurs if a large part of the population is at risk of being expropriated by the government, ruling elites, or other agents. The former set of political, economic and social arrangements (abbreviated "inclusive institutions") ensures that a broad cross-section of the population can benefit from their investments (not only, for instance, a small group of large landowners).

One example for their view is the different behaviour of the inhabitants of the mainland of Southeast Asia on the one hand and the Australia/New Zealand region on the other. Southeast Asia was traditionally characterized by institutions that were not conducive to economic growth. The most extreme case was Kambodsha during the 1975–78 period, when the Red Khmer aimed at creating an extreme version of agrarian communism, with the effect of two million human victims. Other countries were much less inhuman, but mainland Southeast Asia was, until recently, ranked low for its institutional and political institutions. Only during the 1990s were economic and political institutions substantially changed. The other extreme of this region is the Australia/New Zealand group that was characterized by growth-conducive institutions over the whole last century. Taking Australia/New Zealand and Southeast Asia together, the institutional quality index has the largest variability compared to all other world regions during the early twentieth century.

Another very famous example discussed by Acemoglu and Robinson are the cities of Nogales, Mexico, on the one hand, and Nogales, US, on the other hand. Both cities are adjacently situated at the border between Mexico and the US. However, the citizens of the northern city enjoy a far higher standard of living. The argument of Acemoglu and Robinson for the role of institutions is that entrepreneurs in Nogales, US, can be sure that any investment in their businesses, and any sacrifice and effort to create innovations, will pay off in the future. The institutional controls of the executive in the US are designed in a way that guarantees this security of investments. In contrast, Mexican institutions are described by Acemoglu and Robinson in a way that they sometimes allow expropriations of returns. Business success is influenced by contacts with political power. For example, the richest Mexican businessman, Carlos Slim Helú, accumulated his wealth not with an innovative product but by obtaining government licences in the telecommunications market. In contrast, Acemoglu and Robinson mobilize the Silicon Valley entrepreneurs as examples for the US focus on innovation. Acemoglu and Robinson focus on cases such as the Nogales twin cities because their geographic proximity makes it unlikely that other factors, such as geography and its implication on the prevalence of disease, could explain the substantial difference in welfare (Sachs and Warner (1997) emphasized malaria in tropical countries, for example). Early human capital differences are also unlikely to be an underlying explanatory variable in this particular case (on human capital, see Glaeser *et al.* 2004).

Institutional designs have been described by a number of earlier studies as growth determinants. Already during the early development of thinking about the political economy, property rights were recognized as important, for example, by Hayek (1960). Most notably, Douglass C. North received the Nobel Prize in economics for applying the institutional design idea to long-run developments in economic history (North and Weingast 1989).

One core issue of institutional influences on economic development is the direction of causation: are institutions really influencing development, or are simply high stages of development associated with good institutions? To tackle this issue, Acemoglu, Johnson and Robinson developed their famous 'settler mortality' variable, which can be used in statistical analyses such as instrumental variable estimation (Acemoglu *et al.* 2001, 2002). The idea is that European settlement decisions were influenced by the disease environments and population densities in the target countries. Where disease environment was more benign, as in countries that became the US, Canada and Argentina, large numbers of Europeans were willing to settle, and they brought their growth-enhancing European institutions with them. In contrast, areas where the first settlers faced high mortality rates, as was the case in West Africa, Europeans tended to implement more exploitative institutions. These types of institutions survived the end of colonialism. Postcolonial governments continued with institutions that were not growth promoting, with catastrophic effects on growth that have persisted until today.

Albouy (2008) and many others formulated doubts about Acemoglu *et al.*'s measurement accuracy, although Acemoglu *et al.* responded with many arguments. Glaeser *et al.* (2004) suggested another causal channel to explain the growth process, namely migrant human capital, which implies criticism of the

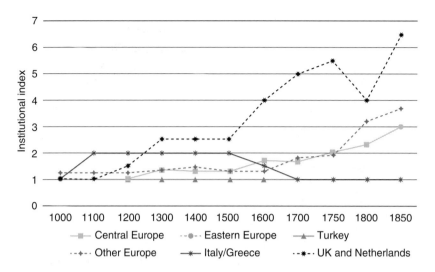

Figure I9.1 Acemoglu/Johnson/Robinson index of institutional protection of capital-owners
Source: based on Acemoglu *et al.* 2002.
Note: the vertical axis represents index values as defined in the source. Other Europe includes France, Iberia, Belgium, Ireland and Scandinavia.

settler instrument: if potential instrumental variables are related through another line of causation, they fail to be good instruments. Settlers might have brought their institutions with them, but primarily, they brought themselves and their embodied human capital, as Glaeser *et al.* stressed. Ogilvie and Carus (2014) wrote recently an interesting critique of many hypotheses of the historical institutional economics literature. Perhaps most provocatively, they reviewed North and Weingast's (1989) view that parliaments of wealth-holders usually promote economic growth. Acemoglu and Robinson (2012) stressed the point that one of the main reasons Egypt, for example, was poorer than England is that the latter had its Glorious Revolution, which changed the political and, subsequently, the economic system (as well as installed a parliament of wealthy people). The institutional protection of capital owners is shown in Figure I9.1, and it becomes clear that England and the Netherlands developed much better and earlier than other world regions. Ogilvie and Carus first consider the issue theoretically and argue that a parliament of wealth-holders does not automatically promote growth policies for the whole economy, but the wealth-holders might be more interested in serving their own aims, for example, by supporting privileges for merchants and craftsmen. They then discuss several cases in which they do not see a growth-promoting effect of wealthy parliamentarians. For example, in the south-west German state of Wuerttemberg, a widely unknown parliamentarian system was created quite early (from the late fifteenth and early sixteenth century). This political system stimulated surprising statements by

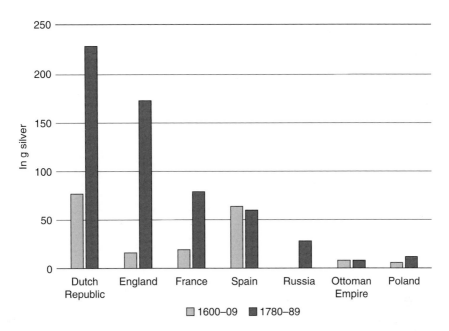

Figure I9.2 Per capita annual fiscal revenues (in g silver)
Source: based on Karaman and Pamuk (2010).

early political thinkers such as Charles James Fox, who remarked that only two constitutions existed in Europe, namely that of Britain and that of Wuerttemberg (Anonymous, 1818, p. 240, cited from Ogilvie and Carus 2014: 420). However, in spite of the industrial and commercial strata being represented in Wuerttemberg's parliament, its policies consisted of preventing economic growth by establishing monopolies, cartels and keeping guilds even longer than the much more autocratic Prussian state.[1] The Prussian rulers were less constrained and, after being motivated by Napoleon's military successes against Prussia, they were able to abolish the old and rather exclusive institutions such as guilds after 1808, whereas Wuerttemberg kept the guilds until 1864. However, this argument might be counterbalanced by many cases in which autocrats installed economic reforms after military defeats, which were, however, not always long-lived or systematic. Ogilvie and Carus add other cases, such as the Dutch Republic between the late seventeenth century and 1800, which caused stagnation, at least partly, by serving the power of already established business elites, at the expense of potential newcomers, although it might be remarked that the Netherlands had already the highest GDP per capita and that zero growth rates might not be as surprising.

However, Ogilvie and Carus' point that the wealthy parliamentarians might serve their own interest rather than the national welfare is well taken. It is the empirical question of how often in human history this was a more substantial growth obstacle than autocratic expropriation threats. Epstein (2000) had argued contrarily to the North-Acemoglu-Robinson view that in the Middle Ages, guild-based regimes were often quite successful. A compromise interpretation was recently put forward by Dincecco (2011), who argued that the combination of constraints on the executive and a high capacity of early modern states to tax would be growth promoting: the latter capacity enabled important infrastructure and human capital investment. The interaction with constraints is important because otherwise, taxes were mostly wasted in wars and other unproductive purposes. In Figure I9.2, it becomes obvious that Russia, Poland and the Ottoman Empire had very low capacities to tax, in contrast with the Dutch republic and England.

In sum, the debate about institutional sources of growth and poverty is an exciting one. Institutional quality has many facets, and it will be important in the future to develop measures and estimates for the various components of institutional quality.

Note

1. The Wuerttemberg parliament had a substantial influence on the crown.

References

Acemoglu, D., Johnson, S. and Robinson, J. A. (2001), 'The Colonial Origins of Comparative Development: an Empirical Investigation', *American Economic Review* 91(5), 1369–401.

(2002), 'Reversal of Fortune: Geography and Institutions in the Making of the Modern World Income Distribution', *The Quarterly Journal of Economics* 117 (4), 1231–94.

Acemoglu, D. and Robinson, J. A. (2012), *Why Nations Fail: the Origins of Power, Prosperity, and Poverty*, New York, NY: Crown Business.

Albouy, D. Y. (2008), 'The Colonial Origins of Comparative Development: an Investigation of the Settler Mortality Data', NBER Working Paper No. 14130.

Dincecco, M. (2011), *Political Transformations and Public Finances: Europe, 1650–1913*, Political Economy of Institutions and Decisions Series, Cambridge University Press.

Epstein, S. R. (2000), *Freedom and Growth: the Rise of States and Markets in Europe, 1300–1750*, London: Routledge.

Glaeser, E. L., La Porta, R., Lopez-de-Silanes, F. and Shleifer, A. (2004), 'Do Institutions Cause Growth?', *Journal of Economic Growth* 9 (3), 271–303.

Hayek, F., von (1960), *The Constitution of Liberty*, University of Chicago Press.

Karaman, K. K. and Pamuk, S. (2010), 'Ottoman State Finances in European Perspective, 1500–1914', *Journal of Economic History* 70, 593–629.

North, D. C. and Weingast, B. R. (1989), 'Constitutions and Commitment: Evolution of Institutions Governing Public Choice in Seventeenth Century England', *Journal of Economic History* XLIX, 803–32.

Ogilvie, S. and Carus, A. W. (2014), 'Institutions and Economic Growth in Historical Perspective', *Handbook of Economic Growth* 2A, 403–513.

Sachs, J. D. and Warner, A. M. (1997), 'Sources of Slow Growth in African Economies', *Journal of African Economies* 6 (3), 335–76.

10 Sub-Saharan Africa

Gareth Austin

Almost all the literature on the economic past of Sub-Saharan Africa has aimed at explaining, directly or indirectly, why the sub-continent is relatively poor. At the end of the colonial period, which for most African countries was about 1960, it was conventionally assumed that very little had changed in African economic history, especially before what, for most of the continent, was the relatively short period of colonial rule. The focus on poverty as the problem requiring explanation sometimes obscures other aspects of African economic history, such as the achievements of African farmers, traders and states, including improvements in food security, and episodes of economic growth. On the whole, however, the historical research carried out over the last fifty to sixty years (since Dike 1956) has used these achievements as means both of qualifying the notions of general poverty and stasis, and as sources of insight into why the overall economic development of the region has not been faster. This chapter begins by introducing alternative explanations of Africa's relative poverty, and then traces the history of poverty and economic development in African economies over successive periods. Finally, we will review the overall descriptions of African economies as historically static and therefore remaining poor, and comment on the major interpretations.

Interpretations

The main explanations for Africa's historic – if relative – poverty can be grouped in different ways: perhaps most fundamentally, external versus internal, and institutional versus resources. The two most influential strands of external explanation for Africa's historic poverty, dependency theory and its rational-choice counterpart, are themselves institutional, in the sense of focussing on the way resources are controlled, organized and exploited, rather than on the resources, natural and human, as such. Dependency theory, which was brought to Africa in the 1970s (Rodney 1972, Amin 1976, see also Wallerstein 1976) is the view that the development of the West was simultaneously – and by the same process – the underdevelopment of the Rest. A rational-choice counterpart of dependency theory was provided by a group of growth economists in the 2000s (Acemoglu *et al.* 2001,

2002, Acemoglu and Robinson 2010, Nunn 2008). Both externalist interpretations are ultra-Eurocentric, attributing Africa's fate to European decisions: during the external slave trades (the largest of which was carried on in European and American ships rather than by North African desert caravans or Arab dhows), and then under colonial rule. Crucially, both externalist interpretations also agree that in Africa the process of establishing capitalist institutions, such as private (as opposed to communal and public) property rights, has not gone far enough to promote market-based economic development. They argue that colonial governments, despite representing capitalist states in Europe, were content to draw Africa deeper into the world market, without establishing the institutions needed for self-sustaining economic development.

One of the two most influential strands of internal explanation also gives primacy to institutions as determinants of economic outcomes. Specifically, it sees indigenous institutions and organizations, from the nature of the state in Africa to such cultural features as extended kinship systems and 'communal' land tenure, as constraints on economic growth. This view with regard to kinship and land tenure was common (though far from universal) among colonial officials, and was reiterated in the 'modernization theory' of the 1950s–60s. While the reasoning behind the earlier formulations has long been discredited by research, their conclusions are partly revived, in a much more informed and nuanced way, in the best of the recent critiques of indigenous institutions (Platteau 2009). Meanwhile, states in Africa – precolonial, colonial, postcolonial – have been criticized from many angles, but the most influential academic analysis, from the early 1980s to the present, has derived from rational-choice political science. This approach, pioneered in African studies by Robert Bates, examines how far the private interests of rulers align with those of the population as a whole, distinguishing the conditions under which rulers will have an incentive to facilitate economic growth from those in which they stand to gain by predation, rewarding themselves and their supporters at the expense of general prosperity. In this framework, Bates has analysed aspects of precolonial, colonial and especially postcolonial political economy, insisting that it has often been rational – for rulers – to maintain policies obstructive to economic growth and public welfare (Bates 1981, 1983, 2005, 2008).

The other main strand of internal explanation starts from an analysis of natural and human resources (or 'factors of production'). This factor endowments framework offers four main propositions. The first is that most of Sub-Saharan Africa, until well into the twentieth century, was land-abundant and labour-scarce. That is, with the technology of the time concerned, the expansion of output was constrained by the supply of labour, rather than of cultivable land and other natural resources. The second proposition is that most of this relatively plentiful land was resistant to intensive methods of agriculture: soils were thin and therefore easily eroded (for example by heavy ploughing); animal diseases such as trypanosomiasis (sleeping sickness) prevented or inhibited the use of large animals over much of the continent, whether in transport or farming; and the extreme seasonality of the distribution of rainfall over the year in much of tropical Africa severely limited the productive uses of land during some months of the year, the heart of the dry season. Proponents of the factors of production approach go on to argue, third, that these resource characteristics help to account for choices of technology, such as the preference for 'extensive' rather than 'intensive' use of land (until the latter became scarce) (Hopkins 1973, Austin 2008). Finally, characteristic institutions of precolonial and (often) colonial Africa such as diverging rather than converging inheritance systems, and reliance on coercion as a means of recruiting labour from outside the household, have also been explained in such terms (respectively, Goody 1976, Hopkins 1973, Austin 2005, Fenske 2012, 2013). A related argument is that low population densities and the constraints on the productive use of land combined to inhibit state formation by making it difficult for would-be rulers to extract large revenues from farmers and pastoralists (Coquery-Vidrovitch 1969, Herbst 2000). The famous 'exception that proves the rule' is the kingdom of Ethiopia. Situated in a relatively fertile region, suitable for ploughs, this monarchy and its ruling class was able to extract an agricultural surplus from peasant cultivators (Crummey 1980), sufficient to sustain what turned out to be one of the most enduring polities on the planet (see also the Highlight Chapter 10.1).

Finally, scholars writing broadly in the tradition of Karl Marx have long contributed to the debate on African development, without ever becoming the orthodox view, even on the political left. While they share with dependency theorists the proposition that capitalism came to Africa from outside, they reject the radical pessimism of the dependency (and Acemoglu *et al.*'s) view of the impact of colonialism in Africa. Instead, they propound a 'tragic optimism': that out of violence and exploitation came advances in technology and the organization of production. They emphasize the extent to which capitalist development has actually occurred, citing in evidence the growth of wage labour over the last century and more, and the growth of education and manufacturing (Sender and Smith 1986, Sender 1999).

African economies, 1500–1650

In this period, even more than later, Sub-Saharan Africa is most accurately seen as comprising a number of regional economies which were not necessarily strongly linked with each other. An example of such a region was the 'Central Sudan', comprising a series of local savannah economies united by trade networks centred in what is now northern Nigeria and southern Niger, extending into Burkina Faso

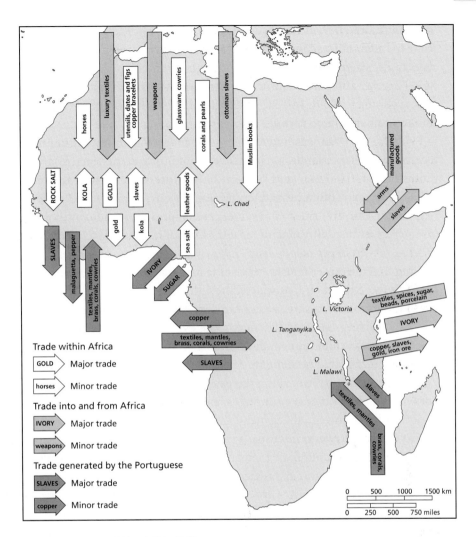

Map 10.1 Trade of Africa 1450–1600
Source: The maps in this chapter were modified by Mina Moshkeri, former cartographer of the London School of Economics, from J. F. A. Ajayi, M. Crowder, P. Richards, E. Dunstan, and A. Newman, *Historical Atlas of Africa*, Harlow, UK: Longman (1985).

and engaging also in trans-Saharan trade (Lovejoy and Baier 1975). However, African networks were not only regional. Trade via the Sahara and the eastern seas was already ancient in 1500 (see Map 10.1), and the institutional framework for long-distance trade across political and cultural boundaries had long been strengthened by the adoption of Islam as a cultural and moral foundation for trust among and with traders. This applies especially to the Swahili-Arab towns of the east coast, and to the courts and trading networks of the West African savannahs.

The fifteenth century had seen the beginning of direct trade with Europe. Portuguese navigators had explored the coasts, partly in order to bypass the

Saharan middlemen in the trade of West African gold to Europe, and partly en route to India. They acquired a string of coastal bases, and inaugurated the Atlantic slave trade when they purchased captives from the kingdom of Benin (in what is now Nigeria) and sold them to African merchants on the coast of what is now Ghana (Rodney 1969). In 1652, the Dutch East India Company founded a colony on the southern tip of Africa.

Evidence on what was happening in the interior is thinner. But archaeologists have shown that 'islands' of intensive agriculture existed across the continent (Sutton 1984, Widgren and Sutton 2004). Intensive agriculture was old; but where it began, it often proved temporary, for environmental or political reasons (e.g., Delius and Schirmer 2014). The great majority of land continued to be used extensively, either cultivated under some kind of rotation system with long fallows, or used for itinerant pastoralism. Likewise, large states existed in certain areas, tending to reproduce themselves in some form over centuries, as around the Great Lakes or the Niger Bend, as well as the Christian kingdom of Ethiopia. But there was no clear trend towards a long-term increase in the proportion of the African population living in states. There is some evidence of expansion of extra-subsistence production and trade in the Zambezi valley, along the east coast and in West Africa. Concentrated settlement, including towns, was also marked in certain areas, such as Zimbabwe, along the east coast and along parts of the Niger river, but without necessarily continuing to expand. While specific local histories were undoubtedly involved, the general constraints of low population density and environments hostile to intensive agriculture are surely part of the explanation.

Yet evidence of cumulative expansion of markets, apparently with expanded production for sale and denser commercial connections, can be found in this period, especially in West Africa (Inikori 2007). Africans took advantage of the opportunities presented by the Atlantic trade in an era where slaves were still only one of several major commodities. A significant feature of Africans' external trades was the large-scale importation of currency materials, such as cowries. This is best documented from trade with the Europeans, who did not accept these materials back in return for other imports: so we can deduce that they were used as currencies only in trade within Africa, testifying to the vitality of internal commerce (Inikori 2007).

Africans also used the Atlantic trade to enlarge their crop repertoire. Following a long history of African imports of crops and crop varieties from Asia, the Portuguese inaugurated an equally important series of imports from the Americas. African farmers adopted these selectively; maize and cassava enhanced calorific returns to both land and labour (Miller 1988, McCann 2005). Meanwhile, however, the emergent plantation system of the European empires – in the Atlantic islands, and then in the Americas – expanded the demand for captive labourers from Africa. Arguably, the size of the African population is un-guessable before its parameters were shifted by the combination of more efficient food farming and much increased slave exports. There is no reason to assume that they cancelled each other out.

Africa during the peak of the Atlantic slave trade, 1680–1800

For west and west-central Africa especially, this period was dominated by an escalation of the Atlantic slave trade to unprecedented levels, responding to the expansion of the Atlantic plantation system. The effects on peaceful production and trade were dire. Not only did the Atlantic market encourage private and state enterprise into slave raiding and slave-trade-stimulated warfare, but wars and raids made the pursuit of peaceful forms of production dangerous: at least parts of the 'Gold Coast' even became net importers of gold (Rodney 1969). On the other hand, those enslaved were overwhelmingly 'foreigners', or people excluded from society for heinous crimes, as far as those who sold them were concerned – contrary to the myth that Africans tended to enslave kin and fellow citizens (the exceptions were mainly in central Africa, as a last resort: see Miller 1988).

Admittedly, the Atlantic trade as a whole still brought certain advantages. Besides the new crops, the currencies that the West African merchants adopted were technically more efficient than their earlier commodity currencies, as was reflected in the expansion of a dual cowrie-and-gold-dust zone in West Africa (Lovejoy 1974). This can be seen as an institutional reform that reduced the cost of doing business; though the developmental benefits of this were limited as long as the business including slaving.

It is impossible to estimate with any precision the demographic impact of the Atlantic slave trade (still less that of the other external slave trades, which are much less documented). For the Atlantic slave trade, at least, we have a pretty good knowledge of the numerator (close to 13 million captives embarked: see Table 10.1), but only a rough idea of the denominator (the population of Africa: see Thornton 1977, Henige 1986). What is clear is that population densities were low relative to Eurasia (Austin 2008a: 590–1), and that, as noted, labour rather than land was the crucial supply constraint on production. We can, however, observe that the external slave trades, including the Atlantic, presumably enhanced inequality. Slave-holding within Africa increased as a joint product of the supply of exports, and there was also a high entry threshold of slave-raiding and trading as a business. All these developments made aggressive states profitable, and aggravated shortages of labour, and of effective demand (Hopkins 1973). Overall, in this time of mortal danger for stateless societies, there was probably a net increase in political centralization.

Table 10.1 Estimated slave departures from Sub-Saharan Africa in the different external slave trades, *c.* 1500–*c.* 1900

Trade	1501–1600	1601–1700	1701–1800	1801–1900	Total
Saharan	550,000	700,000	700,000	1,200,000	3,150,000
Red Sea	100,000	100,000	200,000	492,000	892,000
East African	100,000	100,000	400,000	442,000	1,042,000
Atlantic	338,000	1,876,000	6,495,000	4,027,000	12,736,000
Total	1,088,000	2,776,000	7,795,000	6,161,000	17,820,000

Key: 'Saharan' includes Nile Valley. 'Atlantic' includes shipments to Europe and the African Atlantic islands. Only in the Atlantic case are the figures based on data good enough to be called estimates rather than 'guesstimates'.
Source: modified from Lovejoy (2012): 19, 46, 138. For the earliest and latest periods, Eltis *et al.* (2008) give lower totals for the Atlantic trade: 278,000 and 3,874,000.

This period has been a focus of the scholarly debate about economic cultures in Africa, specifically on the question of whether resources in precolonial economies were allocated by the price mechanism, or by non-economic principles such as command and custom. Karl Polanyi devoted his last book to a study of the kingdom of Dahomey, claiming that the prices in its many markets were fixed (Polanyi 1966): a view comprehensively falsified by subsequent research (Hopkins 1973, esp. 6, 69–70, 112, Law 1992).

At the Cape, the importation of slaves, who were primarily used on large wine-growing estates, made for high living standards among the white population in the eighteenth century (Fourie 2012). Within Sub-Saharan Africa as a whole, however, European rule remained rare, localized and literally peripheral. On the east coast, the late eighteenth century witnessed the start of a fight-back by the Omani dynasty against Portuguese control of towns, forts and harbours (Sherrif 1987, Alpers 2009).

Markets, slaves and states, 1800–80

This period can be characterized by two contrary impulses, both of which lasted into the colonial era: the pressure for abolition, first of slave trading and then of slavery itself; and, in contrast, the continuation and actual expansion of the other slave trades in and from Africa, and the expansion of slavery within Africa. We saw from Table 10.1 that the British act to abolish the slave trade, in 1807, was unable to prevent an additional 4 million slaves being embarked to Atlantic destinations, especially Brazil and Cuba, before the last ship sailed in 1867. Meanwhile, the

Saharan, Red Sea and Indian Ocean slave trades appear to have reached record levels. The latter was especially intense in the 1850s to early 1870s, with the development of elaborate slave-raiding and trading networks, notably via Tanzania.

At the same time there was a major expansion of commodity production for both regional and extra-African markets in West Africa and parts of East Africa, such as the kingdom of Buganda, which until mid-century had no regular or direct trade with the coast and beyond (Reid 2002). The expansion in West Africa was partly a function of the transition from the export of slaves to what abolitionists called 'legitimate' commerce, especially palm oil and peanuts (Hopkins 1973: 124–35, Inikori 2009). Much of it, however, was an unintended consequence of the creation of the Sokoto Caliphate in 1804. At its height, this was the most populous African state of the period, occupying most of north-central and north-west Nigeria and parts of what are now neighbouring countries. Its commercial prosperity was based on internal peace and market integration, an extensive export-trade network run by Hausa merchant diasporas and regular enhancements of the labour supply through the importation of 'pagan' captives as slaves (Lovejoy 2006). Kano, its commercial capital, became the biggest manufacturing centre in the region, exporting cloth all over West Africa, as was described by the German explorer Heinrich Barth from his visit in 1851 (Barth 2011[1857]: 125–9).

The growth of commodity production both increased demand for, and was facilitated by, the increased use of slaves within much of the region: especially in West Africa (almost ubiquitously) but also on the eastern coast, from Somalia down to Tanzania (Cooper 1977). Labour coercion in the pastoral economies of South Africa took a different form: the appropriation of the labour of young adult men for herding and warfare by the Zulu monarchy and its imitators. With both models of labour coercion, the position of women tended to be reduced relative to men: females are thought to have comprised the majority of slaves within Africa (Robertson and Klein 1983), and the elevation of the warrior role was at the expense of the status of ascribed female roles (Mandala 1984).

Historians have paid much attention to the issue of changes in the character of African states in this period. Several partly distinct tendencies may be distinguished. First, there was a jihadist wave in western, central and eastern Sudan (the savannahs south of the Sahara, from Senegambia to what is now the republic of Sudan). This wave, of which the formation of the Sokoto Caliphate by Uthman dan Fodio was part, made Islam a mass rural religion for the first time in much of the region concerned, as distinct from being limited mainly to rulers and merchants. The Caliphate introduced the Islamic repertoire of taxes, a feature of which was light taxation of artisanal production and commerce, facilitating economic expansion (Lovejoy 2006). Second, the Zulu kingdom has been seen as a new kind of state in southern Africa, a patrimonial military autocracy rather than a 'tribe', which became the model for both 'offensive' and 'defensive' states in the region, such as the Ndebele and Lesotho kingdoms, respectively. This view has been much debated (Hamilton 1995). For economic historians, it is worth noting that Lesotho, for example, showed that 'defensive' nineteenth-century states, at least, could provide a setting favourable to the growth of agricultural and artisanal production for the market (Eldredge 1993). Third, the late nineteenth century saw major efforts by kingdoms to 'modernize' to meet the threat of European imperialism, as in the cases of Ethiopia (with some success, defeating the Italian invasion of 1896) and Asante (in Ghana; ultimately unsuccessfully). One can again argue that the greater success of Ethiopia was made possible by its long-standing environmental exceptionalism, which permitted the rulers a logistical foundation inconceivable for other African kingdoms (see Highlight Chapter 10.1 by Marjolein 't Hart).

The colonial era, 1880–1960

Within the long history of European overseas empires, the partition of Africa is notable for its compression in time, and even more for its relative lateness. The timing does not fit everywhere south of the Sahara, but most of the territory and population were subjected to colonial annexation some time during the European 'Scramble' for Africa, 1879–c. 1905; and most recovered their independence around 1960. Both the lateness and speed of the partition are partly explained by technological changes which made it both more attractive and less costly for European countries to invade Africa. The progressive industrialization of Europe and North America created new or at least massively enlarged markets for a range of agricultural and mineral products from Africa. Meanwhile, the cost of coercion for the European powers was reduced by the adoption of quinine against malaria, and by advances in military and transport technology. While none of this made the partition of Africa inevitable, European confidence in their own power, coupled with fears within individual European countries that their rivals would make further annexations in Africa and monopolize its resources if they did not do likewise, helps explain how the Scramble began and was sustained.

It is important to distinguish different types of colony in Africa: settler econo-mies (or, 'settler-elite', when compared to colonies elsewhere in the world where the indigenous population were almost totally displaced, unlike in Africa) in which most of the land was reserved for European use, especially that of individual farmers; 'peasant' colonies, where Africans retained almost all the land; and plantation/concession colonies, in which large areas, but not necessarily the majority, of the land was alienated to European companies. To simplify the comparison, we will concentrate here upon the extremes, the settler and 'peasant' colonies.

In the settler economies, African farmers responded rapidly to opportunities to produce crops for the markets provided by towns and mines (Arrighi 1973, Palmer and Parsons 1977). Initially, African real wages also tended to be high, reflecting labour scarcity and the fact that Africans still often had access to land (for example, Harries 1982: 143, 161 n.). In response, the governments of settler economies embarked on policies aimed at driving Africans out of the produce market and onto the labour market: by reserving land for European use, and restricting or prohibiting African tenancy on European-owned land (Arrighi 1973, Palmer and Parsons 1977, Mosley 1983). By the late 1920s and especially by the mid-1930s it was clear that African production for the market in Southern Rhodesia and Kenya was resilient despite these policies, even during the Great Depression. In response, government policy shifted towards taxing such production, directly or indirectly, rather than trying to eliminate it (Mosley 1983). In South Africa, with by far the biggest proportion of whites to blacks, the original colonial policy against high income for blacks was more successful. Black real wages in gold mining were ratcheted down during the 1890s and 1900s by the creation of a private monopsony as well as by the state policies mentioned above, and did not regain their 1911 level until 1972 (Lipton 1986: 410). Charles Feinstein has illustrated quantitatively that without such wage repression the South African gold mining industry could have been only a small fraction of its actual size by the early 1930s (Feinstein 2005: 109–12).

Meanwhile, the peasant colonies were the setting for the 'cash crop revolution': a widespread expansion of export agriculture by African producers during the early colonial period (Austin 2014a). But their participation was varied in nature and degree. The growth was dramatic in a handful of colonies, where African traders and farmers responded as risk-taking entrepreneurs to the opportunities presented by the continued expansion of markets in the West for produce that could be grown efficiently in Africa. Where farmers could produce for export without imperilling their own food security, they did so with alacrity, as with cocoa beans in Ghana and Nigeria, and peanuts from northern Nigeria. Elsewhere, they resisted, until reassured by improved provision of transport or storage, as in western Uganda (Tosh 1978). The demand for labour created by this expansion attracted seasonal migrants into the cash-crop zones from areas that lacked the soils and/or access to transport required for profitable production. Thus male migrant labour flowed from Rwanda into Ugandan cotton production, from Mali into Senegalese peanut cultivation, and from the savannah of northern Ghana and what is now Burkina Faso, into cocoa growing in the forest zone of southern Ghana (see Map 10.2). In the more prosperous 'peasant' colonies, Nigeria and Ghana – whose main actors are more accurately described as indigenous small-scale capitalists rather than peasants (Hill 1997[1963]) – Africans were not only pioneers of the adoption of exotic crops, notably cocoa beans, but also of lorry ownership (Hopkins 1978, Drummond-Thompson 1993).

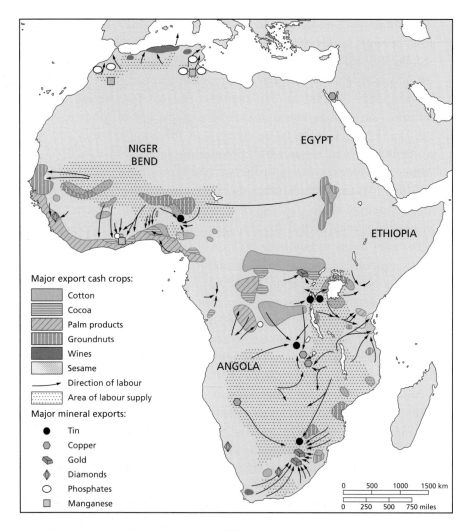

Map 10.2 Export specialization in Africa, *c.* 1928
Source: see map 10.1.

Colonial rule was intended to be cheap: the local administrations faced a combination of constraints on their fiscal capacity and therefore on their freedom of manoeuvre. They encountered broadly the same obstacles to political centralization as their African predecessors had faced, especially the difficulty of extracting revenue from domestic agriculture (Frankema and van Waijenburg 2014). In addition, they had problems arising from the nature of the colonial enterprise: the imperial requirement that colonial administrations balance their budgets, and the need to avoid provoking resistance and thereby the expense of suppressing it (Gardner 2012). From these constraints followed the characteristic colonial reliance (more so in the British case, less so in the French) on 'indirect rule', i.e., rule through the chiefs or

Table 10.2 Overseas investment in Sub-Saharan Africa, 1870–1936 (nominal British pounds)

	Aggregate	Per head of population
Union of South Africa	554,681	55.8
Southern and northern Rhodesia (Zimbabwe and Zambia)	102,403	38.4
Angola and Mozambique (Portuguese)	66,732	9.8
Belgian Africa (Congo and Rwanda-Burundi)	143,337	13.0
French colonies	70,310	3.3
British East Africa (Kenya, Uganda, Tanganyika, Malawi)	110,189	8.1
British West Africa (Nigeria, Ghana, Gambia, Sierra Leone)	116,730	4.8
All European-ruled Sub-Saharan Africa (including Sudan, Zanzibar, but excluding Portuguese Guinea)	1,221,686	<12.7

Source: Frankel 1938: 158–9, 169–70.

emirs. This system was intended to harness the legitimacy of indigenous authorities to colonial ends, especially in order to limit the need to employ expensive European personnel. In *c.* 1939 the supposedly 43 million (actually many more) inhabitants of British tropical Africa were presided over, at least nominally, by a combined total of 2,339 white administrators, judges, police and soldiers: over 18,000:1 (Kirk-Greene 1980). Foreign investment in the African colonies, private as well as public, was similarly minimal: only mines attracted large flows of capital. A study published in 1938, by S. H. Frankel, remains the only attempt at a comprehensive count. According to his figures, 42.8 per cent of all overseas investment in European-ruled Africa south of the Sahara went to South Africa. This represented £55.8 per head in South Africa, but only £4.8 per head in the 'peasant' colonies of British West Africa, and only £3.3 per head for the French colonies (Table 10.2).

Settler administrations employed indirect rule, but were less constrained fiscally than the administrations of other colonies, especially where they became self-governing. South Africa became independent (as a dominion within the British empire) in 1910, as a white-minority regime. Southern Rhodesia became self-governing internally, with the same type of regime, in 1923. Both settler governments, especially South Africa, had the advantage of access to royalties from mines that were unusually lucrative by colonial African standards.

The distinction between types of colony had important effects on the medium and long-term economic outcomes, for African welfare and structural change. European colonization did not in itself alter the economic incentives to holders of power to use coercion in labour recruitment. Hence, besides using forced labour

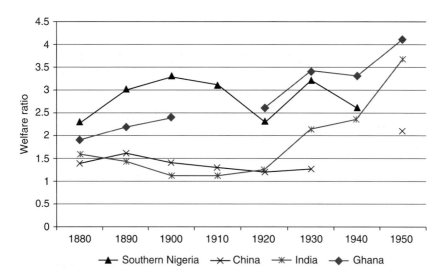

Figure 10.1 Average real wages in cities of southern Nigeria, Ghana, China and India, 1880–1950
Source: based on Frankema and van Waijenburg (2012); growth rates of China/India from www.clio-infra.eu.

themselves to varying degrees, many colonial administrations took years or even decades to implement their international commitments to abolish slavery. In the peasant colonies, where most of the slaves were located, it was the growth of export agriculture that allowed the formal abolition of slavery to become an economic and social reality, by providing opportunities for former slaves as hired labourers or as small independent peasants (Austin 2009). The growth of export agriculture enabled the African real wages to rise earlier, higher and more resiliently in the more prosperous peasant colonies than in the settler colonies. Until the Second World War at least, real wages in the cities of British West Africa were equal or higher than in those of South and East Asia (Frankema and van Waijenburg 2012; see Figure 10.1). Crucially, the retention of rights to land going further than the minimum subsistence plots onto which Africans were mostly crowded in settler colonies, gave the inhabitants of peasant colonies greater bargaining power (Austin 2005), which was reflected in higher incomes and physical welfare (Bowden *et al.* 2008). This also had implications for human capital formation in African countries, because parental investment also depended on wage expectations: in Africa in general and West Africa in particular, numeracy was also higher than in South Asia (Figure 10.2).

We have noted that African opportunities for entrepreneurship in the broader economy were also greater in peasant economies. This was least so, however, where a significant proportion of African labour was commandeered by the state, as in the French system of *corvée*, abolished only in 1946. Again, even under the relatively liberal regimes of British West Africa, Africans faced a

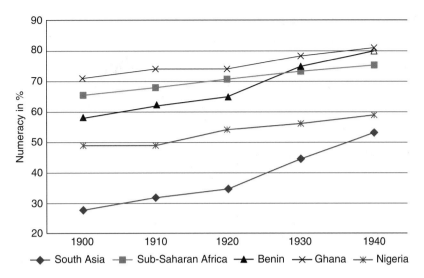

Figure 10.2 Numeracy in South Asia and Sub-Saharan Africa (total), and in selected west African countries
Source: calculated from Crayen and Baten (2010); www.clio-infra.eu.

fundamental asymmetry in the structure of competition. Whereas the markets peopled by Africans were highly competitive, those dominated by Europeans had a very strong tendency for competition to be restricted by collusion, including formal cartels (Hopkins 1978, Olukoju 2001–02, Austin and Uche 2007). African traders, farmers and pioneer bankers struggled against this with varying degrees of success (Hopkins 1966, Nwabughuogu 1982). Still, the economic space for African initiative was even less where they lacked a foundation in commercial agriculture, as was very largely the case in the settler colonies.

The story was different with manufacturing. In 1960, the two African countries with the largest shares of manufacturing in output were South Africa, at about 20 per cent (Lipton 1986: 402), followed by another settler economy, Southern Rhodesia, and then the Belgian Congo, where industry was concentrated in the copper-mining province of Katanga. According to Peter Kilby's data (see Table 10.3), in no other country in the sub-continent had manufacturing reached 10 per cent of GDP. In various ways, the precocious development of manufacturing in South Africa, southern Rhodesia and the Belgian Congo owed much to their mining sectors. But political conditions were critical too: as an unexpected result of a free trade treaty during the Scramble for Africa, manufacturers in the Congo benefited from access to neighbouring colonial markets. Above all, in South Africa and Southern Rhodesia, settler-dominated parliaments gave governments the mandate to pursue import-substitution industrialization, from 1924 and 1933 respectively. By contrast, in the largest 'peasant' economy, Nigeria, and in the – also 'peasant' – colonies with the

Table 10.3 Output and manufacturing in selected African countries in 1960 (US 1964 dollars)

	Population (millions)	GDP ($ m)	Income per head ($)	Manufacturing output ($ m)	Manufacturing/ GDP (%)
Southern Rhodesia	3.6	751	206	120.2	16.0
Belgian Congo	14.1	910	58	127.4	14.0
Senegal	3.1	678	218	64.4	9.5
Kenya	8.1	641	79	60.9	9.5
Uganda	6.7	583	87	37.9	6.5
Ghana	6.8	1,503	222	94.7	6.3
Cameroun	4.7	511	109	30.6	6.0
Ethiopia	20.7	1,021	49	61.3	6.0
Northern Rhodesia	3.2	511	155	28.1	5.5
Ivory Coast	3.2	584	181	31.0	5.3
Sudan	11.8	909	77	43.6	4.8
Nigeria	40.0	3,500	88	157.5	4.5
Angola	4.8	726	151	31.2	4.3
Tanganyika	9.6	671	67	20.1	3.0

Key: Southern Rhodesia is now Zimbabwe, Belgian Congo is now DR Congo, Northern Rhodesia is now Zambia, Tanganyika is the mainland of what is now Tanzania and Sudan includes what is now the independent republic of South Sudan.
Note: the very approximate nature of some of these figures must be underlined. All the population totals are questionable, for example, especially that of Ethiopia, for which no census had yet been taken. The size of food crop production is estimated in all cases, partly by assumption based on the estimated size of population.
Source: Kilby 1975: 472.

highest income per head in colonial Sub-Saharan Africa, Ghana and Senegal, even the modest levels of manufacturing recorded in 1960 reflected very late expansions, as European firms sought to preserve their markets by establishing factories before independence arrived (Kilby 1975).

We can roughly distinguish three overlapping sub-periods within the relatively short period of colonial rule. The first saw the conquests and the establishment of colonial administrations, overlapping with a time of relatively high prices for primary commodities and general expansion of world trade, which ended with the First World War. The second was the 'heyday' of colonial rule, when it was seen as fundamentally stable, but troubled by the disruptions to the world economy of the Depression and the Second World War. The third was 'late colonialism' and decolonization: characterized by greater government taxation and regulation of produce markets (the introduction of export marketing boards, giving the state a monopoly of exporting which became a key source of taxation), somewhat greater willingness of imperial governments to spend in the colonies, and the emergence of explicit struggles for independence rather than simply reform. This period-ization works best for the 'peasant' colonies, the largest category, and least well for the settler colonies, where the white populations sought to avert majority rule, and for the colonies of Portugal, which fought wars against independence movements from 1961 until the revolution in Portugal itself in 1974.

In the long run of African economic history, arguably the two most positive developments of the colonial period were the introduction of mechanized trans-port, partly by African initiative in the case of lorries in West Africa, which was particularly important in a region over much of which disease had previously prevented the use of animals in haulage on the farm and in transport; and the beginning of the continuous increase in population, a trend which began at different times in different colonies, but in most places probably within 10–15 years after the global influenza pandemic of 1918 (Manning 2010, Frankema and Jerven 2014).

Independence and African economies, 1960–present

The economic policies and performances of individual African countries have varied and changed across the half-century and more that has now elapsed since independence in most of Africa. Subject to that crucial qualification, two general-izations can be made: that it is possible to distinguish two sub-periods of policy, with the 1980s as the watershed; and that we can identify three sub-periods of economic performance, with 1973–75 and c. 1995 as the turning points.

On policy, the 1960s and 1970s saw an intensification of the trend, in place since 1939, towards greater state intervention in African economies. Conversely, 'Structural Adjustment', in the 1980s, was a crucial transition: from administrative to market mechanisms of resource allocation. The liberal economic regimes established in that decade essentially continue to the time of writing.

In the earlier period a handful of countries adopted far-reaching socialist policies, whether 'African' (Tanzania) or 'scientific' (Guinea, Benin and from 1975 the newly independent former Portuguese colonies, including Angola and Mozambique). But the main difference was between the franc zone countries and the rest. The former comprise most of the former French colonies: deciding against monetary independence, and therefore retaining a freely convertible currency, state intervention in the franc zone mostly stopped short of quotas on imports and internal price controls. Before Structural Adjustment, on average they had lower inflation and higher economic growth than most of their Anglophone counterparts (plus Zaire-Congo), who adopted their own currencies. Except for Kenya, which in most years maintained a fairly high degree of convertibility, in tropical Africa most non-franc currencies became highly over-valued and not freely convertible. This in turn generated a proliferation of other controls over volume and price. In some cases this led to episodes of economic contraction rather than mere stagnation, for example, in Congo (Zaire), Ghana, Guinea, Tanzania and Zambia. Because the proliferating controls created plentiful economic rents, such policies tailored easily with kleptocracy in the more extreme cases, as in Ghana in much of the 1970s, and most notoriously, under Mobutu Sese Seko in Zaire (now DR Congo), for decades before his overthrow in 1997.

In the era of economic liberalism, the franc zone countries stood out in the opposite direction: the value of their currencies was fixed, albeit to a European currency that was itself floating: the French franc and then the euro. In 1994 the African franc was devalued by 100 per cent against the French franc, to try to assist African exports. On the whole, the franc zone countries (now numbering fourteen, totalling about 150 million people, including Guinea Bissau and Equatorial Guinea, respectively former Portuguese and Spanish colonies) have not outperformed the rest since Structural Adjustment in the 1980s.

The years *c.* 1960–73/75 saw economic growth outpacing population growth in most countries, but on average only by about 1 percentage point. In the second sub-period, 1973/75–*c.* 1995, the aggregate story was slow or negative growth: the early-colonial (and post-Korean War) boom was ended for most countries by the Organization of the Petroleum Exporting Countries (OPEC) oil shock of 1973, though often with a slight lag; whereas a handful of major oil exporters (Nigeria, Angola, Gabon) jumped into rapid growth and forms of 'Dutch disease' (the oil-fuelled appreciation of the currency diverted resources away from alternative exports). The adoption of Structural Adjustment produced dramatic economic improvements in Uganda and Ghana, but in aggregate, the decade or so that followed the policy transition was one of stagnant or even negative growth (Figure 10.3 and 10.4). Finally, the years from 1995 to the time of writing have seen aggregate growth at 4–5 per cent a year, including at least 2 per cent a year per capita.

A striking feature of post-colonial economic history is that, except for Botswana (the single year 2010 apart), no country in Sub-Saharan Africa has grown well throughout the whole period to date (Jerven 2014: 75–102). Many have had a major period of fairly fast growth, sustained for a decade or more, and a similarly extended period of stagnation or actual decline (Berthélemy and Söderling 2001). A classic comparison is Ghana and Ivory Coast, two neighbours with very similar environmental and demographic characteristics,

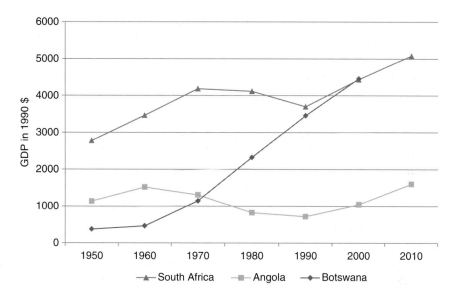

Figure 10.3 GDP per capita in Angola, Botswana and South Africa, 1950–2010s
Source: www.clio-infra.eu.
Notes: Y-Axis in Geary-Khamis dollars (1990). The years refer to the beginning of each decade.

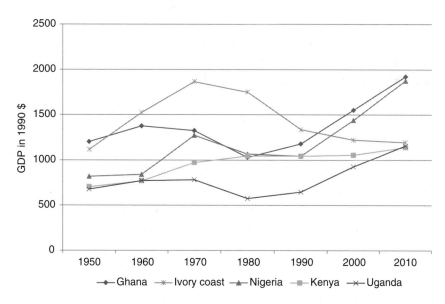

Figure 10.4 GDP per capita in Ghana, Ivory Coast, Kenya, Nigeria and Uganda, 1950–2010s
Source: www.clio-infra.eu.
Note: Y-Axis in Geary-Khamis dollars (1990).

both of whom have boomed and slumped, but at opposite times (Figure 10.4; Eberhardt and Teal 2010). Pessimists might suggest that the alternation of boom and bust conceals a very low 'natural' rate of economic growth, but the ups and downs have both lasted too long for that to be plausible. A more likely explanation is a combination of policy 'mistakes' (often reflecting both vested interests and, albeit in exaggerated form, the conventional developmental wisdom of the time concerned) and political instability, the latter tending to be partly the result of the former, but to then be reinforced by it.

The first decade or so of economic liberalization has been described as 'lost' in terms of economic growth and declining expenditure on health and education. As signalled above, two of the most spectacular under-performers of the era of state-led development policy, Ghana and Uganda, recovered rapidly (Figure 10.4); but the general picture was dismal. The major issue is how far this was the result of the new policy paradigm, and how far it was attributable to the fact that the introduction of Structural Adjustment policies roughly coincided with a severe downturn in world commodity prices. Proponents of economic liberalization argue that the post-1995 boom would not have been nearly as large, nor sustained through the Western financial crisis that began in 2008, were it not for Structural Adjustment in the 1980s (Ndulu *et al.* 2008).

Politically, South Africa rejoined the continent just in time for the post-1995 boom. The economic significance of the fall of the apartheid regime needs to be seen in context of the reinforcement to the system of segregation that followed the National Party's introduction of formal 'apartheid' ('separate development') after its victory in the 1948 election (in which blacks and most other non-whites did not have the vote). The party's narrow victory represented a path not taken: the ousted United Party government had started to advocate a loosening of the existing segregationist rules in response to evidence that the migrant labour system within South Africa was breaking down, with soil erosion in the over-crowded African 'reserves', the growth of illegal African 'townships' around the white cities and unrest among the black population in both rural and urban areas (Wolpe 1974). Until the late 1960s, or even the beginning of the 1970s, the National Party's reassertion of militant white supremacism seemed to pay off economically, with rapid growth and an influx of foreign investment (Figure 10.3). But even before the Uitenhage massacre of 1985 triggered the township revolt that cost the government its control of black urban areas, undermining foreign confidence in the regime and specifically in the currency, the economy had fallen into stagnation and then decline. GDP per head fell at an average of 0.6 per cent a year over the period 1973–94 (Feinstein 2005: 145–7). Already from 1967, well before the international oil price shock of 1973, the marginal efficiency of investment had been falling, gradually then rapidly. In other words, the amount of additional units of investment required to generate one more unit of output rose (Lewis 1990: 132–3). While short-term events contributed to this, the most plausible interpretation of the underlying upward trend was that the economy needed more skilled labour if it was to continue growing, but was being held back by the 'apartheid premium': the fact that highly discriminatory education provision, as well as de jure and de facto racial discrimination, made skilled labour in South Africa very expensive by international standards (Lipton 1986, Nattrass 1991, Feinstein 2005). The economic logic of the political events that were to come was illustrated by the fact that, in practice, blacks began to move into semi-skilled positions vacated by the increasingly educated white workforce (Mariotti 2012). This context does much to explain the encouragement given by big business in South Africa for the negotiation of a transition to black majority rule, which culminated in the first universal suffrage election in 1994, won by the African National Congress under Nelson Mandela.

At the time of writing, economic growth has never been as widespread across Sub-Saharan Africa as it has been during the last eighteen years, if the (distinctly problematic) national income statistics are to be believed (Jerven 2013). In the perspective of African economic history, the question is whether this boom will lead to greater structural change than its predecessors. Like the pre-1914 and post-1950 booms, it has been led by high overseas demand for African primary products. This time agricultural exports have been less important than in the past, compared to mineral exports (including energy), which are non-renewable and, because of their huge economies of scale, more conducive to inequality. On the other hand, it is arguable that Africa is now better placed to receive the 'flying geese' of manufacturing investment, thanks to a relatively cheaper and better educated labour force than it had at the time of independence (Sender 1999).

South Africa aside, why have African economies not grown faster since independence? While externalist arguments focus alternately on protectionism and excessive competition in world markets, the most influential analysts have concentrated on domestic political economy, perhaps in interaction with foreign elites (as with Bayart 2000). In the early 1980s, Bates argued that post-colonial governments represented distributional coalitions. In most cases, the coalition was primarily urban: hence governments were content to tax export agriculture, even when the result was to so discourage farmers from reinvesting that the economy as a whole shrank. Ivory Coast and Kenya, Bates suggested, were exceptions that proved the rule: their rulers were themselves large cash-crop producers, and they desisted from imposing penal rates of taxation of export agriculture, with the result that their economies were doing well (Bates 1981). However, the proposition that most African governments were over-taxing exporters but had no reason to change their behaviour (a 'stable high rent-seeking equilibrium') was surely falsified by the fact that, within a few years, almost all of them had adopted Structural Adjustment. Indeed, by its nature, the general switch from administrative to market means of resource allocation entailed in the World Bank-sponsored Structural Adjustment programmes must have reduced drastically the scale of economic rents (which may be defined, in effect, as surpluses above what the recipients would receive in a competitive market). Thus it seems odd that in the late 1990s leading economists reiterated the claim that rent-seeking was Africa's main economic constraint – albeit now attributing it to 'ethnic fragmentation' rather than urban bias, a much-criticized move (Easterly and Levine 1997; compare the comments of Hopkins 2009). Economic rents remain part of economies in Africa, as elsewhere, being generated in recent years by such redistributions as privatizations and, in South Africa, the 'Black Economic Empowerment' programme. The view that Structural Adjustments were 'captured' by the existing elites (Chabal and Daloz 1999) fits some cases, but does not do justice to the much intensified competition in other economies. But again, not all economic rents are negative for economic growth (Austin 2008b: 1017–19).

It can be argued that the most fundamental change of the whole post-independence period to date was demographic: the growth of population accelerated after 1945. There were signs in some countries that the final phase of the 'demographic transition' had begun by the 1980s, with the fall in mortality being followed, after a gap of decades, by a slight downturn in birth rates, especially among educated women. The tragedy of HIV-AIDS, which became manifest in the 1990s, especially in southern and parts of eastern Africa, particularly affected able-bodied people, and thus reduced the growth of the labour force. Land surpluses persisted in some areas, especially in DR Congo and South Sudan. Even so, the late twentieth century and the start of the twenty-first century saw, on the whole, further steps in the historic transition of Sub-Saharan Africa from relative abundance to relative scarcity of cultivable land (for the extreme case of Rwanda, see André and Platteau 1998).

In agriculture, the result was to create new pressures towards intensification, i.e., raising the ratio of labour and/or capital applied per area of cultivated land. The question is what sort of intensification is predominating. Is it the negative sort, where more hours of labour increase output, at least in the short run, but with lower overall productivity, for example when the often major reductions in fallow periods permanently depleted the soil fertility? Or is it the positive kind, where increased pressure on land stimulates innovation? That debate continues, with international programme of research into higher-yielding varieties of seed aiming to resolve the question positively. The queries, however, remain the environment and the extent to which African farmers can shape the pattern of innovation (Mutsaers and Kleene 2012). So far, higher-yielding varieties have required more water and more petroleum-based inputs (chemical fertilisers and insecticides), neither of which are cheap for most African farmers (Richards 2010).

Review (1): Africa, poor and static?

Let us return to the traditional description of Sub-Saharan Africa, as poor and economically static. According to a classic study, in 1800 in what is now mainland Tanzania, 'men measured out their lives in famines' (Iliffe 1979: 13). Land abundance was no guarantee of subsistence where population was scattered, soils infertile and animal assistance lacking in arable production. But very widespread access to land certainly helped, in Sub-Saharan Africa generally (Iliffe 1987). In West Africa, despite the Atlantic slave trade, evidence on heights for the first half of the nineteenth century suggests that people there were, on average, as tall as those in southern Europe (Figure 10.5, Austin *et al.* 2012).

For the colonial period as a whole Africans grew taller. In certain countries this applied even from the early part of the period, according to detailed studies both in the relatively prosperous 'peasant' (or small African capitalist) economy of Ghana, and more surprisingly, also in the settler colony of Kenya (Figure 10.6, Moradi 2009, Moradi *et al.* 2013). A larger sample of countries, however, indicates for males that average heights in Africa slightly declined during the early years of colonial rule in most of Africa (being 0.57 cm less in 1930 than in 1900), before rising quite strongly in the late colonial era: 2.43 cm more in 1960 than 1930 (Baten and Blum 2012; see also Interlinking Chapter I8 by Baten and Inwood in this volume on the average decline from precolonial times and the substantial increase during late colonialism). Tanzania in Figure 10.5 is an example of this pattern. The

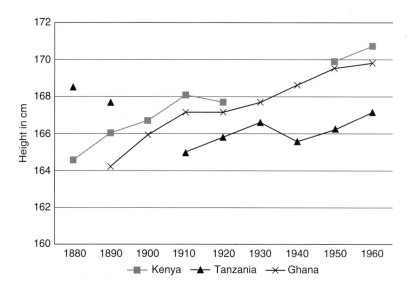

Figure 10.5 Height trends in Ghana, Kenya and Tanzania, 1880–1960s (male)
Source: www.clio-infra.eu, calculated on the basis of Moradi (2009), Moradi *et al.* (2013) and other sources.

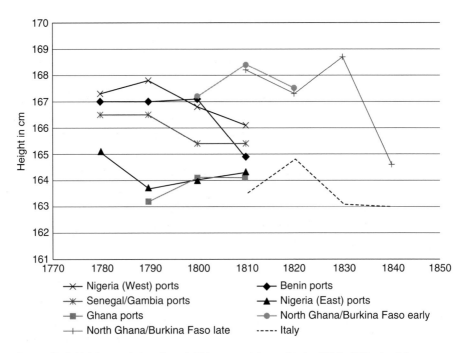

Figure 10.6 Height trends in selected African countries and Italy, 1780–1840s (male)
Source: modified from Austin, Baten and van Leeuwen (2012).

reported decline in heights for the early colonial period in mainland Tanzania is consistent with strong evidence that the late nineteenth and early twentieth century saw a devastating combination of animal and human epidemics, as an unintended side-effect of the local German invasion, and of the Italian invasion of Somalia (Koponen 1996). The latter brought Indian cattle to Africa, introducing the rinderpest virus. This devastated herds in eastern and southern Africa in the 1890s, damaging or destroying livelihoods and in some cases leading to famines. Turning to infant mortality, differences between the political forms of European domination made for contrasts between countries that would not be predicted on economic potential alone. Given the much greater mineral wealth and investment in South Africa, compared to anywhere in tropical Africa, it is remarkable that the infant mortality rate among the black population actually rose, from 254 in 1910–20 to 302 in 1920–30. In Ghana, the rate moved in the opposite direction, from 295 to 110 (Bowden *et al.* 2008: 161).

In the 1980s and early 1990s it was commonly suggested that, with the notable exception of Botswana, real incomes per capita in Sub-Saharan Africa were generally not significantly (if at all) higher than at the time of independence. Yet there had certainly been major advances since independence in education and health, including of women (Sender 1999). Between *c.* 1995 and the time of writing, despite violent conflicts in several countries, the overall economic trends have been positive: in incomes, education and public health.

On the productivity of labour – as the scarce factor in precolonial times, and often later too – we have already noted that there were major environmental constraints on productivity in agriculture. This applied also to the supply of raw material for a key precolonial industry, cotton textiles, because planting more cotton meant less time for planting food crops (Tosh 1980). The antiquity and longevity of the external slave trades seems to imply that the productivity of unskilled African labour, in commercial terms, was higher outside than inside Africa during that era (Austin 2008b: 1006; for context and perspective, Austin 2008a). The external trades did not end because that had ceased to be the case, but rather because they were suppressed. Again, precolonial technologies tended to be relatively simpler and less productive than those used in Eurasia (Austen and Headrick 1983). But there were qualifications: the iron smelting technique used in western Africa produced higher-quality metal than the imported competition, and declined because of exhausting the supplies of fuel (charcoal) rather than because of competitive inferiority (Goucher 1981). The environmental obstacles to agricultural intensification in African conditions remained costly, helping to account for the failure of European plantations in Ghana and colonial mechanization in Tanzania (Austin 1996, Hogendorn and Scott 1981). But in the nineteenth and early twentieth centuries Africans, especially in West Africa and Uganda, took advantage of the emergence or expansion of overseas markets (following the Industrial Revolution) for various crops that could be grown profitably in African conditions, to turn the availability of land into a competitive advantage, raising their own labour productivity in the process (Austin 2014b).

Indeed, despite the difficulties of quantifying income per head in precolonial and even colonial (and postcolonial) Africa, it is clear that there were episodes of economic growth in particular regions, sustained over decades: for example in much of West Africa in the period of 'legitimate commerce', between the beginning of the decline of the Atlantic slave trade and the onset of the European partition of Africa; and again in the more prosperous 'peasant' colonies and – accompanied by coercively-squeezed African wages – in South Africa (Austin 2008a, Jerven 2010, 2012, Feinstein 2005). Since independence, the aggregate picture was of slow growth until 1973–75; then a period of stagnation and even decline; followed by faster and more widespread growth since 1995, sustained by the Chinese-led commodity boom.

Overall, the general view of Sub-Saharan Africa as characterized by low average real incomes is broadly upheld during the long period reviewed in this chapter, but with significant qualifications. There were episodes of economic growth, especially at national and regional level. Very importantly, economic development is more than economic growth. Africans have worked for centuries towards improving their food security and incomes in agriculture, above all by the selective adoption of exotic crops and crop varieties, and by further trial and error experimentation with those already adopted. In this sense, attempts to achieve a 'green revolution' in food crop production in Africa fit into an old, indeed ancient pattern. Africans have also worked to improve the productivity of labour during the dry season, taking opportunities to extend the agricultural year where possible, and/or to develop off-farm sources of income (Austin 2008a).

Review (2): economic development in Africa – dynamics and constraints

Returning to the interpretations introduced at the beginning, it is clear that interactions between internal and external elements, and between resources and institutions, have been critical in determining the paths and patterns of development in African economies. This is exemplified by the external slave trades. The internal constraints on labour productivity in agriculture and manufacturing in Africa made it possible for the export of captive labour to be profitable for the parties to the sale; but without the external market, there would have been no slave exports.

While the resource endowment of the time helps explain why the external slave trades were rewarding for captors and buyers, they damaged the wider economies of the region, notably by the violence they entailed and encouraged, and by their reinforcement of labour scarcity. Thus an economic explanation for the export of captives from Africa, while necessary, is insufficient. A political condition was also required: the willingness of political authorities, small or large, to participate. Joseph Inikori has argued persuasively that this was facilitated by political fragmentation: the absence of huge empires capable of enforcing, on a wide scale, the interest of states in avoiding the large-scale sale of their own subjects (Inikori 2003).

The old claims that Africans were unresponsive to market opportunities are refuted by numerous examples, including the 'cash-crop revolution' in the peasant colonies, and studies of more recent African entrepreneurship (Forrest 1994). Indigenous institutions, such as systems of group-purchase of land used by the pioneers of the Ghanaian cocoa industry (Hill 1997[1963]), illustrate that in some cases African institutions were well suited for exploiting the opportunities presented by the growth of overseas markets for crops that could be grown on African soil.

Crucially, an institution which facilitates economic growth in one period may hinder it in another, when resource ratios have changed. The colonial government of Ghana repeatedly debated whether to introduce compulsory registration of individual titles of ownership. It never did so, not least because the existing indigenous system of land tenure had proved to provide the security of tenure needed by farmers wanting to plant tree crops, a form of investment that took several years to begin to produce a return. Though the soil itself belonged to the community, presided over by a chief, crops planted on it belonged to the person who planted them. This guarantee was evidently sufficient to induce farmers to plant on such a scale as to raise Ghana's cocoa exports from zero to the largest in the world in twenty years (*c.* 1891–1911), and then proceed to multiply it five times from that level in the next twelve years (Hill 1997[1963], Austin 2005). But by the beginning of the twenty-first century, the situation in the same region of Ghana had changed. With land now very scarce, because of population growth and expanding markets for agricultural produce internally as well as externally, the elders of the land-owning communities tended to assert their own property rights, but to limit and dispute those of 'stranger-farmers', even when the latter had been there for decades. The result was that, in total contrast to the period when cocoa farming began, strangers were now investing less in their farms (now commercial food farms) than the locals, not daring to leave their land fallow for long in case someone challenged their ownership (Goldstein and Udry 2008).

Another example of an institution that favoured economic growth (though in this case, at high human cost) in one period that became a hindrance to it later, is labour repression under the system of segregation and apartheid in South Africa. The cheap labour produced by this system made possible the early success of the South African mining industry, facilitating the import-substitution industrialization on which the government embarked in 1924. But we have seen that, by the 1970s, apartheid had become a brake on corporate profits and macroeconomic growth, hindering the transition to higher total factor productivity, because the latter required the employment of much more skilled labour – which the apartheid system made relatively expensive. Both the changing significance of indigenous land tenure systems in relation to agricultural investment, and the declining utility of labour coercion as a tool of profit and growth, illustrate the necessity of considering the changing historical contexts when we search for the long-term determinants of economic development. This sense of changing contexts is, arguably, insufficiently present even in the sophisticated reinvention (as in Platteau 2009) of the traditional argument that indigenous institutions were a brake on development. It is even more lacking in attempts to find causal relationships for changes over very long periods by a static comparison of two far-separated periods, without tracing the intervening changes (Austin 2008b).

A 'static geography' approach to the analysis of African economies has no attraction for economic historians, who are highly aware that resources change, especially because of human responses to the resource ratios that happen to prevail at any given time. In a dynamic context, it is useful to think of 'paths' of development (Austin and Sugihara 2013). In this case, the characteristic precolonial choices of technique and institution are to a large extent explicable as responses to a situation where land was relatively abundant but labour scarce. One example is land-extensive agriculture: maximizing returns to labour and conserving and restoring soil fertility by extended land rotation, growing more than one crop in the same field, and leaving occasional trees, and more than occasional roots, in place (Austin 2008a).

Another is social applause for high fertility. When mortality rates fell in the early and mid-twentieth century, the preference for large families helped to produce a population 'explosion' (Iliffe 1989). Conversely, an institutional approach needs to be tempered by realism about resources. If the main obstacle to foreign investment in Africa was institutional, there would surely have been a very high level of such investment during the colonial period, when the risk of expropriation was generally negligible. Rather, the main problem was a lack of opportunities for embodying capital in forms that would be profitable in African environments (Austin 2008a).

As already hinted, this grim situation may be changing. The population of Sub-Saharan Africa increased at least six times during the twentieth century. African workforces are not only much better educated than at the time of Independence, in global terms African labour is also cheaper than before. This strengthens the logic for reembarking on industrialization, using labour-intensive methods where possible (Austin 2013). At the time of writing, however, African real wages are only now being overtaken by Chinese ones, and most African governments have a long way to go before they can promote the process as effectively as the 'developmental state' model requires (compare Mkandawire 2001). This chapter is not the place to examine the political dimension in detail, but it can well be argued that the most damaging colonial legacy for economic development was the impetus that 'indirect rule' gave to the strengthening (in some cases, creation) of ethnicity as a mode of mobilizing support in struggles over limited resources (Mamdani 1996, qualified by Spear 2003). This is as distinct from the creation of a sense of national solidarity, which makes it easier to ask citizens to accept sacrifices, as is necessary, for example, when states seek to accelerate, by policy interventions, the transition from a comparative advantage in primary products to one in manufacturing.

Finally, and in contrast to the Eurocentric interpretations of dependency theory and of some rational-choice writings, it is necessary to underline the importance of African agency, i.e., African influence over African history. Even under colonial rule, Africans' decisions were decisive in the achievement of the 'cash crop revolution' in the more prosperous 'peasant' economies, and in the failure of the attempt to drive Africans out of the produce market in settler economies – except, very largely, in South Africa itself. In the post-independence era, specifically in the 1980s, the decision of most African governments to agree Structural Adjustment programmes with the IMF and World Bank, in exchange for big loans, was, in case of the economies in greatest difficulty, often in large part the result of a fiscal crisis resulting from producers and consumers bypassing official markets, and thereby not paying taxes. And, literally at grass-roots level, African farmers continue to produce new varieties of seed through trial and error on their own farms (Richards 2010).

Conclusion

The study of Africa's economic past has been overhung by the question of abiding poverty: why has economic growth south of the Sahara not been faster? This chapter has emphasized both the validity of the question, and the need to qualify it by recognition that there have been both episodes of economic growth (usually concentrated in particular regions) and trends towards economic development in the broad sense, including greater food security. The major theoretical and historiographical approaches to African economic history variously emphasize external and internal influences on economic growth, and the respective importance of institutional and resource conditions. Such economic development as has occurred over the centuries, and the constraints upon it, are indeed the result of the interaction of both pairs of opportunities and constraints. Despite the importance of foreign slave buyers, colonial administrations and multi-lateral financial institutions, African economic history has always been greatly – often decisively – influenced by the decisions of Africans themselves, especially in responding to their own environments. Finally, as is also hinted above, there is much research to be done in African economic history, a field in which there is probably more new work being done today than ever before (Austin and Broadberry 2014).

Further reading

Austin, G. (2008a), 'Resources, Techniques and Strategies South of the Sahara: Revising the Factor Endowments Perspective on African Economic Development, 1500–2000', *Economic History Review* 61 (3), 587–624. A critical review and restatement of one of the major approaches to the explanation of Africa's economic trajectory over the long term.

Bates, R. H. (2005), *Beyond the Miracle of the Market: the Political Economy of Agrarian Development in Kenya*, 2nd edn, Cambridge University Press. An impressive example of the rational-choice political science approach to African economic history and political economy.

Feinstein, C. H. (2005), *An Economic History of South Africa: Conquest, Discrimination and Development*, Cambridge University Press. The best economic history of the country, combining insights from both sides of the long-running 'liberal' versus 'radical' debate about whether racial segregation and apartheid helped or hindered economic expansion, 1652–1994.

Frankema, E. and van Waijenburg, M. V. (2012), 'Structural Impediments to African Growth? New Evidence from Real Wages in British Africa, 1880–1965', *The Journal of Economic History* 72 (04), 895–926 (a partly richer version was published by the Center for Global Economic History, Utrecht University, as

Working Paper 24, 2011). An ingenious and thought-provoking example of a recent wave of studies that are enriching our quantitative sense of the evolution of bargaining power and living standards.

Hopkins, A. G. (1973), *An Economic History of West Africa*, London: Longman, reprinted several times. A classic, full of ideas, beautifully written. While many of the statistics in it have been superseded by subsequent research, this is still the best introduction to thinking about the economic history, not just of West Africa, but of Sub-Saharan Africa generally.

Iliffe, J. (2007), *Africans: the History of a Continent*, 2nd edn, Cambridge University Press. Provides valuable context for economic historians: erudite and incisive, clearly written, if dense in content.

Inikori, J. E. (2007), 'Africa and the Globalization Process: Western Africa, 1450–1850', *Journal of Global History* 2 (1), 63–86. Incisive long-term perspective, focussed on market expansion within West Africa before the height of the Atlantic slave trade.

Mandala, E. (1984), 'Capitalism, Kinship and Gender in the Lower Tchiri (Shire) Valley of Malawi, 1860–1960: an Alternative Theoretical Framework', *African Economic History* 13, 137–69. A densely-written but profound case-study exploring broad themes.

References

Acemoglu, D., Johnson, S. and Robinson, J. A. (2001), 'The Colonial Origins of Comparative Development: an Empirical Investigation', *American Economic Review* 91 (5), 1369–1401.

(2002), 'Reversal of Fortune: Geography and Institutions in the Making of the Modern World Income Distribution', *Quarterly Journal of Economics* 117 (4), 1231–79.

Acemoglu, D. and Robinson, J. A. (2010), 'Why is Africa Poor?', *Economic History of Developing Regions* 25 (1), 21–50.

Alpers, E. A. (2009), *East Africa and the Indian Ocean*, Princeton University Press.

Amin, S. (1976), *Unequal Development: an Essay on the Social Formations of Peripheral Capitalism*, Hassocks, Sussex, UK: Monthly Review Press, French original, 1973.

André, C. and Platteau, J.-P. (1998), 'Land Relations Under Unendurable Stress: Rwanda Caught in the Malthusian Trap', *Journal of Economic Behavior and Organization* 34, 1–47.

Arrighi, G. (1973), 'Labor Supplies in Historical Perspective: a Study of the Proletarianization of the African Peasantry in Rhodesia' (first published in Italian 1969, English 1970), reprinted in G. Arrighi, and J. S. Saul, (eds.), *Essays on the Political Economy of Africa*, New York: Monthly Review Press, 180–234.

Austen, R. A. and Headrick, D. (1983), 'The Role of Technology in the African Past', *African Studies Review* 26, 163–84.

Austin, G. (1996), 'Mode of Production or Mode of Cultivation: Explaining the Failure of European Cocoa Planters in Competition with African Farmers in Colonial Ghana', in W. G.Clarence-Smith (ed.), *Cocoa Pioneer Fronts*, London: Macmillan, 154–75.

(2005), *Labour, Land and Capital in Ghana: from Slavery to Free Labour in Asante, 1807–1956*, University of Rochester Press.

(2008b), 'The "Reversal of Fortune" Thesis and the Compression of History: Perspectives from African and Comparative Economic History', *Journal of International Development* 20 (8), 996–1027.

(2009), 'Cash Crops and Freedom: Export Agriculture and the Decline of Slavery in Colonial West Africa', *International Review of Social History* 54 (1), 1–37.

(2013), 'Labour-intensity and Manufacturing in West Africa, 1450–2010', in G. Austin and K. Sugihara (eds.), *Labour-intensive Industrialization in Global History*, London: Routledge, 201–30.

(2014a), 'Explaining and Evaluating the Cash-crop Revolution in the "Peasant" Colonies of Tropical Africa: Beyond "Vent-for-surplus"', in E. Akyeampong, R. H. Bates, N. Nunn and J. Robinson (eds.), *Africa's Economic Development in Historical Perspective*, Cambridge University Press, 295–320.

(2014b), 'Vent for Surplus or Productivity Breakthrough? The Ghanaian Cocoa Take-off, *c.* 1890–1936', *Economic History Review* 67 (4), 1035–64.

Austin, G., Baten, J. and van Leeuwen, B. (2012), 'The Biological Standard of Living in Early Nineteenth-century West Africa: New Anthropometric Evidence for Northern Ghana and Burkina Faso', *Economic History Review* 65 (4), 1280–1302.

Austin, G. and Broadberry, S. (2014), 'Introduction: The Renaissance of African Economic History', *Economic History Review* 67 (4), 893–906.

Austin, G. and Sugihara, K. (eds.) (2013), *Labour-intensive Industrialization in Global History*, London: Routledge.

Austin, G. and Uche, C. U. (2007), 'Collusion and Competition in Colonial Economies: Banking in British West Africa, 1916–1960', *Business History Review* 81 (Spring), 1–26.

Barth, H. (2011[1857]), *Travels and Discoveries in North and Central Africa*, vol. II, Cambridge University Press.

Baten, J. and Blum, M. (2012), 'Getting Tall but Unequal: New Findings and Background Evidence on Anthropometric Welfare in 156 Countries, 1810–1989', *Economic History of Developing Regions* 27 (Supplement), S66–85.

Bates, R. H. (1981), *Markets and States in Tropical Africa: the Political Basis of Agricultural Policies*, Berkeley, CA: University of California Press.

(1983), *Essays on the Political Economy of Rural Africa*, Cambridge University Press.

(2008), *When Things Fell Apart: State Failure in Late-Century Africa*, Cambridge University Press.

Bayart, J.-F. (2000), 'Africa in the World: a History of Extraversion', *African Affairs* 99 (395), 217–67.

Berthélemy, J.-C. and Söderling, L. (2001), 'The Role of Capital Accumulation, Adjustment and Structural Change for Economic Take-off: Empirical Evidence from African Growth Episodes', *World Development* 29 (2), 323–43.

Bowden, S., Chiripanhura, B. and Mosley, P. (2008), 'Measuring and Explaining Poverty in Six African Countries: a Long-period Approach, *Journal of International Development* 20 (8), 1049–79.

Chabal, P. and Daloz, J.-P. (1999), *Africa Works: Disorder as Political Instrument*, Oxford: James Currey.

Cooper, F. (1977), *Plantation Slavery on the East Coast of Africa*, New Haven: Yale University Press.

Coquery-Vidrovitch, C. (1969), 'Recherches sur un mode de production africain', *Pensée* 144, 3–20. Appeared in English translation in, among other places, M. A. Klein (ed.), *Perspectives on the African Past*, Boston: Little, Brown and Co., 1972.

Crayen, D. and Baten, J. (2010), 'Global Trends in Numeracy 1820–1949 and its Implications for Long-Run Growth', *Explorations in Economic History* 47 (1), 82–99.

Crummey, D. (1980), 'Abyssinian Feudalism', *Past and Present* 89, 115–38.

Delius, P. and Schirmer, S. (2014). 'Order, Openness, and Economic Change in Precolonial Southern Africa: a Perspective from the Bokoni Terraces', *Journal of African History* 55 (1), 37–54.

Dike, K. O. (2011[1956]), *Trade and Politics in the Niger Delta, 1830–1885*, Oxford: Ibadan, Foreword by Gareth Austin.

Drummond-Thompson, P. (1993), 'The Rise of Entrepreneurs in Nigerian Motor Transport: a Study in Indigenous Enterprise', *Journal of Transport History* 14, 46–63.

Easterly, W. and Levine, R. (1997), 'Africa's Growth Tragedy: Policies and Ethnic Divisions', *Quarterly Journal of Economics* 112 (4), 1203–50.

Eberhardt, M. and Teal, F. (2010), 'Ghana and Côte d'Ivoire: Changing Places', *International Development Policy Series* 1, 33–49; or 'Le Ghana et la Côte d'Ivoire: une inversion des roles', *Revue internationale de politique de développement* 1, 37–54.

Eldredge, E. (1993), *A South African Kingdom: The Pursuit of Security in Nineteenth Century Lesotho*, Cambridge University Press.

Eltis, D. *et al.* (2008 plus updates), *Voyages: the Transatlantic Slave Trade Database*, www.slavevoyages.org, last visited 10 October 2014.

Fenske, J. (2012), 'Land Abundance and Economic Institutions: Egba Land and Slavery, 1830–1914', *Economic History Review* 65 (2), 527–55.

    (2013), 'Does Land Abundance Explain African Institutions?', *Economic Journal* 123, 1363–90.

Forrest, T. (1994), *The Advance of African Capital: the Growth of Nigerian Private Enterprise*, Edinburgh University Press.

Fourie, J. (2012), 'An Inquiry into the Nature, Causes and Distribution of Wealth in the Cape Colony, 1652–1795', PhD dissertation, University of Utrecht.

Frankel, S. H. (1938), *Capital Investment in Africa*, Oxford University Press.

Frankema, E. and Jerven, M. (2014), 'Writing History Backwards and Sideways: Towards a Consensus on African Population, 1850–2010', *Economic History Review* 67 (4), 907–31.

Frankema, E. and van Waijenburg, M. (2014), 'Metropolitan Blueprints of Colonial Taxation? Lessons from Fiscal Capacity Building in British and French Africa, *c*. 1880–1940', *Journal of African History* 55 (3), 371–400.

Gardner, L. A. (2012), *Taxing Colonial Africa: the Political Economy of British Imperialism*, Oxford University Press.

Goldstein, M. and Udry, C. (2008), 'The Profits of Power: Land Rights and Agricultural Investment in Ghana', *Journal of Political Economy* 116 (6), 981–1022.

Goody, J. (1976), *Production and Reproduction: a Comparative Study of the Domestic Domain*, Cambridge University Press.

Goucher, C. L. (1981), 'Iron is Iron 'til it Rust: Trade and Ecology in the Decline of West African Iron-smelting', *Journal of African History* 22, 179–89.

Hamilton, C. (ed.) (1995), *The Mfecane Aftermath: Reconstructive Debates in Southern African History*, Johannesburg: Wits University Press and Pietermaritzburg: University of Natal Press.

Harries, P. (1982), 'Kinship, Ideology and the Nature of Pre-colonial Labour Migration: Labour Migration from the Delagoa Bay Hinterland to South Africa, up to 1895', in S. Marks and R. Rathbone (eds.), *Industrialisation and Social Change in South Africa*, Harlow, UK: Longman, 142–66.

Henige, D. (1986), 'Measuring the Unmeasurable; the Atlantic Slave Trade, West African Population and the Pyrrhonian Critic', *Journal of African History* 27, 295–313.

Herbst, J. (2000), *States and Power in Africa: Comparative Lessons in Authority and Control*, Princeton University Press.

Hill, P. (1997[1963]), *The Migrant Cocoa-Farmers of Southern Ghana: a Study in Rural Capitalism*, 2nd edn, Hamburg: LIT, Introduction by G. Austin.

Hogendorn, J. S. and Scott, K. M. (1981), 'Very Large-scale Agricultural Projects: the Lessons of the East African Groundnut Scheme', *African Economic History* 10, 87–115.

Hopkins, A. G. (1966), 'Economic Aspects of Political Movements in Nigeria and the Gold Coast, 1918–39', *Journal of African History* 7 (1), 133–52.

(1978), 'Innovation in a Colonial Context: African Origins of the Nigerian Cocoa-farming Industry, 1880–1920', in C. Dewey and A. G. Hopkins (eds.), *The Imperial Impact*, London: Athlone, 83–96, 341–42.

(2009), 'The New Economic History of Africa', *Journal of African History* 50 (2), 155–77.

Iliffe, J. (1979), *A Modern History of Tanganyika*, Cambridge University Press.

(1987), *The African Poor: a History*, Cambridge University Press.

(1989), 'The Origins of African Population Growth', *Journal of African History*, 30 (1), 165–69.

Inikori, J. E. (2003), 'The Struggle Against the Transatlantic Slave Trade: the Role of the State', in S. A. Diouf (ed.), *Fighting the Slave Trade: West African Strategies*, Athens, OH: Ohio University Press, 170–98.

(2009), 'The Economic Impact of the 1807 British Abolition of the Transatlantic Slave Trade', in T. Falola and M. D. Childs (eds.), *The Changing Worlds of Atlantic Africa: Essays in Honor of Robin Law*, Durham, NC: Carolina Acedemic press), 163–82.

Jerven, M. (2010), 'African Growth Recurring: an Economic History Perspective on African Growth Episodes, 1690–2010', *Economic History of Developing Regions*, 25 (2), 127–54.

(2012), 'An Unlevel Playing Field: National Income Estimates and Reciprocal Comparison in Global Economic History', *Journal of Global History* 7 (1), 107–28.

(2013), *Poor Numbers: How we are Misled by African Development Statistics and What to do About It*, Ithaca, NY: Cornell University Press.

(2014), *Economic Growth and Measurement Reconsidered in Botswana, Kenya, Tanzania, and Zambia, 1965–1995*, Oxford University Press.

Kilby, P. (1975), 'Manufacturing in Colonial Africa', in P. Duignan and L. H. Gann (eds), *Colonialism in Africa, 1870–1960*, Cambridge University Press, 475–520.

Kirk-Greene, A. H. M. (1980), 'The Thin White Line: the Size of the British Colonial Service in Africa', *African Affairs* 79 (314), 25–44.

Koponen, J. (1996), 'Population: a Dependent Variable', in G. Maddox, J. Giblin and I. N. Kimambo (eds.), *Custodians of the Land: Ecology and Culture in the History of Tanzania*, London: James Currey, 19–42.

Law, R. (1992), 'Posthumous Questions for Karl Polanyi: Price Inflation in Pre-colonial Dahomey', *Journal of African History* 33 (3), 387–420.

Lewis, S. R. Jr. (1990), *The Economics of Apartheid* (New York: Council on Foreign Relations Press.

Lipton, M. (1986), *Capitalism and Apartheid: South Africa, 1910–84*, Aldershot: Gower.

Lovejoy, P. E. (1974), 'Interregional Monetary Flows in the Precolonial Trade of Nigeria', *Journal of African History* 15 (4), 563–85.

(2006), *Slavery, Commerce and Production in the Sokoto Caliphate of West Africa*, Trenton, NJ: Africa World Press.

(2012), *Transformations in Slavery: a History of Slavery in Africa*, 3rd edition, Cambridge University Press.

Lovejoy, P. E. and Baier, S. (1975), 'The Desert-side Economy of the Central Sudan', *International Journal of African Historical Studies* 8 (4), 551–81.

Mamdani, M. (1996), *Citizen and Subject: Contemporary Africa and the Legacy of Late Colonialism*, Princeton University Press.

Manning, P. (2010), 'African Population: Projections, 1850–1960', in K. Ittmann, D. Cordell and G. Maddox (eds), *The Demographics of Empire: the Colonial Order and the Creation of Knowledge*, Athens, OH: Ohio University Press, 245–75.

Mariotti, M. (2012), 'Labour Markets during Apartheid in South Africa', *Economic History Review* 65 (3), 1100–22.

McCann, J. C. (2005), *Maize and Grace: Africa's Encounter with a New World Crop 1500–2000*, Cambridge, MA: Harvard University Press.

Miller, J. C. (1988), *Way of Death: Merchant Capitalism and the Angolan Slave Trade 1730–1830*, London: James Currey.

Mkandawire, T. (2001), 'Thinking about Developmental States in Africa', *Cambridge Journal of Economics* 25 (3), 289–313.

Moradi, A. (2009), 'Towards an Objective Account of Nutrition and Health in Colonial Kenya: a Study of Stature in African Army Recruits and Civilians, 1880–1980', *Journal of Economic History* 6 (3), 719–54.

Moradi, A., Austin, G. and Baten, J. (2013), 'Heights and Development in a Cash-crop Colony: Living Standards in Ghana, 1870–1980', African Economic History Working Paper Series, AEHN WP 7 (Lund, Sweden).

Mosley, P. (1983), *The Settler Economies: Studies in the Economic History of Kenya and Southern Rhodesia 1900–1963*, Cambridge University Press.

Mutsaers, H. J. W. and Kleene, P. W. M. (eds.), (2012), *What is the Matter with African Agriculture? Veterans' Visions between Past and Future*, Amsterdam: KIT.

Nattrass, N. (1991), 'Controversies about Capitalism and Apartheid in South Africa: an Economic Perspective', *Journal of Southern African Studies* 17 (4), 654–77.

Ndulu, B. J. *et al.* (eds.) (2008), *The Political Economy of Economic Growth in Africa 1960–2000*, 2 vols., Cambridge University Press.

Nunn, N. (2008), 'The Long-term Effects of Africa's Slave Trade', *Quarterly Journal of Economics* 123 (1), 139–76.

Nwabughuogu, A. I. (1982), 'From Wealthy Entrepreneurs to Petty Traders: the Decline of African Middlemen in Eastern Nigeria, 1900–1950', *Journal of African History* 23, 365–79.

Olukoju, A. (2001–02), 'Getting Too Great a Grip: European Shipping Lines and British West African Lighterage Services in the 1930s', *Afrika Zamani* 9&10, 19–40.

Palmer, R. and Parsons, N. (eds.) (1977), *The Roots of Rural Poverty in Central and Southern Africa*, London: Heinemann.

Platteau, J.-P. (2009), 'Institutional Obstacles to African Economic Development: State, Ethnicity, and Custom', *Journal of Economic Behavior and Organization* 71 (3), 669–89.

Polanyi, K. (1966), *Dahomey and the Slave Trade: an Analysis of an Archaic Economy*, Seattle: University of Washington Press.

Reid, R. J. (2002), *Political Power in Pre-colonial Buganda: Economy, Society and Warfare in the Nineteenth Century*, Oxford: James Currey.

Richards, P. (2010), 'A Green Revolution from Below? Science and Technology for Global Food Security and Poverty Alleviation', retirement address, Wageningen University, 18 November; published online.

Robertson, C. and Klein, M. A. (eds.) (1983), *Women and Slavery in Africa*, Madison: Wisconsin University Press.

Rodney, W. (1969), 'Gold and Slaves on the Gold Coast', *Transactions of the Historical Society of Ghana* 10, 13–28.

(1972) *How Europe Underdeveloped Africa*, London: Bogle L'Ouverture.

Sender, J. (1999), 'Africa's Economic Performance: Limitations of the Current Consensus', *Journal of Economic Perspectives* 13 (3), 89–114.

Sender, J. and Smith, S. (1986), *The Development of Capitalism in Africa*, London: Methuen.

Sherrif, A. (1987), *Slaves, Spices, and Ivory in Zanzibar: Integration of an East African Commercial Empire into the World Economy, 1770–1873*, Athens, OH: Ohio University Press.

Spear, T. (2003), 'Neo-traditionalism and the Limits of Invention in British Colonial Africa', *Journal of African History* 44 (1), 1–27.

Sutton, J. E. G. (1984), 'Irrigation and Soil-conservation in African Agricultural History', *Journal of African History* 25 (1), 25–41.

Thornton, J. (1977), 'Demography and History in the Kingdom of Kongo, 1550–1750', *Journal of African History* 18, 507–30.

Tosh, J. (1978), 'Lango Agriculture During the Early Colonial Period: Land and Labour in a Cash-crop Economy', *Journal of African History* 19 (3), 415–39.

  (1980), 'The Cash Crop Revolution in Tropical Africa: an Agricultural Reappraisal', *African Affairs* 79 (314), 79–94.

Wallerstein, I. (1976), 'The Three Stages of African Involvement in the World Economy', in P. Gutkind and I. Wallerstein (eds.), *The Political Economy of Contemporary Africa*, Beverly Hills: Sage, 30–57.

Widgren, M. and Sutton, J. E. G. (2004), *Islands of Intensive Agriculture in Eastern Africa*, Nairobi: James Currey.

Wolpe, H. (1974), 'Capitalism and Cheap Labour-power in South Africa: from Segregation to Apartheid', *Economy and Society* 1, 425–56.

H10.1 Why was Ethiopia not colonized during the late-nineteenth-century 'Scramble for Africa'?

Marjolein 't Hart

By 1870, 10 per cent of African territory was controlled by Europeans. Twenty years later, this had risen to 90 per cent due to the infamous 'Scramble for Africa'. Only two African states, Ethiopia and Liberia, remained independent. Liberia had been colonized by Afro-Americans, which explains its special position, but what lay behind Ethiopian resistance to European colonization? And why did most of Sub-Saharan Africa succumb during the 'Scramble'?

Let us begin with the last question. The obvious differences in military technology were not decisive; various trade linkages ensured that rich African rulers were able to procure guns. Sub-Saharan Africa had counted several powerful and vast empires for centuries, such as Mali, Songhai, Asante, Oyo, Kanem-Bornu and Mutapa, often supported by rich mineral resources such as gold. However, the political economy was usually founded upon patrimonial linkages and loyalties, not upon land. In contrast to Europe, clear-cut boundaries did not exist and territorial control was weak. This precluded the levying of substantial taxes upon the populace of a particular territory. In addition, population densities were low, and most inhabitants subsisted on herding or rain-fed cultivation with plots that lay fallow for most of the time (Austin 2008). It is virtually impossible to levy taxes upon nomads or wandering farmers. As a result, the bulk of the revenues of African leaders came from trade in slaves, ivory or gold; fiscal proceeds consisted mainly of export duties and tributes imposed upon neighbouring populations (Herbst 2000, Lonsdale 1981, Thies 2007). These fiscal resources proved extremely vulnerable when Europeans expanded their control over African territories and trade (Law 1989, Falola 1989). In addition, the logistic advantages of the European military, based upon sturdy fiscal structures at home, secured regular funding for (African) troops and the development of superior communication techniques (telegraph) that turned out decisive time and again. A further problem was the sudden inflation after 1850 of the cowries, the dominant currency of numerous African states, which directly affected the revenues of local rulers. Europeans had started to ship large loads of these shells to Africa in exchange for African goods (Nwani 1975).

By contrast, the political economy of Ethiopia was much more robust. Its fiscal revenues stemmed mainly from taxes on land. Moreover, effective control over territory and boundaries enabled the rise and persistence of powerful institutions supported by writing and administration, just like in most advanced states in Europe and Asia. Trade was less dependent upon cowries, since payment was made in gold, salt or iron. In the last decades of the nineteenth century tax revenues were plentiful, which facilitated the defence against European incursions. These developments, in turn, ultimately relied upon the advanced agriculture, which was based on a long-standing environmental exceptionalism of the area vis-à-vis most other sub-Saharan societies. Ethiopian peasants were among the few African peoples to have adopted the technology of the plough, and some areas even yielded two or three harvests per year. The spread of domesticated crops and animals was substantial, and was facilitated by the temperate climate of the Ethiopian highlands, which was closer to that of the Mediterranean than tropical Africa. This allowed for irrigation and intensive food production and ensured a steady income from taxation (Pankhurst 1961, McCann 1987, Crummey 1990). In short, state formation had been much more resilient and durable in Ethiopia than in most of Sub-Saharan Africa, thanks to highly developed agricultural production and fiscal structures that facilitated the maintenance of a permanent governmental administration.

References

Austin, G. (2008), 'Resources, Techniques and Strategies South of the Sahara: Revising the Factor Endowments Perspective on African Economic Development, 1500–2000', *Economic History Review* 61 (3), 587–624, 600–01.

Crummey, D. (1990), 'Society, State and Nationality in the Recent Historiography of Ethiopia', *Journal of African History* 31 (1), 103–19, 107–08.

Falola, T. (1989), 'The Yoruba Toll System: its Operation and Abolition', *The Journal of African History* 30 (1), 69–88, 70.

Herbst, J. (2000), *States and Power in Africa: Comparative Lessons in Authority and Control*, Princeton University Press.

Law, R. (1989), 'Slave-raiders and Middlemen, Monopolists and Free-Traders: the Supply of Slaves for the Atlantic Trade in Dahomey *c.* 1715–1850', *The Journal of African History* 30 (1), 45–68, 68.

Lonsdale, J. (1981), 'States and Social Processes in Africa: a Historiographical Survey', *African Studies Review* 24, 139–225, 177–78.

McCann, J. (1987), *People of the Plow: an Agricultural History of Ethiopia, 1800–1990*, Philadelphia: University of Pennsylvania Press, 39–40.

Nwani, O. A. (1975), 'The Quantity Theory in the Early Monetary System of West Africa with Particular Emphasis on Nigeria, 1850–1895', *Journal of Political Economy* 83 (1), 185–94, 191.

Pankhurst, R. (1961), *An Introduction to the Economic History of Ethiopia from Early Times to 1800*, London: Lalibela House, 179–220.

Thies, C. G. (2007), 'The Political Economy of State Building in Sub-Saharan Africa', *The Journal of Politics* 69 (3), 716–31, 719.

Conclusion

Joerg Baten

In this volume, twenty-seven authors from many different countries and all world regions have jointly written a history of the global economy. They have considered a set of development indicators for income, health (height), education (numeracy), democracy and institutional quality that allowed the identification of periods of welfare improvement or decrease in all world regions. Insights could be obtained into the economic history of Africa, Asia, the Middle East and other world regions – important parts of the world that could not be studied using such a comparative, non-Eurocentric and long-term development approach before. This global approach changes the way we understand the economic history of the world.

What can be learned from this book? It is certainly impossible to summarize all the results regarding global economic development of this volume in a short conclusion. The only strategy that we can follow – in order to round up this volume – is to emphasize some recurrent themes that were discussed in several chapters. One of the most fascinating findings was the large mobility between countries that developed faster and others that lagged behind. It has often been overlooked by historical descriptions of Africa, for example, how some countries and regions experienced growth spurts and rapid educational development during phases of their development. In west Africa during the nineteenth century and again during late colonialism, the development of 'rural capitalist' peasants (Austin) was quite promising, even if later civil wars and problematic institutional designs ended this. Similarly, Poland and other parts of east central Europe experienced a period of surprisingly high welfare after inviting skilled Jewish immigrants and setting constraints to the king in the sixteenth century (again, this governance system became problematic later). These less well-known examples of development episodes are not as present in the historical narratives because they later failed. However, failure was not always predetermined; economic history allows us to identify the reasons for success and failure. In this volume, we also included the hitherto little discussed countries and episodes of development.

A number of factors have been identified in the chapters as promoting or retarding growth, and these apply to many of the historical cases discussed here. One factor about which many (but not all) scholars agree is the role of inclusive institutions that encourage entrepreneurial talent and innovative ideas and ultimately stimulate growth. However, it has proven difficult to install this set of institutions. For example, when Acemoglu and Robinson published their book *Why Nations Fail: the Origins of Power, Prosperity and Poverty* in 2012, they introduced it with the great hopes of the 'Arab Spring'; the authors hoped that after removing extractive tyrants, inclusive institutions would lead to higher welfare in the Middle East. However, it turned out that many Middle Eastern countries did not follow this path but rather turned to civil war and religious struggles. Similarly, when eastern Europe adopted seemingly growth-promoting, capitalist institutions in the 1990s, the scale of unwanted side effects and backlash movements was shocking.

In contrast, for countries that had accumulated human capital over a long period, changes in institutions appear to have been accomplished more easily, such as in South Korea after the end of its dictatorship phase or in Germany after the end of national-socialism. Human capital consists of many different components, such as reading, maths skills and other abilities. Recent research identified numerical skills as the most decisive human capital component for economic development; therefore the authors of this volume studied numeracy intensively. For example, basic numeracy was quite high in East Asia, and this fact might explain the growth of the world region during the last century: first in Japan, then in South Korea, finally in China. Part of the decision about human capital investment is exogenously driven by religious motivations as formulated in specific traditions (reading the Torah or Bible, for example) or by the heritage of ancient traditions (as in the Chinese case). Specific views rather than the religion itself are decisive; for example, the Jews were not exceptionally skilled before the Pharisee reformation in the first century CE. The East Asian obsession for astrology and calendars kept numerical skills alive in a period when income was low and schooling difficult to finance. Gender equality is also crucial here because it often had a strong impact on the education of subsequent generations. Only educated mothers can provide home schooling.

In addition, an important determinant of development is the ability of the central government to tax. Several authors described how the interaction between this ability and the constraints on the executive authority had an influence on infrastructure and schooling investment. Ability to tax without constraints on the ruling powers leads to increased levels of warfare in contrast.[1] If a ruler did not need a justification of his expenses, he often overinvested in military equipment and armies.

Of course, wars and civil wars were not only detrimental because less was invested in education and infrastructure. Fishback addressed this issue using the example of the US during and after the Second World War. He observed that some Americans have a misguided notion that wars are good for the economy. The Second World War provided a counter-example. While of course the main losses of lives and physical capital took place in Europe, the North American war production did 'cost' 40 per cent of overall gross domestic product (GDP) during the peak period. After the Second World War, a substantial amount of GDP was used for cold war armament.

In the economic history of the last five centuries, colonial empires played an important role, and their economic effect was repeatedly evaluated in the present volume. For example, Roy draws a multi-facetted picture of South Asia during the colonial phase: while he finds that agricultural real wages (or grain wages) stagnated during this period, he obtained the impression that some Indian historians overemphasized the colonial exploitation effects. While agriculture tended in fact to stagnate during the colonial phase, this period was not only a 'Dark Age', because in the urban centres there was a surprising diversification and development, for example. After independence in 1947, GDP growth was faster, but productivity stagnated.

Finally, openness in labour and product markets was a recurring theme in this volume. However, while in the last decades the effects were on average positive, trade openness did sometimes have adverse effects on poor countries, as stressed for the Latin American case for the early twentieth century. Williamson described how the developing world grew in the early nineteenth century, but its income increased less than that of western Europe and North America. He identifies trade specialization and subsequent deindustrialization in some regions as a main determinant of global inequality.

In conclusion, a substantial number of factors influences success or failure in certain periods and countries. Our list of growth factors is certainly incomplete, but those mentioned above have played a role in a substantial number of situations. Young adults deciding about their economic future, and policymakers and those that influence political and economic decisions, can all improve welfare on this planet by gaining insights from economic history.

Note

1. Fishback describes the North American success with constraining the executive.

Index